The Library of Co

Veterans History

Since You Asked
Arizona Veterans Share Their Memories

Since You Asked Arizona Veterans Share Their Memories Volume III
Conceived, edited, designed and published by
Cactus Shadows High School
Arizona Heritage Project
P.O. Box 426
Cave Creek, Arizona 85327
USA

ISBN 978-0-615-14112-1

Illustrations and logo design by Kyle Hobratschk
Layout by Mark A. McCullough

Page 1 photo: GI holding helmet with Vietnamese kid (Courtesy of Steve Goldsmith)
Previous page photo: "Guiding a "bird" (CH-47 helicopter) into Fire Support Base Apollo is a Big Red One soldier from the 1st Battalion, 28th Infantry—the 'Black Lions' (Photo provided by Jim Siket, US Army photo by Sgt. Chris Parsons, 14 November 1969, #P0944).
Opposite page photo: Arlington National Cemetery (Courtesy of Barbara Hatch)

Veterans

World War II

Korean War

Cold War

Vietnam

Operation Iraqi Freedom/ Gulf Wars

Table of Contents

Foreword

Arizona Heritage Project 2006-2007 participants in the Association of the US Army building in Washington, DC (front to back, left to right): Jill Quintero, Kevin Hildebrandt, Alex Doss, Carolina Nick, Cindy Garcia Barraza, Lt. General Roger Thompson, Kelly Wilcox, Libby Day, Lauren Byrd, Barbara Hatch; Colonel John Davies (ret), Amanda Poincelot, Patrick Ward, Sergeant Major Leroy Bussells (ret), Lt. Colonel Isabelle Slifer (ret), Kirk DiGiacomo, Natalie Omundson, Greg Gorraiz, Kyle Hobratschk, Mark McCullough, Dr. Ed Berger, Kasey Burton (Photo taken by Lt. Colonel Stan Crow)

After 160 veteran interviews in three years, people periodically ask me, "Why do you do it?" To paraphrase Elizabeth Barrett Browning, let me count the reasons…

- Fifteen Arizona Heritage Project students delivered 98 veteran interviews to the Veterans History Project in Washington, D.C. for permanent archiving in the Library of Congress. They also presented the project to the Association of the U.S. Army and the National Council of Social Studies. Their professionalism left me speechless.
- Students spend before and after school and sometimes lunch hour working in the project corner of the room, which has become their "office." Seeing them create history while recording history is a teacher's greatest reward.
- We have the opportunity to learn history first-hand from those who lived it. Gobel James was a prisoner of war in the Hanoi Hilton for 56 months. While incarcerated, he heard the fire of the Sontay rescue, which our veteran Jim Morris led. Stories overlap.
- We record the memories of our veterans before they are lost. This past year our dear friend Ed Splain, WWII survivor of Iwo Jima, Guadalcanal, Bougainville, and Tulagi passed away. When I kissed him on the forehead to say goodbye, he looked at me kindly and said, "Thank you, my dear." God speed, Ed.
- We met more of the local veterans at Cave Creek's Wild West Days and Veterans Day activities, including the mother of Michael "Sergeant Rock" Marzano, who was killed in Iraq. We are proud to bring you his story, written by his mother Margy Bons, owner of The Unique Boutique.
- Vietnam veterans are finally telling their stories. We are a catalyst. We say thanks.
- Cactus Shadows graduates/veterans came back to visit: Chris Stull (Army), Jessica Beazley (Coast Guard), Buck Skowronek (Marines).
- Thirteen veterans and their wives bought me a lifetime membership to the Association of the U.S. Army and presented it at a faculty gathering. I was humbled. I know their stories and the level of their sacrifice. Mine is small.
- AHP students mature into poised young adults ready for careers. I will hear from them.
- Older AHP students model leadership for the younger ones. The torch is passed.
- Even when we work, we laugh. Who can forget the Christmas Tree Lot, or doing cartwheels on the Capitol lawn in D.C.?
- Students learn that all wars end. The enemies of yesterday are friends today. World War II veterans Dieter Loeper, German army, and Kenny Dahlberg, American flying ace, welcomed Jeff, Kyle, Mark, and Lauren into their homes while they teased each other about being imprisoned in opposing camps—and their golf game!
- When the veterans attend the reception in May, sometimes in uniform, they walk a little taller, sit a little straighter, smile a lot wider. They get to know each other.

For a third year, we are proud to share the memories of the remarkable men and women who gave of themselves to defend this country. When I hear of more veterans eager to tell their stories, I can only answer, "Next year." How can we say no?

Barbara Hatch
Advisor

Prologue

The Arizona Heritage Project has presented us with experiences that far outweigh the academic education we receive in high school. The classroom setting offers a teacher, classmates, and textbooks; our project offers veterans, peers, and stories. These do not supplement our education, but rather augment life skills. This project has provided us with opportunities to enhance not only our abilities in communication, writing, and leadership, but also extraneous skills in exhibiting, illustrating, and woodworking.

The multi-faceted project required us to obtain new roles as we gained a higher level of proficiency when communicating with veterans ranging in age from their early 20s to their 90s, along with a variety of student personalities in the project. Interviews served as an opportunity to hone our communication skills while bridging generation gaps. Our veterans gained a sense of closure, and we gained respect for America's servicemen and women. We observed each pause, sigh, and cry to help document every story shared for our publications. Beyond retelling their accounts through essays, illustrations depicted the scope of each war through the veterans' point of view.

Aside from interviewing veterans, our most pleasurable experience was building an exhibit to complement our books. Without the experience of a museum curator, our plans led us through trial and error as we struggled to find the best way to honor our veterans visually. We accumulated a garage full of photographs, medals, weapons, and memorabilia. The opportunities were boundless. With sketches, power tools, wood, and close friendships, over eight months of labor led us to construct an exhibit ready to proudly represent community history.

In addition to our veterans' histories, we have created pieces of our own history working on the Project. Three years of intense research with a select group of students have enabled us to chronicle our memories in annual scrapbooks. Flipping through these pages reminds us of the stories we can now enjoy together. The freshly sealed wood we stickily stumbled onto and struggling to dress an overweight mannequin in a petite vintage service uniform highlight only two of the thousands of shared memories. We now understand the true definition of history. It is neither in classroom lectures nor chapters read in textbooks. Instead, history is experience and the pleasure of documenting it.

Our history on the project has just begun. Although we will graduate high school in 2007, new Project members will continue our mission with a fervid passion to learn and preserve. A trip to Washington D.C. to present our work to the Library of Congress, National Association of the U.S. Army, and the 86th Annual Social Studies Teacher Conference provided satisfaction to graduating members who saw the results of their hard work and powerful enthusiasm for new members. These active members have a desire to contribute their best to thank our veterans for their service. Their history and our history will continue for as long as this passion endures.

Lauren Byrd
Kyle Hobratschk

Introduction

We speak of Veterans Day in reverent tone because that day honors all military men and women of our combat forces, both living and dead. This is the origin of Veterans Day.

In 1921, an unknown World War I American soldier was buried in Arlington National Cemetery. This site, on a hillside overlooking the Potomac River and the city of Washington, D.C., became the focal point of reverence for America's veterans.

Similar ceremonies occurred earlier in England and France, where an unknown soldier was buried in each nation's highest place of honor (in England, Westminster Abbey; in France, the Arc de Triomphe). These memorial gestures all took place on November 11, giving universal recognition to the celebrated ending of World War I fighting at 11 a.m., November 11, 1918 (the 11th hour of the 11th day of the 11th month). The day became known as "Armistice Day."

Armistice Day officially received its name in America in 1926 through a Congressional resolution. It became a national holiday 12 years later by similar Congressional action. If the idealistic hope had been realized that World War I was "the War to end all Wars," November 11 might still be called Armistice Day. But only a few years after the holiday was proclaimed, war broke out in Europe. Sixteen and one-half million Americans took part. Four hundred seven thousand of them died in service, more than 292,000 in battle.

Realizing that peace was equally preserved by veterans of WWII and Korea, Congress was requested to make this day an occasion to honor those who have served America in all wars. In 1954, President Eisenhower signed a bill proclaiming November 11 as Veterans Day.

On Memorial Day in 1958, two more unidentified American war dead were brought from overseas and interred in the plaza beside the unknown soldier of World War I. One was killed in World War II, the other in the Korean War. In 1973, a law passed providing interment of an unknown American from the Vietnam War. But none was found for several years. In 1984, an unknown serviceman from that conflict was placed alongside the others. To honor these men, symbolic of all Americans who gave their lives in all wars, an Army honor guard, the 3d U.S. Infantry (The Old Guard), keeps day and night vigil.

A law passed in 1968 changed the national commemoration of Veterans Day to the fourth Monday in October. It soon became apparent, however, that November 11 was a date of historic significance to many Americans. Therefore, in 1978 Congress returned the observance to its original date.

The focal point for official, national ceremonies for Veterans Day continues to be the memorial amphitheater built around the Tomb of the Unknowns. At 11 a.m. on November 11, a combined color guard representing all military services executes "Present Arms" at the tomb. The nation's tribute to its war dead is symbolized by the laying of a presidential wreath. Finally, the bugler plays "taps."

Frank Sackton, Lieutenant General, USA (ret)

Association of the United States Army

Certificate of Appreciation

Awarded to

Cactus Shadows High School
Arizona Heritage Project

for

your exemplary efforts to document the tremendous contributions
of the veterans from the State of Arizona to the freedom of the
United States of America.

November 30, 2006

Gordon R. Sullivan
General, US Army (Retired)
President

I had the good fortune to learn of and meet the students of Cactus Shadows High School as a result of my own participation in the Library of Congress's Veterans History Project. Since I am local to the Washington, D.C. metro area, I was asked to participate in a demonstration the students gave to history teachers at the National Council of Social Studies in the Washington Convention Center in December 2006. The demonstration focused on the nuts and bolts of conducting the project; my part was as a mock interviewee to show the audience how the interview process progressed. The students were engaging and interested, and made me feel very comfortable throughout the interview.

Prior to the demonstration date, I was given the first two volumes of *Since You Asked*. I was fascinated and impressed by both the stories and the professionalism these students possessed in obtaining and writing up the

interviews. I was not disappointed when I met them in person. Each and every one was polite, enthusiastic about the project, and enamored of the veterans they met and interviewed. I was thrilled and honored to be a part of their demonstration and doubly honored to be asked to write the Introduction for Volume 3.

In the aftermath, I have received thank you letters from the students who interviewed me, with regrets that it was only a demonstration and not an actual, recorded interview! What a class act—no pun intended!

Since meeting these young adults, I have questioned my own complacency in documenting both my own service in the United States Navy during the 1980s and 1990s, as well as the many relatives, now deceased, who served our nation in World War II or Korea. As a result, I am determined to find as much information as I can about my father's service in the Merchant Marines during World War II and share it with both my family and the Library of Congress's Veterans History Project. I also plan on interviewing several of my father's relatives and friends who can remember Dad as a young (17 years old!) sailor on a merchant vessel in the Pacific theater. At this point, that is sadly all I know of him and his history.

Our nation has a history of forgetting our veterans after the conflict in which they served is over. I think it is wonderful that the Arizona Heritage Project is bringing together young people who do not just learn the human experience of the military and war in their history classes, often limited to boring and sterile accounts of battles, strategic goals, and individual military and political leaders. Never do they read about the common Foot Soldier, Sailor, Airman, Marine, or Coast Guardsman's duties within those conflicts, or the sacrifice of the family and friends who remained behind to support the war effort. The Arizona Heritage Project, in conjunction with the Veterans History Project, is changing that. While most veterans are proud of their service to their country, some never return; some return, but are neither physically nor mentally the same, and these things too need to be known about the history of war. Perhaps as more young people come to learn the human toll that war brings, war as a vehicle for resolving conflicts will cease. That can only be a good thing.

Darlene M. Iskra

Darlene M. Iskra
Commander, USN (retired)

VETERANS
HISTORY
PROJECT

Serve, Preserve, Honor

December 28, 2006

Mrs. Barbara Hatch
Arizona Heritage Project
Cactus Shadows High School
P.O. Box 426
Cave Creek, Arizona 85327

Dear Barbara,

As Program Officer and liaison to the Veterans History Project for classrooms and youth groups I have had the honor and privilege of working with hundreds of teachers and students from across America. While all efforts are appreciated, I can honestly say that few have displayed the level of enthusiasm and just plain hard work exhibited by you and your students at Cactus Shadows High School.

I know that you are well aware of the urgency involved in the collecting of our veterans' wartime experiences, and I am sure that I speak for all the veterans whose stories you have saved for future generations when I say "Thank You" for your extraordinary commitment and efforts.

The Veterans History Project could not have reached its current level of success without the enthusiastic support of volunteer historians like those participating in the Arizona Heritage Project at Cactus Shadows High School. On behalf of the staff at the Project, I want to express my appreciation for all you have accomplished.

I look forward to continuing to work with you and your students towards our common goal: to honor America's war veterans.

Sincerely,

Tim Schurtter

Veterans History Project / Library of Congress / 101 Independence Ave., SE / Washington, DC 20540-4615
Telephone: 202-707-4916/888-371-5848   Fax: 202-252-2046   Email: vohp@loc.gov   www.loc.gov/vets

The LIBRARY of CONGRESS
Washington, D.C.

In 2006, fifteen self-directed, motivated learners from Cactus Shadows High School in Cave Creek, Arizona went to our nation's capitol. They delivered to the archives of the Library of Congress ninety-eight veterans' oral histories they had collected. While in the capitol, volumes I and II of, *Since You Asked, Arizona Veterans Share Their Memories*, were presented to the Association of the United States Army. The students also presented their project to teachers at the National Council of Social Studies convention. At every turn they were honored for their amazing contributions to our history. I had the honor of being in the company of those young heroes and their Master Teacher, Barbara Hatch.

When master teachers like Barbara Hatch work with students they unleash individual powers long restrained. Individuals become motivated and self-directed as the learning of applicable facts and concepts accelerates. The student becomes his/her own teacher. When the positive energy of students is focused and unleashed on a project such as *Since You Asked*, amazing things happen. The process each student goes through to make a gift of scholarship to his/her school, community and nation, results in internalized information, patterns, and connections. Within hours, experiential learning takes the student well beyond the expectations of the closed classroom.

The Arizona Heritage Project provides support to master teachers who dare involve students in the greater community where they can make a contribution. Master teachers are not tellers of knowledge. The master teacher orchestrates opportunities. This role centers on organizing situations and events so that a desired effect or outcome is achieved. In Arizona Heritage Projects the "teacher" sets the parameters and keeps learners focused. The teacher's role is to develop interrelated learning and processing skills and learning situations that require great effort and self direction from students. This observation from a Cactus Shadows High School sophomore captures the essence of great teaching and true learning:

It's like in school everything was done and my job was to learn it. That was before I got into Mrs. Hatch's AHP project. This is the first time I had to think and plan and solve problems because the information hadn't been recorded before. It was up to me to discover and record history. I did. I made a contribution.

One experiences the depth of teaching ability when, at every turn, each student is challenged: "I don't know, let's find out." "Will those of you who know how this works teach the rest of us?" "We know where we want to go, figure out how to get there." "Now you know what you don't understand. Ask questions. Do the research. Figure it out."

English and Social Studies teachers debate whose students get the most out of AHP projects. The English teachers see advancements in writing, reading, speaking and editing skills. They marvel at the motivation of students who have been empowered. Social Studies teachers observe students who take responsibility, do background research so they are able to interview an elder, learn to sort and weigh information and prepare their work for archiving. They see connections to the real world and expand their ken into the realities of our times in preparation for their future. Parents and community members come into the classroom as resources at the request of the students. Broad learning communities form.

Book Three, as presented here, is testimony to the power of those who can legitimately say to our children: "We need you."

Dr. Ed Berger, Arizona Heritage Project State Coordinator
American Folklife Center, Library of Congress
Sharlot Hall Museum
Prescott, Arizona

World War II

In the Second World War, men and women from all walks of life came together to create an ethnic melting pot of cultures and races across the United States of America. They were bound by honor, patriotism, a strong sense of duty, and care for the guy next to them. The title "The Greatest Generation," coined by Tom Brokaw in his book of the same name, was earned to the fullest by the actions of the soldiers who fought for freedom, but they have also earned the title "The Humblest Generation" in my mind, because they don't see themselves as heroes, but merely soldiers doing their duty when their country asked them to. Most veterans will tell you, "Oh, I didn't do much," but they did. They were all comrades depending on each other in the face of insurmountable odds. They defeated a powerful coalition of nations: the Axis powers.

In the end, that great melting pot of many different races and cultures had two things in common: they were all Americans and they fought for the greater good. Because of their great efforts, our country, and the security of the world, is what it is today.

Patrick Ward

Joe Anderson

June 1942 - July 1945
South Pacific

The Greatest Generation

An Interview with Joe Anderson
By Natalie Omundson and Joe Anderson

Most stories are best told by the original narrator. An attempt to interpret Mr. Joe Anderson's account of his Marine service would dilute the significance of the story. So here, in his own words, is Mr. Joe Anderson's story:

One June 2nd, 1942, I, Joe Anderson, at the age of 20, enlisted in the United States Marine Corps.

Along with 30 other recruits, I, a Minnesota native, boarded a train for the long ride to the San Diego Marine Recruit Depot. Due to wartime conditions, boot camp was shortened to eight weeks as opposed to the twelve weeks required today. The dedicated drill instructors were allowed to touch the Boots, sometimes with a quick kick or a slap. Upon completion of this experience, we were transported to nearby Camp Elliot to join the Ninth Marine Regiment. Three weeks later, we hiked to Camp Pendleton, some fifty miles north. We were the first combat troops in this huge military installation. I became a member of Fox Company, Second Battalion, Ninth Regiment, a member of a 60mm mortar squad. Strenuous training in the hills around this vast camp made us anxious for action.

On the rainy night of 24 January 1943, our Regiment boarded a ship to an unknown destination. After several days at sea, we were advised that we were headed for Auckland, New Zealand. Upon arrival, after twelve days at sea, serious training commenced, including three sixty-mile hikes.

We left New Zealand in late June, and arrived at Guadalcanal on 6 July. Our camp was in a coconut grove, reportedly owned by Lever Brothers, the soap manufacturers. On the third night, a few friends were visiting me when we heard a diving airplane. Jokingly, I said, "It sounds like a Jap to me." I was right. The pilot dropped a string of bombs in the only area of the grove which was not occupied by troops. However, that night foxholes were rapidly dug, much deeper than they were before. Our training continued, and included patrols into the jungle and mountains. In spite of the mandatory use of Atabrine pills, numerous cases of malaria were occurring. Japanese planes appeared every moonlit night, but appeared to be mostly scouting the area. While on guard duty at storied Henderson Field, I accidentally encountered a college friend of mine. Bob Hanson was a Marine pilot, flying Corsairs. On his three tours of duty, he shot down twenty-five enemy aircraft. On the day before he was to return to the States, he was killed in a strafing run. At the time of his death, his only decoration was an Air Medal. He received the Medal of Honor posthumously.

In August, I transferred from Fox Company to Battalion Headquarters. Bougainville was to be our next stop. On 1 November 1943, our Division landed at Empress Augusta Bay on the island of Bougainville. The reason for this landing was principally to establish an air base. We landed in a swampy area with light resistance. However, about five minutes later, three Japanese Zeroes, flying low, strafed the landing craft that was still coming in. Fortunately, there were only a few casualties. The second biggest enemy on this inhospitable island was the weather and environment. Heat, high humidity, mud, and daily rains that sometimes filled our foxholes made waiting for enemy action almost a relief. The completion of the air base by the Seabees allowed the famous Black Sheep Squadron, commanded by the irrepressible Pappy Boyington, to fly attack missions in the northern part of the island. After fifty-four days, the army relieved us and we set sail back to the almost pleasant—by comparison—confines of Guadalcanal. Replacements were received and training continued, including a few practice landings in preparation for our next experience.

We said farewell to Guadalcanal on 6 June 1944 and headed north to the Marshall Islands en route to the Marianas, where we were scheduled to recapture the American possession of Guam. The harbor in Kwajalein was an unforgettable sight, one of the largest in the world. There were hundreds of ships, including battle wagons, aircraft carriers, cruisers, destroyers, cargo ships, and, of course, troop transports. The Northern Task Force escorted the Second and Fourth Marine Decisions to land on Saipan. We sailed later for Guam, but were called back to Eniwetok (the westernmost of the Marshalls) because of the impending huge naval battle between the American and Japanese fleets. When we finally got clearance to land on Guam, they fed us a steak dinner about three o'clock in the morning, and joked nervously about how condemned men ate a hearty meal.

We clambered down the cargo nets into the bobbing landing craft and headed to the rendezvous area and then took amphibious tractors over the coral reef surrounding Guam. There was sporadic enemy fire on the beach, but we ran into a dried-out rice paddy and were greeted by substantial artillery, mortar, and machine gun fire for about forty-five minutes. We finally were able to move ahead onto high ground and complete the day's mission. During the night on Guam, the Marines would go into their foxholes, while the Japanese wandered around all night, sometimes initiating Bonzai charges led by a screaming, sword-waving Japanese officer. On one terrible night on Fonte Ridge, our battalion was subjected to, and repulsed, three of these attacks. There were many heroes that night; the most prominent was then Captain Louis Wilson, who received the Medal of Honor. He later became Commandant of the Marine Corps. The Guam campaign lasted about three weeks. The Guam natives, called Chamorros, were very nice people. The U.S. Navy took over Guam in 1898 after the Spanish-American War. The Navy had run the island until the Japanese took over on 10 December 1941. Because of the American influence, the Chamorros were very patriotic and even composed songs such as, "Sam, Sam, my dear Uncle Sam. Would you please come back to Guam? I don't like Sake…I like Canadian." After the campaign, we received many replacements, including some draftees, as we prepared for the next action.

Coincidentally, on 19 February 1945—D-Day for the Fourth and Fifth Marine Divisions to land on

Japanese Zero crashed in the water off Guadalcanal

Iwo Jima—the Third Division sailed north and remained offshore in floating reserve. My regiment was called in on 24 February to capture the second airfield and the ground beyond. On the way in, to the far left, we could see the famous American Flag waving on top of Mt. Suribachi. Forward progress around the airfield was limited sometimes to a hundred yards a day because of the fierce resistance. As a volunteer stretcher bearer, I can attest to this. Private Wilson Watson from our G Company was a galley cook, and due to some minor transgressions, wound up in a rifle squad carrying a Browning automatic rifle. Although wounded, he captured a small promontory by himself. He survived, and his actions rewarded him with the Medal of Honor.

When the carnage was over, more than 6,000 Marines and Naval personnel had made the supreme sacrifice. Another 20,000 were wounded. The enemy fared even worse. Of the original garrison of 21,000, only 1,000 survived and were captured. Psychologically, the capture of this island fortress—only 600 miles from the Japanese mainland—was a severe blow. Many crippled B-29 Bombers returning from raids on Japan used Iwo Jima as an emergency landing strip, thus saving many airmen's lives. The regiment returned to Guam, and the veterans of the three campaigns sailed home. They were given thirty-day leaves and reassigned to various Marine and Navy facilities around the country.

After the war, I moved to New York. For a brief time I served as a flight attendant for Pan American World Airways, which afforded me the opportunity to travel extensively to Europe and Africa. After several other career changes, I went to work for Airsupply Company, a division of the Garrett Corporation, a California-based aerospace organization. I also met my wife, Evelyn, who resided in New York. We got married there and later transferred to Columbus, Ohio, where we raised our

son and daughter. My final four years with the company was as Midwest District Manager, based in Indianapolis. I retired in 1982, and we moved to beautiful Hilton Head Island, South Carolina, where we resided for fourteen years. During that time I became a charter member and officer of Parris Island Museum & Historical Society. On my numerous visits to this famous recruit depot, I was able to often witness the modern training of Marine recruits. A reminder to all was a banner over the main street of

The 2nd Battalion, 9th Marines, 81mm Mortar Platoon

the Parris Island base which proudly proclaims: "Welcome to Parris Island, Where the Change Begins."

In 1996, Evelyn and I decided to move to Scottsdale, Arizona and have enjoyed this beautiful part of the southwest for ten years.

Perhaps Tom Brokaw was correct when he titled his book *The Greatest Generation*. After all, we survived the Great Depression and sixteen million of us served in the armed forces during WWII, wholeheartedly supported by the civilian population in various capacities.

William Barnett

June 1941 - June 1947
South Pacific

Willow Walls and Typhoons

An Interview with William "Barney" Barnett
By Libby Day

William Barnett, who goes by "Barney," enlisted in June of 1941. He left a small town called Fond du Lac in southeast Wisconsin to go to boot camp in Great Lakes, Illinois. When he finished boot camp, he was to choose a training school of his choice. Barney chose to be a signalman and ended up in Toledo, Ohio, where he graduated signalman training and came out a Seaman 2nd Class. In a short period of time, Barney was on his way to his training center on Treasure Island in San Francisco, California. Barney was only on Treasure Island for two weeks before he was sent off to a cargo ship headed for New Zealand. Just after his departure, Pearl Harbor was bombed on December 7, 1941.

The crew of the cargo ship was sent immediately to wartime conditions, which made Barney's job as signalman all the more important. The ship stopped for brief layovers in Wellington and Auckland, New Zealand, and continued on to Sydney and Melbourne, Australia, and then continued on to Tasmania. After spending a few nights in Tasmania, the crew shipped back up to Pearl Harbor, refueled, and was on its way to the Eniwetok Islands. After finishing business in the islands, Barney's captain got an order transferring him to Pacific forces in the North Pacific and the Aleutian Islands.

By this time Mr. Barnett had advanced to a 3rd Class Signalman and was transferred to the Aleutians, where he was based in Attu and Adak. During this time they took many of the islands, including Amchitka, Kiska, Attu, and Adak. Here Barney was in charge of the communications tower and had the 6-to-6 watch. This meant he was in charge of all communications between his ship's communication and the ships in Adak Bay from 6 in the morning to 6 in the evening. At one point it was believed there were Japanese camps on the island of Kiska. American ships surrounded the island; it was bombed and strafed for three weeks. When the ground troops went onto the island, there was not a person on it. There was evidence of the Japanese being there—stores of supplies, ammunition, and other items they had left—but they were gone. The way Mr. Barnett figures it, submarines must have come in and gotten the Japanese troops off the island. This would have been possible because radar had not yet been highly developed.

In the Aleutians the weather gets very hostile in the winter months. One of the effects is "Willow Walls." A "Willow Wall" is a very strong wind, so strong that a person can lean into the wind at a 45-degree angle, and then all of a sudden the wind switches direction and knocks him flat on the ground. This type of wind was a danger to planes that were strafing or training near mountains because all of a sudden they got smashed into the mountainside. It was also during this time that Barney's mother died. Most servicemen are allowed to come home for a few days when family members die; unfortunately, Barney was not allowed that luxury. "I couldn't understand. I didn't make a better cannon than anybody else, but I never got to come home."

Barney even considered returning to the U.S. for his mother's funeral without permission. He reflected on one sailor who got so "stir crazy" in the Aleutians, he secretly stockpiled food and fuel on a Higgins boat. One day after transporting supplies to shore, he did not return. When the officers realized he was not to be found, they sent a destroyer to look for him. They found him two days out to sea heading for the United States. It is doubtful he could have reached the U.S. in a small craft battling the high seas of the north Pacific. He was brought back to the ship and spent time in the brig. Levels of punishment on a ship ranged, in order of severity, from a report, to Captain's mast, to a general court martial, to prison, to dishonorable discharge. Barney was not willing to take those risks.

After successfully completing his two-year assignment in the Aleutians, Barney was transferred back to his base at Treasure Island in the middle of 1944. Because he had already served two years he was granted unconditional liberty, and for three weeks all Barney had to do was check in at six o'clock in the morning; after that he was free do as he pleased. Suddenly Barney and his crewmates were transferred to Miami, Florida, where they ran the Venetian Hotel. "We ran it just like a hotel. You answer the phone, call the officers down, and are responsible for getting the mess boys to serve the dinner, supper, and breakfast for the officers." After spending all the money he had saved while serving in the Aleutians, his next assignment was Orange City, Texas. He was ordered to help put a ship in commission, an ATA, or Auxiliary Ocean Tug, to be exact.

Before making it to open ocean, Barney ran into a few complications. Just before the crew was headed down to Galveston, Texas, on their shakedown cruise, Barney had a, shall we say, bit of a run-in with the shore patrol. "The shore patrol came along and I had my hat on the back of my head—you are always supposed to carry it two fingers above your eyebrow. He [the shore patrolman] told me to tip my hat and I gave him an obscene signal. They put me in handcuffs and took me to the brig [jail]." Fortunately, Barney had an understanding judge who let him out at 6:00 in the morning so he could make it back to his ship in time to get underway.

From Texas the crew headed down to the Panama Canal via Key West, Florida. Without incident they traveled back into the Pacific. Unfortunately bad weather made cooking impossible. "You couldn't keep anything on the broilers, so they gave us the ice cream, wafers, and soda crackers that they had," Mr. Barnett commented, referring to the limited victuals available during a typhoon off the

Ship being put into commission. Colors and commission pennant being hoisted.

coast of Okinawa. Barney was one of the lucky ones; he did not get seasick.

Some of the new recruits on board could not handle the sharp pitch of the ship and came down hard with seasickness. Barney and a crewmate decided

of the time of day or night, when the ship crosses the "IDL," all pollywogs are ordered on deck to serve at the will and pleasure of King Neptune, who is selected from all the shellbacks.

Headquarters after surrender, Yokoska, Japan

The initiation differs on each ship depending on the whim of King Neptune. In our case, there were 15 of us pollywogs. We were stripped of all clothing and blindfolded. Then our heads were shaved and some sticky substance painted on our bodies. We were forced to drink something I can only compare to vomit. There were other indignities we had to endure, which goes on until "King Neptune" seems to think we have suffered enough, at which time we are given a certificate signed by King Neptune and his court. Believe me, that certificate is something you guard for the rest of your enlistment because if you cross that line again and can't produce the certificate, you have to go through the initiation all over again. I'm proud to say I'm a certified "shellback."

to have a bit of fun with the guys. "We went down and got a big piece of fat off the meat. We put it on a string and pulled it in and out of our mouths. All the new recruits were heaving over the side of the ship." By the end of a two-week period, the foodstuffs previously available were considerably lacking. Lucky for the sailors, the storm was also running low on energy.

As Barney's ship was on the way to New Zealand and Australia, it is necessary to cross the International Date Line. Because he was a Seaman 1st Class having never been out to sea, he had no idea what would happen once they crossed the "line."

If you've never been across this hallowed line, you're in for a rude awakening. First of all, the men who previously crossed this line are called "shellbacks"; those who are to be initiated are called "pollywogs." Regardless

Barney held onto that certificate.

Off Okinawa the crew saw a few Japanese ships, but they were never bombed. They did have one *kamikaze* that came at them, but it missed the ship entirely and was shot down. Being on a small ship, they were able to use a zigzag course to divert. They made their way to the Philippines, and to most everyone's relief, the ship's grills were back in action. The men could eat again.

By this time it was July 1945 and the war was over. Barney and his company were assigned to be part of the surrender in Tokyo Bay. They sat about three miles off the *Missouri* with a pair of binoculars. "I saw Tojo and MacArthur standing on the deck of the *Missouri*—saw the entire surrender."

Barney was on the first ship granted liberty in Tokyo, Japan. He was lucky to be on the starboard side of the ship and was one of the first off the ship. He traveled down to Yokohama and saw all the damage done by the American air raids. In Yokohama, the fleet patrolled and hauled barges for four months before Barney was transferred back to the United States, where he continued hauling barges.

For a year the crew shipped in and out of San Diego, California, and ran up and down the coast from San Diego to Fresno to Portland, Oregon, and to Seattle, Washington. They hauled flat barges that carried supplies for the APLs, or Auxiliary Personnel Lighters, large ships also known as Barracks Barges. They housed supplies, doctors, and fresh produce among needed items. APLs are usually situated at any base or in any war zone.

After six years in the United States Navy, Barney came home in June of 1947. He returned to Madison, Wisconsin, where his dad was living as a traveling salesman for a pharmaceutical company. His father had remarried and Barney decided he would rather not live there. Instead, he moved in with a couple who had an extra room that he rented. During this time Barney worked as an auditor for Kroger. He traveled often and was lucky to find his future wife, Ruth, at a small restaurant in Freeport, Illinois. Ruth was fresh out of school and had moved to Illinois with a few friends to work as a medical technician at a hospital in Freeport. It was the night Ruth and her friends had come to town, and Barney and one of his junior auditors were out having dinner at the same restaurant as the girls. "I saw her, liked her, asked her out, and that was that." They were married in her hometown of Anderson, Indiana. Ruth and Barney recently celebrated 56 years of marriage.

After working for Kroger for four years, Barney was offered a job in Junction, Texas. The newlywed couple moved down there and purchased their first home on the GI Bill—a modest three-bedroom house for $15,900. The couple now resides in Fountain Hills, Arizona.

Of the many lessons Barney learned during his time in the service, there was one piece of information with which he wanted to end. "If you are ever in a position to direct people, war is never a solution. There is nothing pretty about war—at all. You should strive in every way to attain peace."

Barney standing between two Aussies

Harold Bergbower

May 1939 - August 1969
Philippines, Japan, U.S.

No Place Like Home
An Interview with Harold Bergbower
By Katie Stotts and Barbara Hatch

"Girls, there is no place like home...there is no place like home. Remember that," said Mr. Bergbower when Mrs. Hatch, Kelly, and I interviewed him. Mr. Bergbower allowed us to address him by his first name, Harold. We all gathered in his living room as he shared his stories and experiences about life, war, being a POW, and what peace and freedom means to him. Harold's story increased my understanding of the hardships, agony, and hopelessness our brave servicemen faced during World War II. But he also shared some fun stories the men used to pass the time and keep their spirits high while in Japanese captivity.

The interview took place on a Thursday, May 11, 2006, in Mr. Bergbower's home in Peoria, Arizona. Harold is 86 years old and was born in Newton, Illinois, on May 11, 1920. We were interviewing him on his birthday!

Harold met his wife Eunice in Decatur, Illinois, in 1946; they had three children together, two sons and a daughter. He enlisted in the Army Air Corps on May 12, 1939. He was 19 years old. In fact, he enlisted the day after his 19th birthday. Harold made the military his life and career. He left the Army in 1969 with the rank of Chief Master Sergeant after 30 years of service to our country.

Harold is a World War II veteran. He was stationed in the Philippines with the 28th Bomb Squadron. He was also captured and held by the Japanese as a POW. He spent time in six different camps: Malabay and Davao Penal on Mindanao, Bilibid and Cabanatuan on Luzon, and Moji and Toyama in Japan.

After Harold enlisted in the Army, he was sent to New York, where he stayed until he boarded the *USS Republic* and was transported to San Francisco, California, by way of the Panama Canal. From California he boarded another ship called the *USS Grant*, which took Harold and his fellow Army Air Corpsmen to the Philippines. He arrived in the Philippines on July 20, 1940, and was immediately stationed at Clark Field working on B-10s. In his time off, Harold rode his Harley motorcycle and played golf to make his time there more normal. A few months later, Harold was reassigned to an emergency landing strip in Rosales. Harold stayed at Rosales until he returned to home base a couple months later.

On December 8, 1941, Harold sat in the mess hall eating his lunch when Japanese bombers flew over, dropping bomb after bomb on Clark Field. The same day across the International Date Line in Hawaii, another group of Japanese bombers attacked Pearl Harbor. Harold was on his way to his duty station when he was knocked out by an incoming bomb. When medics found Harold, they pronounced him "dead" and sent his body to Fort Stossenburg. A few hours later Harold woke up in the morgue where his "dead" body had been placed. He crawled out and walked back to Clark Field, where medics cleaned him up and sent him off. "I had a sore head for a while."

Harold hitched a ride to Rosales to get his possessions. The driver told Harold he would return to give him a ride back to Clark Field. Harold agreed, and said he would wait until the man returned. A couple hours passed, then a couple days, until five days had passed and the man in the truck had not returned. As Harold's hopes fell, the Filipino scouts of the 26th Cavalry came over the hill on horses. "You better come with us. The Japanese troops are about an hour behind us."

With no other choice, Harold accepted and traveled with the Filipino scouts. On horses, Harold and the scouts fought a delaying action back to Bataan. Thanks to these men, Harold missed being taken prisoner and sent on the Bataan Death March. From Bataan the men took an outrigger to Cagayan on the island of Mindanao, which took five to six days. When they reached Cagayan, Harold left the Filipino scouts and took a truck to the Bulangi River, returning to his squadron, who were on infantry duty along the river. A Japanese patrol caught Harold and took him prisoner.

The first camp Harold and the hundred captured Americans were sent to was Malabay, on Mindanao, where they gathered wood for cooking. Their next stop was Davao Penal Camp, also on Mindanao. Harold stayed here from 1942 until August 1944, growing rice, sweet potatoes, and okra for the Japanese troops. "The camp was fairly nice, but still strict. We grew potatoes and many different types of food for the Japanese soldiers." While in the rice paddies one day, he caught a snake and took it back to the camp and ate it. "Snake is good eating! You were lucky if you caught a snake. It was the only real food in the camp." Unfortunately, the rice the prisoners grew was sent to the Japanese troops, while inferior rice was shipped in for the prisoners—full of worms. "You girls got a good stomach? Man, I've eaten so many worms, hundreds of thousands of them, I guess." Seaweed was another staple. The okra and sweet potatoes Harold grew were sent out of the camp along with the rice. Little wonder Harold's weight dropped to 78 pounds in Davao.

Conditions in Davao were so bad, ten men escaped and eventually made it back to the United States. Normally the Japanese guards did roll call every half hour. Each time they yelled "Count off!" they noticed ten men were missing. The rule was that if one man escaped, ten were shot. Fear rose in everyone, not knowing if they were the one chosen to be shot. But luck was in Harold's favor. Since the Japanese factories needed men to work, they decided not to kill any of the men. Towards the end of Harold's time in Davao Penal, he befriended a guard. One day the guard caught a cobra in the rice paddies. "Eat the heart and you will live a long and healthy life," said the guard. Harold accepted the heart and ate it. But snakes could not deter malnutrition.

In August 1944 the POWs boarded a "hell ship" to Luzon. "Hell ships" are the term given to the overcrowded boats the Japanese used to transport

POW Christmas under tinsel, 1944

prisoners from one location to another. Harold remembers approximately 1,000 men crammed in so tight, they had to stand. On their entrance to Manila Bay, an American torpedo struck the ship because the Japanese refused to place a Red Cross insignia on the side, which would have saved lives. The torpedo crippled the ship, but did not sink it. Once again luck was on Harold's side. The guy next to him was not so fortunate. "He's dying, and you can hear he's trying to breathe, trying to get his breath because it's so hot, stinky, and urine and feces, the top and the deck and the hull down below, and that stuff is running over. You just sat in that much down below [holds his hands about 6 inches apart], guys laying in it dying. It's unimaginable."

After arriving in Luzon, Harold spent some time in Bilibid Prison near Manila, where there was not much work for these emaciated prisoners. A truck took them to Cabanatuan shortly thereafter, where they did some farming. In September they rode back to Bilibid to prepare for transfer to Japan as slave laborers.

Japanese guards gathered all the men and began loading them into train cars with an overwhelming number of POWs in cars with a capacity for only 100. Cars usually held over 150 men. They stood so tight against each other, it was hard to breathe. Even if their legs gave out, they would still be standing because there was no place to fall. But the train cars were not the worst. When Harold and the other POWs were moved to Moji, Japan, they were loaded onto more "hell ships," tiny ships that transported POWs overseas to Japan or other countries. Since all trains ended near the ocean, more and more POWs were shoved onto these ships with little room. In the ships all the POWs were given one bucket of rice and one bucket of water. "You were lucky to be in the front where you could get some water and food. In the back, more men die." While on the hell ships, Harold watched as many of his comrades died right next to him of dehydration and hunger. One day at sea, Harold's ship was under fire from American planes. The men began to shout in the desperate fear they would sink. Later, Harold found out the Japanese didn't paint the Red Cross on the side so American planes would shoot at them. They didn't know there were POWs on board.

Harold was sent to another camp in Toyama, Japan. Unlike the first camp, this camp was very strict and guards frequently killed and beat the prisoners. At Toyama, Harold shoveled ore into furnaces. In the ore room, temperatures would rise to 114 degrees. "My eyes would get burnt and it would feel like you

got a ton of sand in your eyes. I couldn't see, and it was really painful—*really* painful." Many men died due to heat and dehydration.

Harold did not know the war ended while he was in Toyama. Unbeknownst to him and the other prisoners, the Americans had dropped atomic bombs on Hiroshima and Nagasaki, on August 6th and August 9th, respectively. One day the guards simply left the camp. The camp commander, a one-armed Japanese captain, stayed until the Americans regained control. Harold then got aboard the *USS Hasbro*, also called *The Rescue*, and threw his prison clothes overboard. The sailors gave the men Navy dungarees, a shirt, and good meal. "Wash—no, scrub,—line up for shots…and the last shot was a shot of whiskey!" He sent a message home to his folks through the Marconi telegram service in Canada; it was delivered to his mother's house by regular mail. Later in the day when she opened it up, she went into shock.

> My father in those days used to call home several times to check on her, and this day she wouldn't answer the phone, so he called the neighbor lady. The neighbor lady went over and looked through the door and saw my mother sitting at the dining room table, but she wouldn't answer the phone. So the door was unlocked by the neighbor lady, who went in and saw the telegram from me: "I'm well, I'm alive, I'm in good shape, and I'm on my way home."

From Japan, Harold went back to the Philippines to a place called the 29th Replacement Depot. From there, he boarded a ship for the United States, arriving in San Francisco about the first part of October. "And boy, when our ship was pulling in, there was all kinds of ships out. There were people waving, cheering, hollering." Harold spent a short time in Linderman General Hospital before continuing on to the Mayo Clinic in Galesburg, Illinois. He called his folks, who came up to visit, and finally got home on Halloween night 1945.

As an enlisted member of the Army Air Corps, while Harold was recovering from his incarceration, he reported to the airbase in Chicago, enlisted in the Army Air Force, and went to the Air Force hospital in Coral Gables, Florida, not too far from Miami. On a six-month leave he returned to Illinois and met a friend of his youngest brother, "and we hit it off pretty good." On April 17, 1945, they were married. Unfortunately, Eunice passed away in May 1997. Harold spent 22 more years with the Air Force, including three years in Japan. When asked if a return to Japan was "tough," considering their treatment of American POWs during the war, Harold remarked, "It was tough for me, but I didn't want to ruin the trip for my wife and three kids." In fact, on one occasion the Japanese played ball with the American kids. Only later did they confess they were a professional Japanese team! He wondered if it weren't "revenge for the war…" But Harold appreciated how safe Japan was for his family. He even saw a footlocker of money left on the street while the carriers stopped for tea on their way to the bank. Nobody touched it.

Newspaper article: "Three brothers are in U.S. Armed Forces"

Harold also returned to the Philippines with his daughter Debra for the 60th anniversary of the fall of Bataan. They stayed at the Manila Hotel and took bus trips to various places involved in the war. The first stop was Camp O'Donnell, the first POW camp in the Philippines.

> Can you imagine trying to bury 500 to 550 guys a day? Each day. There was probably 60 to 70,000 people in Camp O'Donnell. One water spigot. Imagine how long you'd have to wait in line to get a canteen full of water. People were dying. Americans were dying like 50 a day; Filipinos were dying like 500 a day… This was in a period of three to four months.

At the Camp, the Filipinos have planted 31,000 trees—one tree for each person that died at Camp O'Donnell. They are also building a compound to resemble the one used to imprison American and Filipino troops.

Harold and Debra also visited Marvalis, milepost number 1 for the Bataan Death March. A large hill with rocks against its face memorializes this event. Debra was very moved by the local woman whose family keeps the memorial clean and watered. The woman told Debra that her older sister was pregnant when the Japanese entered the Philippines. They were all working in the fields when a Japanese soldier came to their house, opened up her sister's womb, and beheaded the baby. Her husband heard the screams. While going to his wife, he was killed; she was left to bleed to death. When the Japanese left, the Filipino people dug graves with their own hands to bury the American and Filipino dead; the Japanese were "flung out into the ocean." Little wonder that, when American ex-POWs viewed the premiere of the movie The Great Raid in 2005, about the liberation of the Cabanatuan POW camp, they cheered. To this day, Harold will not own Japanese products, even a car.

Though Harold was fortunate to be with the Filipino scouts during the brutal death march on Bataan, he thinks about those who were caught in the Japanese attack.

> You take Bataan, probably 20 miles wide and 40 miles long. You put 90 to 100,000 people in that little area with absolutely nothing coming in from the outside. How long can you survive? Every plant that's edible on Bataan was eaten and every animal was eaten: snakes, cobras, pythons, monkeys. At least one-third of the troops were sick [with] malaria, dysentery, typhoid. No food. We were down to 800 to 1,000 calories a day. Ammunition was obsolete. And the people that made the march were sick. If you fell down, you couldn't get up. They bayoneted you or shot you, put you out in the road where the tanks would run over you. Absolutely nothing left.

Harold will not forget them.

A few years ago Harold moved to Peoria, Arizona, to live next door to his daughter and teach golf at a local high school. This is where we found him on his 86th birthday, cake on the counter, to celebrate surviving the hardships of the war. Though he will probably have nightmares tonight, "thinking about it again," getting up to watch History Channel shows where "the good guys got the white hat and the bad guys got the black hat," this afternoon we will eat cake and celebrate Harold's 86 years. At home. He and his daughter wonder if that cobra heart added to his longevity…

Happy 86th Birthday, Harold.

Harold, back row second from right, with fellow POWs at reunion

Norman Butler

September 1942 - February 1946
Panama, Cuba, South Pacific

"Let Those Men Go!"
An Interview with Norman Butler
By Kelly Wilcox

A seaman's worst nightmare: a kamikaze plane hitting his ship. Fortunately, Norman Butler was not aboard his first ship, a PC, or patrol craft, when it was hit, wiping out a third of its crew.

With not-so-great financial conditions after the bombing of Pearl Harbor, Butler left Kings College in Delaware to go back to his job at Weston's Electrical Instrument, which he had for eight months, until a girl down the street informed him his name was to be in the next draft. He had to do something. His mother desperately did not want him near any sort of war, so he chose the Coast Guard. When his future brother-in-law took the Marine physical with Norman and passed, she would not sign the papers for Norman to become a Marine. "She thought being in the Coast Guard, you'd stay on the coast. I didn't."

Norman enlisted in Manhattan and saw basic training in Brooklyn, not too far from home. His first assignment was to a rich man's house in Tampa, Florida, with "palm trees growing in the center of the room" and a servant who filled his wine glass whenever it was empty. He was then sent to Sarasota to patrol a nearby beach on Siesta Key. The U.S. feared enemy infiltration along the Atlantic coasts. Norman had more trouble with snakes. Whereas Arizona, where he is retired, has rattlesnakes, the cottonmouth was feared in Florida—"and they don't rattle!" An occasional cormorant spooked from the breakwater often gave the men a scare until they learned to kick the pilings to flush out the intruder.

Blackout conditions were the norm. A friend of Norman's who smoked thought he could conceal his cigarette behind a fisherman's shack; the blackout warden off Sarasota detected it and rowed over during high tide to chastise the offender. Norman flashed his buddy to warn him. The men with machine guns could not find the smoker and had to pull their boat back across the harbor at low tide through the mud. But mostly Norman and the other men walked and patrolled, encountering more mosquitoes and egg-laying turtles than enemy invaders.

In Daytona, Norman was given an IQ test by the head of his station, a high school principal. Finishing on top, Butler was given the option to go on invasion or go to service school. He said, "I just got married! I'm going to service school!" He was sent with his wife to Groton, Connecticut, home of the Coast Guard Academy, where he graduated third in his class of 200, earning him a single stripe. He chuckled. "A stripe in the Navy is worth two in the Army!" The Coast Guard is part of the Navy during wartime and the Treasury during peacetime. Unlike most of the men, Norman always had a car while at the Academy, "so we had fun."

Norman spent two or three months in Miami in a motor pool for an admiral, living in subsistence quarters off base with his wife before being transferred to a small patrol craft, or PC, whose responsibility was to monitor the waters of the Caribbean and Gulf coasts. Unfortunately the ship was in bad shape when Norman boarded, in the process of a complete overhaul. As an electrician, Norman went around the ship and "just twisted" and fixed everything "because I didn't want anything wrong if we had any action."

The PC was made for shore duty rather than large ocean crossings, but rarely did they get a berth as they patrolled near Guantanamo Bay or the other islands in the Caribbean; they usually anchored offshore. Because the ship was not made for heavy seas and was light, it rolled in the waves more than heavier craft. Norman was constantly seasick. Diesel fumes did not help. A bucket was his constant companion. In Hawaii, they finally put Norman off the ship at Sand Island to ease his illness. But more about that later.

Norman was on duty when a man fell off the boat. They sent in a small rescue boat and found there was a shark circling the man who fell in. The man survived; however, the man who jumped in to save him did not resurface. "The shark got him."

Because the patrol craft was a small ship, it left the sailors relatively free of danger from torpedoes because the ship was so small and light the torpedoes would pass under it. Due to its small size, the PC was also able to go into the ports of Iwo Jima and get radio signals and send them back to the bigger ships so they could map out bombing coordinates around the island for the Marines. It served as a great middle ground between the smaller and larger ships until attacked by a kamikaze. "I'm glad I didn't stay on that ship because a kamikaze hit that ship, right where I would have been, and they lost a third of their compliment…and I was not there."

After his time on the PC, Norman was transferred to two different DEs, or destroyer escorts. They did a lot of convoys between South America and Texas. They traveled through the Panama Canal to San Diego, an experience Norman found quite interesting, though he was shocked by the poverty of the Canal Zone towns and swore he'd never again leave the United States after the war. "This country [the United States] is so good, so clean. I will never want to go to another country."

Later, when Norman was dropped off in Hawaii at Pearl Harbor due to seasickness, his main job on the island was to make sure the buoys would go light and dark at certain times, and by certain times, we do not mean by the hour. We are talking tenths of a second. This is probably not an ideal job for a man prone to seasickness. He was good at what he did, apparently much better than what they had before at the island. The buoys had problems once or twice a week so he decided to fix that. "I lubricated everything my way—petroleum, by the way—but when I left Hawaii, we were only going out once a month, so it must work." Another task he had was to set up the harbor lights at different angles. Ironically, these lights were very high up in the middle of the water on swaying structures, once again not an ideal job for someone as seasick as Norman. Despite his seasickness, he climbed the towering 200 to 300 feet needed and repaired the lights.

Norman's primary job was maintaining the ships' electrical systems. He monitored the flow of electricity, be it direct current on the PC or alternating current on the DE, kept the generators humming, and the batteries charged. The many cables that distributed the electricity were also Norman's responsibility. He would have favored stacking the cables in a trough on the ceiling, or "topside," rather than on a rack, however, to keep them cleaner. "That's not a place for dirt! But you know, I do what they say." When the men on the ships twisted the cables of the sound power telephones, Norman had to fix those too. Another responsibility was preserving the balance of the ship's gyroscope. This was a challenge when other men tampered with it while Norman was on liberty. One time another sailor turned off the scope, causing it to "tumble." Fixing it cost the Coast Guard $10,000.

Refueling at sea was a tricky operation as lines from tankers had to be transferred to Norman's craft along with bumpers to keep the two ships from colliding. This was more difficult in the Atlantic, where the water was choppier, than in the Pacific. One reason the men hated to see the refueling tanker pull alongside was it meant they would not see land for a while. "If we're going to be refueled at sea, that means we're going to be out again. It'd be another month! You could see a ship and you could see an island, but you never got to it. That's the way it was."

In a way, Norman was also an entertainer. At least, he was the one who showed the movies on the PA to the other soldiers on the island. He did not, however, partake too much in watching the movies, at least not so much as he did washing his clothes! This was a perfect time to use the washing machine they had built out of old scraps and gears to do a "wet wash." During movie showings, the laundry area wasn't crowded, and he had a bit of time to himself.

Norman in full uniform.

Next to his base in Hawaii was an Italian prisoner of war camp. In this camp, Norman took care of the "brig"; he kept the men in order. Though Norman described such a post as "meaningless and scanty," this position took much dedication, patience, and understanding. Even with prostitutes and other immoral distractions on the island, Norman kept his head up and spirits high, remembering his wife back home.

The "greenies," men who had just gotten out of training, were stationed around the camp. Norman and his buddies would mess with them a bit, just because they were not yet acclimated to military life. Norman and his men would torment them, chucking pebbles at them, but not big stones! One prank they used on these greenies concerned a bulldozer on site. They took the bulldozer and turned it on, then headed it straight for the Pacific Ocean—with no driver to control it.

The Provost Marshall, who was the Army officer in charge of the camp there, would come out with his chief, and the bulldozers didn't have any lights on them so you couldn't see anything, and they'd say "Halt, halt!" But there was nobody on it, and the thing would be aiming towards the Pacific, and he'd have to jump in and shut the whole thing down!

When Norman was asked about fun times that occurred during his service, incidents such as those at the Italian prisoner of war camp were mentioned. Though they weren't the nicest incidents to the other party involved, Norman did have some fun with it. "So we did a few things like that. It wasn't right, you know, but what am I to say?"

Norman did not stay stationed too long in Hawaii, maybe three or four months, before he was transported to the *Peterson* for a short time until transferred to the *Marchand*, one of five flag ships in the Coast Guard. This second ship was a pleasant experience when, upon his arrival on the *Marchand*, he encountered someone he knew. "When I went out on the *Marchand* from Hawaii, guess who the head of the electrical group was—he was my instructor in the Academy. I could do no wrong!" The *Marchand*, along with the other four ships in the fleet, headed towards the South Pacific. In their best efforts they attempted to cross the equator at the same time, during which Norman and his shipmates were transformed from pollywogs to shellbacks! The *Marchand* next made its way to Guadalcanal, where they received a berth in the harbor.

There was constantly work that needed to be done on the *Marchand*; Norman made many substantial improvements. No one wanted to have management duties in the battery room, which was dirty and just a mess. However, Norman took it as a challenge, and not only did he clean it up and organize the battery room, he made waterproof connections from the batteries to wherever they were on the ship. This was definitely not a petty job.

One humorous incident Norman recalls at Guadalcanal was when a man on a scooter came with orders for their captain. Norman and his crew stole the scooter, disassembled it, and hid it in the engine room! Something else that's funny that still sticks with Norman today was that the natives would do just about anything for peroxide. This seems pretty strange; however, peroxide was a cheap way to change their hair color from black to a lighter color such as brown or blonde.

One may think sleeping is one of the few times a sailor gets to himself. Think again. Norman was on dry deck, but still sleeping with the fishes! On destroyer escorts the men were supposed to sleep "topside" to keep away from mosquitoes that transmit malaria. They slept on the bow of the ship, thinking they were safe, so slept soundly— for about five minutes. Then flying fish would spring up onto the deck. Despite this damp and malodorous inconvenience, the sailors simply threw them off the deck in the morning. Looking back, Norman can't help but laugh at his naiveté as a young sailor, especially the fact that he also slept on an ammo box when on deck. If he had rolled off, he would have most definitely been shark bait. Norman laughed, "But when you're young, you do those things, you know."

As the war wound down, Norman was put on air-sea rescue, "in case anything happened while bringing the fellas back." Many of the Army and Marine men returning home didn't even have their own water and had to eat the diet of powdered food on board ship. Though most people think all ships have the best food in the armed forces, think again. "We had everything aboard ship. Like, I'm used to having powdered milk and green syrup for pancakes, powdered anything, powdered eggs, anything! You think we're supposed to have the best? Forget it!" In port they had fresh food; when that ran out at sea, powdered food was the normal fare.

His ship stopped in the Russell and Phoenix Islands to pick up Marines, eager to get home. The weary soldiers thought rolling around on the ship would make it go faster. "But you can't make a ship go faster. That's silly to use up your fuel that way." The ship usually did 15 to 20 knots coming back to the States, but could do 30 in an emergency. "Nobody did that unless they had to." While passing the Pacific islands, Norman noticed the damage. "No trees at all—crazy. They destroyed everything."

Norman's ship did not stop in Hawaii. It continued through the Panama Canal up to South Carolina. For a while, Norman wasn't sure when he was going to get out, because of his selfish skipper. "I had an order to get out, and we all had enough points to get out, but the skipper thought it'd be nice to prolong his assignment, his time, you know. So we went to South Carolina. They overruled his orders, and radioed Washington anyhow, and Washington radioed back, 'Let those men go!' So he had to turn the ship around." Norman boarded a train in Jacksonville, Florida, for New York, where he mustered out and joined his wife.

After returning home, Norman used his experience with electrical systems in his civilian life. He made thermometers for Alaska, then got a job with a wiring company. He became wiring inspector later on, "where they did the work and I looked at it; that was the best thing!" He eventually bought a house in 1946. Now residing in Fountain Hills, Arizona, with his wife Allie years after the war, he still doesn't forget what happened. As for every sailor, being in the Coast Guard shapes who you are, your courage, your strength, your compassion, and your patriotism to your country.

Though he was brought up on guns, Norman never liked them. Once when he was in charge of a brig, he took the men to lunch and tried to "convert" them to cleaner living. One man who was drunk all the time on torpedo juice, they simply put in the attic until he sobered up. Norman also took care of a 40-year-old coxswain retired from the service who found himself drunk much of the time, though he was a "happy drunk." If a man escaped from the brig, the sailor on guard had to serve his sentence. So Norman told the men, "Don't go, 'cause I can shoot," though he admits he never could have shot another American soldier. The enemy were another matter. He even gets choked up when he thinks of how poorly some of the men treated a collie he befriended while patrolling in Daytona. Remember, Norman joined the Coast Guard so he would never have to hurt anyone. This gentle man was able to live up to that promise.

His mother would be proud.

Lyle French

August 1941 - January 1946
England, N. Africa, Italy

Surgical Marathon

An Interview with Gene French about her husband Lyle
By Nicole Liebgold

"Hi, Dad! When are you coming home?" Lyle nearly fainted. He was calling his wife Gene to tell her he was finally coming home after three long years of overseas service in World War II. To his surprise, it was his three-year-old son Fred, whom he had never met, that answered the telephone and spoke to his father for the first time, not only devoid of all baby talk, but in complete sentences. He later told his wife, "I knew he was three years old and I knew about the size he would be, but it never occurred to me he could talk and answer the telephone."

At the age of twenty-seven, Lyle French was sent to Birmingham, England, on October 5, 1942, to serve in World War II. Coincidentally, his first son was born that very same day. Their meeting would have to be postponed because a new chapter of Lyle's life was just beginning. Lyle had joined the Reserves while in medical school to help with expenses. In July of 1941 he was called to active duty at O'Reilly General Hospital in Springfield, Missouri, a "brand new hospital" managed by the Army, but which did not have any patients. Lyle was made Chief of Surgery and Chief of Anesthesiology. Ironically their surgical instruments were packed in gauze and Vaseline inside 12x4-inch metal cans left over from World War I. After December 7, patients began to arrive. From there, Lyle was sent to Fort Sill, Oklahoma, to join the 26th General Hospital as a neurosurgeon, three years after graduating from the University of Minnesota. Gene came with him, but not as a nurse because she was married. The nurses at that time were all Red Cross recruits. Besides that, she was pregnant.

The 26th General Hospital, formed in World War I, got orders to proceed to England. Not wishing to leave Gene in Oklahoma seven months' pregnant, Lyle drove her back to Minnesota. Fred was born the same day Lyle was shipped from Oklahoma to New Jersey, and then overseas. Lyle did get the message he had a son.

After a "pretty treacherous journey" to England, Lyle lived in some red-brick apartments and worked with the 26th. The American invasion of North Africa changed his status. The 26th General Hospital was sent in boxcars, "like cattle," to Constantine, Algeria, where they set up a tent hospital. From Constantine they moved across Algeria, eventually settling in Oran.

They took under their wing anyone who was wounded, including Germans, on whom Lyle had no difficulty operating. He already spoke a fair amount of German. Back when Lyle was a teenager in Mankato, Minnesota, his high school burned down. The kids from his school were temporarily relocated to another high school in New Ulm, Minnesota, where almost everybody spoke German. Since they would be spending a year at this school, necessity forced Lyle to learn German, not knowing how helpful it would one day become.

Thankfully, due to Africa's intense heat, they did not have wetness or pneumonia to harbor infection, which greatly reduced the number of patients in the tent hospital. The hospital's only misfortune was that sheets mysteriously disappeared on several occasions. They eventually discovered that after the nurses hung the laundry out to dry, the local Arabs stole their laundry and wore the stolen goods around town.

After the fall of Africa they moved to Bari, Italy, on December 2, 1943, becoming seasick on the LSTs used in the crossing. The 26th took over an Italian hospital formerly run by the Italian army. The night Lyle got there, Bari harbor was bombed during a German surprise attack in the biggest bombing since Pearl Harbor. All of the ships in Bari harbor at the time were destroyed, including the one belonging to the 26th General Hospital. Fortunately Lyle and the majority of his peers were not on the ship at the time of the bombing. The only two casualties from their unit were the unfortunate men who had stayed onboard to guard the medical equipment from potential theft. Their efforts were in vain because most of the medical supplies were destroyed anyway in the bombing, and the two men guarding them were killed. Not only was the surgical equipment lost, but the men's Christmas presents as well. The soldiers' families had sent their presents early; the men were saving them on the ship to open on Christmas Day. The 26th General Hospital was left with no supplies or Christmas presents, so they sent Lyle and another man to Naples to borrow supplies from neighboring units.

During this expedition, Lyle was detached to the British army, who needed a neurosurgeon; theirs had been killed in the African campaign. Lyle went up Italy with that unit for a short time before returning to the American army, this time to the 170th Evacuation Hospital. This hospital was constantly under fire and was blown up on several occasions. One time, after twenty-four hours of intense surgery, the unit was bombed and the patients Lyle had just operated on were tragically killed.

Through Lyle's time in the service he was able to save many lives that might have otherwise been lost. On April 14, 1945, ten men from the 10th Mountain Division, who had been injured in the attack on Hill 913 in Italy, were brought to the tent hospital for treatment. One of these men was none other than former US Senator and Presidential Candidate Bob Dole, who had been shot in the shoulder. This injury resulted in the paralysis of his right hand and arm, an affliction the politician still deals with today. During surgery, Lyle found small bone fractures in Bob's neck that he had to remove with forceps. Also, Mr. Dole developed a hematoma and had ruptured blood vessels that caused him to lose a significant amount of blood. After the surgery, Dole remembers being in a hospital building when he regained consciousness, but this is inaccurate because Mr. Dole's first surgery was completed in the tent hospital. Not too long ago, Gene received a copy of Senator Dole's book *One Soldier's Story*, which stated, "Years later Dr. French sent me his handwritten notes regarding my condition that day. He told me there is no question that I had sustained a severe injury not only of the bones but also of the nerves, in part from shell fragments and in part from the loss of blood because of the hematoma and the ruptured blood vessels. Within twenty-four hours Dr. French operated on ten men from the 10th Mountain Division's attack on Hill 913. In notes that he later recorded in his ledger of patients he treated that day, the doctor wrote about me."

On a separate occasion, Lyle found himself in another frenzied twenty-four hour surgical marathon that left him extremely fatigued. He decided to take a nap in a nearby foxhole. He nestled into the hole and, using his Valpack as a pillow, dozed off to sleep. Sometime during his nap, 170th Evacuation was shelled. Lyle awoke disoriented and confused, probably thinking the scene around him was a dream. He heard the unmistakable sound of a shell coming his way. Before Lyle could react, a shell fragment pierced the Valpack and a large piece of shrapnel "welded" to the mess kit on which he was resting, missing his head miraculously by only a couple of

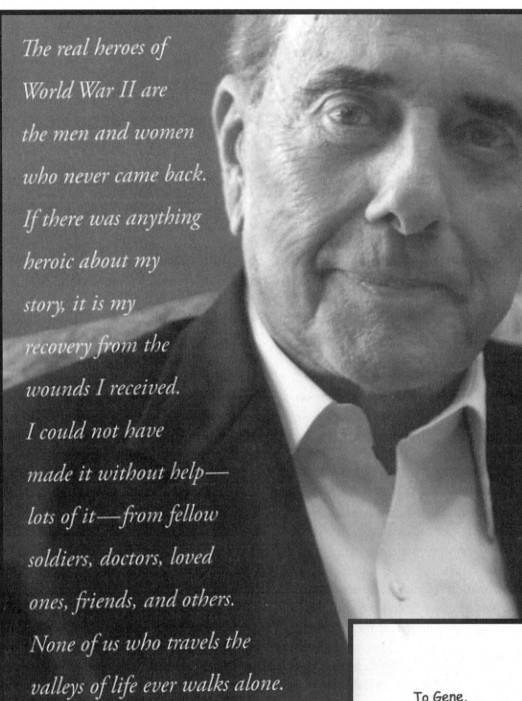

The real heroes of World War II are the men and women who never came back. If there was anything heroic about my story, it is my recovery from the wounds I received. I could not have made it without help— lots of it—from fellow soldiers, doctors, loved ones, friends, and others. None of us who travels the valleys of life ever walks alone.

To Gene,
Whose husband,
Dr. Lyle French,
saved my life in Italy

Bob Dole

inches. The bullet also pierced Lyle's two medical volumes behind his head.

In 1944, Lyle and his family expected him to return home shortly because of his two years of service. He was sent to Naples to board a ship that would reunite him with his wife and introduce him to his son. He was to spend a night in Naples and leave the next morning. Unexpected things seemed to happen to Lyle when he was asleep because he found himself shaken by another soldier who told him he had just been promoted from Captain to Major. This meant he would have to spend another year in Italy with the 170th Evacuation Hospital.

Several times, Lyle was asked to operate on patients secretly. In Venice, he was kept in the basement of a church across from St. Mark's Square for several days, operating by lantern light. The patients were both American and Italian. On another night, Lyle and a few other surgeons were taken on a plane to perform some kind of emergency surgery. The mission was top secret and Lyle was not told where he was going or upon whom he would be operating, but judging from the length of the flight he guessed it must have been in Yugoslavia. He suspects the patients were upper level staff officers, but he never knew for sure. After his job was over, he was taken out by cover of darkness and flown back to the hospital. For some reason Lyle was never told why their mission was a secret.

Lyle was finally allowed to return home in September of 1945 and landed in Boston. From Boston he was sent to Wisconsin, where he was formally discharged. After three long years of being away from home, Lyle was reunited with his beloved wife Gene, who had been working as a neurosurgical nurse while Lyle was overseas. The two found there was no strangeness between them despite their time apart, and their lives essentially reverted to the way they had been before the war. When Lyle was overseas, the two were able to keep in touch through V-Mail, a system where soldiers would handwrite letters that were photographed by the Army on 4x6 pieces of paper and sent to their wives or other family members. Gene also kept busy with her nursing, until the strain of working and raising her son became too much.

This child didn't have much of a mother and he didn't have a father because we operated in those days from eleven o'clock in the morning 'til nine o'clock at night, plus being on call. I was on call twenty-four hours a day. I was the only neurosurgical nurse and so if they had an emergency, no matter what time of day or night it was, I had to go to the hospital and work. After about a year I decided that this was crazy. So I quit that job, went downtown, and tried working in an office. I did that for maybe six months and I thought no, so I gave up, went to California for Christmas with my father and sisters, and stayed 'til the war ended.

Gene thinks young women today may have more difficulty coping while their husbands are overseas. Seeing them on television, talking on the phone, or corresponding through computers could make the pain of physical separation more severe. Gene had the

Lyle with shrapnel welded to mess kit

support of the other doctors' wives and their families; she was also a nurse.

The transition from the war zone to the workplace was not very difficult for Lyle because throughout everything he was still a doctor. He returned to the University of Minnesota where his old position was waiting for him. His war experiences aided him in the writing of his master's thesis on the early repair of peripheral nerves. At the time, wounds were first cleaned and bandaged to be operated on at a later date. It was Lyle's idea that it would be better to operate right away after an injury, rather than waiting, while the wounds were freshly severed. This

26th General Hospital beds, Constantine, Algeria

is because nerves retract as soon as they are cut or injured, leaving a gap where the nerve would otherwise be. If they could resuture those nerves quickly enough, the patient would heal significantly better because those nerves could then regenerate if they were reattached. This resulted in the patient being able to use that limb again.

After his return home he completed his schooling, receiving his Master's Degree and PHD from the University of Minnesota. He found that his military service was "invaluable" because of all the trauma surgery he had performed overseas. When he returned, he went back to doing primarily neurosurgical procedures. The general surgeries he performed in the high risk atmosphere of a war zone helped him hone his surgical skills.

After the birth of their second child, Lyle became a professor at the University of Minnesota and also the head of the department. He would stay with the University working as the first Vice President for all of the Health Sciences until 1982. He was President of the Neurosurgical Society of America from 1957 to 1958, and President of the American Association of Neurosurgical Surgeons from 1973 to 1974. He was also the President of the Academy of Neurosurgery. He received the Harvey Cushing Medal from the American Association of Neurosurgeons and

had the Lyle A. French Chair named after him at the University of Minnesota Medical School.

Lyle French passed away unexpectedly on October 19, 2004, at the age of eighty-nine. He was diagnosed with congestive heart failure in June of 2004, but the cause of his death was that his kidneys stopped functioning after a cardiac arrest. In the months prior to his death he received one final honor in June, the Neurosurgical Society of America Service Award, and celebrated his sixty-third anniversary with his wife Gene in September. From interviewing Gene it was obvious the two had an exceptionally strong bond and that they were truly life partners.

As a whole, Lyle French's military career was like an epic three-year surgical marathon, during which he saved countless lives in a myriad of locations, moving from surgery to surgery at a relatively rapid pace.

Phil Goan

July 1943 - April 1946
France, Germany, U.S.

The Bottom of the Heap
An Interview with Phil Goan
By Allison Wooten

Phil Goan, a young college student at the age of 18, was ripped from his American college lifestyle and thrown into the war-stricken region of Europe during the final and most brutal stages of World War II. He served as a mortar gunner for the 276th Infantry Regiment of the 70th Infantry Division. This is his story.

Phil Goan's war memories start in the year 1939 when he was only fourteen, long before a gun was ever put into his hands. His family lived next to a thickly accented German who was close friends with Phil's father, and it was from this man that Phil first learned of Germany's politics, and the possibility of America going to war. His senior year of high school, Phil attempted to join the Navy; however, he flunked the eye exam and therefore was not able to enter the military. "That summer my buddies had decided that we were all going to go in the Navy, and I went in the Navy with them as far as the basement of our post office, and I flunked reading the eye chart. I was very tall and they said, 'Can you read that E?' And with one eye I could read it just perfectly, and I didn't notice that with the other eye I couldn't, so they said, 'Well, walk forward until you can read it,' and I walked forward until I hit my head on a steam pipe, and that ended my career in the Navy three minutes after it started."

In 1943, just a few days after Phil's 18th birthday, he was drafted. Being a college student, among other things, Phil believed he would be sent to A.S.T.P.—Army Specialized Training Program. However, upon entering Macon, Georgia, to his horror he learned he was to be sent to Camp Wheeler I.R.T.C., or Infantry Replacement Training Camp, as Phil saw it, "the bottom of the heap." It was a typical boot camp where "their mission was to train us physically and demoralize us mentally." But being a fit, young eighteen year old, he got through camp without any considerable struggle.

After Camp Wheeler Phil was sent home on a two-week pass, during which he was stricken with appendicitis. After a harsh recovery he arrived at his port of embarkation two days late and was immediately put in the guard house, with stitches still in his side. He was expected to leave for Europe after two days in the guard house but was still recovering from his appendicitis and in no shape to fight a war. On the day of his departure he was allowed to see the inspector general who, upon seeing Phil's condition, told him he needed to go to the hospital, not into combat.

When his stitches were removed, Phil was sent to Fort Leonard Wood, Missouri, where his real military career began. He was assigned to the 70th Infantry Division and sent off to Europe on a troop ship called the *USS West Point*, a converted luxury liner stripped of its luxury and now used to transport GIs to Europe and enemy prisoners on the return trip. Due to the speed of the ship they traveled, without escort, straight south of Boston, across the equator and the south Atlantic "where presumably there were no subs," through the Strait of Gibraltar, and up the coast of Southern France. They landed on a beach somewhere in southern France. As for where in southern France they landed, all Phil can tell is "we landed in the dark of night on a pebbly beach, wasn't sandy, it was just pebbly with big hillsides right behind it, and there was no town, there was no sign board, there was no light, and there were no Frenchmen so I don't really know where we landed."

From their arrival they hiked to the town of Marseilles, where they boarded boxcars that would take them to the combat zone—in their case to the town of Bischwiller, a small town on the edge of the Rhine River, near Switzerland. Part of their combat was fought across the Rhine River. Phil tells how the machine gun shells would skip across the river and harass the soldiers on the other side. This was an extremely intense battle, with the untrained GIs fighting against the highly experienced and equipped Waffen SS division. By the end of this battle only 35 of the original 187 American soldiers remained.

The final battle for Phil was the battle for Forbach. "It was an industrial town that the Germans held, but we wanted it for the gateway to Saarbrucken. This was our division's mission." It was a steep mountainous area, and the

men approached the town under the cover of darkness. They dug in for the night on top of a hill on the outskirts of town. In the morning when they awoke, they were shocked to see that in the darkness they had dug their foxholes right underneath the second story window of a house; in a combat zone this is a place you never want to be. Sleeping in a bunker with the enemy above you is basically the same as sleeping in a death trap.

That morning Phil and another GI entered the town of Forbach. They intended to scope out the town for the rest of the platoon, but as they walked around to the front of the house under which they had been so dangerously "dug in" the night before, they spotted a German soldier "standing at parade rest by an artillery piece." Both Phil and his German enemy took a shot at each other but only succeeded in making a lot of noise. Phil and his buddy headed towards the building they had intended to investigate, and as they did, eight "Krauts," or German soldiers, came out and surrendered to him. "They came out of the house with their hands up." Phil and his buddy marched the men back to the wine cellar where their company CP was and turned them in. For his heroic actions Phil earned a Bronze Star; it was mailed to him when he returned home to Billings, Montana. His

Soldier with "Welcome to Forbach, Through Courtesy of the 276th Infantry Regiment." (Courtesy Men and a Time Remembered, *H. Lynn McGuire, Andrew J. McMahon, Philip C. Lester)*

more instant gratification, though, was that he got one of the German soldier's P-38 pistols and some German sausage, which at that time he appreciated even more than the weapon.

They were never short of ammunition, but they were always short of food, and they all got very skinny. Phil is 6 feet, 4 inches and a healthy 215 pounds now, but upon returning from Europe he was about 129 pounds and at the time only 6 feet tall. The men had K-rations and maybe a hot meal once a month, but they were too far away from the trucks that delivered the food and the blankets. People weren't anxious to get up near the front lines to give them any supplies because of how dangerous it was. The troops were terribly neglected because of their location, and it wasn't until about a month later that they were given their first change of clothes and underwear and their first shower.

Everyone carried a heavy load. Phil was ammo bearer for a mortar and had a canvas piece over his front and back to carry four heavy mortar shells in front and four in back, and on his pistol belt he clipped a .45-caliber pistol, a couple of hand grenades, a first aid kit, a canteen, and a shovel. One of his buddies had to help him stand up. Phil talks very little of these hardships, nonetheless, and even goes so far as to say it was not the Germans that were their greatest enemy but the cold. Their uniforms were thin olive jackets, incapable of providing the warmth necessary for the temperatures they were in. The biggest issue was their feet, which were never warm. "They were not frozen, really; they were just never warm and never dry. My Mom used to knit socks and mail them to me. I would pin them in my field jacket so my back would get the socks warm and hopefully somewhat dry so I could change them

every two or three days. I only had the two pair, the ones on my feet and the ones pinned in my jacket."

As the soldiers traveled deeper into Forbach, they faced greater resistance, and the capture of Forbach turned out to be an "immense battle" that lasted over a week with the Germans retreating slowly,

R and R in France 1944, Phil standing in the snow next to a tent

street by street, block by block. After conquering Forbach, and while his division was still creating plans as how to best cross the Saar, Phil became sick with a common case of yellow jaundice, otherwise known as hepatitis. He was taken to a hospital in Verdun, France, where he remained until the end of the war.

When the war in Europe ended, Phil and his buddies made plans to escape the hospital, in fear they would be sent to combat in Japan if they waited around for their reassignment. So they escaped the hospital, which was built like a prison, and Phil hitchhiked back to Germany where he met his company in the town of St. Gore. It was said Hitler kept his yacht in this town, but it was supposedly sunk by the time Phil and his friends arrived. They stayed in a nice castle, and "fiddled and diddled" around until they were all transferred somewhere else. Some men were sent home, but Phil was assigned a clerk typist job with the 3rd Infantry Division Headquarters after trying out for the basketball team. This was merely a job to keep him busy until the serious military action ended at St. Gore around the spring of 1946. There was still policing to be done, but his training was in combat and not compatible with the formal code of behavior that an occupational role entailed. He didn't follow military protocol, such as saluting his superiors and so forth. "In combat it was dangerous to call attention to the executive officers," as he learned early on when both lieutenants in his company were picked off by snipers. The closest Phil got to being in an occupation army was guarding a brewery in a Kassel, Germany. Phil and his men had to keep the GIs from the beer to save it for the Officers Club. The beer was called Adolph Kopf, and Phil remembers it fondly.

When asked about the damages he saw, Phil responded that they didn't have a tank or howitzer at the time and so little structural damage was done to the buildings, but they did damage roofs and windows. "Infantry are after the people, not the buildings generally." The houses were stone, but sometimes the soldiers used white phosphorous grenades to burn them down. He remembers with guilt going into a home and bumping into a chandelier because he was so tall, then pulling it down and breaking it for no reason. The one town he does remember as greatly damaged was the city of Cologne. The army sent him to Cologne to count gas masks for no apparent reason and "Cologne downtown was just rubble from the bombers." The airplanes did miss the Cologne cathedral, fortunately, and it stood marvelously amongst all the rubble; however, he later learned it was only the exterior that remained intact, while the interior was severely damaged.

But the war brought Phil to dislike some things as well. To this day he does not like the 4th of July because of all the loud banging fireworks, and he doesn't have much love for the French people either. He feels the French did very little to help fight their own war, even though America was in this war defending the French. "We did better trying to bum potatoes and eggs off of German housewives than we did the French."

Phil was not the only one in his family recruited to World War II. He has two brothers. One was a pilot that flew a PBY, a big flying "boat" used to get MacArthur out of the Philippines, and a military air transport. The other was a mechanic in North Africa. His brother the mechanic was ironically the one to die in a plane wreck.

Phil recently ran into an old war buddy who had sent him on a sort of suicide assignment during the war. He had sent Phil out to be the signal man in a foxhole to watch for approaching German troops. Phil waited in the hole until night, and then returned to his platoon without ever seeing any German troops or hearing from the ambush party behind him. What he never knew was that the squad to his rear had been "shelled" and most of the men were casualties. Once again it was ironic that Phil had been put in harm's way so that other men would be warned of the approaching enemy, and instead the enemy took them by surprise and Phil ended up being too far ahead of the squad to be in danger.

Phil was one of the last soldiers to arrive home. He married his wife Joan in 1949 and didn't talk about the war or tell any war stories until the last few years. It has been only recently that he has come in contact with some of his very close friends from the war. In fact, he just had a reunion in Scottsdale this summer with some of his old buddies.

Phil is living a comfortable life now and appreciates the VA benefits he receives. He has come to respect the German people who, during the war, were always very "civil," at least to the extent their duties would allow. And though this war has by necessity had a great impact on his life, it does define the man he is today.

Anthony Gray

August 1942 - December 1945
Pearl Harbor, South Pacific

Dungaree Navy

An Interview with Anthony Gray
By Barbara Hatch

     Tony Gray is one of 16 million men who served their country during World War II. A farm boy from Winamac, Indiana, who had never seen the ocean, Tony left trade school to join the Navy at the "ripe age" of 20.

     With American losses at Pearl Harbor, the Navy needed replacements, and they needed them fast. After three and a half weeks of boot camp in San Diego, Tony and three other recruits were selected for training in what was whisperingly referred to as "radar." While the remaining 156 men in Tony's unit quickly found ships, Tony and the others were transferred from Mare Island to Pearl Harbor to Treasure Island, just missing their ships by a few days. Finally Tony got aboard a new Liberty ship, the *USS Celeno*, AK-76, in January 1943.

     This apprentice seaman added another first to his list: he saw fighter planes. As part of the "dungaree Navy," his ship's job was hauling cargo to American bases in the South Pacific.

> …all kinds of machinery and welding machines, well, let's see, every type of construction equipment, materials, building materials, supplies, military supplies, food, medical—just everything that wartime needs required. That was the type of cargo that we had…And then we were loaded with primarily aviation gas and bombs to take up to Guadalcanal—the Solomon Islands. But instead of going to the Solomon Islands from New Zealand, we were sent back to New Caledonia and unloaded and then we got another load of general cargo, generally building materials, harbor nets, big buoys for holding the nets over the harbor entrances where submarines couldn't get in to where ships might have been berthed in a kind of a protected area around the islands, particularly on Tulagi island or even around Guadalcanal.

In his 25 months aboard the *Celeno*, his ship stopped in Noumea, New Caledonia; the Solomons, including Guadalcanal; the New Hebrides; Fiji; and New Zealand. They were busy.

The USS Celeno

Your job was doing physical types of things—loading, unloading cargo, keeping equipment maintained that you used, whatever it might be, whether it was winches or motors or air conditioners or refrigeration. The deck gang [was] maintaining lines, the ropes and all the other kinds of equipment that was being used. That was your job. And each person had something in the gang that they were with, or the group that they worked with, that they should be responsible for doing. And of course, there was always something that needed doing.

Hauling cargo was not without risk. On June 16, 1943, spotters near the Solomons reported 120 Japanese planes approaching Guadalcanal, site of heavy ship concentration and the Army's Henderson Field. At 1:30—red alert! Despite heavy anti-aircraft fire, the *Celeno* took four hits. Fifteen men were killed, 19 burned and maimed. Japanese skip bombing blew holes in *Celeno's* side; water came aboard. Another craft pushed the ship to the beach while uninjured sailors accounted for casualties and damages. Eventually it was decided the ship could be salvaged. It was towed back to the United States, passing under the Golden Gate Bridge on September 30, 1943, repaired, then retrofitted to haul both cargo and troops to northern Pacific islands where the action had moved. "That was one major action that a lot of new sailors that had never seen anything like that in their lives, why, rescuing the, you know, dying, and people who were damaged, or people who were injured, particularly by strafing and shrapnel and fires. Those are deadly things aboard a ship." One frightening moment occurred when another sailor commented, "I thought you were dead." Turns out another man

aboard the ship also bore the name Gray. Since men rarely addressed each other by their full names, preferring nicknames like Red or Curly or Tex, mix-ups happened. Tony simply replied, "No, that was the other guy."

Besides loading and unloading cargo, the "dungaree Navy" kept men busy maintaining the ship. Because ships rust in the salt air, men constantly chipped paint and repainted. "Clean and sweep down fore and aft" started every morning. Seamen removed cigarette butts, paper—the debris of life aboard ship. Of course, radiomen had their regular jobs. When Tony became Quartermaster, he kept sea charts updated and logged the ship's daily activities. After suffering through the apprentice days of "destination unknown" when leaving a port, Tony thought it might be more interesting to know where his ship was headed, "to kind of be in the know what was going on 'cause everything else aboard a ship is usually considered 'scuttlebutt.'"[1] At Ie Shima and Okinawa from May to July 1945, Tony kept track of typhoons that threatened American ships. The *USS Hamul*, his new ship, was in three. He remembers "green water" coming over the bow as the ocean rose up. He was grateful the commander took the waves head-on. Getting hit sideways could capsize a ship.

Quartermaster duties, however, meant less R & R. In a port like New Zealand, men got either port or starboard liberty, meaning half the crew stayed on ship while the other half went ashore. But there was always a Quartermaster on duty with the officer of the deck. Time off in ports, though, was welcomed. Tony mostly remembers the liberties of New Zealand's "stike and eggs" and the chance to drink real milk. Although Tony never liked the milk from his dad's "straw stack dairy," it was a relief to get away from the ship's powdered milk and "Marine butter," thick enough to hold up in warm climates. "They'd have a 10-gallon can with fresh milk sitting on the table there and you'd just help yourself. Most of it was almost SPAM and milk, I mean, when you had a chance. I don't know how many 10-gallon cans they'd go through a day, but every time you walked by, you'd grab a cup of milk and down it and enjoy every drop of it."

Unfortunately much of the ship's cargo was delivered to small war-damaged islands devoid of ports. There Tony spent his time beachcombing for souvenirs, trading his two beers for other men's two Pepsis, which he could bring back aboard ship. Per Navy regulations, alcohol was not permitted at sea. This farm boy avoided the gambling on payday. One older carpenter's mate named "Pop" wore a money belt that resembled a loaf of bread; when the ship reached port, he wired his winnings home. Tony decided early on, "Ooh, boy, that's not for me."

Neither a reader nor writer, mail did not provide much distraction from daily chores. Going from one island to another, letters took months to catch up with the men. By the time they arrived, "the corners were worn off, kind of tattered and shredded." Parcels in metal boxes further chewed up the letters; some were inevitably lost along the way. Sadly, it took two weeks until Tony heard his father had passed away. A Red Cross radiogram informed him while he was in the Solomons. "If advisable, please inform Seaman Gray father passed away April 19th." Some of his father's letters did not reach him for nearly three years—after he died. What further irritated the men was the three or four "fellas" who received daily newspapers. Sailors saw the large mail bags, hoping for letters,

Anthony in full uniform.

finding them filled instead with out-of-date newspapers. Of course, censors cut out any G.I. references to ship locations in their letters, causing girls back home to wonder, "What is he trying to tell me?"

Tony served until August 1945, when two atomic bombs ended the war. He vividly remembers the exuberance of the sailors. "People just went crazy… without authorization of course, they started shooting anti-aircraft guns, the high artillery shells, tracers were flying everywhere" until the skipper called "general quarters," returning men to their battle stations. This quelled the celebrations. Though no one was injured on the *Hamul*, exploding shells and raining shell fragments led to casualties elsewhere. "That was the exuberance that people felt, that the war was going to be over."

Having taken little R & R while at sea, Tony hopped an early ship home. In January 1945, on his first trip back, he accompanied 2,000 war brides from New Zealand and Australia and their children, along with a group from India who called themselves the FBI, the "Forgotten Bastards of India." At war's end, Tony sailed on the *Wesson*, which acted like a "taxi" back to the States for returning G.I.s. When the *Wesson's* skipper was ordered to tow a recaptured American ship back to Pearl Harbor, however, he conveniently "forgot to hitch his tow in Guam," commenting, "To hell with this. We're going home!" Tony never knew what happened to that skipper.

Going "home," for Tony, was bittersweet. His mother had died in February of 1940, his father during the war, his siblings had homes of their own. The farm on which he had been raised "was gone." After a short homecoming, Tony decided to take a "vacation" in Chicago to visit a Navy buddy, perhaps shop for civilian clothes. In Fowler, Indiana, all he could acquire was a Samsonite suitcase and a new pair of Florscheim shoes! Even the Chicago department stores still reflected wartime scarcity. After several stops, someone mentioned Carson, Pirie, and Scott had gotten a big shipment in the boys' department. Of diminutive stature, Tony got a top coat, a suit, and two white shirts. "They were boys' sizes—and they fit!"

While in the Navy, Tony dreamed of owning a car. He'd saved his cash. He was ready to buy a car "right now!" But cars were still scarce unless you were willing to pay "under the table several times what they were worth, which my Irish temperament would not permit me to do." Instead he enrolled in the Agriculture School at Purdue University on funds from the G.I. Bill. "Being a farm kid in the Depression, you never had a snowball's chance in hell of ever going to college if you didn't have the money. And, of course, farmers never have any money." Putting up with attic accommodations in the Agriculture/ Engineering building—heaven after sleeping on ships—until locating off-campus housing, Tony graduated in June 1949 with a Bachelor of Science degree in General Agriculture.

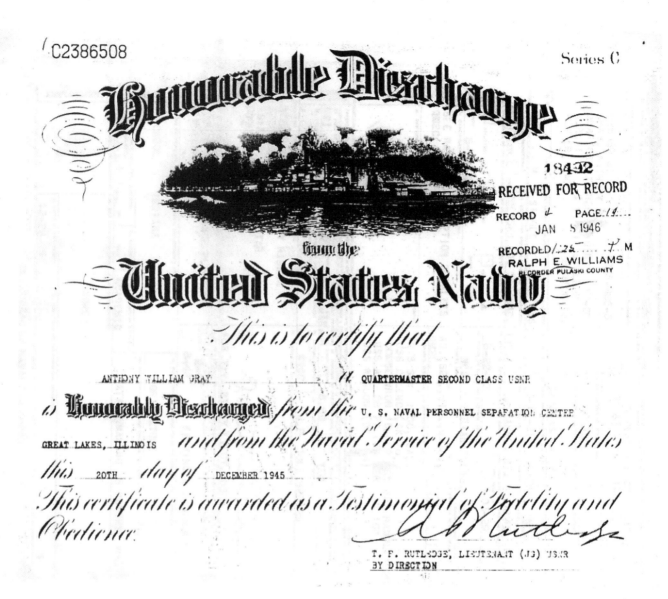

Honorable Discharge

from the

United States Navy

This is to certify that

ANTHONY WILLIAM GRAY   A QUARTERMASTER SECOND CLASS USNR

is *Honorably Discharged from the* U. S. NAVAL PERSONNEL SEPARATION CENTER

GREAT LAKES, ILLINOIS *and from the Naval Service of the United States*

this 20TH *day of* DECEMBER 1945

This certificate is awarded as a Testimonial of Fidelity and Obedience.

T. F. RUTLEDGE, LIEUTENANT (JG) USNR
BY DIRECTION

18432
RECEIVED FOR RECORD
RECORD 4   PAGE 19
JAN 5 1946
RECORDED 125   P M
RALPH E. WILLIAMS
RECORDER PULASKI COUNTY

When asked what his Navy service meant to him, Tony revealed his Midwestern farming values. He didn't think his story was unique or he had done anything special. He was simply one of 10 million others the Navy had given a "liberal education."

I had experiences in living and working with people that you would never have an occasion to experience in your lifetime under different circumstances. I mean, you discovered that a lot of things that you might have considered very important really don't amount to a damn as far as anything important is concerned. That living your life with peace of mind is something that you really kind of have to plan for. You can't be concerned about things that are not of importance to you, keeping in mind that humanity, we all should have a goal, and that we should realize that we are on this earth for a comparatively short time. And the things that we do have quite an impact not only on ourselves but on those around you.

He thinks back on his war experience with amazing peace of mind. "If you use the philosophy of having each day one that for your having been there or doing what you did, helps not only yourself but helps others, you have a tranquility that's kind of unshakeable." He knows his generation left the world a bit better than they found it.

Not bad for a bunch of farm boys in dungarees.

Emery Hildebrandt

1942 - 1946
North Atlantic, South Pacific

Old Nameless

An Interview with Emery Hildebrandt
By Kevin Hildebrandt

Born in South Dakota, Emery Hildebrandt served as a signalman aboard the ship named for the state in which he was born, though no one would know it. Being raised a farm boy, Emery learned to never question his elders, especially those higher in rank, and when he entered the Navy that was expected. "I was a pretty naïve little guy—still am. The situation was, I would do anything anybody would tell me to do that was in authority. I seldom questioned anything."

So it was that, beckoned by the world's war and the attack on his country, Emery took upon himself the responsibility for defending that country and enlisted in March of 1942. Leaving Oregon State University at the age of twenty after attending for two years, Emery took the train to San Diego. He found his niche in the Navy, where he felt he was safe. At the time, he never thought of great danger or death.

At least *I* didn't think we were in much danger. I never was worried or felt like I'd lose my life or something. On board that ship we were safe. We had thousands of tons of steel around us.

That is why the Navy suited him, although he began to second-guess his decision on choosing the Navy when he stepped aboard his first transport ship.

There were thousands of us on that ship, everybody puking and vomiting because everyone was sick. The "heads" were just terrible and everybody— I can remember that it was the saddest thing that I saw, just riding in that transport ship to Hawaii. I got real sick out on the sea, and I didn't know whether or not it was a good idea for me to be in the Navy or not.

Upon arrival in Hawaii, however, Emery began to feel the reason he was there. Looking at the destruction of Pearl Harbor and knowing the frightening terror of this invasion, he knew it was what he needed to do. "I don't think I ever hated the Japanese, or I never had any feelings about them. I just thought it was the loyal thing to do." It was in doing this "loyal thing" that Emery found himself the signalman of the *Old Nameless*, as it later came to be known. After only six weeks of boot camp and training, the ship and its neophyte crew entered the Pacific war zone and the oncoming fire of Japanese Zeros.

Her name was nowhere on the hull, and crew members were told not to mark anything with *USS*

Signalman Emery on left

South Dakota. Captained by Thomas L. Gatch, the *Old Nameless* and her crew were reported by papers and throughout Japanese news to have been sunk, but that was not the case. The mysterious ship was part of a new line of state-of-the-art ships with increased firepower and quickness; consequently, the Navy wanted to avoid confirming its identity, so this "sunken ship" quickly became the lethal weapon in Pacific combat.

Emery was in the communications branch of the ship as a member of the signal crew. Learning how to send Morse code on a flashing light to let other ships know what they were doing, they also maneuvered flags that were raised for different meanings. However, as the *Old Nameless* became more powerful with its potent twenty and forty-millimeter guns and was transformed into more of an anti-aircraft ship, Emery also trained on the guns and turrets in order to effectively use this firepower in encounters with the Zeros.

We were practicing all this time as we were sailing south out of Hawaii. They always

talked about the captain taking a bunch of men that had no skills and had been in boot camp maybe six weeks, and got on the *South Dakota*; we taught them how to be gunners. That is essentially what happened. We became an anti-aircraft base. We could put up a wall of fire so the Japanese couldn't get in. So we practiced all the time shooting at these drones as they were flying by.

The drones and short training would have to be enough, because the pressure came soon after entering the Pacific. There were many night battles, and it was all about protecting islands from being overrun by the Japanese and playing offense by taking the islands back for the United States. From Guadalcanal and the Battle of Santa Cruz to Savo Island in the Solomons, *Old Nameless* was there in formation, putting up their "wall of fire" to protect the aircraft carrier *Washington* and to take down Japanese planes. At that, they managed okay. In the Battle of Santa Cruz they shot down thirty-two of these planes, and at Guadalcanal they were credited for sinking four enemy cruisers. But during these battles, Emery was put in the sick bay with injuries.

In the battle of Santa Cruz, while working on the guns of the ship, reloading and carrying magazines, Emery was hit by the strafing bullets of Japanese aircraft.

A lot of the bullets were hitting the bulkhead as I was carrying magazines to a twenty-millimeter gun. So I got hit and sprayed because I had turned my back from the way it hit. It hit the bulkhead, and all this metal hit my butt, my back, the backs of my arms, and the backs of my legs. So they picked out a lot of stuff. I was sort of bleeding a lot, but none of it was my organs. I was just lucky that it didn't sink in any deeper. Once in a while I can feel one in my leg.

After the ship was repaired, Emery departed on the *South Dakota* across the Atlantic to Scotland, where they were to defend American transports from the United States to Russia from German torpedoes. But the torpedoes never came. So for the better part of three months, the crew "just sat around and ate mutton." The fun and relaxation of the European lifestyle was soon trumped, however, by calls for assistance in the Pacific, where the *South Dakota* returned to battle.

In a night battle on Savo Island near Guadalcanal, the *South Dakota* was defending the island from a Japanese invasion.

We were credited for sinking four enemy cruisers. We also lost forty-three sailors as a result of shell fire from the Japanese ships. The *South Dakota* lost all radio contact with other ships and land facilities and the Japanese thought they had sunk the *South Dakota*. Our Captain, `, cautioned the crew and officers to not send any messages, and the Navy personnel wanted to avoid confirming the *South Dakota's* identity. It was then called *"Old Nameless,"* and it continued to be a lethal weapon of the Pacific.

It was in this battle that Emery was set afire by a shell that pierced the ship not more than five feet from him.

I was on the bridge and it hit through a bulkhead, and it was kind of like a fireball and it set me afire, but luckily it also pierced a water pipe that was going to a floor above us, and all I felt then was the spray of water. It was just miraculous that I didn't get burnt more or injured more.

He was one of the more fortunate sailors in this incident for, as he stumbled through the turmoil, a fellow sailor asked Emery if he would take off his shoe; however, when he looked down, there not only was no shoe, but the entire leg had been removed from the wounded sailor's body. Emery's injury put him in sick bay for a period of time, but he refused the advice to transfer to New Caledonia because of talk about its being a leper colony.

After recovering, Emery spent the rest of his career aboard the *South Dakota* until he received an honorable discharge in 1946 after his battle with tuberculosis and the torture of the prison-like hospitals to which he was confined.

I then went to a Memphis hospital and then I went to a New York Hospital, and then I was transferred to Corona in California and then to North Permanency in Vancouver, Washington, and then to the Veterans' Hospital in Portland, Oregon, and then home. But during that time the treatment of tuberculosis was rest, so I lay in bed for most of that year. That was about as bad as the war—maybe worse.

Over Emery's thirty-eight months of military service, he experienced many events that left him with feelings of great sadness and shock, such as the burial at sea of forty-three sailors placed in canvas bags along with a five-inch shell in each bag to carry the body deep under the water. On the other hand, there was also the joy and celebration of the crew as they watched, through a telescope, the peace treaty being signed by United States and Japanese officials on the battleship *Missouri*, anchored near the *South Dakota* in Tokyo Harbor. Emery was also awarded various ribbons, such as a Purple Heart; a Gold Star in lieu of a second Purple Heart; a Good Conduct medal; an Asiatic Pacific Ribbon with 13 bronze stars; a Philippine Liberation Ribbon with 2 bronze stars; and a European-African-Middle Eastern Ribbon. In the end, Emery came out of the war no longer a naïve boy, but a grown man with memories that would be with him the rest of his life.

So many things happened out there. It is sort of terrible to have to go to war. You should be, probably, always an anti-war person but, I don't know, it seems like people are their greatest enemy.

Nothing could be truer than that. A signalman aboard the most infamous ship in World War II is calling war what it is—a nightmare.

Emery Hildebrandt was discharged from the war to become a professor at Oregon State University and now leads a terrific and healthy life with his wife in Corvallis, Oregon, at the young age of eighty-five. But more than that. More than his title or the ship on which he served is the man Emery became. He is a grandfather who has inspired me to be more, and to live in the hopes that I can achieve as he has—not his rank in the Navy, but to get as much out of life as this wonderful man has done to achieve *his* rank in life.

I love you, Grandpa.

Bruce Hilsee

February 1944 - October 1947
Atlantic Ocean, France

Living in Reverse
An Interview with Bruce Hilsee
By Barbara Hatch

A pot of artificial hydrangeas sits just inside Bruce's front door. They remind him of his apartment in Milan, where he lived for 15 years while working for Honeywell. They remind him of a 15-year-old Italian girl whose father wanted her to sing "Un Sera di Maggio" in English, "One Night in May," to entertain the American and British embassy staff who worked near the bar where he played piano. They remind him of the fur coats that got on the tram each day as he left for work. They remind him of a lifetime of memories that sometimes keep him awake at night, but are delightful to ponder from a comfortable armchair in his living room.

Many veterans consider their military service the most dramatic event in their lives. Certainly Bruce's 324 parachute jumps—one from 41,000 feet—were memorable. But it's the people Bruce met and the places he visited in 134 countries that keep him awake at night. "I got too many memories."

Few trace their military career back to grade school, but Bruce does. Skipping second grade meant he would graduate at 17. In 1944, young men were off to war before the ink dried on their diplomas. Normally the military would not admit a boy until he was 18. Bruce looked around his class and noticed there were 46 kids—23 girls and 23 boys—and knew he was not going to sit alone at graduation with 23 girls. He joined the Army at age 17. The enlistment office didn't ask and he didn't tell. "That's a fact."

Fort Rucker, Alabama, was his first stop. By his own request his next assignment was jump school at Fort Benning, Georgia; he joined the 101st Airborne, headed to Fort Bragg. They became members of the 82nd and two or three weeks later were on a ship out of Norfolk, Virginia, bound for Europe. They could just see the spires of a church in Nantes, France, when the captain announced the war was over and they were returning to the States. It took a month to get back.

Bruce's crew was billeted at Camp Shanks, an embarkation point on the Hudson River above New York City, waiting for the rest of the 82nd to return from the war. To celebrate V-E Day, Bruce was swept up in a parade through New York's streets, complete with ticker tape raining down on his head. His mother, father, and sister witnessed the event. The chilly September weather had Bruce wearing a sweater beneath his Eisenhower jacket; each soldier also received campaign cords to place on their shoulders to match those in the 82nd who had seen combat. Bruce gets very emotional recalling one veteran who "must have had 60 ribbons hanging down from his chest on both sides." He was not sorry, though, to miss the war in Japan, which had ended in August.

When Bruce got back to Fort Bragg, he volunteered for a five-man parachute test platoon. They tested various parachute designs from different altitudes, everywhere from 500 to 10,000 feet. Bruce is proud to report he always landed on his feet "because you want to be standing up with your rifle if the enemy's right there." On occasion they jumped from a Flying Boxcar, a C-119, into the Gulf of Mexico. These jumps were designed to test the ability of a mechanism on a pilot's boot that was designed to sense water and automatically release the Air Force pilot's parachute and keep it from dragging him down underwater when ejecting over water. A Navy boat picked them up and took them back to an awaiting cruiser.

One night after dinner Bruce's captain came in his barracks to tell him to report to the airfield at 6:30 in the morning, dressed and ready to go. Bruce found it odd there was no airplane on the runway. Entering a side door to the hangar, men in civilian clothes attached tabs to his body similar to those for an EKG, with wires emerging from a hole in the side of his jumpsuit to a box strapped on his thigh. Two oxygen tanks hung from his waist to the backs of his knees. He carried one reserve parachute on front and two on his back, with three release cords. "I weighed a ton! I couldn't even walk." He had to be carried outside to a high-altitude silver weather balloon that carried a silver single-man gondola so tall he could barely peer over the top.

When the Captain gave the word, the weather balloon rose in the air until Bruce could see the Atlantic Ocean in the distance. At 38,000 feet he opened the latched door of the gondola and stepped out. "I wanted to fall as quickly as possible because the gauges around my waist indicated I'd used more oxygen than I thought just getting to this altitude. So I pointed my toes and dropped straight down to about 17,000 feet and pulled my first chute. Then lying out flat to study where I was with relation to Fort Bragg

and realizing I was using too much oxygen, I pushed the release button and dropped out of my parachute. I resumed free-falling to about 8,000 feet and pulled my second chute and pulled the risers as hard as I could to dump air and direct me back towards Fort Bragg. I knew I didn't want to land in the ocean." He released the second chute and free-fell to an altitude about as high as the Eiffel Tower and pulled the reserve chute on his chest. He landed standing up about four miles from the airstrip at Fort Bragg. He made this jump eight times.

Word got around about the "daredevil" who lived in Barracks A. Sitting in the PX having a beer, he heard people wonder "who this guy is." His fellow jumpers knew, of course, but other than that, "I never told anybody." He admits to being scared but not worried. He was 17, and he had jumped many times. He trusted the parachute packers at Fort Bragg, but he heard of situations where men who had packed their own chutes got the lines twisted, keeping the chute from opening. "And you cry at night 'cause you lost your buddy in the next bed." Seeing a "streamer," a man plunging to the ground in an unopened chute, was not a pleasant memory. Bruce saw six or seven of them. But all in all, he pays tribute to those men who came before, the soldiers who during World War II hooked up to a line on their C-47s that launched them into the void. He saw several who were caught around the midsection when they hesitated on their jump and were hit by the plane's tail. He preferred landing on his feet. As "crazy" as these times were, Bruce has never jumped since. Three hundred and twenty-four was enough.

When he left the service he got a job cooking hamburgers in Ocean City, New Jersey. One day a letter arrived from the Pentagon looking for soldiers to send to Korea. They offered Bruce a 1st Lieutenancy to go Airborne. At his physical, the doctor gave him all the tests, checked his heart, and asked about his legs. He admitted to having "nervous legs," and having to get up and walk around. But when the doctor asked if he "wet the bed," Bruce said yes, "every night." He returned to Ocean City and cooked hamburgers and never heard from the military again. "So I guess I got discharged from the military, or didn't, wasn't called up because I wet the bed. I don't, but that's what I said 'cause I didn't want to go to Korea!" Instead he majored in math at the University of Maryland.

A job at Honeywell helped Bruce fulfill a childhood dream. When he was six, his father subscribed to *National Geographic*. Bruce lay in bed at night looking at the pictures and said, "Damn. I gotta see this someday." At Honeywell he read every book on how to make gasoline, plastics, cement, or power dams. If business meetings ended on a Friday, he changed his return flight to Sunday night so he could look around, but "not like a tourist. I wanted to see how people lived, what their life is like. I'd go into bars in the dingiest parts of towns and sit there and talk to guys with tattoos up and down their arms." He saw Victoria Falls, the Taj Mahal, Robben Island while Nelson Mandela was incarcerated, the Eiffel Tower, the pyramids at Giza, the largest power dam in the world on the border of Brazil and Paraguay. But it is the people Bruce remembers the most.

First, the famous ones: Saddam Hussein at the dedication of a refinery in Kirkuk; Josip Broz Tito of Yugoslavia; the sister of the Queen of Holland, who gave him a Cartier lighter; King Juan Carlos of Spain, from whom he received a wood statue of the Man of La Mancha; Prince Adam of Liechtenstein; Saudi princes.

None compare to the "little people" he met by chance. He gave 10 piasters to a ragged boy begging near the pyramids, warning him not to tell the other boys who would take it away from him. This added up to about "two bucks," about 100 days of begging. "And I kept his hand there and slowly let go and stood up. All of a sudden a big smile burst on his face 'cause he realized what I was saying. Things like that mean something, you know." At the bottom of a 400-foot cliff in Portugal he roasted sardines, broke bread, and drank wine with a man who spoke no English. They drew pictures of their children with the appropriate gender indicators to distinguish between the two. "He had three boys and a girl; I had two girls and a boy." They watched the sunset over North Africa and talked the whole evening. He went fishing one day after work with a man from Surinam. "He's got bare feet, pants rolled up to here, he's a dark-skinned fella, and I'm in the boat fishing." When Bruce looked out, thousands of piranhas swam around the man's legs but did not attack. "You and I stand there, we're going to get our legs eaten off." Why don't they? Is it their diet? Genes? Bruce wonders about those things. Another time he met the Reverend Jim Jones in a Guiana bar and asked him to sign a dollar bill. Jones was the leader of a cult that existed in the jungle. He jokingly told Jones he thought he'd "go down in history." Little did he know that two years later Jones and his 913 followers would commit mass suicide by drinking poisoned grape juice.

Bruce gets worked up when friends and neighbors close their minds to learning about other cultures, particularly relating to Islam and Arab people. Walking down the streets of Riyadh one day, he bumped into a cleric, causing him to spill his papers on the ground. Bruce conveyed his apology in Arabic and invited him to an outdoor café where they "took" a coffee. The Arab man explained Muslims don't eat pork because they died of trichinosis when the meat spoiled in the desert. Yet, "very few Muslims know that." While standing in Damman on the Persian Gulf during the call to prayer he met an old robed Arab who asked him to join him in prayer in his office since he was too old to pray at the mosque. In the office the old man reached behind his desk and handed Bruce a copy of the King James Version of the Bible while he held the Koran. "Now we can pray together." Bruce commented, "Does that sound like a Muslim terrorist?" On the other hand, he has no issue with the removal of Saddam Hussein after Bruce sat at dinner one night with an Iraqi family when Saddam's Republican guards broke in and took the family's 14-year-old son for the Christian divisions who fought in Iran. These boys were sent into combat "without any guns or ammunition just to find out where Iran had their artillery guns. And all the boys were slaughtered. That's an evil man." He also recounts the savagery of Saddam's two sons, who kidnapped girls off the streets, took them to an arena, stripped them naked, then shot them from the stands with high-powered rifles—not to kill them, just to watch them bleed to death. "That's why we should've taken him out." But Bruce disagrees with Americans who think every Muslim "should be shot dead tomorrow." He's seen both sides.

Bruce has traveled so much his passport has pages glued to pages. They tumble out of his passport like an accordion. He spent so much time in Saudi Arabia, he was able to negotiate visitation rights for a woman whose Saudi husband took their child back to Arabia and did not allow the mother to visit. Bruce even gets Social Security from that country. He flew Lufthansa so often, he and the flight attendants addressed each other by their first names. On one return flight after his parents visited him in Milan, he looked so exhausted the stewardess offered him a bed in first-class. "Mr. Hilsee, you're in business class. You can have that bed in first-class if you'd like it."

Jessica and I could not get enough of Bruce's stories. When I asked him to offer some "profound words" to the "feisty" 17-year-old seated to my left, Bruce first told her to go to school all the way till the end, "but have a dream that you want something to happen in your life, like I had at six years old. You want to see the world or you want to be an aviator, make up your mind to do it. And figure out every castle you want to see and make sure you get it done. Whoever you want to be or whatever you want to do with your life, do it. A lot of people sit and talk, 'I wish I had done this. I wish I had done that.' It doesn't have to be something glamorous." He is sad his wife does not share his memories.

Bruce in full uniform

You'd think Bruce's military memories would be lost in the lifetime he led after his service. But he comes back to that gondola. "That's blazoned in my mind… I could see the ships out at sea. I remember opening the door. I remember the first step, but I don't remember falling. It was an aluminum gondola with a door and an aluminum latch. This silver balloon high above me, maybe five stories, with nylon strings going up. I always have that image."

But Bruce had to finish with "one last story," this one about his great grandmother, the second of seven children farmed out to relatives when her mother died at the age of 36 and her father could not care for them. She eloped. Her husband enlisted in the Civil War, was shot, captured, and incarcerated at Libby Prison in Richmond, Virginia. His wife, Bruce's great grandmother, "rented a horse and buggy, got a pass through Union lines, got a pass through Southern lines, drove from Philadelphia to Richmond in a horse and buggy, paid a hundred dollars, and got her husband out of jail." She nursed him back to health. They had a child—Bruce's grandmother. "If my great grandmother hadn't done that, I wouldn't be here," he told us, overcome with emotion.

Most people live a quiet life, then retire and travel. Bruce jumped out of airplanes, traveled, and *then* retired—with his memories. Many memories of a life lived in reverse.

Dick Hoover

December 1942 - August 1971
Italy

"If Your Plane Wants to Commit Suicide, Let It"

An Interview with Dick Hoover
By Callie Adair

During Night Fighter Pilot training in 1944, Richard "Dick" Hoover was flying a P-70 Night Fighter aircraft when the intercom to his Radar Operator malfunctioned, and he was not able to receive flight directions from his Radar Operator. They were performing a practice "head-on" interception, and without any direction from the Radar Operator, a near head-on mid-air collision happened. The other aircraft, the "bogie," was only about 50 feet above as it passed over. He could actually see the exhaust pattern of the other aircraft. "That was the closest near fatal incident I ever experienced."

Dick enlisted in the U.S. Army Air Forces on December 7, 1942, the first anniversary of Pearl Harbor Day. After completing pilot training at Luke Field in Glendale, Arizona, then Night Fighter pilot training at Hammer Field in Fresno, California, he was deployed to Italy to fight in World War II. He was based in Pisa and Pontedera, not far from Florence. Even though he was combat ready as a P-61 Night Fighter Pilot, Dick was assigned to the 416th Night Fighter Squadron to fly the prestigious English "Mosquito" Night Fighter Aircraft. Being one of only 31 American Night Fighter Pilots to fly the Mosquito, he considers himself "E Paucibus Unum," or "One of Few."

His check-out in the Mosquito was brief. The Operations Officer, Captain Jim Urso, told Dick, "Read this Pilot's Information Manual carefully because tomorrow you are going to check out in the Mosquito." The next day he reported to Captain Urso, who said to him, "'Do you see that man standing next to that airplane? He is the crew chief for the Mosquito. His name is Sergeant Dwyer, and he will show you how to start the engines. It flies just like any other airplane. Keep all the instruments in the green and you will have no trouble.' And that was my check-out."

With all his talent for flying, and a large dose of youthful feelings of infallibility, Dick crashed a Mosquito. The Mosquito is a relatively small twin-engine airplane with two large Rolls Royce engines. It could fly faster and higher than a P-38. Only the German ME-262 jet fighter was faster. The Mosquito was made of plywood. If an engine failed on take-off, it would usually result in a crash. When Dick had his crash on take-off, it was in the daytime. He was checking out the airplane in preparation for that night's mission. The port [left] engine failed on take-off, and he knew he could not make it because the engine caught on fire and the fire spread throughout the cockpit. He called the tower and told them he could not make it and he was going to belly the airplane in, which he did. Both his Radar Operator and he walked away from the crash. Like they were told in training, "If the airplane insists on committing suicide," let it, but try not to be part of the suicide. The old saying applies, "Any landing you can walk away from is a good landing." Dick has a photo on his bedroom wall of the crashed Mosquito from which he walked away. "That's my wrecked Mosquito." When his roommate crashed in the Mosquito, the plane flipped when it lost an engine on takeoff. He did not survive.

Before January of 1945, most of the missions were patrol. Pilots were "vectored" to a location of suspected enemy activity to shoot down enemy planes. In January the mission was changed from patrol to "night intrusion." Pilots were ordered to fly low at night to hit targets on the ground—trains, train stations, "whatever you could shoot at." Without sophisticated radar, low flying at night was dangerous. Besides anti-aircraft fire, there was the risk of flying into hills or buildings, "things we didn't see." By April, there were not many enemy planes still airborne. The Germans lacked aircraft and fuel. On one mission in Italy's Po Valley on April 22, 1945, twelve Mosquitoes went up; only four returned unscathed. They were shot down by German anti-aircraft fire. This was a daytime low-level mission, the only one

A crashed "Mosquito"

the squadron flew. That's the reason for the high casualty count. Dick was still in the hospital with burns after his accident, "so I was not privileged to go on that mission. I probably would have got shot down." Dick was happy to return to the P-61, a "forgiving airplane." The Mosquito was like a thoroughbred race horse; the P-61 was more like a

work horse." He felt at home in the P-61. After May 8, the official end of the war, the pilots were told to "fly around and try not to get killed." There were still accidents, particularly when the weather was bad. Planes then did not have the sophisticated instruments that modern planes possess today. While with the 416th Night Fighter Squadron, the P-61 assigned to Dick was named *The Great Speckled Bird* after a country religious song. It had distinctive bumblebee stinger marks painted on its tail. Dick has a photo of it on his wall and a model hanging from his living room ceiling. He loved that plane!

There were also fun times between the missions. The officers received one bottle of whiskey each month. Dick, as part of the lower rankings, got last pick. He ended up with "Old Overholt," rye whiskey that was terrible. Dick used it to trade for items that were hard to get. Another story Dick likes to tell is about Colonel Banks, the 416th NFS commanding officer. Everyone called him "Buster," not because he was such a good guy, but because he would "bust" [discipline] them! One time he called in the mess officer to complain about the food. Banks told him to fire the cook because he was "skinny." "Skinny cooks don't know how to eat. Get me a fat Italian cook who can speak Italian." From then on the food improved because the cook could speak the language.

After the end of the war, General Eisenhower decided to have the first official air show at "Skippo" air base in Amsterdam, Holland. Dick was asked to fly the P-61 and was the first official demonstration pilot of the P-61 for the Air Force. On his way to Amsterdam, he forgot to pick up the orders to go to

Amsterdam, so he landed at Munich and telephoned the squadron for advice. He was told to proceed and "act like they owned the place" because they had just won the war. When a person monitoring the call "found out I was one of Eisenhower's selected boys, showing up without orders," they sent a telegram to the 416th NFS commander, signed by Dwight D. Eisenhower himself, to dispatch proper orders to Lieutenant Hoover to fly to the Netherlands to be the P-61 demonstration pilot. "How many lieutenants get a personal telegram from Eisenhower?"

Dick's favorite flying days were when he was able to fly his own airplane wherever he wanted. "When you fly somebody else's [airplane], it's, 'May I? May I? May I? When you fly your own airplane, you don't have to ask, 'May I?'" Flying numerous different airplanes, including the P-61, the English Beaufighter, the Mosquito, and the P-70, Dick accomplished what not many pilots have. At a recent Night Fighter reunion, "I was the only pilot there that had flown all four night fighter aircraft that we used in World War II." Yet another reason he is "one of a few"—*E Paucibus Unum.*

When Dick finally decided to settle for good, he had a choice between Florida and Arizona. "I chose Arizona." At the end of the war, many states gave their veterans a bonus of $100. Arizona gave two-and-a-half acres of land to its veterans. Many veterans found this bonus insulting. They refused the land, even as a gift, because they thought it was worth nothing. Dick was able to get eight of these parcels for about $500 an acre to add up to a total of 20 acres; he now lives on this land. At the time it was barren desert, but he liked the cactus plants. According to him, one of the saguaro cacti on his property is said to be the largest in the world.

If the airplanes hanging from his living room ceiling and the photos on his bedroom wall are any indication, Dick is proud of his flying days.

In WWII there were four major night fighters, airplanes. That's the Black Widow P-61, which you saw hanging out there. This is the P-70 that flew, and the other one that I showed you out there. This is the Mosquito here. And this is called the English Beaufighter. I flew that one also. When I went to a reunion in Wright Patterson [AFB] about three or four years ago, I was the only Night Fighter pilot there that had flown all four night fighter aircraft that we used in WWII.

Dick Hoover now resides in Scottsdale, Arizona, with his wife Norma. He is an artist, making bowls out of desert trees in the garage of his house. He is proud of the successful asphalt business he established over the years. He is involved with the reunions of his fellow Air Corps members. Ironically, the location of his house carries many memories of his flying days. Back in 1943, when stationed at Thunderbird Army Air Base Number II, now Scottsdale Airport, the area where they practiced aerobatics—loops and rolls—was "right here, where I now live."

A telegram from General Eisenhower

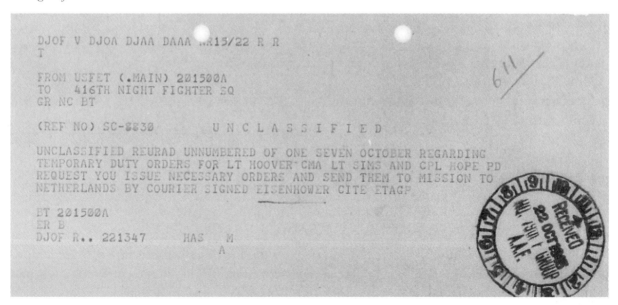

Kenneth Huff

July 1, 1942 - July 1, 1946
Iwo Jima, Okinawa

The Ninety-Seven Days of Okinawa
By Ken Huff

I was commissioned an Ensign in the Naval Reserve early in 1941 and served four years on active duty, followed by fifteen more as an active reservist, leaving the Navy as a Commander. The following condensed excerpt is taken from a war memoir I composed for my children, and relates to one period of my service. At that time I was commanding officer of the *USS LCS (L) 35*, a 170-foot, lightly armed, rocket firing ship employed in connection with amphibious landings. What follows are my memories of that engagement.

Sunday. April 1, 1945. Easter Sunday. April Fools Day. D-Day. It was day one of the ninety-seven we would spend before again turning south toward Leyte Gulf. It was a beautiful morning as we took position 2,000 yards off the landing beaches. The sea was calm, the sky clear, and the weather warm, bordering on hot. The six Division 7 LCSs preceded the landing craft and at 700 yards fired ranging rockets, followed by a full salvo at 500 yards. Dust and smoke obscured the shoreline as the ships turned out of the path of the small LCVPs, their guns firing shoreward hopefully, but without any visible effect. Then, in an almost surreal way, we became spectators of the landing drama unfolding before us. We anchored 2,000 yards from shore, flanking and well out of the way of the steady flow of LSTs, LCMs, and other amphibious ships bringing their materiel to the beach. There was little visible reaction from the enemy, and except for the intermittent sound of the big bombardment ships' guns offshore, there was a kind of calmness about the scene. Reports of the progress ashore indicated that all was going well. As we relaxed in the sun, we concluded that cleaning up this business was going to be an easy task, and we spoke of an early return to Leyte.

First doubt about the reasonableness of that opinion came with the first air raid in the early evening. "Flash Red" was the radio warning that an air attack was imminent. All ships went to General Quarters, and when ordered, our ships commenced making smoke to obscure the Hagushi anchorage area. We watched with astonishment as a Jap Val (designation of a plane type) dove through a barrage of anti-aircraft fire to crash on the deck of an unloading cargo ship. Four more air alerts, and four more calls to stand at GQ, rounded out the night, and our first day at Okinawa. It was an ominous omen of things to come.

What was to come in the following ninety-six days exposed us to conditions, experiences, and sights that were revelations in our young lives. Many hundreds of "Flash Reds" destroyed any semblance of daily routine or of normal sleep. Most of the raids came at night, sometimes six or seven in sequence, and occasionally single ones that lasted all night. Each one necessitated that all hands turn out to man their duty stations. For the first two months, except for two nights, I slept in my clothes, sometimes including my shoes. On some occasions it was simply on a pile of life jackets placed on the deck of the pilothouse. The lack of schedule and routine itself became our only routine. When we anchored at night, we took up a position upwind of larger ships. If enemy planes came close enough to warrant, we activated our smoke generators, which produced a dense, sweet-smelling, oily white smoke. And, because we anchored from the stern, that smoke enveloped us first before drifting with the wind to blanket other ships present. As a result, every topside surface on the ship took on a greasy coating. Usually we were groggy from lack of sleep, and while we waited action developments, sleepy silence prevailed, broken only by the steady rumble of the smoke generator at the stern. The radiomen monitored and relayed reports about enemy plane location and counts. Shore-based radar directors guided combat air patrol planes (CAP) toward targets, and when one was sighted visually, the pilots radioed, "Tally Ho." Sometimes if the action was in our viewing range, we could then watch a burst of fire, and finally follow the burning enemy plane as it spiraled toward the ground. On one night we counted sixteen such sightings.

Every means was used to keep the Japs from getting to the anchorage area. To that end, radar picket stations were established around the entire island at distances of about fifty miles. At each, one or two destroyers, plus two or three LCSs, patrolled back and forth, providing early radar warning of approaching flights and also a wall of anti-aircraft fire when the planes were within range. As a consequence of their forward location, these stations were the most subject

Ken aboard ship

to attack by the *kamikaze*. We were tense as we monitored reports of incoming flights toward our northernmost station, or toward the ones adjacent. On nights of the full moon, every individual felt that he was personally under the eye of a marauding enemy. We watched as a Jap Val slipped through the curtain of AA fire to crash into the destroyer *Bryant* 2,000 yards on our beam. The damaged ship immediately increased speed and concentrated on fire control, while we moved to where survivors were seen in the water. We picked up five living and three dead of those blown overboard by the explosion, and watched three other dead without life jackets sink beyond our reaching hands. Crews of the larger ships referred to smaller ones, such as the LCSs, as "undertakers" or "pall bearers" because of the role we played in that way. Dozens of ships were sunk by *kamikaze*, and dozens more were disabled.

Our daily duties were varied, and changed frequently. Occasionally an enemy did make it into the anchorage area. One bright afternoon the security situation was "Flash White," which indicated an all-clear condition. Suddenly we heard the sporadic firing of a few guns, and as we looked toward the source, we saw a single Tony (designation for a particular plane model) approaching at perhaps 200 feet off the water. It was headed for an LSD anchored just beyond and a little astern of us, but initially it appeared to be heading right for us. As it passed astern at a distance of about 1,000 feet, 20-mm shells from the *35*'s guns stitched along the fuselage and the plane crashed near, but short of its LSD target. That big red circle marking on the plane became an indelible memory for all of us. During a night raid a plane, unseen and unheard, swept overhead and disappeared after straddling us with six small bombs, one close enough that spray and a few metal bits pattered aboard. On other, more lazy days, the division simply lay at anchor, spaced across the wide entrance to the harbor at Naga Wan. We guarded against the incursion of suicide boats, or "skunks," as they were called. Other days and nights were spent patrolling near shore, on watch for suicide swimmers. The anti-swimmer weapon was a stick of dynamite that was to be activated and flung into the water to kill any concussion. Ashore, the battle had moved to the far south end of the island, but for those aboard ship, the events there that were of consuming interest to the Army and Marines went unnoticed. For us, the battle was being fought at sea against an enemy in the air. There, 4,000 sailors were lost, and ashore, 30,000 Americans died.

Beyond the various assignments, and beyond the excitement and the moments of terror, there was boredom to occupy our time. There were even moments of relaxation, especially as the campaign wound down. Morale was amazingly high, and in spite of living closely together in crowded, cramped, and Spartan conditions, the crew got along well. And they were healthy. We listened to "Tokyo Rose," a nightly broadcast in English hosted by a Japanese-American broadcasting from Tokyo. It offered the latest stateside musical hits, as well as commentary about the approaching American forces. She described the scenes and actions we were actually a part of every day, but in terms at such variance from reality that the reports were a source of humor. In the later days, liberty parties could go ashore and accumulated dental

Ship 35 looking beat-up

work could be taken care of. The dentist office was set up in an old high school, and while the quality was good, the equipment was field style. A foot treadle activated the drill! The small boat carrying the parties to the landing usually paused to view a sunken Jap destroyer sitting upright as though ready to sail, with only the top of its mast above water. It was an eerie sight in the crystal clear water. At the landing site the

Marines had erected a sign reading, "Over the body of 10,000 Marines, MacArthur returned to the Philippines." The message reflected the disdain in which the Corps held him.

The liberty parties came back relaxed and with fleas. Off and on until we departed Okinawa, fleas were a minor annoyance and nuisance. But far and away the most important moments had to do with mail. The Navy made every effort to move it in both directions. Inevitably, incoming service was erratic. Sometimes we went for two or three weeks without any mail at all, and then would be deluged with 15 or 20 letters apiece. Mail sent in February finally arrived in May, but on the other hand, service from the States frequently took only six days. Whether fresh or ancient, the arrival of mail sacks always raised spirits on the ship. It was an elixir that outshone all others, and moved all negative emotions to the background. The mail also brought V-discs, recordings of all types of music with broad appeal, as well as V-magazines that were small editions of popular ones without advertising. Ongoing boredom could always be put aside through the auspices of one more "Condition Red" announcing the likelihood of yet another set of "visitors" from the north.

On June 30th the Battle of Okinawa was declared officially ended. The next day I celebrated the anniversary of my third year on active duty. If I had thought about it, I might have considered how the past ninety-one days had changed me, for indeed they had. If nothing else, I was a veteran of two campaigns, and a much more experienced officer. I don't think I ever lacked self-confidence in my role as commanding officer, but I was more at ease in it now. I had learned at Iwo Jima and Okinawa that I could be very afraid, and still function as if by rote.

But now it was time to move on to what we knew would unquestionably be the mother of all battles, the invasion of the home islands of Japan. So, on that ninety-seventh day, July 6, 1945, eleven ships of Flotilla Three formed into two columns and proceeded on a southerly course at ten knots toward San Pedro Bay, Leyte, P.I. Our twelfth ship, the *LCS 33*, remained at the island of Okinawa, sunk on the picket line.

Bob M. Johnson

March 1942 - August 1945
France, Germany, Austria

Tabasco and Trumpets
An Interview with Bob M. Johnson
By Kasey Burton

In the dead of night, staccato shouts punctured the dark surrounding him as he jammed himself deeper into the corner of the garden wall. He was determined no one would get him from behind. From what he could decipher of the yelling, the Germans knew he was there. Terrified, all Bob could do was wait.

After eight hours, the others finally remembered they left Bob behind and returned to save him from his trap in no-man's-land, where approximately 30 or 40 Germans had been wandering around. Just how did Bob end up in this situation?

When Bob was drafted, he was sent to Camp Roberts for basic artillery training. Upon the completion of his training Bob traveled to Fort Ord. At Fort Ord, Bob didn't receive what he would specialize in. Much to his surprise, he found that the military had looked into his high school records and seen he had been a member of the band. Of the 30 artillery members, 29 were made cooks, and Bob, who played the French horn, was placed in the Army Band.

Though the band was easy duty, Bob eventually grew restless. He persuaded his wife to allow him to enter the Air Corps. After arriving in Amarillo, Texas, Bob joined the thousand from which 200 would be chosen for training. Bob was selected to become a part of the 200 and was sent to "what is now part of the University of Minnesota, but it was Morehead State Teachers' College." The teachers' college had been converted into training grounds where the men absorbed three years' worth of college education in one and a half. "I remember even having to go into the bathroom to study because that's the only time I could find to do it!" All of a sudden, however, Bob's training was for naught. The need for pilots had unexpectedly disappeared, and the 200 men were dumped into the infantry. Knowing the effect of the infantry on his uncle, Bob was devastated. "That was about the worst thing you could've done to me."

Luck was on his side. He discovered the band was in need of a member, again the French horn. "I thought, 'Well, maybe this is something that's meant to be. Maybe this is gonna save my life.' And it did."

Bob was still trained and sent overseas, but instead of fighting on the front lines, he became part of an intelligence unit called G-2. Bob's responsibility was to transport prisoners where the Army needed them. He was assigned a partner, Vincent Petinelli, and together they "practically wore out that Jeep in Europe." In fact, the pair went through several Jeeps. The two mostly used armored Jeeps; however, the armored Jeeps were so often damaged, they ended up with a normal one.

The head of G-2 was a German Jew who had escaped Germany in 1939. He decided to join the American army, and when his past was discovered, the army put his knowledge to full use by placing him in charge of G-2.

This German Jew was in command when Bob became responsible for Karl and Ilse Koch, the commandant of Buchenwald and his wife, the "Bitch of Buchenwald." Isle and her husband were guilty of horrible atrocities. Ilse is known for her lampshades of Jewish skin, as well as selecting prisoners to be killed for their tattoos. In dealing with Karl Koch, who of course refused to speak, the German Jewish commander told Bob and the others to take him out and have him dig his grave. They marked the outline for him and handed him a shovel. Upon the completion of his grave, the men decided he needed a cross. They fashioned it out of wood, and told him to write his name and date of birth. "Then we said, 'All right, now put down today's date as the date of death.' He decided to talk."

As for Karl's wife, Bob was only required to transfer her to Army Headquarters. "You would never believe it. She was kind of a nice gal. I mean, you know, she was going to be nice to us, because obviously we were in charge." Even so, one of Bob's fellow band members, David Rickard, remembers Bob stating that transporting Ilse Koch gave him a creepy feeling.

The German Jewish commander's talents were effective with common soldiers as well. When they were in Echternacht, Belgium, trying to get into Germany, the men were fighting up a hill against pillboxes. They managed to take some prisoners, and the commander got each and every one of the prisoners to reveal how to access the pillboxes. "Just

think how many men he saved... I have to believe he saved over a hundred soldiers."

Bob not only transferred single prisoners, but large groups. Bob and his men were required to search the prisoners and take away any dangerous objects. One of the items Bob disliked taking was guns. "He [Petinelli] and I would have to go out and take their beautiful guns and wrap them around a telephone pole." The guns were often hand-carved, gold inlaid, and very well-made. "We'd take the firing pins and throw them away or bury them or something so they could never use them again." He also recalls how bad the prisoners reeked. The German soldiers often carried cheese, bread, and butter. The butter went rancid, the cheese went green, and the bread "was so hard you could pound nails with it." This, coupled with the fact that they hadn't bathed for months, led to quite the aroma.

Despite rampant looting and souvenir-gathering, many chose not to take German guns. If you were found with a German gun, you would be shot with it. This didn't deter all the men; Bob knew an officer who took advantage of his position. "This guy must've shipped home a dozen rifles and I don't know how many pieces of stuff, because he could get away with it." One of the other valued prizes was a camera. "Everybody wanted a gun or a camera." Bob himself had a camera with which he took at least a hundred pictures during the war.

Transporting Ilse Koch, the Bitch of Buchenwald

Bob encountered several close calls while driving with Petinelli in their Jeep. Petinelli and Bob usually couldn't get food when they traveled. The divisions they ended up with wouldn't give them food because they didn't know who they were. The two often lived off the land or with what they could find. "If we could find a chicken, we had chicken." On one occasion, Bob, Petinelli, and two other soldiers heard of a kitchen in the rear. They decided to take advantage of the four-mile distance to get some food. They were on a little country road and began to approach a small area thick with trees. Bob, who was behind the wheel, began to get a bad feeling about the place. "Something says, 'You better get out of here in a hurry,' and I could just feel my skin crawl." Bob floored the pedal and passed through the wooded area as quickly as possible. Later on, as they were eating, the group was approached by someone who asked if they had heard what happened. It turned out another Jeep had been passing through the wooded area and was ambushed. "They were probably German troopers that were trying to escape." All the Americans in the Jeep were killed.

Another time, in the mountains, Bob was driving a six-by-six in the rain late at night with no lights on, to prevent detection by enemies. He was transporting a load of eight or ten prisoners. He accidentally made a wrong turn, realized his mistake, and made a U-turn to correct it. When he turned around, there was a tree drawn across the road. It wasn't a very large tree, so Bob just drove over it, but "I'm telling you, you never had a feeling like that in your life… you just know that you're going to be killed." Luckily they made it out of the area with no further problems, but Bob continued to be on the lookout for the men who had pulled the tree across the road.

Throughout the war, Bob and Petinelli were strafed seven to nine times. They were considered MIA three times, usually when they ran out of maps and got lost. Once, the Jeep got overturned in the front yard of a farmer. Bob and Petinelli decided to escape the cold and the rain by going into the farmer's

house. The two just walked in. The family fed them fried eggs and let them sleep in the house. "They could've slit our throats right there." Another time, the two men were driving along next to an airfield. Bob knew they were going to get strafed, so he steered sharply to the side into a field to get away from the plane. When the Jeep came to a halt, Bob jumped out and started running. He soon noticed Petinelli wasn't with him. "I walked back to where the Jeep had stopped, and he wasn't in the Jeep. I looked all around

Bob and the band driving through European town

there and he comes a-crawlin' out of a culvert. I don't know how he ever got in that culvert, but that was funny, really."

The end of the war finally came. As it drew closer, President Franklin Roosevelt died. On this day Bob was guarding 5,000 prisoners in eastern Germany. Alone. He was in charge of the collecting point for prisoners, who "were being captured by the hundreds." Despite the obvious danger, Bob had no worries. Those who could speak English would tell him they were glad to be alive. "They were glad that the war was over. They weren't going to go anyplace, but somebody had to be in charge of them." Bob showed them a picture of his father-in-law and his house and the car they had, which happened to be a Cadillac limousine, "but that was a different story."

At the finish of the war, Bob was stationed just east of some Russian troops. It struck him as odd that the Russians could enter American lines, but not vice versa. It was decided the Americans would hold a reception for the Russian officers. The band members hadn't seen their instruments for six to eight months, but the Army provided them. The band was instructed to play the national anthems of both the United States and Russia. The men were successful in their execution of the American national anthem; however, as they began to play the Russian anthem, they were ordered to stop. They had played the wrong song—an old tune from the time of the tsars. "That was the end of that."

Because Bob had the most combat service of those he was with, he was given the first leave when the war ended. He was sent from Krimichau, Austria, to Brussels for a week of "R and R." After the allotted time, Bob and his friend, someone from the medical department, couldn't find their divisions. There they were, combat soldiers–dirty, smelly, unshaven, lost, and AWOL. One officer suggested they go down to Frankfurt, which they did. Initially they had no luck there, either, and were forced to eat with the Displaced People, or DPs. Eventually an officer told the two they could probably catch their divisions on the *autobahn*. They got on a truck headed that way and hoped for the best. Soon Bob saw a truck with his division, going the other way. He leapt on this truck, leaving all his possessions behind. "They said, 'Well, you don't belong to us anymore. You're detached to the 30th Division.' And that's how I ended up in the 30th Division."

Finally, Bob was sent home. Because he had a rough time in combat, a colonel promised him and Petinelli a stateroom on the *Queen Mary*. "I was the last man to get on the *Queen Mary* before it shipped out. When I walked in, they closed the door." When they got to the stateroom, it was jam-packed with soldiers. There was nothing they could do to get them out, so they wandered around trying to find a place to stay. They'd sleep in the hallways, but were always kicked out because they weren't supposed to be blocking the passageways. The military even had to drain the pool so more men would have a place to eat. Bob and Petinelli finally ended up in the isolation ward, where men were infected with dangerous diseases. "We hung our signs—diphtheria, smallpox, scarlet fever, anything we could find. Nobody bothered us." Four days after boarding, the men arrived back in America.

Bob remained a part of the Army for 90 more days. He was given three thirty-day leaves before the system was capable of handling his discharge; it was that overcrowded. Once discharged, he and his wife traveled to South Dakota to visit their families, and then headed back to Salinas, California, where they lived for "thirty-some years." Bob now lives in Mesa, Arizona, with his wife Ann. The two will soon sell their house and move to the sun-soaked shoreline of The Villages, Florida.

As Mrs. Hatch and I readied ourselves for departure, Bob mentioned in an off-hand comment that he was selling his old vinyl records. "Do you think I could buy a record off you?" I inquired. He and his wife insisted it was completely unnecessary for me to buy one. Instead, they gave me a record, free of charge. The artist is Joe Leahy, a man Bob was friends with earlier in his life. The title? *Tabasco and Trumpets.*

Karl Koch "digging his own grave"

George Kelloff

Sept. 1942 - March 1946
Pacific: Noumea, Solomons, New Caledonia, Okinawa

Marian, Mindanao, Mogmog, and Movies

An Interview with George Kelloff
By Kasey Burton

It was just another Sunday evening. The Kelloffs had finished dinner and Mr. Kelloff flicked on the radio. The commentator, H.V. Keltenbun, was urgently relaying the tragic news. Pearl Harbor had been bombed. The family understood the gravity of the situation, but still felt confusion. "Where's Pearl Harbor?" Upon clarification of the location, both George Kelloff and his brother Mitchell wanted to enlist.

Unfortunately for George, he was obligated to stay behind because his brother enlisted. It became his duty to take care of the family's movie theater when his brother left. George had to buy the film, run the projectors, and keep the theater in order. Luckily, he was able to teach his sister Edna how to manage all aspects of the business and went off with his friend Louie Ricketorn to Denver to enlist. The two arrived at the Marine office, prepared to sign up. The Marines were willing to accept Louie; however, they turned down George because of his flat feet. Louie refused to join the Marines without George, so they directed the pair across the hall to the Navy. They signed up. The Navy sent Louie to Chicago and George to San Diego. They didn't see each other again until after the war, both blessedly intact.

Boot camp was rough for George, as it was for everyone. "They got you up at daybreak, and they kept you marching, and it was hell!" He often heard his fellow soldiers weeping at night, homesick. They got leave every now and then, though, which turned out very lucky for George. On his very first day of leave in San Diego, he was walking down the street, and much to his surprise he ran right into his brother! The two immediately called home to report the news, thrilled that they could be together.

Upon completion of basic training, the men were tested to determine their capabilities. It was discovered George could type, and he was asked if he knew shorthand. When he responded in the negative, he was put on a train along with several others and sent to Boston, Massachusetts, to report to Brian Stratton Business College to learn shorthand. The train ride was an uncomfortable one because the train lacked air conditioning. The only air they could get was from opening two windows, which allowed the smoke in, covering them in soot.

George studied typing, shorthand, and Navy paperwork for four months. While in Boston, he was impressed by the kindness of its residents. One of his fondest memories was going to the Boston Symphony Orchestra to hear Marian Anderson sing opera. Not only was she the first black person George had ever seen, but at the end of her performance she called all the sailors up on stage, sat them down, turned her back to the audience, and sang *Ave Maria* to them. It was one of the most beautiful songs he ever heard.

After he finished his studies, George was sent to Washington, D.C. to work in the Bureau of Ships. During his six-month stint in D.C., he often went to the USO, where he would do impersonations. One night, he competed in a talent contest. He did impersonations of Franklin Roosevelt, Wendell Wilkie, and other important figures of

Marian Anderson

the day. He tied for first with an opera singer. After the show, he found out that Eleanor Roosevelt had been in the audience. She came backstage and spoke with him for a short while, congratulating him on the accuracy of his impersonations.

George was able to leave Washington after women started coming in as WAVES to fill clerical positions that would free the men for combat. During World War II, women were not sent to combat. He boarded the *USS Mindanao*, a repair ship, as yeoman and they headed toward New Caledonia, anchoring at Guantanamo Bay, Cuba, to get supplies. After passing through the Panama Canal, they were ordered to "general quarters," where they were supposed to go in case of an attack. "This is not a drill!" a general shouted. It was thought there were Japanese subs in the area, and they were preparing for an attack.

Fortunately, the attack never came. "That was the first scare I ever had."

Throughout the 28-day trip from D.C. to Noumea, New Caledonia, George was most excited about his opportunity to become a shellback. He had seen the pride of the shellbacks about their status and desired the position of shellback as well. As they approached the International Date Line, all the pollywogs were ordered to strip and run through a line of men who smacked them with paddles. At the end of the line was a fat, sweaty man, whose bellybutton they were ordered to kiss. The fat man represented King Neptune. At the end of this ceremony they were given certificates authenticating their shellback status. "After you had gone through that line, your bottom was sore for about a week… It was quite a proud moment for a young 17-year-old boy."

The ship stayed in New Caledonia for only a short time, moving on to the Solomon Islands to do repair work. One day, a captain informed the crew that some Marines were going to come aboard. The Navy sailors were ordered to stay out of the showers and mess hall while they were in use by the Marines. "When those Marines came out of the jungle, I looked at my feet and said, 'Thank God you're flat.'"

A short while after the Marines had returned to the jungle, the ship set sail for the New Hebrides Islands to ready themselves for the invasion of the Philippines. On November 10, 1944, at 8 o'clock in the morning, the men on the *USS Mindanao* were called to muster. After their names were read, they returned to their duties. An hour later, George was sitting at his desk below deck. In the middle of his paperwork, he heard an explosion and the ship lurched. The lights disappeared, forcing George to feel his way through the hallways until he reached the deck.

He emerged into smoky air, confused and concerned. As he stepped onto the deck, he tripped and fell. Lying on the wet deck, he waited for the air to clear. As the smoke settled, he realized he had stumbled over a dead body. "The devastation on topside was something I'll never forget. It was hell." Limbs were scattered about, and for five days afterwards bodies floated to the surface.

This tragedy was the result of the *USS Mt. Hood*, an ammunition ship next to the *Mindanao*, exploding. It killed all 400 crew members aboard. The accident—ruled a mishandling of ammunition—also took the lives of 27 crew members on the *Mindanao*, as well as injuring 170, some of whom ultimately died. "After it was over I had to put the office back into shape again." It became George's responsibility to do the paperwork for the men who had died and the men who were injured and to find replacements. "They're all individuals, you know. They're not just numbers."

Forty days later, the *USS Mindanao* was back at sea. Because they hadn't been able to be a part of the Philippine invasion, the *Mindanao* was sent to Mogmog Island. Once they were organized, they prepared for the invasion of Okinawa. Soon it became a matter of waiting for orders. They ended up going to Okinawa for only a short time. "By the time we got there, it was practically over with." Though their stay was relatively short, they still did what they could to repair as many ships as possible.

Explosion on USS Mount Hood.

The day the war ended, George was sitting in Mass. A man came running in, shouting the news. Excitement filled the room, and as soon as Mass was over, everyone was saying, "We wanna go home! We wanna go home!" The long and costly war was over.

Unfortunately for George, he was forced to stay behind and watch his fellow crew members go home. He had to stay behind to do the paperwork for those leaving and those coming in, as the Navy was unable to find a replacement for his position. The officer assigned to go ashore everyday and find replacements was only able to grab two or three a day.

Finally, the officer getting replacements got frustrated with going ashore to bring back only a few men. He approached George and said, "Kelloff, I'm going to send you ashore tomorrow." The next day George went ashore, rented a Jeep, and drove to the Replacement Depot. Resigning himself to the long line, he waited for an hour and a half to reach the inside of the tent. George approached the desk where a chief yeoman, like himself, was sitting. "What the hell are you doing in here?" the yeoman asked. "Well," George responded, "The executive got tired of coming over here every day, and he was only getting two and three people so he sent me over to see if I could do any better." The yeoman asked, "Well, how many do you need?" George replied honestly, "'All you can give me.' He gave me *twenty*." George's success made him the hero of the day. However, the executive officer, pleased with George's results, told him, "Great job! You're going back tomorrow!"

The next day George again went ashore and waited in the long line. "I got in there and this chief looks at me and he says, 'You back?!' I said, 'Yeah, you gave me so many yesterday that the executive sent me back today.' He said, 'I'm giving you two today.' …That was the last trip."

During his six-month stay in Buckner Bay, Okinawa, George managed to make the best of it. Every fourth day the men received chips for two Cokes and two beers. Unfortunately, the beer and soda were always warm. George didn't drink; he was merely collecting the beer chips to make a little money. He went to the man in charge of the ice on the ship and said he'd trade a duffel bag full of ice for a beer. The man traded him, and George filled the bag with his warm beer. After the beer chilled, he went around and started shouting, "Cold beer! Cold beer!" Others gathered round and asked if he really had cold beer. He told them he did, and they asked what his price was. He told them he'd give them a cold beer in exchange for their warm beer and one dollar. This way, he made money and never ran out of beer.

At last, after six long months of waiting, George found out a replacement was coming. He went ashore and boarded a converted carrier to bring him home. George sailed across the Pacific to San

Francisco. As they sailed under the Golden Gate Bridge, all the sailors were topside screaming, yelling, and celebrating their return. "We were home!"

George was released in San Pedro with an honorable discharge. He took a bus home to Colorado, where he worked in his father's grocery store by day and his mother's theater by night. For a while he attended Trinidad Junior College, but eventually started a band called "George Kelloff and his Orchestra," in which he played trombone and saxophone, and sang. It was through this band that he met his wife Edna Mae. He was playing at a gathering, saw her, and knew he had to meet her. Not long afterwards, the two married. George then quit the band, opened a drive-in, and returned to college on the GI bill. He went back to school at Adam State College, where he majored in political science and music.

Using money they had saved from their coffee shop, North Café, the couple built a motel surrounding their drive-in, so that guests could watch the drive-in movie from their rooms. This motel, still in existence in Monte Vista, Colorado, was named Movie Manor Motel. It started as a small motel with 14 units, but grew to 60.

If you have occasion to visit Colorado, drive on in. Where else in America can you lie in bed, watch a movie on an enormous screen while sipping a cocktail, and then roll over and go to bed? You just might find George visiting from his home in Arizona, talking about the war, the movie business, his band, meeting Marian Anderson and Eleanor Roosevelt, and the Arizona sunsets he has traded for that movie screen.

Najib and George in front of family home in Aguilar after being discharged as a Chief Yeoman

Louis Kraft

March 1942 - September 1945
England

You Can Call Me Al
An Interview with Louis Kraft
By Barbara Hatch

Louis was 5 or 6 in 1919 when "Uncle Al" left the trenches of France. "Al" had changed his name from Isaac to avoid discrimination. Though Louis doesn't remember many details of Isaac's military service, he remembers the "puttees" Isaac wound around his shins to keep the mud out of his boots. Young Louis was ordered to share his bed with Uncle "Al" and not ask too many questions. Louis does remember Isaac telling him never to expose himself. "Don't volunteer, and don't try to progress in the Army. Just be a good soldier. Make a bed properly and be a good guy and do what you're supposed to do, but don't try to run the Army!"

Growing up in Boston between the wars, Louis graduated from college and got a job with Lever Brothers, "the soap people." He saw a future with this company. The Army had other plans.

Fort Devens, Massachusetts, was Louis's first stop. Older than most, Louis interviewed other draftees to determine their "proper slot" in the Army. "A fellow that was a baker, for the most part, ended up in the kitchen doing work in the mess department." Select questions determined if the man was telling the truth. There were no women in the camp at that time because the Army did not yet accept that women could do the clerical work to free the men for the infantry. "They were an afterthought, I think." Basic training taught Louis to march, maneuver, and clean a rifle, but soon after he headed to the 5th Port of Embarkation in New Jersey to be shipped to Greenock and Gourock in Scotland, then on to England and France to handle supplies going to the troops.

Louis did not say much about crossing the Atlantic on the *Queen Mary* with 20,000 other troops. In Glasgow, the 5th Port split into three divisions. Louis headed to Bristol, England; the other two were sent to Wales and London, respectively. Liberty ships arrived from the States, supplies coded with the name of the depot to which they would be delivered. Louis's job was to meet the ship, climb aboard the rope ladder, get the stowage plans for each hatch, and prepare for offloading. Each Liberty ship had five hatches. Supplies were "scientifically loaded" to prevent the ship from tipping, and camouflaged. Stevedores offloaded supplies to convoys of trucks for delivery to military depots. Army units would get supplies from these depots, "clothing, airplane parts, cigarettes, liquor for the Officers' Clubs, PX supplies, tanks, women's clothing, jewelry, engines, airfield equipment, medical supplies." Louis knew the value of supplies in winning the war. That included keeping the soldiers "comfortable." The U.S. sent not only artillery, food, and clothing, but doctors and dentists. If the Army bombed a bridge, troops needed the equipment to repair it. The United States even supplied European civilians. "We did everything possible to make the people, the natives of France, and even Germany, the civilians in Germany, more comfortable than they were before the war." In fact, so many jeeps and artillery were sent, "millions and millions of dollar of this stuff" remained in France and Germany at war's end.

Supply handling was not without danger. Six days after Allied forces landed in Normandy in June 1944 on D + 6, Louis found himself aboard a Norwegian coastal vessel offloading supplies onto four-wheeled, propeller-driven trucks called DUKWs because they could go into the water, then drive ashore to deposit goods on waiting trucks. The Army created a sort of "reef," or breakwater, to make landing easier by sinking ALCOA (Aluminum Company of America) ships offshore. Until the 9th Air Force eliminated German guns in hillside pillboxes, however, even supply delivery was not safe. German shells peppered Louis's craft. Louis didn't say what the other 19 men aboard did, but he hid under an overhang called a "combing" until the shelling ceased. Bodies of dead GIs floated past. "As I remember, there was a lot of fighting going on." As for the Norwegian coastal vessel, many merchant ships found themselves trapped in England when the war started. German subs kept them there. The English drafted them for the war effort.

Louis and friend with helmets

After the heavy fighting moved east, Louis followed the Army through St. Lô to Rouen, France, where he and his men found refuge in a schoolhouse. His job remained the same: go up the Seine River, pick up stowage plans, and get the gear ready for offloading onto trucks. On occasion his limited French allowed him to act as interpreter.

Gasoline took precedence over other supplies. Patton's 3rd Army moved very fast in pursuit of retreating German troops; gasoline kept his tanks on the move. Though some of his fuel came from North Africa through Italy, Louis remembers wooden cases of gasoline arriving through France as well.

"Pilferage" could be a problem. Black marketers stole railroad cars of cigarettes to sell for profit. Some men traded "war souvenirs" for cash to ship-bound sailors eager to bring home trophies. The biggest problem was liquor. Some of the stevedores "weren't very nice and broke open anything they suspected was drinkable. Now, they also drank shaving lotion, and we had a few guys we had to ship to the hospital. Some of them went blind." It was probably denatured alcohol. As a rule, Eisenhower's Secret Servicemen limited their court-martials to bigger theft, not bothering with the minor incidents of selling a few spent artillery shells or other trinkets.

Louis's work consumed his days, but evenings were free. German prisoners of war cooked and did routine KP. "Long days" and free nights allowed the unmarried Louis to attend the Folies Bergères with some French girls. Next thing he remembered was waking up next morning in a French firehouse. When asked how he got there, Louis responded, "Taxi!" When questioned further he admitted he "probably had too much to drink," but the French people "took good care of me and put me to bed…because we were very respected by the French."

Louis made French friends. When the Germans surrendered in May of 1945, he was invited to a party with a French family he had met. They all shared a love for music.

They were the nicest people I met while I was there. His name was David. You pronounce it DAH-VEED. And she [his wife] had a beautiful voice. She could sing that song, "Old Man MacGregor and His Farm." You know that one? I don't remember the words to it, but she'd get up there. She sang it in

English with a French accent. I remember that. And they had a whole group of neighbors and musicians and they included me so I went there and I included Cronin and took him with me.

Old McDonald still has that farm.

Louis came back to the United States by ship. Actress Barbara Stanwyck bought him a drink in a New Orleans hotel while he was assigned to Camp Plauche, training to go to the "Orient." Fortunately the United States ended the war in August by bombing Hiroshima and Nagasaki so Louis could stay in the States. He was "separated" at Camp Fannin, Texas, in September 1945. Was he happy? "Oh, yeah. I was ready to call it quits."

Louis married Edythe in 1945 or '46. They have two sons and a daughter. Lever Brothers offered Louis two months' salary to resume his prewar job, but his father needed him more. After working briefly for a friend's shoe business—"I suspect his father wanted me for one of his daughters"—he joined his brother, helping his dad sell ladies' hats. At that time, Catholics and Jews both covered their heads during religious services. His mother made hats for politicians' wives. Louis and his brother bought up most of the millinery stores in New England, keeping the owners supplied with inventory from New York. They handled the bookkeeping and used their "tremendous buying power" to keep the store stocked with the best fashions. They traded hats for sportswear when the Pope said Catholics no longer needed to wear hats in church. "He did a job on us!" The popularity of denims, with Louis's New York buying connections, made this new business profitable. Inexpensive Asian imports did not yet compete with American-made goods. Louis admits he recently bought a mail-order seersucker suit from Singapore since today, "The whole world is a buying company."

Though Louis feels strongly about each American serving his country when called, military service was never his calling. He never achieved higher than Private 1st Class. As his uncle Isaac suggested many years before, he did his job and did it well, but he had no desire for promotion or heroics. He admits the role of supplies in winning the war, but "it was just an episode in my life, and each day was a waiting period to get out." He never attended 5th Port reunions. He used the G.I. Bill's low-interest

4% loans to buy his first house, then settled down to work and a family. Though Louis's sons showed no interest in the armed forces, he reminded them, "If you're called, you go. This is your country."

Today Louis and Edythe live in the retirement community Classic Residence in Scottsdale, Arizona. Most of the men and some of the women who live there served in World War II. When I reminded Louis he and his neighbors make up Tom Brokaw's "Greatest

Louis with arm draped around fellow GI

Generation," he turned to Edythe and quipped, "You'd better be nice to me!" She responded in the offhanded manner of those who have been married for 60 years. "All right. Talk some more about WWII."

I asked Louis to sum up his war service in a sentence. That's all it took. "I feel that every healthy individual in the United States of America should go to the defense of their country or when their country calls them for help."

Uncle Isaac would agree.

Allan Kramer

July 1940 - February 1946
Mediterranean, N. Atlantic, Caribbean

Navy Pioneer

An Interview with Allan Kramer
By Kirk DiGiacomo

"Look back over your forebears in this country. They have fought many wars, and made it possible to have what you had. Many of them died, and now it's your turn." It was 1940, and by June of that year patriotism drove Allan Kramer to enlist in the United States Navy's V-7 program. "And there I went for the next five years." This program took him on an apprenticeship: a one-month cruise to Panama as a seaman. After the Navy let him go back to school for the next year on the condition he would return for three additional months of midshipman training on the *USS Illinois*, where he learned skills necessary to be an officer. With the war in Europe already in full swing, the United States saw the need to ready its armed forces. "But I remember Professor Seavy. It was a very moving talk, and very persuasive to me."

Kramer received his commission in September of 1941. After receiving his commission, he went to the district intelligence office in the Third Naval District of , where he didn't do much except wait for orders. Then he was transferred to Harbor Entrance Control in New London, Connecticut, a joint Army-Navy facility. While there, he protected Long Island Sound from invasion by the Germans. In the "ol' days," two Coast Artillery units were manned by the Army and Navy. He stayed there until he received orders at the beginning of the next year to a fleet minesweeper, the *USS Staff*. Minesweeping was "something you do only on occasion," but convoy was the chief activity of the ship, as well as various types of anti-submarine gear and means of protection for the ship.

Kramer got on the *Staff* soon after its commission. They worked around the coast and engaged in convoys to the Caribbean. An encounter occurred in 1940 while Allan was on the *New York* battleship in passing through the Panama Canal. United States seamen and a Japanese freighter going the opposite direction were within ten feet of one another on the "streets" of the canal. Japanese photographers were stationed on the freighter to take photographs of the American battleship. While the two weren't to be in opposition for another year and a half, it was eerily foreshadowing of what was to come for the Americans.

American ships waged fire against elusive German subs while in the Caribbean; they dropped numerous depth charges on the shipping routes which

Germans traversed. Until 1943, submarine tactics proved incredibly effective, but use of blimps and many new anti-submarine ships, coupled with great

Yale men aboard USS New York

communication to ships from the air, helped derail this successful system.

Following this came the United States's first invasion, North Africa, at the end of 1942, and Allan incidentally missed sailing due to being in the hospital because he had pneumonia. He finally boarded the *Staff* to North Africa in 1943, and upon the squadron's arrival at the large Mers el-Kébir port, the war was still being carried out. His duty was to sail on escort ships in the Mediterranean Sea with the purpose of conducting anti-submarine operations.

Along with preparation for minesweeping, which everyone engaged in, Kramer also was a gunnery officer, a communications officer, and a navigator. Also a central part of the daily routine was standing watch, a task divided into four-hour segments. Rotation of tasks was typical for junior officers, and he along with twelve other officers had to do different tasks depending on what was needed, whereas with convoys, it was "just a routine life," remarks Allan.

Then they planned for a major invasion of Sicily, which was the first invasion of continental Europe, something they "trained and trained for." When arriving in the sun-drenched country, Allan remarks that it was "just like in the movies," with

vessels similar to those later depicted in World War II commentaries. The invasion of Sicily came in July of 1943, and the squadron's job for the landings was to go in close to the shore and point the way to the beach for the landing craft. The landing was very easy, with little but a scattered effort from Italian forces attempting to repel them. The Germans didn't get around quickly enough to thwart the invasion. Shortly after these landings in Sicily, the plan was for the Army to go around the coast in both directions and try to get the entire island contained, but German divisions held them up so they planned another landing in the city of Agrigento on the southern coast of Sicily.

The problem with controlling Agrigento was that it was very well-defended. The squadron's job was to sweep the mines so landing craft could get in, and bypass the obstacles the Army encountered while they subsequently moved west. They took eleven ships, and Kramer was on the flagship of the division, leading the way for the others.

The mechanics was sweeping, but everybody's protected except the first ship, because somebody had to be in front. We had the squadron commander on board and we swept all day long, and they were shooting at us all day long, and they never hit anything from the shore. We had ships shooting. Shooting back we had two great big ships, with big guns on them, shooting over us to hit the shore. And then they shot back at us, and we shot back at them.

Firing between Americans and enemy forces amounted to "nothing much really happened except a lot of noise."

While the firing was going on, the ship hit a mine, which blew a hole in the bottom of the ship and put it out of commission. They were towed into one of the captured little ports in Sicily, where a Navy repair ship came along and patched them until they could be dry-docked and receive better patching. They stopped for repairs in Bizerte and Mers el-Kébir.

Finally, due to failure from three out of four engines, coupled with body damage from collision, they were towed across the Atlantic Ocean in November 1943 during the biggest hurricane in World War II. Were Kramer and his fellow seamen nervous during the hurricane? In what he describes as "phlegmatic" behavior, he as well as his fellow crew members lived through the situation.

> Nobody was particularly scared. If we were going to drown, we were going to drown. We never missed a meal. We didn't have much choice. If anybody said, "Would you like to get off and ask for a hotel, dancing?" Yes, we all would have, but we couldn't. So they just had to do it. When we had our shooting and when we hit the mine, with minor exceptions I'd say there was no running around in confusion to speak of, and every officer did just what he had to do. If the ship was going to sink, it was going to sink and somebody would pick us out of the water. And I'm no hero either... I think the idea of personal danger is different. I would think if you're in a foxhole, you'd figure somebody's shooting right at you, but when you're on a ship it isn't that way. Maybe if you were under air attack and you saw them coming at you, you'd think they were all aiming right between your eyes, but when everything is at long range in the ship, I think a lot of people didn't have any fear of danger.

The general feeling was "they'd rather not be there, but they had a job to do."

In Norfolk, Virginia, all on board were transferred due to severe ship damage. Kramer received leave for a while and upon coming back was sent to Yorktown, Virginia, for mine craft school and learned all about minesweeping. Due to Navy expansion as the war continued, they needed more and more officers, so he was there for a couple of months being trained, experiencing a "very nice life." Following this training, he was sent to another school in Little Creek, Virginia, where he did more work on and off ships than in classrooms—actions he practiced until 1944.

Allan was then assigned to a new fleet minesweeper, the *Intrigue*, but he didn't have any "excitement" with this ship. He operated mainly in the Caribbean, running to Panama and into the North Atlantic escorting commercial vessels. Fortunately he never actually did any minesweeping onboard this ship. After time on the *Intrigue*, he went to train as a flag lieutenant, a personal assistant to an admiral. He was in a class of about twenty at Harvard University. Six months through the training at Harvard the war ended. The Navy did not "throw us out right away, but obviously they weren't going to need us so I just went on." Simply put, from here he got out of the Navy, went home, and went back to law school in 1945.

Allan remarks on how comfortable his lifestyle was on a daily basis while he was in the Navy. As an officer, his quarters were better than the average sailor's with special-order cooks, caretaking mess attendants, and more comfortable provisions. "We were always well-supplied. We never ran low on food, oil, ammunition, or clothes." They even had a Dutch baker who had emigrated to the United States but was too old for combat duty. He said the United States had been very good to him and he wanted to pay it back in some way. Imagine a ship with pies, cakes, and fresh bread! When the ship hit a mine, the baker unfortunately broke both legs and his arm and had to be taken off the ship. Allan never found out what happened to him.

Even when Allan's ship was sent up to the North Atlantic, they were supplied with fur-lined boots and winter gear. He noted the desperate shortages the Germans experienced, particularly with fuel. Allan's ship, on the other hand, could refuel at sea with tankers that never stopped moving. "The thing that always impressed me as absolutely marvelous is that [the United States] could take from practically a standing start in 1940, build up an organization like this with people like me that didn't know anything about the Navy, and beat the Germans and the Japanese and the Italians." Proper supplies played a big part. To pass the time on board they sometimes watched movies. Only one of these movies stands out to Kramer, but not for ordinary reasons. While watching the movie *Laura*, sailing was smooth until a boiler exploded and the cabin needed cleaning and repair. He remembers that movie to this day.

It was surprising to me that even during World War II, some men "cooked up reasons" to get out of going to war, but some just dodged the draft and headed to Canada. Allan understands that happening in Vietnam or perhaps in Iraq, but he never considered not serving. "You couldn't be opposed to World War II. You just couldn't," states Kramer. He shared the same mentality as other servicemen: "I didn't plan to go to World War II, but I sure thought it was likely to happen, and if it was going to happen I wanted to be there."

Navy men in uniform (above), signed names on back of photo (below).

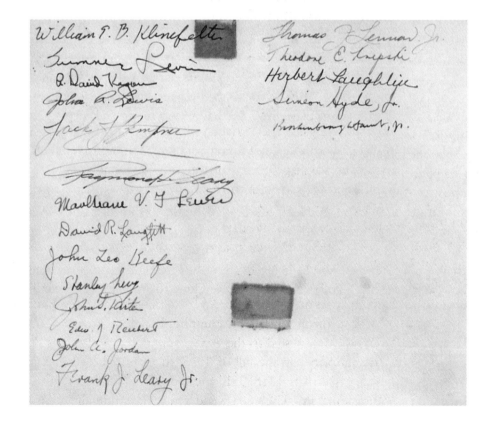

Glen Lytle

1942 - 1946
Europe

It's All About Family

An Interview with Glen Lytle
By Jeff Tully

One of the privileges of an Arizona Heritage Project member is the ability to allow friends and family the opportunity to interview their loved ones who served in the armed forces and thus preserve important pieces of family history. When Mrs. Carmen Sterner asked me to interview her son Ryan's great grandfather, Glen Lytle, I was happy to do so, and enjoyed an afternoon with Glen and his family in what would be my last interview as a student of Cactus Shadows High School.

Upon meeting Glen I was struck by his earnest humility and easy going demeanor. Greeting me by name and presenting me with a warm handshake, he introduced himself as "Glen" and made me feel immediately at ease. The respect and love his daughter Judy, her husband Richard, and granddaughter Carmen had for Glen was apparent throughout the interview, as they took great pleasure in reminding him of key events and filling in the details on anecdotes they had heard many times before.

As a member of a field artillery outfit in World War II, Glen fought and suffered alongside the "infantry boys" of Patton's Third Army, and his stories reveal the importance of infantry support—those men who work extremely hard to aid the soldiers fighting directly on the front lines. Modest about his own contributions to the war effort, Glen nevertheless was an integral part of the 12th Artillery Corps and left me with a greater understanding of the sacrifices every soldier made for his country.

Glen's story began as a student at Kansas State in 1936. "In order to make things a little easier going to school," Glen informed me, "people went into the ROTC. That's so every dollar you can save would make school that much easier. It was an all-day Saturday deal. We didn't have school, but we had ROTC all day Saturday." ROTC members looking to join for a third year were automatically enlisted in the Army, and in 1938 Glen was enlisted and given his serial number. "In the fall of 1938, that would be when I actually had my serial number, which is 17165051," he recalled. "I'll never forget it." After leaving Kansas State in 1939, Glen wandered a bit, eventually going to the University of

Nebraska. "I was just kind of in limbo during those years. You did pretty much as you pleased. The Army didn't pay attention to you, or anything else."

Unfortunately, after a little more than a semester of study, "things got pretty rough" and Glen was forced to go back to work, transporting truckloads of beer from Omaha to Milwaukee and back. "It was a 24-hour job to get from Milwaukee to Omaha or vice versa," Glen said, chuckling. "The top speed of those trips in those days was 35 miles an hour." Glen would later take a job at the H.P. Law Company as a warehouse truck driver. While at H.P., Glen met and became well acquainted with a man named George Metcalfe. Neither suspected what fate had in store for these soon-to-be soldiers.

In 1941, Glen got married and moved to Douglas, California, where he secured a "well paying" job. "I was making 65 cents an hour. We thought that was a hell of a job." Glen's daughter Judy was born, and a year later Glen was set to move back to Nebraska with his wife and young daughter. It was not to be. "The minute I left Douglas, the Army just grabbed a hold of me like that, and said, 'You got to go to the service now.'"

Glen's engineering background coincided with the advent of radar technology, and the Army sent Glen to several schools to become familiar with various radio and television broadcast techniques. After he completed the requisite training, he was assigned to his outfit. "I'd been assigned to an outfit," he recollected, "but I'd never seen it. It was a field artillery outfit, and it was a 288 FOB, what they called a field observation battalion. It ended up being in the Third Army in the front battalion in the 12th Artillery Corps, which was the artillery for the Third Army." Boarding a train heading for New York, Glen was then loaded up and shipped across the Atlantic. The sailors threw explosives overboard to root out the U-Boats that were still running across the Atlantic. "The destroyers were circling our fleet all the time," he mentioned. "I saw a lot of U-Boats blowing up." Finally landing at Glasgow, Scotland, Glen worked alongside the rest of the 12th Artillery to prepare for the D-Day assault on Normandy Beach.

Sailing from Glasgow to participate in the invasion of Normandy, Glen's ship "laid out there in the bay for six days while the infantry boys were getting a foothold so we could run the trucks and the tanks up on the top." When asked about the carnage of the initial invasion, Glen replied gently, "The bloody stuff is not fun to talk about. I mean, hell, everybody's heard it a thousand times." Landing a little further deeper into Normandy at Le Havre, the men endured German dive bombers, which claimed many ships. "They got a lot of ships," Glen told me, "but there were so darned many of them. We didn't outsmart the Germans; we just outnumbered them. We had so much more of everything than they had. That's the only way we ever got through and onto that beach."

Once the American tanks were established behind the "infantry boys," the Third Army began to push in earnest, and five days after Glen landed he was in Paris. "Everyone turned tail and ran. The Germans were well trained and good soldiers, but when they say all that power, they turned yellow. They hightailed it back and they kept on running." Glen witnessed the capture of such cities as Bastogne. Finally the Germans turned to make a stand along the Siegfried Line, and Glen found himself at the Battle of the Bulge. "They brought up their big stuff then. We made quite a mess there for awhile."

Equipped with the dreaded Tiger tanks, the Germans pushed back at the American infantrymen in what Glen called "the roughest [fighting] that I was ever in." Having pushed so hard and so quickly, the American supply line was struggling to catch up, and the convoy of men, tanks, and artillery was at a standstill, the tanks and trucks having run out of fuel. "We were completely out of gas, and here come these Tiger tanks, and frankly, everybody retreating on us. There were maybe a hundred of us," he informed me. "The artillery didn't really have any place for us to go, because we tried to stay with our equipment—me and my radios and other stuff." Faced with the advance of the tanks, Glen took command, as "I was the only sergeant left in this little slump." Wondering what would happen if the artillery was fired off its mounts, Glen directed his men to lay the guns down on the ground, and then tried to destroy the tanks. "We tried one, and that just blew the tank all to smithereens. And we got seven of them, and they just turned tail and ran. That broke that push. The next day we got gasoline, and we started moving on again. But we sure put the fear of God into them. We got six or seven of their big Tiger tanks, you know."

Around this same time, the previously American-held city of Bastogne fell to the German offensive, and so the Third Army marched back to

76

retake it. The Germans had entrenched themselves within the city wall, so "our planes dropped bombs. The bombs didn't get them. We sat there for thirty, forty-five days, shelling them, and shelling them, and shelling them." Finally, the 90th Infantry was called in from Italy. "They had filled it all up with guys from the States," Glen recalled sadly. "I'm talking about young guys, kids, nineteen and twenty, you know, new draftees." They were sent into the city to reclaim it from the Germans. "Oh God, that was a mess. That's where I got my overshoes," he explained, obtaining shoes from one of the casualties of the 90th Infantry to keep his feet warm in the bitter cold of the season. After the disastrous offensive from the 90th, American tanks were deployed and finally broke through to the beleaguered town. Glen recalled the sight that greeted him within the city, evidence of a failed 101st Airborne attack on the town a while back. "One side of the square was lined up with the 101st Airborne, stacked

Photo of the tents and camp in 1944

up, six, ten high. The Germans had put them in sacks, like bags, on both sides. They took care of the 101st Airborne. And they keep bragging about the 101st Airborne," he commented sorrowfully. "That's what I think of, every time I hear them. They didn't last very long in Europe."

Glen wouldn't have lasted very long himself if he didn't have God looking out for him, as he told us when recalling an episode with his radio tank and best friend Radick. A couple of days after breaking the Siegfried Line, Glen and his radio gear were situated with the rest of the 12th Artillery along the Rhine River,

waiting for pontoon bridges to be set up; the Germans had destroyed all brick and mortar structures. One night, after moving the radio tank—Germans could pinpoint the location of the tank from radio signals—Glen woke up suddenly and went outside to relieve himself. "Why I ever did, I don't know, but I walked maybe a hundred feet over to where a few trees were, and about that time, a shell came in and blew the tank up to smithereens along with my best friend at that time," he recalled sadly. "He was operating the radio. He was from Worchester, Massachusetts, and it was the dirty job I had when the war was over, to talk to his folks. He never had a chance. I wouldn't have had a chance if I stayed in there. God was taking care of me, I guess."

Glen didn't escape the war without a scratch, however, as shortly after that incident a shell exploded near his location. "It had to be some kind of mortar shell or something. Anyway, if I was very close to a shell, I wouldn't be here today to tell about it," he informed me. Shrapnel from the shell exploded and sank into Glen's legs. "I was picking the damn pieces out," he said laughing, "and it was bleeding." Walking down to the medics' station, Glen was treated, but no record was made of his injury, and he was deprived of a Purple Heart, a fact he related to me good-naturedly, too humble to be bitter with the oversight.

That's not to say Glen remained undecorated. One of his most humorous anecdotes related the beginning of his close relationship with a man he referred to simply as his "Colonel." Communications at the time revolved around the limited range of the Army telephone, which worked on a push-to-talk basis. "You let up and you hear," Glen explained. There was an eleven-mile limit to what could be sent over a battery-operated telephone. Glen had a novel idea: install amplifying devices within the button one pushed to talk. "I thought, why can't we have one of these on each telephone, and when you push to talk, it amplifies your signal going out, and maybe we can get another ten miles out of it. So we tried it. And it worked!" His commanding officer, the Colonel, thought it was a fantastic idea. "He said, 'Draw that up for me, Glen!' He called me 'Lytle' all the time!" Glen said, laughing. "He said, 'And write me a little note how you figured this out, how you made it work.' So it's part of the job. I just did it. He sent it in. He got a Silver Star; I got a Bronze Star. That's why he took me with him every place after that."

The convoy continued its tour through Europe, making 25 to 50 miles of progress per day. Eventually reaching the Czechoslovakian border, the American forces were greeted by the sight of a Russian army. "Facing us was the Russians. We sat there with guns on each other, while President Franklin D. and Stalin had their conversation and decided we weren't going to fight. The war was over then, you see."

The hard work did not stop with the cessation of hostilities. Glen and his comrades were occupied with releasing concentration camp prisoners from the death camps in Bavaria. "They were all just starved to death," Glen remembered. "The Germans didn't have enough to feed themselves, let alone feed their prisoners." As the sole authority in the area, American battalions were used to keep order in the occupied countries. "We'd be the governor; we'd be the governing body of that country," Glen told me. "Of course, we'd take everything we wanted, but we didn't steal from them or anything. We did eat their food." On one occasion, Glen and his buddies went to hunt deer, much to the consternation of a local farmer, who believed it to be against the law. "We finally explained to him that we couldn't find any law, except us. We were the law," Glen said, chuckling. "He thought it was a great deal afterward. He helped us clean them and everything else."

With seven million GIs in the occupied areas of Europe at the time, it was just a common fact that not all would be able to return home. "I had 85 points," Glen said, "and that was not enough for a discharge, but it was too many to be sent to the South Pacific. So I had to stay in Military Government, although they broke up our outfit. There wasn't field artillery anymore." Glen's colonel requested Lytle be transferred with him to the 90th Infantry Division. Glen arrived and met his Colonel, wondering where the other high-ranking officers were. "I asked him, 'Where's the First Sergeant?' He said, 'Well, you're the First Sergeant.' I said, 'I can't be. I've never been a First Sergeant.' 'You are now,' he said," Glen told me, laughing.

Glen spent the rest of his time in Europe assisting the displaced persons who came out of Hitler's concentration camps. "You have never seen anybody so tickled to see anybody as they did us," Glen told me, describing the adulation that greeted him and his fellow soldiers as they liberated and assisted various refugees. "Boy, I'm telling you, we were welcomed with open arms."

Time not spent on duty was rare, but Glen spoke of occasional poker games and the near-futile attempts to take baths. "I'll tell you about baths," he said, grinning. "The infantry boys, about every two weeks, they'd get a few days off to go back and clean up." Artillery personnel, having no replacements to man the stations, never got such a chance. "I had whiskers that long!" Glen said, stretching out his arms. "That steel helmet, you know, in the middle of wintertime, that's hard thing to take a bath in." "We looked like a bunch of apes," Glen joked. "It's no wonder we scared the Germans. It would scare me, to look at us."

Though it seemed an eternity since he first landed at Normandy, Glen was shipped home to the

Glen and buddies next to garbage signs in 1944. Glen is second from the left holding the newspaper.

U.S., though it took the better part of a month before he was reunited with his family. First was an excruciatingly difficult visit to Radick's parents. "I didn't want to go. But it was Radick, and he was my friend. So I decided that, well, by golly, it had to be done, and I'd appreciate it if someone did it for me. So I went up and spent two days with them. That was a crying mess." Next was an attempt to wrangle a discharge out of the Army so he could return to civilian life and not have to worry about being reactivated. "I spent two weeks at Fort Leavenworth, Kansas, before I got a discharge. They were bound and determined that I was going to sign up for the Reserves, you know. They offered me a permanent Master Sergeant's promotion, which is supposed to be a good deal. I don't know how good it is," he told me, smiling. All the promotions in the world would not have kept Glen from returning home.

And what a welcome it was. "We were treated just like royalty when we came back." Glen received a Buick convertible from a friend, and was told, "You don't owe me a thing. You drive it as long as you want to. When you get a car of your own, why, you can give it back." A grateful bank allowed him to forgo the down payment on a nice house. "They were trying hard to make things good for the GIs. They don't do that today." The best part about getting home, however, was the family waiting for him.

As I listened to Glen's story, I began to understand that his experiences in the war didn't define who he was as a person. It was his relationships with his family and friends that gave meaning to his life. His close relationships with grandsons Ryan and Tyler Sterner, current and former students of Cactus Shadows High School, respectively, gave him more pleasure than any glory he had won during his fighting days. I realized that in documenting Glen's story, I was preserving that history for the family who loved him.

I am especially glad I had a chance to do so, as Glen Lytle passed away from natural causes on September 2, 2006, well before he would have been able to see his account published in this book or attend the reception and book signing in May 2007. Though his family is no doubt saddened by this loss, I hope they are able to take a small bit of comfort in the fact that Ryan and Tyler's great grandfather will never be forgotten, as his story is archived in the Veterans History Project at the Library of Congress in

Glen (right) and a friend walking

Washington, D.C. On behalf of the Sterner, Hauptman, and Lytle families, I would like to urge families not to take for granted the opportunity to preserve these memories.

Bob Parsons

April 1942 - October 1946
November 1955 - January 1972
Philippines, Japan, Korea, Vietnam

Wearing Out Your Welcome

An Interview with Bob Parsons
By Kasey Burton

It's 6:15 in the morning and I'm staring out the kitchen window, watching tiny drops of rain shake themselves free of the battered clouds above. Though the sun has yet to make an appearance, the air conditioning sleepily sighs to life. Its low, steady breath raises goose bumps on my skin, so I wander around the house until my feet find my room. As I enter, the computer catches my eye, but I look away. To ignore its judgmental stare I begin readying myself for school, yet its glare remains fixed. It's been a more than generous amount of time since I last saw and first met Robert Parsons, an Army veteran that served in three wars. Much to my frustration, the words with which I may craft his story still manage to elude me. Another glance out the window reveals the end of the fragile storm. I cannot allow my frustration to keep me from this. After the day has retired and the moon begins to approach friendlier skies than the sun first encountered, I settle down and bring the computer to life. I am determined to unravel the words tangled in my mind.

He was supposed to be a teacher. It was perhaps his last choice for a profession; however, it was what his father wanted. "I'd sit and listen to my mother and he [his father] describing these small-town politics and I said, 'No way I wanna go through *that*.'" To avoid complying with his father's wishes for him to go to teacher's college, Bob became a truck driver. His plans for a life on the road were soon altered, for on April 11, 1942, Bob was drafted into the United States Army to fight in World War II.

He left his home in Providence, Rhode Island, for induction at Camp Devens, Massachusetts. After spending a week there, he traveled down to Fort McClellan, Alabama. Upon completion of basic training, Bob remained as a truck driver. Unfortunately, the Army's insistence that his position couldn't be filled kept him from promotion. Despite their claims, he applied for a year at Camp Davis, North Carolina, for anti-aircraft training. Though lacking previous anti-aircraft experience, he was accepted and graduated quickly, becoming a "90 Day Wonder" and a second lieutenant.

After graduation Bob was sent to Camp Hulen, Texas, to another anti-aircraft unit. He trained there for some time, and was then sent back to the headquarters battery at Fort McClellan. Four months later, headquarters battery was transferred to Fort Bliss, Texas. Bob remained there for a few months, but seized the opportunity a transfer project offered.

Someone was needed to transfer a trainload of Puerto Ricans to Fort Knox, Kentucky, for conversion to the tank department. Bob signed up for the job. He was given the responsibility of making sure everyone stayed on the train. However, it was a long ride, and his patience soon wore thin. "After the first day, I wanted to get off myself. So we would stop out in the boondocks to let the fast freight train go by." He called the sergeants up and informed them that should any of the Puerto Rican soldiers go missing, they were going to get the blame. Another situation that arose while escorting the soldiers came as quite a surprise to Bob. One morning, while on their way to Fort Knox, a sergeant came into Bob's office. He informed Bob there was some unrest growing among the men. Bob inquired what was upsetting the men. Apparently, on one of the small hand-held radios one of the Puerto Ricans had brought along, they found out they were no longer going to receive overseas pay. "I kinda got a kick out of that. They were getting overseas pay in the United States." Bob apologized for the situation, though it still brought a smile to his face.

Once this task was completed, Bob was allowed a few days' leave to visit his family back in Rhode Island. By the time Bob got back to Fort Bliss, he had been promoted to 1st lieutenant. However, also during his absence, the headquarters battery had been disassembled. Consequently, he was sent to Fort Ord, where he was trained to join the Far East Command. After training he caught the *General Sturgis* in Oakland with approximately 100 officers and 6,000 enlisted men. No time was wasted, for the night they arrived the ship set off for New Guinea. After a short stay of two nights, they set off once again, this time part of a convoy headed to Manila. The trip was painfully slow, for though the *General Sturgis* had decent speed, the traders present in the convoy kept the group dragging along at about 8 knots an hour.

While on the *General Sturgis*, Bob became acquainted with the process of becoming a shellback. He had to run through an obstacle course, prodded along by small jolts of electricity and whacks with paddles from the men lining the course. Next, Bob sat down and a blindfold was tied around his head.

He was then ordered to kiss King Neptune's belly—the stomach of the biggest, fattest man on the ship. As they took the blindfold off, Bob was shocked to see the rear end of King Neptune looking him in the face. "You wonder whether you've kissed his bellybutton or what happened!" The last action was Bob allowing himself to be blindfolded once more and shoved down a slide into a container of used dishwashing liquid. "This is just what they do to the innocent Army guys." He recalls members of the Navy having to either shave a track through their hair or sheer half their hair off.

It was a five-day journey to Manila harbor, and as the boat sailed in, the names of sunken ships lining the harbor's floor decorated the entrance. Bob stayed in the reception center for a week, and was then assigned assistant motor officer of Headquarters Company Far East Command. Bob remained at this job for three months, until the war ended.

Though Bob had enough points to return home, he decided he would volunteer to go to Japan. His arrival in Japan was delayed five days when a sandbar caught his ship in Manila. Eventually the ship was freed and he arrived in Yokohama in mid-September 1945. He was assigned to Transportation Headquarters Company of the Far East Headquarters in Tokyo. Though these were MacArthur's headquarters, Bob never met him. He did happen to meet MacArthur's wife Jean, however, on two separate occasions—both at the Ginza while Bob was shopping. Captain Hogan, Mrs. MacArthur's guard, called Bob over because he recognized him. This was because Captain Hogan had to go through Bob to get vehicles for their travel. Bob found himself extremely impressed by Mrs. MacArthur. "She was a *real* lady." After a short chat, each went on their way, but he was forever impressed by her manners. Bob was stationed there for several months and then received orders to transfer back to the United States. Upon receiving these orders, Bob requested a discharge. Two weeks after he left the Army, he encountered Mrs. MacArthur again at the Ginza. She recalled him from the last time they met, and asked, "Captain Parsons, what are you doing in your civilian clothes?" It took him by surprise that she remembered his name, and they once again commenced a small conversation.

Bob met a girl named Keiko through a business partner in Japan while he was a motor officer. It was through local Japanese businessmen he acquired certain items for Army vehicles, such as side curtains. He often went to lunch with these men. On one occasion, one of the businessmen brought along his 17-year-old granddaughter. Though Bob could not speak Japanese and she could not speak English, the two managed to become friendly. Eventually, Bob and Keiko began going out. Though her father wasn't thrilled about the situation, the two eventually married after Bob was discharged from the Army.

Shortly before discharge, Bob managed Headquarters Far East Command's baseball team. Creating the lineup for each game was no easy task. "If I put officers in, then enlisted men would complain, and if I put enlisted men in, officers would complain." It was a bit of a Catch-22, but he managed. Despite the fact that it was merely a recreational military team, Bob had several notable players on his team. He had a guy, "last name was Tanaka. He was the Mickey Cochrane of Hawaii. He was such a good baseball player." There was also a man named Jack Swift who played first base. He played professional ball in Birmingham. Among all these good players, however, one stood out. One day, a big, tall man walked up to Bob asking to try out as a pitcher. Bob agreed, and was wowed by what he saw. "This guy could really fire." It turned out that though the man, Vic Starfin, was working for the Army, he was actually a Russian national and a professional Japanese baseball player. At first Bob took everything Starfin said with a "grain of salt," but eventually Vic showed Bob films of himself pitching against Babe Ruth. One evening, after Bob reentered the Army, Vic came in and asked Bob if he wanted to

Bob at his desk in Vietnam

go out. Bob declined, saying he didn't want to get on the plane to Korea the next day with a hangover. It was a strange sort of luck. Unfortunately, while he was out, Vic ran into a streetcar and died. It was quite lucky for Bob, despite the loss of his friend.

Bob remained out of the military for nine years, first entering the Department of the Army as a civilian working as a civil custodian. He would go into the houses of Nazis who had been kicked out of Tokyo and inventory their belongings. It was mostly just the usual items one would find in a well-off household, though there were some discrepancies when it came to artwork. Bob and his partner often had to send paintings in for evaluation. "Neither one of us, the other guy or I, knew much about arts." After filling this position for a while, Bob became garage manager for the Army and the Air Force Post Exchange.

While he was out of the Army, Bob purchased a boat called *Udemon*. It was a small boat, 42 feet long, but Bob fixed it up, and he and his buddies often took it out. "In fact, I was playing golf, and then I bought the boat and I quit playing golf 'cause I liked the boat... I wasn't much of a golfer, anyway." The boat moved too slow to use water skis, so Bob attached a sort of surfboard and people rode on that instead. On one occasion, Bob had several buddies on the boat for a fishing expedition—unsuccessful, but quite the expedition nonetheless. It was a bright, sunny day, as many were, and the men were riding along on the surfboard. One of Bob's friends went to get on the surfboard, and Bob stopped him, asking if he wanted a life jacket. "Nah, I don't need it, I don't need it." As they got going, the man managed to fall off. The boat wasn't particularly quick, and it took a full five minutes for them to circle around and get him. The tough guy had lost his upper dental plates and couldn't eat anything for days. Needless to say, the next time he wore a life jacket. Unfortunately, when Bob returned to the United States he had to get rid of the boat.

In December 1955, Bob reentered the Army as a corporal. He was immediately shipped to Korea, but returned for a short time to legalize his marriage to his wife, get his two oldest sons into school, and get ID cards for all for them. Once he completed these tasks he was sent back to Hui Jumbu in Korea to drive Quonset huts up to the DMZ for men to live in. Upon finishing this fifteen-month tour, Bob returned to Japan and his family. He was stationed fifteen miles from Tokyo at Camp Drake, where he continued to work in transportation.

Bob then received orders to move back to the United States. He was stationed at Fort Ord, California, which mainly functioned as an infantry training center. As they settled into their new home, Bob's family got their citizenship and they bought a house. Their new home was located in Marina, a town not far from Fort Ord. Bob ended up being assigned athletic and recreation sergeant for CDEC, Combat Development Experimental Command. Bob did not get to rest long in his new position, for after a few months he was sent back to Korea for another fifteen-month tour. This time he was a part of the Vehicle Utilization Inspection Team, a group that investigated military advisement detachments and decided if they were fully utilizing their vehicles. The men in the inspection team traveled everywhere from Seoul to Pusan. After completing his second tour, Bob returned to his former position at Fort Ord, remaining there for a year and a half.

After a year and a half, Bob was sent to Ingrandes, France. Once again, his family was left behind as he traveled off to his next station. He had been in France for six months when General Charles DeGaulle suddenly forced all American troops out of France. Bob's entire truck company drove to Kassel, Germany. He was a large contributor to the driving duties due to his experience on the road. "If I didn't drive, I'd have to ride with some of them. Some of them were so inexperienced that they couldn't even back these semi-trailers up when we'd get someplace. I'd have to do it." He didn't have to drive, but preferred it to sitting behind a desk all day. Bob never found out why they were booted out of France. He said the French weren't particularly nice people, but figured the Americans had probably overstayed their welcome. "My favorite saying is, 'Everywhere the military has been, they've worn their welcome out.'"

Sadly, while Bob was in Europe, his wife passed away. His journey had steered him properly, though, for he became friendly with a German woman

Bob on a muddy road in Vietnam

who later became his wife. He left Germany and went to Fort Bliss, Texas, for approximately eight months, then volunteered to go to Vietnam where his son Robert Parsons Junior, a Marine, was headed. He was stationed in what was then Saigon (now Ho Chi Minh City) with Headquarters Company Transportation USAFV. After five months, he was promoted to E-7, Sergeant 1st Class, and then moved to Long Binh, about ten miles outside Saigon, to a fully constructed headquarters for the USAFV. After staying there a short time, he returned to the United States to Fort Sam Houston in San Antonio, Texas, as operations sergeant in the medical motorpool. After a year he returned to Vietnam.

Bob was stationed at Dong Ha, where there was oftentimes constant artillery fire. Because of the constant artillery threat, they were moved six miles back to Quang Tri. Bob's job was to shuttle 5-ton trucks with supplies from the Qua Viet River to Dong Ha. He was transferred to Mannheim, Germany, for a year and a half before returning to Vietnam. His son had enlisted in the Marines and had been shipped to Quantico, Virginia, where he became a commissioned officer to be stationed in Da Nang, Vietnam. Fortunately Bob was stationed there as well. Because of this, the two often spent time together when Bob Jr. came in from the field. The pair sat around and talked, played pool, drank a few beers, and enjoyed each other's company. Bob's son, much to his pleasure, went home before him. Shortly after his son's return to America, Bob, sick with hepatitis, was medevaced to Okinawa, Japan, to recuperate. While healing, Bob, approaching his 55th birthday, received his discharge orders. He returned to Fort Ord and was officially discharged January 1, 1972.

While in Vietnam, Bob earned two Bronze Stars. He received the first star on March 2, 1968, for meritorious service against hostile forces. Bob received a second Bronze Star with a V on May 18, 1969, at Dong Ha. There Bob came under fire approximately two or three times a week. On one of these occasions, the Viet Cong hit a maintenance shop containing several trucks. One of the damaged trucks began burning, threatening the trucks around it. A 1st Sergeant turned to Bob and said, "Come on, let's go." The two rushed out amidst the rain of shells and began dispersing the trucks. The other sergeant got behind the wheel of a functioning truck while Bob wrapped a chain around the front of a truck in the maintenance shop. The sergeant drove the truck away while Bob began chaining up another. Together the two managed to disperse the trucks as well as any danger of a major explosion. "If somebody had asked me if I'd ever do that, I'd say, 'Heck no,' but under the spur of the moment, if one guy's going, what the heck, you have to go, you know?"

Bronze Stars were not the only awards given to Bob. He received a plaque from his platoon in Vietnam. This plaque reads:

> Sergeant First Class Robert Parsons is one of the few individuals who has gained the affection and respect of all those he has come into contact with through the forms of sincerity and outstanding ability to get the job done. We can only hope that others will have the privilege of his association to the men of these 363 troops who will always represent the finest the Army has in its ranks.

It is this plaque that means the most to Bob. He valued his men very deeply. He never asked them to do anything he wasn't willing to do. For example, whenever he and his men had to haul ammunition, he drove the lead truck. "How could you ask the rest of them to go out if you're going to be sitting in some fairly safe place?"

After his final exit from the military, Bob entered college. He was 55, but ready for the studying ahead of him. He took courses such as English, Ancient History, California History, and Political Science. Bob worked at a veterans' center in the evening so he could attend school during the day.

He begins slowly, avoiding the camera's unrelenting stare. He eases into the conversation with a recitation of the basics of his service, where he had been, what his position was. It all seems rather formal. However, as he begins to speak of transferring the Puerto Ricans, a crack seems to appear in his uncomfortable countenance. Through this crack shines a touch of light. It's the light of the man behind the military. It becomes a matter of time before he forgets the watchful eye of the camera and falls into natural speaking. Though he never meant to spend his life in the military, it seems to have steered him well. It's beautiful to watch his pride glow as he displays the plaque his platoon gave him in Vietnam. These memories flow through my mind, and I happen to glance out a window. It's been quite some time since I began to write this essay, yet once again the night sky embraces a gently glowing moon. The story seems to have come full circle. I didn't know where to start and now I don't know where to end. All I can say is, I am grateful to Bob. I am grateful for his time, his story, and his life, and that he was willing to share all of this with me.

Mortared motor pool, Vietnam

Al Pempek

1940 - 1944
Panama, England, Germany

Tell Me About My Boy

A Tribute to Al Pempek
By Kyle Hatzinger, West Point 2006
Edited by Barbara Hatch

Background: Kyle became interested in Albert Pempek, a relative, when his uncle found the picture of Al (above) in a shoebox, with only the words "Al" scrawled on the back in his grandmother's handwriting. He later discovered that Al, born September 21, 1916, was attending a Chicago Bears game at Soldier Field on December 7, 1941, with his sister Catherine when the attack on Pearl Harbor was announced. All military personnel were to return to their stations. Al reported to his unit at Midway Airport, and then found himself flying three-seat O-47 reconnaissance planes out of Panama with the 108th Observation Squadron from January 1942 until November 1943. In lighter moments, he liked to trap monkeys with baited coconuts! Sergeant Pempek graduated from multi-engine pilot training at Brooks Field, Texas, was integrated into a new bomber crew in Salt Lake City, did Air Combat Training with his crew in Blythe, California, then eventually joined the Mighty 8th Air Force's 448th Bomb Group in England in June 1944. Before his departure for the European theater, from which he would not return, Al married Mary Jane McKelvie, a young rubber factory employee from Illinois who "met" Al when she picked a serviceman to write to. This soon-to-be lieutenant, according to Mary Jane's sister-in-law Joan McKelvie Deuger, "looked like Errol Flynn with his moustache." Mary Jane's son Gary remembers Al "whittled me a wooden P-38 plane" and was the "nicest guy I ever saw." He regrets not having the chance to spend years with a man many felt would have been a "great father." The loss of Albert Pempek and his crew is told by his West Point descendant, Kyle Hatzinger, in the story below:

On November 6, 1944, a B-24 Liberator from the 715th Bomb Squadron was lost on a mission to Minden, Germany. While the Air Corps may have viewed the loss as "one bomber," there were ten men killed in action, all of whom had next of kin that needed to be notified. The crew consisted of 1st Lieutenant Frank Genarlsky (Pilot), 2nd Lieutenant Albert Pempek (Co-Pilot), 2nd Lieutenant Walter Ford (Navigator), 2nd Lieutenant Ralph O'Neil (Bombardier), Technical Sergeant Paul Novichenk (Flight Engineer), Technical Sergeant James McLaughlin

(Radio Operator), Staff Sergeant Lewis McMahan (Left Waist Gunner), Staff Sergeant Joseph Yates (Right Waist Gunner), Staff Sergeant Albert Cole (Tail Gunner), and 1st Lieutenant Alton Kraft (Nose Turret Gunner). One crew member, Al Pempek, was married, while the others were single. Most had siblings, but all had parents anxiously awaiting their return. Crews were usually known by their pilot; thus when the "Genarlsky Crew" is referenced, it refers to the whole crew. The plane was also identified by its serial number, 42-50820, and its nickname *OUR HONEY*, featuring its nose art of a scantily clad cowgirl. There were also group and squadron identifiers on the vertical stabilizers to allow for visual identification in flight. There were many redundancies in visual identification so a crewman in another plane in the formation could easily report which aircraft was lost, despite the radio silence exercised over enemy territory. On this day, these visual means of identification would be needed.

The Genarlsky Crew was but ten of over 400,000 U.S. servicemen who were lost from 1941 through 1945. There were also over 100,000 listed as missing in action (MIA). Behind each person in the statistic were the friends they served with and the family waiting back home for their return. When the soldier's unit and the War Department received word that he was killed or missing, a chain of events was set in motion that produced effects that, in some cases, are visible today. Each family and each person within that family chose how to deal with their loss in a different way. Throughout the six-year ordeal the ten families of the Genarlsky Crew experienced from November 6, 1944, through the final burial of the crew in November 1950, a failure of some systems that were in place to deal with casualty assistance, coupled with the lack of information, caused many relatives of the deceased crew to have lingering questions to this day.

The target for the 448th Bomb Group's November 6th mission was the Mitteland Canal at Minden, Germany. This canal, along with the Dortmund-Ems Canal, was one of the most important inland waterways that supported the German industries along the Ruhr River. The bombing of these targets was part of a larger post D-Day effort by the Allies aimed at the German transportation systems.

Thirty-three planes of the 448th departed from Seething Airfield at 0730 hours on November 6, 1944. The "wheels up" time for 715th Bomb Squadron was around 0745 hours. The planes took off at thirty-second intervals, taking about 17 minutes for the entire group to clear Seething Field. At 0915, the 448th was met by 176 more planes from the 93rd, 392nd, 446th, 453rd, 458th, 467th, and 491st bomb groups over the North Sea at an altitude of 13,500 feet. *OUR HONEY*, piloted by 1st Lieutenant Frank Genarlsky, was the second plane to the left from the lead plane in the lead squadron. P-51 Mustangs from the 479th, 364th, and 357th Fighter Groups comprised the fighter escort for this mission. Even though German fighter sightings were becoming more infrequent, German fighter production peaked in September and the Luftwaffe (German Air Force) was still a force to be reckoned with.

The bomber crews faced two direct threats from the enemy: fighters and flak. By 1944, there were over 2,000 flak batteries in Germany alone which, by the fall, were expending about 16 million rounds of ammunition a month. These flak guns would account for the downing of 5,400 American aircraft, over half of the total downed during the war in Europe by the Luftwaffe. The 8th Air Force suffered 54,539 planes damaged by flak during its campaign in Europe. *OUR HONEY* would soon become one of

Bomber crew, Al in center below engine

the ninety 8th Air Force bombers to be destroyed by flak in November of 1944.

At 0955 the flight crossed over Holland at 20,000 feet, continued 16 miles east-northeast of Zwolle, then turned right on a southeasterly course in the direction of Enschede. After passing over Ahaus, the formation turned left and headed east-northeast towards Greven. This was the IP (Initial Point), at which time the formation commenced the bomb run to the target. There had not been opposition until the formation came to this point, approximately 2 miles northwest of Greven, almost directly north of Muenster. From this point until after the bombs had been dropped, it was essential for the aircraft to fly straight and level regardless of the peril in order to ensure a successful bomb run.

At 1033 hours, just after the IP and north of Muenster, flak struck OUR HONEY. With the low formation to his left, Lieutenant Genarlsky turned the plane to the right as he lost altitude to avoid a possible mid-air collision. Lieutenant John Jordan, a pilot with the 713th Bomb Squadron flying in the Lower Left formation on 6 November, recalled that a B-24 with such damage,

[W]ould fly pretty good. The only catch is that you couldn't keep up with the rest of the formation. That left you with two options: first, you could look for and try to reach, and join, a formation of B-17s. With one engine out, you still had the speed to stay with them and use their firepower for protection. The second [option] you didn't want to have to do. It meant flying across Germany trying to reach the coast all by your lonesome.

What happened after Lieutenant Genarlsky left formation until the plane crashed is unknown, and unfortunately it is the piece of information the next of kin most crave. Instead of heading straight west towards Holland, the plane took a southwestern azimuth. This could be attributed to a number of factors, both internal and external. With number two engine out, assuming all others were still operating, the plane would naturally pull left. The main concern at this point was to keep the aircraft under control and to ensure the crew was okay. Lieutenant John Jordan remembers, "There were a lot of 8th Air Force planes in the air that day," and Lieutenant Genarlsky

may have been seeking a group of slower B-17s he could latch onto for protection while getting back to England. The plane traveled south-southwest for approximately 15.5 miles, or about 5.48 minutes. Between the German towns of Atenberge and Temming the plane turned right and traveled southwest for another 4 miles (1.6 minutes). It is at this point that the plane is presumed to have jettisoned two of its bombs, as there were two craters found that matched the type of ordnance OUR HONEY was carrying that day. One bomb is presumed to have hung up in the bomb bay because the load for the Minden mission was three 1000-pound bombs and only two craters were located. The plane continued southwest for another 5.28 miles, which took a little over two minutes. At this point, for some unknown reason, the plane could not remain in the air any longer. Author Jeffrey Brett, citing an account of a German farmer, offers more detail as to what happened as the plane went down. According to the farmer, "The plane struck a telephone pole and crashed, catching fire almost immediately. Quickly after crashing, the plane erupted in an explosion evidently from the one bomb that was not jettisoned." While there is no concrete proof there was a bomb hung up, there were still plenty of things aboard the aircraft to cause a catastrophic explosion upon impact. This included the ammunition, fuel, and oxygen tanks, all of which were in plentiful quantities on board the aircraft.

Upon the group's return to Seething Air Field, the Army began the process of determining the fate of the Genarlsky Crew and ultimately reporting the findings to their families. Sadly, this process was almost second nature for squadrons in the 8th Air Force, having been done far too often since 1942. This process began with a post-mission interrogation of all crews participating in the day's mission. Each crew would be brought into the same room where earlier in the day they had been briefed for the mission. Because of the limited view each position on the aircraft offered, it was essential to get each crewman's viewpoint because one man may have seen an incident that the rest of the crew could not. These reports determined the status of the crew. The other three bomb groups also submitted reports, which the 448th reviewed in hopes they contained some insight into the disposition of OUR HONEY. Unfortunately, no information other than what was ascertained from the interrogation report was found and, as a result, each crewman was listed as Missing in Action (MIA).

With the information gathered from the interrogation reports at hand, the group S-2 [intelligence] began to prepare a Missing Air Crew Report (MACR) for *OUR HONEY*. The MACR would essentially be an open file until the status of the crew became killed in action (KIA), or returned to military control (RMC). One set of documents that could potentially shed light on the fate of the bomber crew were called *KampfFlugzeugeUSA* (Battle Planes USA, shortened to "KU") Reports. The Luftwaffe prepared these reports on downed Allied planes and turned them over to the Red Cross. Contained in these files would be the location of the aircraft wreckage and the fate of any crewmembers. However, these files could take months to be forwarded from Germany to England. In the meantime, the Army had to notify the next of kin that their relative was MIA.

During World War II, the grim task of notifying the next of kin did not fall upon specific members of the Army; it was the Western Union Company. It was not a military officer or senior non-commissioned officer; rather, it was an informally dressed man or boy with a busman's hat. Notification

As the Army searched for remains, it also had to process the personal effects left behind by those missing or killed. Regardless of status, the effects had to be moved from the unit as there were replacements that needed the billets. As a result, after the unit conducted an initial inventory of effects, they shipped everything back to the United States. The destination was the Army Effects Bureau in the Kansas City, Missouri, Quartermaster Depot. Here items were carefully inventoried to ensure everything that was documented as being present overseas was still there. They laundered soiled garments, removed anything that was property of the government (for enlisted soldiers this included all uniform items), converted foreign money to U.S. currency, combined with any the U.S. funds the decedent already possessed, and converted it to a money order. The Bureau held this money order and the package of personal effects for a time before it was sent to the next of kin.

The Genarlsky Crew's situation was not unique because many men's remains were unrecoverable due to being in enemy-controlled territory. As early as 1943, the Army was looking into how they would deal with the immense undertaking of finding and burying war dead after gaining control of all areas. The Quartermaster Corps expanded to include a Memorial Branch, which could coordinate with the next of kin of war dead and ensure their wishes were carried out. Part of the Corps' reorganization included the Graves Registration Service Branch, whose grim job it would be to locate, exhume, and hopefully identify the remains of U.S. soldiers in both theatres. By V-E Day, Graves Registration estimated it had approximately 25,000 bodies to locate and recover throughout Europe.

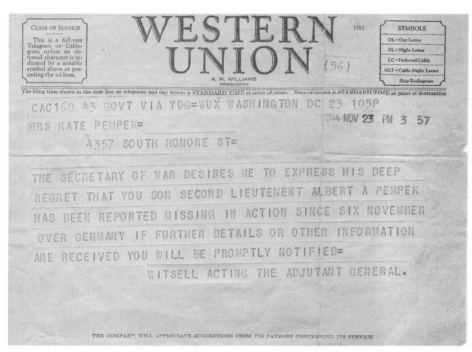

did not come on a piece of stationery; rather, typed lines of all capital letters pasted on yellow paper composed the message. Sometimes there was no punctuation included, which made the message difficult to decipher.

The successful location of isolated remains was largely a grass-roots campaign by the Army. Bilingual posters were put up in towns throughout Germany, asking those who might have had information about Allied servicemen buried in the area to come forward. There were also ads placed in the newspapers and announcements made during radio broadcasts.

The most critical phase was obviously conducting a proper and accurate investigation. This responsibility fell upon the Investigating Team, comprising a leader, interpreter, and a driver. Upon arrival at a destination, the team leader met with influential members of the community, to include the mayor, police chief, priests, local physicians, cemetery attendants, and anyone else who was known to have knowledge of an incident or burial location. Team leaders became very good at keeping an ear open for any rumor or bit of gossip, as anything mentioned in passing could be either a breakthrough clue for that investigation, or evidence of a previously unknown set of remains.

The next stage in remains recovery was the actual exhumation of the gravesite and then the attempt at identifying the remains. The identification team searched for clues by conducting an intense anatomical examination, where all "deviations from the normal" were noted, such as fractures, amputations, etc. They explored all remaining flesh for any foreign objects like identification tags or jewelry that may have become embedded in the tissue. A special cleaning process designed to bring out laundry marks and other indications of identity was performed on all clothing. Any personal effects were examined for revealing clues as well. In all cases the analysts constructed tooth charts and, flesh permitting, made fingerprints.

When all identification work was complete, the remains were then shipped to a military cemetery for internment until a final decision was made regarding their disposition. The body was wrapped in a clean mattress cover and placed in a casket. If the remains were unknown, an "X" was marked on the casket followed by a series of numbers. Beginning in 1947, the majority of unknown remains were sent to Neuville-en-Condroz, Belgium, where a cemetery was being established and the Central Lab was located. A total of 1,600 sets of remains were sent to the lab: 348 were identified, 206 were "believed to be identified," 943 "possessed clues [for identification]," and 103 remained as unknowns.

Congress created a program called the "Final Disposition of the WWII Dead" on May 16, 1946. The intent of this program was to offer all families with a loved one killed overseas the option of bringing home their decedent's remains or leaving them buried overseas. If they elected to keep their loved one overseas, no further action was required. If they chose to bring him home, a cemetery and a funeral home first had to be identified. On average, this process took about a year. The government covered all expenses from transportation to final burial. Once the burial was complete in the U.S., or the family chose to leave their loved one overseas, the case was considered closed. For the Genarlsky Crew, it was a six-year ordeal filled with lingering questions and frustrations that were not laid to rest, even when their loved ones were interred at Rock Island Cemetery in 1950.

When a family says "goodbye" to someone leaving for military service during wartime, it is understood they are also saying, "Maybe I'll never see you again." The story of the Genarlsky Crew's downing on November 6, 1944, and the pain their next of kin experienced in searching for answers is an interesting one to an outside observer, but it is made personal when one of the crewmen, Albert Pempek, is a relative of the author. When George Yates wrote his first letter with question marks after every fact because even 60 years later he did not have satisfaction as to what happened that day, it was easy to imagine the Pempek clan felt the same way. After interviewing Pempek's sister, Catherine (Pempek) Gourley, and sister-in-law Joan (McKelvie) Deuger, this was confirmed. Thus, the research of what happened to the Genarlsky Crew required an examination of the effectiveness of the Army casualty reporting system in order to determine why the Pempeks and other families were left with so many unanswered questions.

When the 448th Bomb Group returned from the Minden mission, the aircrews executed the same process of post-mission interrogation they had been doing the past year in the theatre. Flight Engineer Don Zeldin from the 715th Bomb Squadron remembered a problem with the interrogation process. They would interview the crewmen immediately after the mission, but would never follow up later in the day or anytime thereafter. Frequently, men would remember additional details, some of which may have been valuable to intelligence, but were never asked again about that particular mission. As the squadron took the interrogation reports to formulate an official statement for the MACR about the fate of the

Genarlsky Crew, they compiled the following statement: "Lt. Genarlsky received a flak hit in the #2 engine which burned for a while but went out. Pilot feathered the engine and plane lost altitude at 5206N-0735 E, and peeled off under control, heading back to England." The MACR lists three witnesses to verify this claim: Lieutenant Sheffield, pilot of the aircraft on the port side of OUR HONEY in the lead formation; Lieutenant Jordan, a pilot in the Lower Left formation; and Lieutenant Hillman, a pilot in the High Right formation. Upon contacting one of these pilots, Lieutenant John Jordan, he replied, "As a pilot flying formation, we didn't have too much time to look around, so we depended on our crew members in the back of the aircraft to keep good records and keep the pilot informed. During debriefing, we shared our sightings with other crew members." The failure to follow up post-mission interrogations was detrimental to gathering the most facts possible.

Furthermore, the 448th Bomb Group submitted its loss report, saying, "One A/C lost by this group, number [42-50]820 Letter E [tail marking]. Received flak hit in No. 2 engine, No. 4 also smoking. Left formation at 1030 just after IP and headed back. Believed to have flown as far as Zuider Zee with 93rd Group." It was almost universally known among B-24 crews that losing one engine of a B-24 was like living on the edge; losing two was flirting with death. Given this knowledge of the B-24's characteristics, the possible loss of the second engine being hit may have made it easier for the next of kin to believe that the plane probably was forced down and that the crew may not have survived. Also, the Army may have been able to judge how far away OUR HONEY could have flown from where it was hit before it would have been forced to land or crashed.

Perhaps one of the most tragic incidents that added to the anguish of the next of kin occurred on November 8, 1944, in Billerbeck, Germany. When the Germans submitted the KU report for the downing of OUR HONEY on the road to Billerbeck, they only listed Lieutenant O'Neil and Staff Sergeant Cole as being identified. What is tragic about this incident is the admitted removal of the crewmen's dog tags and other personal effects from their remains, mentioned in a letter between German officials. As also described, the crewmen were buried in a single mass grave by the Germans, allowing the remains to intermingle and probably preventing any identification from being possible after that point.

November 23, 1944, was Thanksgiving Day in the United States. Ten mothers were sitting down to Thanksgiving dinner that afternoon with the thought that their son was missing another holiday from home. Undoubtedly, each held out hope that their boy would be home by that time next year. That hope was shattered by a knock at the front door. A man was there to deliver a Western Union telegram stating that their son was missing in action, and if any further information was received, they would be promptly notified. It was not the worst news that could have been received, but the lack of information surrounding their disappearance brought great anxiety. Three days later, a follow-up letter arrived to each home from the Adjutant General. This letter offered no further details of the downing, but explained what was meant by personnel being listed as MIA and that the Army was doing everything it could under the restraints of war to locate MIAs. The letter closed, promising that another letter would be generated once additional information was received or three months' time had expired.

Not all families would receive meager information because the KU report telling that O'Neil and Cole were KIA was forwarded to the Americans on 9 February 1945 and their next of kin were subsequently notified. There would be considerable delay in passing further information to the Cole and O'Neil families regarding other members of the crew and the whereabouts of remains. By 1946, Mrs. O'Neil was prompted to write to the Adjutant General.

My son...was listed as missing on Nov. 6, 1944...then on Feb. 10, 1945 I received a telegram saying Germans had said he died that day which I do not believe to be true... [This] is the most cruel way to torture a mother, talk about Jap and German torture this is slow death. I have been under doctor's care for almost a year just with worry the Doctor has told me... Please if you have any information...won't you let me hear from you this drives me insane too.

There was nothing the Adjutant General or the Quartermaster Corps could do in response. It was merely forwarding the best information available at the time. The war was still ongoing and it would be some time before the Graves Registration teams would even start to search for isolated graves, much less be able to positively identify O'Neil's remains.

Another incident that would further the confusion when Allied teams exhumed grave number one at the Billerbeck Cemetery was the addition of the remains of another airman, Harold Rial, a tail gunner aboard B-17 44-6607. In thick clouds, Sergeant Rial's plane collided with a plane to its right. He plummeted 23,000 feet to his death. Rial's location was not far from Billerbeck, so the Germans buried his remains with the crew of *OUR HONEY*. While Rial's burial party did leave identification with his remains, their crude burial method would hinder future identification efforts.

The Army, much like the families of the Genarlsky Crew, held out hope they would receive word that the crewmen were prisoners of war (POWs), or perhaps they had made contact with the Resistance and were hiding out. By November 7, 1945, no word or evidence was received, and the Army gave up its official search.

In the fact that twelve months have now expired without the receipt of evidence to support a continued presumption of survival, the War Department must terminate such absence by a presumptive finding of death... The finding does not establish an actual or probable date of death; however, as required by Law, it includes a presumptive date of death for the termination of pay and allowances, settlement of accounts and payment of death gratuities... I regret the necessity for this message but trust that the ending of a long period of uncertainty may give at least some small measure of consolation.

Until the war ended and the area was under Allied control, there was not much more to do.

The 3046th Graves Registration Company arrived in the vicinity of Billerbeck in early 1946, despite the fact that the area was technically in the

British zone of control. Making up these companies were soldiers who had not quite acquired enough points to rotate home and were merely biding their time. One member of a Graves Registrations unit commented on his gruesome task: "We picked them

The crash site

up, began our burial details, and vomited our insides out... Eventually, as the days dragged on, our loathing for our jobs increased." Only the company commander was actually a member of the Quartermaster Corps; the rest of the men had only seen death on the battlefield. Now they experienced death personally for a much prolonged period of time.

Despite these shortcomings, the 3046th Graves Registration Company did locate the Billerbeck grave in February of 1946. The remains were heavily fractured from the catastrophic explosion and were suffering from a year and a half of being buried en masse with no protection from the elements. As a result, they had become what would later be described as "hopelessly intermingled." Miraculously, one body had clothes which could still be read. An I.D. bracelet bearing the name "Ralph O'Neil" was found on the wrist which matched the name on the clothing. An eventual match with dental records would constitute sufficient evidence for identification.

There were still sets of remains from the Genarlsky Crew, and the five bodies buried in the Billerbeck Cemetery could not be assumed to be members of the crew without more evidence. In April

1947, the five unknowns in the grave were taken to Neuville as part of the process of consolidating the investigation. In July 1948 the original crash site was exhumed. There they found pieces of the B-24, the "missing" remains of the Genarlsky Crew, and personal effects. These effects included a ring with Albert Pempek's name inscribed and a lighter belonging to Paul Novichenk. Between the documentation of the six bodies in Billerbeck Cemetery, the discovery of the missing bodies at the crash site, the personal effects, and the portions of the plane, the Army finally had enough evidence to warrant a group identification for the remains in question.

Word reached the families of the Genarlsky Crew and Harold Rial in April of 1950 that the remains could not be individually identified despite the best efforts of the Army and they would be brought back to the United States and buried at a national cemetery centrally located amongst the next of kin. In the case of the Genarlsky Crew, since there were next of kin in all corners of the United States, the burial would be at Rock Island National Cemetery, Illinois.

Presentism cannot be used to judge the Army's actions during the six-year process in bringing the remains of the Genarlsky Crew home. That is, the communication and technology standards of today cannot be used to evaluate the poor information exchange of the pre-computer era. However, the Army

Rock Island burial

did hold itself to a standard with which they can be judged, and it failed both in what it had the ability to do and what it ought to have done. Granted, the sheer number of dead and missing cases during World War II made it difficult to devote considerable attention to one case over another. The Army reported in 1946 that the most frequent question posed was, "Tell me about my boy." Simple questions could not always be answered due to many factors such as the number of casualties to process, wartime secrecy, and a lack of manpower. What is inexcusable, however, are such errors as not proofreading a letter before it was sent to an already hysterical mother, or double checking addresses to the name on the identification bracelet prior to shipment. Such simple errors caused a lot of needless grief for the next of kin, and severely damaged their faith that the Army was not only doing the best it could, but that it even knew what it was doing.

Unfortunately, the need for casualty notification has continued since World War II, but changes have been made to the process. A relative of an airman lost in the Ploesti raid, Italy, in 1943 remarked, "When I see how families of soldiers are notified today, they don't know how easy they have it. It's still horrible, but today if it happens, a representative from the military comes to your door, not some Western Union boy with a telegram." Instead of a cab driver delivering the telegram, in Vietnam and the first Gulf War a military delegation, usually including a chaplain, delivered the sad news. Regardless, the news was just as devastating.

Furthermore, up through the Vietnam War, after the notification, too often families were left to fend for themselves against the Army bureaucracy. Now there is a dedicated assistance officer for each family. This new system has not proved seamless, however. Perhaps the most high profile instance has been the case of Corporal Pat Tillman, who in 2004 was killed in action in Afghanistan. Initially, Tillman's family was told he died from enemy fire, but further investigations only now are revealing Corporal Tillman died as a result of fratricide.

Some of the problems are the same as in World War II: wanting to view the body (now families are allowed by regulation; in World War II honor guards were told, even to the point of using physical restraint, to prevent this from occurring), and asking for details of their loved one's death. Other problems arose from the processing of personal effects. The processing center, now located in Aberdeen Proving Ground, Maryland, has been blamed by families for losing or damaging effects that have been logged as reaching the facility in good order. One mother summed up her thoughts by saying, "I know these are little things…What makes it important is that my son was good enough to go over there and fight, but is not important enough to get his stuff back to his family."

Researching one case study begs the question, "What can possibly be learned about casualty reporting?" The casualty notification process was and still is unique in that for each case there was a completely different set of circumstances and facts available that dictated how the investigation was conducted. Most importantly, almost every case was the Army's only chance to "get it right." The next of kin of a dead soldier did not care if the previous 20 cases were executed perfectly, and the following 20 cases were executed perfectly. All they cared about is how well their individual case was handled. This made or broke their attitudes towards the Army for the rest of their lives. Such consideration is important when remembering that this process is occurring almost daily in Iraq and Afghanistan, using the lessons learned from past experience. While the technology is better, the number of dead is considerably smaller, and most sets of remains are recovered immediately, the stakes for the Army remain the same. With each notification, there is only one chance to get it right when a next of kin says, "Tell me about my boy."

Virginia Rewick

1943 - 1945
Scotland

A Red Cross Heart

An Interview with Jinny Rewick
By Kelly Wilcox

It's funny when someone as philanthropic as Virginia "Jinny" Rewick describes her noteworthy service as an average task. "As far as I was concerned, my service was volunteering, you know, typical." You could say volunteering was in her blood. Her father was a doctor and her mother was a nurse, so it wasn't difficult for Jinny to find it in her heart to help. Many people have served and are currently serving our country. During World War II, Jinny served with as much dedication and pride, by helping restore the spirits of the plane crews who flew over the dangerous anti-aircraft fire of Europe. She was a member of the Red Cross in Scotland.

Jinny graduated from Cornell University in 1941 with a Bachelor of Science degree. After further training at Illinois Institute of Technology, she worked for the Army Ordnance Department as part of a training team that traveled the country conducting safety classes at a number of ordnance plants, "so you wouldn't blow yourself up with black powder."

Although Jinny felt her war efforts were meaningful and rewarding, she had a "hankering" to do more, "so with my mother's consent I joined the Red Cross and never one minute regretted it." Jinny first arrived at a Red Cross base in Glasgow, then served in Edinburgh, and finally at Buchanan Arms, in a small Scottish town called Drymen. This was where she felt she fulfilled her best duties, as Red Cross Director. Her principal efforts were to keep the GIs occupied and entertained while they were on leave for a one-week "R & R." At times she felt like an amateur psychologist, since many of the men needed someone to talk to. These conversations would sometimes last into the "wee small hours," and much of it was an outpouring of personal thoughts, or memories of loved ones at home—wives, families, and girlfriends. "The stories were both joyful and sad, including some unfortunate 'Dear John' letters and the morale-shattering results suffered by some of the men I came to know." Buchanan Arms housed 44 men (four to a room) from U.S. bomber crews. They would arrive as complete personnel units from each bomber, ranking from commanding officer to the lowest-rated airman on each aircraft.

Many of the boys that went to Buchanan Arms were "flak-happy" from being shot at by German anti-aircraft fire on their bombing runs over the Continent. "They had just seen enough flak to last them a lifetime." Among these men there was some drinking, as can be expected among young GIs with such life-threatening assignments. At Edinburgh, there was an incident where a sailor got a bit hostile and quarrelsome. However, Jinny didn't bother with him. After eight cups of coffee, he began to "hang on me and hug me." He then asked Jinny to help him put his jacket on. Because it was a sailor's jacket, it fit snugly and had a square collar, thus fairly difficult to put on. "When I reached under the pea jacket to pull down the collar, all of a sudden I heard an earsplitting popping noise." Jinny was certain she had been shot, when in fact a cork had exploded out of a bottle of "kickapoo joy juice," denatured alcohol and grapefruit juice, in the sailor's jacket. "It'll kill you, but it gave them what they wanted." All in all, Jinny felt very safe in her working environment. The men in each air crew looked out for each other, and mishaps were rare.

Jinny recalls a harrowing experience driving from Edinburgh to Drymen. Her journey started at about 5 p.m., which in Scotland was about as dark as night. This was her first experience driving on the left side of the road, and there was a blackout. Headlights were hooded, exposing only small slits of light, and roadside lights were off. Being unfamiliar with the roads, Jinny prayed for her safety and finally reached Buchanan Arms. As she says, "You talk about being scared!"

Right across the street from Buchanan Arms was an Italian prisoner of war camp, converted from an old castle. Oftentimes, Jinny would pass those in the camp and they became friendly, though she did not speak Italian and the Italian prisoners did not speak English. One of them gave her a small gift, a hand-crafted wooden name plate, which she has to this day. "He presented that to me one day at a meeting at the fence, which was just barbed wire, just regular prison fencing, and I don't even remember his name. But he would chatter away and when he gave me this I cried, I really did, because I was so touched to think he would spend his time doing something like that." Buchanan Arms was by far Jinny's favorite place in Scotland. Everything was in harmony—the GIs, the workers, and the spirit. "Buchanan Arms was special because

RIBUNE-SUN, San Diego 12, California, Wednesday, March 20

Placard Appeals for Red Cross Aid

Virginia Rewick, formerly a Red Cross field director in Scotland, holds up a "Give" placard in the current mercy appeal for a goal of $628,000. Mrs. Rewick now is a member of the campaign staff.

Fund Nearing $200,000 Mark

Jinny in newspaper regarding Red Cross Fundraiser

the boys appreciated it so much." Though it was open to all Allied servicemen, only Americans were there. The British soldiers had other facilities. Jinny also had a nice room overlooking a garden, accommodations she considered "top drawer."

Meager British rations, like tripe, were "not very good," but Jinny made sure the men eating them felt special. Tables were set with white tablecloths, and the men ate with silver cutlery—ersatz, but "silver" nonetheless. There were even candles. "And when they'd come in looking a little ratty, from a long trip or whatever they came from, they'd start cleaning up for dinner. They knew it was special." The head manager at Buchanan Arms ordered the food, and Miss Jarvie, the cook, made it edible. Once she saved "every little bitty piece of butter that she could get" to make Scottish shortbread. It may not have been as good as one gets today, but "it tasted good to us."

Dairy products were few. Besides rationing, the American military did not allow milk, eggs, or cheese because they did not pass "certification." Small wonder Jinny weighed a scant 95 pounds while in Scotland. She almost disappears in a photo taken in her office. "The desk was bigger than I was!"

Christmas is a day that many veterans remember, away from their families. Jinny remembered Christmas as anything but glorious; however, they were able to obtain a Christmas tree. Despite the beautiful countryside that surrounded them, and the lush pine trees, they had nothing to decorate their bare tree besides pine cones. Deciding to spark the creativeness of the servicemen, she held an ornament-decorating contest. The winner would receive a small book of poems by Sir Walter Scott as a prize. It was astonishing how quickly this caught on. There were soon ornaments all over the tree, but that was not all. The day before Christmas, a man from Army Air Corps came to deliver Jinny a package. Puzzled as to what it could be, she opened the package and found lights, but not just any lights. They were airplane landing lights that the boys had strung for *their* Christmas tree.

To help pass the time during R & R, the GIs played cards, bingo, and board games. Ping pong balls were in short supply; however, once in a while a GI would rustle up a new batch of balls. Jinny one time thought she was engaging in an innocent game of checkers with some of the guys when she discovered they were playing for money. The red checkers were worth two dollars and the black were worth four dollars. This was no pocket money. Unaware of the stakes, Jinny continued playing, and luckily for her, she won! "Fortunately I won, but I thought, I'm in real trouble if the Red Cross ever finds out that I soaked these boys... I won a hundred and fifty dollars. In fact, $150 was my salary for one month while I was in the Red Cross—not bad for winning a simple game of checkers."

Jinny would "organize" dances occasionally. They did what they could with what they had, most of the time forced to listen to a highland band in kilts playing bagpipes, or settle for the scratchy records previous tenants left behind. Local dances were held outside of Buchanan Arms, where everyone in the community got together and taught them the Highland fling. These dances were never really planned, because a man could be there one day and

gone the next. They were more of a "pick-up thing." The famous Scottish singer Sir Harry Lauder came up once and put on a show. "He must've been maybe five-feet tall, a very famous singer, and we were able to get him to perform for us, you know, gratis." In the community, the Duke and Duchess used to open their home every Wednesday for tea. Jinny remembers the Duchess getting all dressed up, and how much the boys enjoyed these outings.

In an untailored and yet humorous manner, Jinny recalls a time when one of the crews commandeered a plane and took her to Dublin for dinner. After an hour's flight, Jinny savored a meal every soldier dreamed about—a luscious and tender

Jinny the snow-woman!

steak! Jinny says it cost the government a "pretty penny." Still, the trip was definitely a well-deserved, overdue treat. Even in Edinburgh, with more men to take care of, entertainment was hard to find. "I mean, you get in a place like Edinburgh, where you can sleep 1,500 men, and there's not much you can do with the number of people that were there. I'd plan bus tours, and where ya' going with no gas, you know? I'd drive around the block. Like all those in wartime service, we had to make do with what we had."

After V.E. Day, Jinny returned from Scotland on the *Queen Mary* along with, according to the newspaper, exactly 14,698 servicemen from the European Theater! And then, after she married, she continued to volunteer with the Red Cross in San Diego, making speeches to raise money for the cause.

Jinny's husband David Rewick also served in World War II. David was in the Navy in the South Pacific, handling supplies. He said his only "claim to fame" was sharing a Quonset hut with the author James Michener. While in the Pacific, David bragged to his

Buchanan Arms living room 1944 - 1945

associates that he was sending a native-made grass skirt to Jinny, and "Boy, wait 'til you see the photo of her in the grass skirt!" He got the photo in due course, but not exactly what he expected. She was outside in the snow, wearing a bandana, heavy sweater, with slacks and boots under the grass skirt, surrounded by three grinning GIs. So much for the grass skirt episode! As a sequel, to this day David does not relish looking at the pictures that flight crews signed for Jinny before they returned to combat, particularly the picture of the "rakish" Colonel with whom Jinny exchanged letters and photos. David thinks the Colonel was "smitten" with petite young Jinny and hoped the reverse wasn't true. "That's the Colonel that I was competing with." Jinny merely laughs, "Oh, my."

Jinny and David returned to Buchanan Arms and Drymen 25 years later in 1970 and visited a pub called the Clachen Arms, where Jinny had taken "the boys" for a "small treat" after dinner before taking

them back to Buchanan Arms, making sure she didn't "lose" any of them. The proprietor during World War II was a man by the name of Tommy Campbell. Out of curiosity, David asked the older man behind the bar if he were in fact Tommy Campbell, to which he received an "Aye, Laddie." David then asked Tommy if he recalled any of the Red Cross Girls who came into that pub about 25 years previously. After a "pretty girl in the corner" was brought to his attention, Tommy instantly recognized Jinny and exclaimed, "Why, that is Jinny Jones! She marched the boys in here for a quaff, and then marched them right back out again, like clockwork."

Jinny received many letters of thanks from the servicemen who stayed at the Red Cross Clubs. "It gives me pleasant memories to think of the things that I did and then kind of remorseful about the things I could've done and didn't. But I met so many wonderful young men." Jinny Rewick touched more lives than she knows, including mine. What stays with me the most about the interview, though, is Jinny's subtle sense of humor. As we looked through a box of pictures, we found a card signed by President Lyndon Johnson. When asked where that came from, Jinny quipped, "I don't know. He probably wrote to me. Thanked me for not voting for him."

I'm glad Jinny got to tell her story, and I'm even more enthralled that I got to hear it first-hand and have the honor of documenting it. During her service, Jinny listened to the soldiers, no matter what their situation. The signed photos of the crews with their airplanes are treasured to this day. I'm glad Jinny now has the opportunity for people to hear her story and experience the impact she made. "I look at my tour of duty with the Red Cross as one of the many highlights of my life. And if I did contribute, I'm grateful, because I made many wonderful connections and met a lot of terrific people."

David Rickard

September 1942 - November 1945
Europe, U.S.

Saved by a French Horn
An Interview with David Rickard
By Alex Doss

David Rickard's World War II days began in the summer of 1942. He was enrolled in his sophomore year in chemical engineering at the Rensselaer Polytechnic Institute when the possibility of being drafted manifested itself. "I did not want to go into the Army, so I had applied at the recruiting offices of the Marine Corps and the Navy in both Albany, New York, and on Long Island where I lived. And because of my eyesight, I was rejected by all of them, so therefore I was what you could call draft-bait."

David was reluctant to return to RPI if he was going to be in the Army before the end of the semester. It would be a waste of money, something his family could not afford. His father's job was eliminated when his place of work, the Florence Stove Company, was ordered to manufacture objects of war by the WPB (War Production Board). Luckily, Mr. Rickard had a number of friends on the East Rockaway Long Island draft board who had no specific knowledge of draft numbers, but advised against a return to college. With a 1-A draft category, there were no civilian jobs available. Dave enlisted in the Army of the United States at the New York City recruiting office on September 24, 1942.

I signed up and took the oath and I was ordered to report back there early the next morning. When I reported back, they put us on a ferryboat and took us out to Governor's Island, an island in New York Harbor between Manhattan and Brooklyn. The whole island is an army base. One of the things that the army did was strip away everything of your persona that they can, make you a nothing, and then build the kind of soldier that they want. They started the process that day on Governor's Island by making all of us take off all of our clothes. We were absolutely stark naked and they put us through intelligence tests. They inoculated us. They gave us medical exams. They fed us lunch out of boxed lunches, all day long completely naked until five o'clock in the afternoon running around on Governor's Island… And then they got us back to our clothes and let us go home with orders to report to Penn Station in Manhattan early the next morning.

The following morning, from Penn Station they took the Long Island Rail Road trains out of Manhattan to the induction center at Camp Upton in Yaphank. All of the draftees were requested to bring three days' worth of clothing and were assigned to barracks; 4:30 a.m. had the boys standing in formation in the bitter cold, movement prohibited, until 7:30 when the sergeant marched them up to the mess hall for breakfast. The remainder of the day Rickard was put through routine classification tests. Everyone was bothered at the lack of information they received about their future. Everything was top secret and all the while Camp Upton was routinely bringing in more and more draftees while simultaneously hauling just as many out. Rickard was soon to realize that by watching the railroad sidings near camp, you could predict the length of your trip by whether you were taken out in day coaches or Pullman sleeper cars. You would have less than a 24-hour trip if you were loaded into the day coaches, overnight if in the Pullman sleepers.

David ended up in a day coach with several other draftees. "The big problem at this point is, 'Where are we going?' It is a weird thing. You are hauled off, you are government property, and you have no right to say, 'What is going to happen?' or 'Where are we going?'" Rickard was pretty familiar with the area, so he found it interesting to study the countryside outside the train where they crept past various familiar landmarks. They passed where the line branched off to New England, rode non-stop through Penn Station, passed the cut-off to the Hudson River heading towards upstate New York and past the turn-off point leading into Pennsylvania, Ohio, Chicago, and the Midwest. They continued on the tracks that took them through Washington, D.C., and into the South.

They were told that all the secrecy was partially due to the priority given to trains hauling military equipment and that the Army was concerned that when their troop trains were stopped to allow priority trains to pass, that the draftees inside the train would be able to communicate their destination with the people outside. So it was a relief when an officer approached the men with their destination just after passing Richmond, Virginia. They were going to become trained medics at Camp Pickett. "There are two fields of work in which medics were used. One

was working as technicians and helpers in hospitals, which would have been a 'safe' assignment," Rickard pauses, "We weren't being trained for that." They were going to be trained for the front lines, picking up the wounded guys, giving them first-aid treatment, and then getting them the heck out of the line of fire and safely into a company aid station. Let's just say that the average mortality rate of a unit wasn't brought up too often.

About five weeks into basic training, Rickard's corporal squad leader and his platoon sergeant requested taking him out into the company street after chow for a "private conversation." At this point in the interview, Rickard leaned forward just so. "You know, when you go through life, you reach points in your life when you have to make a decision. Am I going this way or that way? And whatever decision you make, from then on, there will always be moments when you wonder what would have happened if you had done the other thing." His commander intimated that his record in basic training was such that they wanted him to stay behind as Cadre for the next class, then promoted to the rank of corporal as a squad leader, and upon completion of eight weeks in training, Rickard would be sent to Fort Sam Houston to the medical training center located there. At the completion of 90 days in OCS, he would become a 2nd Lieutenant in the medical department. "And I thought, well gee, that sounded pretty good," Rickard smiled lightly.

Rickard wanted to be an officer for all the obvious reasons, but the thought of becoming an officer in command of a bunch of medics in the front line of combat slowed his acceptance of this offer. This was where the decision-making comes in. His squad leader offered a second choice. It turned out his commanding officers weren't the only ones Rickard had impressed. The medical center's band heard him play bugle calls and wanted him to join them. "And I thought, 'Boy, sitting in the band at Camp Pickett, Virginia—my whole outlook on the war was that I'd rather be a live coward than a dead hero.' So I thought playing in the band at Camp Pickett for the rest of the war was a wonderful opportunity. I went into the 28-piece band as first horn and it was a pretty good outfit." But life in the band quickly became too much of nothing. "My life ambitions—what I wanted to do all my life was to get myself a good education, find the right gal, marry her, have kids, settle down and have a nice home. That was my ambition. And the army, the government, grabbed me out of that to be in the army for the war, which I was glad to do, as I felt we had to win that war. But if they put me in this spot, where I sit around all day long not doing a damn thing, I resented it. I would have done more for the war effort by being at RPI studying chemical engineering."

Pentagon was being built, but it was not finished yet. The war was being administered by Army brass and Navy brass in Washington and their estimate at the beginning of the war was that there was going to be a great need for engineers and technical people. So they organized a thing called the ASTP, which stood for Army Specialized Training Program, and

The band

The band had morning rehearsals maybe two or three times a week. They played at afternoon retreat ceremonies four or five times a week, an uncomfortably early reveille ceremony here and there, and the occasional dances where David could attend with the band but have fun as well because the French horn was not included in swing or jazz bands. David found it pleasant but was upset at the lack of progress in his life. They had Class A passes; they could come and go as they pleased. It became just so pointless and too totally boring. The monotony was interrupted that year with the production of a Christmas pageant for the men. Rickard had a demanding solo in Irving Berlin's "White Christmas." He laughs about having to repeat that song seven times before the show could continue. By January, however, David was tearing his hair out.

I was going crazy just sitting there doing nothing. And at that point, the army— remember there was a War Department, there was not a Department of Defense. The

that was to train guys that were in the Army as engineers, and they put that out if you wanted to apply. Boy, I was the first in line.

Rickard was one of ten or twelve in Camp Pickett accepted to the program. He was placed in the advanced group in Washington, D.C.'s Georgetown University where he studied basic civil engineering because chemical engineering was not offered. After three weeks, the ASTP students were put on the Red Arrow Limited, a train departing from Washington to Detroit, Michigan, where they switched trains for Ann Arbor to continue their studies at the University of Michigan. The university quickly converted its beloved frat houses into company barracks for the "Ass Trap" students. Rickard was put in the Beta Theta Pi house during the three-month semester with a week's furlough to follow. Every three months, he returned home to visit his family. This schedule went year round: three months study, a week off, three months study, a week off, and so on, beginning April 1, 1943, for twelve months. At the end of that year, Rickard and the "ASTP" company were to be commissioned lieutenants in the Army Corps of Engineers. David was also able to experience life in the Michigan marching band and as first horn in the University of Michigan concert band under Dr. William D. Revelli. "It was a wonderful experience to play with him, and in addition to being a student for a year, you can't have Army life better than that."

It was well into David's last semester before graduation when the "Powers that Be" in the War Department realized there were too many infantry fatalities; they needed replacements quickly. So they busted up the ASTP program. Two weeks before David would have received his commission, they shipped him out to Camp McCoy, Wisconsin, as an infantryman of the 76th Infantry Division, a basic rifleman in Company B, 417th Infantry Regiment.

They threw a rifle at me and I was not a happy camper. I did not go for that at all. So we were into basic training for the infantry and I managed to let the bandmaster know that I could play the French horn and I got transferred to the Division band, which was entirely different from the first band I was in. This was a 56-piece band, bigger sound, more professional; the music we played was much better. We had two 18-piece dance bands. One played sweeter dance music. The other was jumping like Benny Goodman and those guys.

Rickard joined the 76th Division Band under the command of a German shepherd pup named Downbeat, the band's mascot. The bandsmen underwent all the training the rest of the infantrymen took. It was no matter of sitting around; it was a matter of being exhausted most of the time. Every afternoon consisted of retreat parades, every morning reveille formations and rehearsals, with the occasional concert and dance. Rickard explained that the band was a crucial part of any military division, not only

for keeping the men's morale from sliding but for supplying the music for the military's formations. During combat, however, the division's band is used at the commanding general's discretion. In this case, the general had the band trained as MPs because when you only have an MP company with 200 MPs policing 15,000 men, that's obviously not enough. So Rickard was trained as an MP and an infantryman on top of his medic training.

David found relief from the excruciating drilling in July when some Special Services guy suggested the 76th Division put on a war bond show.

We had a trombone-playing arranger who had worked with Paul Whiteman and Ferdé Grofé, who was the composer of the "Grand Canyon Suite." The arranger wrote these absolutely beautiful arrangements of the popular songs of the day and this show had gorgeous music. However, when we started rehearsing it, the guys in the band laughed ourselves silly. It was the stupidest, most mawkish, sentimental pile of garbage we ever heard. When we put that show on at the first stop, what we did not realize was that this Special Services guy who wrote it knew more than we did about who our audiences were going to be because the audience was made up almost entirely of women who had loved ones away in the service. There were times when the music was so soft that we could hear sobbing in the audience. You could see the Kleenex and the handkerchiefs over the footlights!

The "Spirit of '76" show was presented 33 times throughout Wisconsin and sold over 3.5 million dollars in war bonds.

By September, the entire 76th Division was put through maneuvers conducted under the watch of General Leslie McNair. When the division was halfway through the maneuvers, they were escorted into a large arena at Camp McCoy, where McNair, the commander of all U.S. Army ground forces, praised their maneuvers, then said, "These maneuvers are over. The status of the 76th Division is hereby changed from a training division to a combat division. The 76th Division is going to war!" I don't need to tell you how that made us feel! So after that, day-by-day, the equipment was packed up and once in a while you would notice that there was a string of barracks emptied and whole units disappeared."

By Thanksgiving, Headquarters Company was just about the only part of the division still operational at Camp McCoy. Rickard had befriended a family down in La Crosse where he often played with the band, and they had him over for Thanksgiving dinner in 1944. This family was living off rations like all other civilians. "When a soldier got invited to dinner in the home of civilians, you knew that they were on ration points. Sugar was rationed; meat was rationed; gasoline was rationed. So were canned vegetables and fats. It wasn't just that they were giving you this food. They were giving you stuff that they could not replace because of their ration points." The La Crosse family obviously had gotten wind of what was happening in Camp McCoy and that Rickard was going to be sent overseas, but to their credit, they didn't say a word.

The next morning, Rickard and all the rest of the 76th Infantry Division Band were loaded into Pullman sleeper cars without the slightest idea where they were going. "The big thing that bothered all of us during that whole period was, 'Are we going to Europe or are we going to the Pacific?' because nobody wanted to go to the Pacific. It was horrible." When they were given German-to-English handbooks, it convinced the optimists they were going to Germany and the pessimists that it was just a roundabout way to baffle the enemy and they were really going to the Pacific. They all breathed more freely when the sleeper car moved toward the east coast. The train of sleeper cars finally arrived at Camp Myles Standish in Boston, which was a P.O.E., a port of embarkation.

Regulations for overseas shipment had the men in distinctive uniforms so that any onlooker in Boston might differentiate a soldier on furlough from a soldier bound for overseas service. The families of the soldiers were not to know where their sons were.

So I'm on the phone collect to my parents, and my mother was a pretty sharp gal at figuring things out. I would double-talk her about things that had happened in the past and stuff like that, and after four or five of these phone calls she said, "Okay, we got it." When my weekend pass came up, I went into Boston and sat down in the lobby of the Statler Hotel. After a while, I saw my parents come through the door. They checked in and registered and Dad, as he walked by, showed the key with the room number. This was strictly not allowed. This was a court martial offense!

They had dinner in their room at the Statler, talked and laughed, but when the room service guy arrived at the door, Rickard hid in the bathroom. Next morning, David stepped into the sunshine and "hopped to" in order to catch the bus back to camp. He cocked his head back towards Boston's Statler Hotel and saw nothing but a field of green jackets emerging from the lobby. "The entire hotel was full of guys who had figured some way to get their folks to come and visit them!"

Twenty-four hours later, Rickard was loaded aboard the *General W.P. Richardson* troopship, where the boys of Headquarters Company were herded into a large room at the rear. The space was smothered with the weight of stacked military bunks. Rickard was assigned a bottom bed but fervently prayed that the guy above him didn't get seasick. At 2:00 a.m., Rickard felt the ship get underway. The next day, off New York, a convoy from Gravesend Bay joined them. The *Richardson* would be the flagship of the convoy headed to Liverpool, England. Rickard dictates that the *Richardson* had the capability to outrun submarines but was forced to travel at six knots through the angry surface of the North Atlantic as flagship of this convoy of some 50 or 60 ships. It was then announced the 76th Division would become an occupational division in Germany as opposed to a combat division because the general feeling was that the war would be over by Christmas. Although this meant the men would be overseas much longer on occupational duty, the assignment would be safer and well away from the lines of fire.

Over the 19-day transatlantic voyage, the only thing that got Rickard's blood pressure up was when the P.A. systems roared to life. "Man your battle stations! This is no drill! Man your battle stations!" It had the sailors donning helmets and yanking the covers off the ship's guns, their gray snouts rounded and fierce, and the troops retreating below deck. "That about put me into a panic. I'm more than a tad bit claustrophobic and I can't think of a worse way to die than being trapped inside a metallic container that is sinking." The panic subsided when the scouts reported back to the mother ship that what they had spotted was nothing more than a deserted vessel. "All they found was a derelict piece of junk. Thank God!"

Overall, the voyage was pretty dreary: only two meals a day, hungry all the time, cramped spaces, and heavy winter days. However, Rickard became fixated with the convoy's operations as they passed into the threshold of English waters. He was on deck when the ships started maneuvering with each other, converging and crossing each other's paths. He couldn't help but think that only three years prior, most of these men that made up the crew probably had never even seen the ocean and now they were piloting massive troopships through the most complicated nautical maneuvering one could witness. "One ocean liner came close enough we could shout back and forth to the people as they passed our bow."

Over a period of time, the convoys split into two. Most of the cruisers and destroyers followed the *Richardson*. When the ship docked in Southampton, there seemed to be some confusion. "Our commanding officers had told us that we were going to Liverpool, so why we were in Southampton?" As the 76th Division got ready to disembark, the officers of the *Richardson* announced over the ship's P.A. system: "We want to tell you how proud we are to have brought the 76th Infantry Division into the war in Europe. We will be following your combat record and we hope you have nothing but victory in your every engagement with the enemy. We congratulate you and wish you the best." This message made no sense to us. At first the men shrugged it off as a captain's being misinformed. "We were loaded into British railroad cars and taken with curtains drawn to Bournemouth, England, a Channel coast resort a few miles west of Southampton."

Reality presented itself on December 21. It was the first day they learned that on December 16 German forces had made a breakthrough against the Allied forces in the Ardennes in the Battle of the Bulge. Rickard's officers explained that the Germans might possibly push the Allies back to the Atlantic. The status of the 76th Division was officially changed to a combat division. They were assigned to the 3rd Army under General George S. Patton. To a soldier, General Patton's 3rd Army was a tough assignment. Even though occupational duty meant they would be in Europe much longer, with Patton their odds of coming out alive were reduced.

Now the men had to repack everything and were required to walk guard along the English Channel.

I remember walking four hours from midnight

Bournemouth

to four o'clock along the deserted beach of the English Channel. Four hours is a long time to walk all by yourself so I figured a way to kill time. Since I had played in symphony orchestras, I knew Beethoven's 5th Symphony all the way through and I figured that if I sang it to myself it would take 25 minutes. I could kill 25 minutes. So I looked down at my watch, hummed Beethoven's 5th Symphony all the way through, looked at my watched again, and only three minutes had gone by.

The entire division was in a part of Bournemouth fenced off from the civilian population. That Christmas Eve Rickard and a small group of musicians walked around Bournemouth playing Christmas carols for different units in the division. "We started playing at around five o'clock in the afternoon all the way to midnight. We had 'leather lips' those days. The last place we played was at the commanding general's quarters, and of course, everything was blacked out. We could see the door open and people standing in shadows and when we finished playing the carols, our general thanked us and made a very effective speech about how he hoped that next year we would be home for Christmas with our families but that in the meantime things were going to be 'rough, tough, and dirty.'" The next day, the musicians were able to attend a performance of Handel's "Messiah" by the Bournemouth Symphony Orchestra and Chorus.

Rickard remained in Bournemouth until January 8, when he was awakened at 0400 and put on trains bound back to Southampton to revisit the docks of their original disembarkation from the *Richardson*. From 0800 to 1500 the men hunkered in the bitter, freezing cold with nothing but K-rations for noon chow. Once loaded on a ship bound for Le Havre, France, just southeast of Southampton across the English Channel, Rickard had two four-hour tours of sentry duty. "I was posted on the poop deck, which is the highest deck on the rear of the ship most exposed to the weather. It was complete suffering because it was freezing and bitter cold." The sergeant of the guard for that shift was a fellow named Cecil Travis, third basemen for the Washington Senators, and when he saw the misery of David's assignment he came out and stood guard duty with him. When Rickard got home, he was listening to a New York Yankees baseball game and the announcer had Cecil as a guest.

It turned out Travis' feet were frozen upon crossing the Channel. He had ruined his career to help out Rickard that night.

Upon crossing the English Channel, the city of Le Havre was so bomb-scorched there was no place for the ship to dock, so the men climbed down landing nets into a Landing Craft Tank and then were ordered to find in the dark the one duffel of the entire division's that belonged to them and get themselves loaded into a truck. This trip was an adventure in itself. They swerved and tore up obscure roads in blackout situations for longer than was comfortable. It wasn't until the tires spat up dust in a stopping motion outside a building in Limésy, France, that Rickard was able again to draw breath. At this point Rickard had been deprived of sleep for 57 consecutive hours. A moment of shuffling and Rickard learned they would get coffee. That was good. However, when light clipped off the metal container into David's eyes, he noticed they were just placing the coffee over the fire. It would take an hour longer before they would get any warmth from hot coffee. A cutting comment here and there and a clichéd blackout later, Rickard was hauled away from the general vicinity.

I was tired. They were going to make coffee for us and this was great. Give me a cup of coffee. And then I saw it. I had been on KP enough that I knew a thing about it. I saw them take these great big metal containers, pour cold water in them, and put them over the fire. That was going to take an hour before the coffee was ready. I said something about that, and at this point, I was so tired I don't know what happened. I blacked out on my feet or something because some guy was standing in front of me and I let him have it verbally, and when he disagreed with me, I punched his lights out! He turned out to be a lieutenant colonel.

Only Rickard's earlier reputation saved him from a jail sentence. Attacking an officer doesn't go over well in the Army. However, they decided "extenuating circumstances" had pushed David over the limit. Instead they were all marched into a princely French mansion, where he slapped his sleeping bag right down on a marble floor and slept 18 hours straight.

By this time, the 76th Division Band had been detached into three segments. One unit was sent to do MP work for the rest of the war. The second unit was assigned to the rear-echelon command post usually made up of clerks—guys who had no idea how to handle a rifle. The rear echelon C.P. is stationed six to 25 miles behind the front lines. The unit assigned to the rear was required to act as security. Rickard and nine others assigned to the forward echelon C.P. would trail from one to three miles behind the front lines, moving the C.P. every day or two as needed, digging and maintaining the latrines and doing guard duty. They were basically the division headquarters' "moving men." The work Sergeant Brophy's ten-man detail had to undergo was more than they could handle and took hours of back-breaking labor to finish. This detail, with a lieutenant in command, had to scout out the towns and decide where the division's facilities would be stationed and then make the move. It was a critical operation because if the Germans knew where command headquarters were located, they could shell a town and the 76th Division would be without any command.

On their move from Limésy to Belgium, they stopped outside Beines, France, and were told the 76th Division was now on the secret list. Every man was ordered to remove his 76th Division insignia and heave the patches onto the roads. "No one was supposed to know who we were, but we left 10,000 soldier patches in the snow!"

The convoys made their way to Champlon, Belgium, where the 10-man detail was ordered to move into a squalid building whose insides had been given the Germans' scorched-earth treatment. It was entirely uninhabitable. They were able to save enough of the building to set up a decent command center, and when every livable space was occupied, there was nowhere for the 10-man detail to stay. An extremely dismayed Captain Fred Haynes had to ask the 10-man detail to pitch a tent in the fields. "The temperature was zero degrees. It was the coldest winter on record in Europe and without exaggeration, if we would have done that, we would have been blocks of ice by morning. There was no way we could survive, and he knew he was sentencing us to our deaths." Haynes bent Army regulation to allow the men to stay the night in the one undamaged house in

a cluster of bombed-out houses about a half-mile from HQ with the stipulation that they keep night watch. The housing provided enough covering to keep the men alive. The next day they took the 76th Division's first prisoner of war, a German infiltrator.

That afternoon the 10 men came back from their duties to find Captain Haynes talking to four civilians at the door of "their" house. Captain Haynes explained to the men that they had to get their gear and move out of the house. Though Rickard couldn't speak French and the Belgians couldn't speak English, he gathered enough to conclude they owned the house. The Allied forces were prohibited from putting people out of their homes, but sleeping outside made Rickard's chances of survival slim.

I had studied French in school but could not speak it. The guys turned to me and said, "Hey, Rickard, didn't you study French? Can you talk to this guy?" So I turned to this man and I figured the only way I could do it was using French words one at a time. "If you say one word to me at a time, I can understand you." He caught on right away. "Oui." I asked him if he owned that house. "Oui." I thanked him profusely and said that we would leave as soon as possible. He went wild with excitement and ran up to me and pointed at my rifle. "Un, deux, trois, quatre, cinq…" He counted ten rifles. "Ten American soldiers can be in my home to protect me and you say that you have to leave? Are you nuts?"

With orders to double the guards' shifts and keep a close eye on the Belgian couple, Rickard and the guys headed to chow. Food was plentiful and they wouldn't be out in the cold that night. As Rickard was washing out his mess kit he remembered there had been absolutely no food in that house. So he went back up to get seconds, closed his kit, and went to the house. Grateful, the couple portioned out their meal and invited David to sit down with them. They got a huge kick out of his first name being "David [pronounced DAH-VEED]" and their being "Monsieur and Madame David." David found out Monsieur David had been a police commissioner in Liège, Belgium, and a Belgian soldier in World War I, flanked side-by-side with American soldiers. "He had heard a bunch of English words and he asked if I could tell him what they meant. I said, 'Sure,' and out of this dignified, very proper gentleman, spewed out the foulest words of the English language!" David laughed. "We became good friends." Every night, David brought them dinner, and every night he stayed up with them. Over time David began to pick up more and more of the rapid conversations in French the couple had with each other, but he kept that to himself in case they said something interesting that might have been kept from him otherwise. Every night for five nights, Rickard stayed up late in the evening with the couple talking until one day the men received orders to move out of there at 3:00 the next morning. The 76th Division was going into the line. In Champlon, they had been in reserve behind the 101st Airborne in the Battle of the Bulge.

Rickard went back to the Davids' house that night, acting as usual in order to give nothing away to the couple, because as much as he liked them, he was still not sure who they might be. Funny, but that was the night Madame David asked how long they would be staying with them. Monsieur David was quick to tell his wife rather severely she should never ask a soldier that question. "It is none of our business. They have come over to save us and some morning we will get up and they will be gone. And all I have to say is 'Kill the Bosch!'" M. David exclaimed wildly. As the conversation drifted, David pushed the matter as to why the Belgian couple wasn't at home the first night of his division's stay. Madame David spoke in French, "Don't tell him!" M. David simply stared back at her and spoke just as quickly, "Twice these people have come over and have rescued us. They are rescuing us right now. If we can't trust him, we can't trust anybody. I think we should tell them the whole story." M. David faced back towards Rickard and spoke more slowly, "I am going to tell you."

M. David said he had a number of friends in Champlon. One was good with bridges. Another was good with railroad tracks. Another was good with trucks and engines. He was good with radios. From his way of telling this, I could tell this was a group in the famed but highly secret Belgian Underground.

M. David's radio was located behind the door from the entryway into their living room.

Opening this door could pin someone against the bookcase in which he had his radio equipment. He would listen to all the short-wave broadcasts from other countries and tell his friends what he heard because German radio broadcast only propaganda, and the truth of its newscasts could not be trusted.

On June 6, 1944—D-Day—he listened to the BBC (British Broadcasting Corporation) announce the landings of the Allied forces on the Normandy beaches and the broadcast by General Eisenhower telling the people of Europe that the invasion was on and they would soon be liberated. M. David naturally related this news to his friends. This news, which they had awaited for four years, was too much for them to keep a secret as they should have and the Germans soon knew that the native population knew about the invasion before the Germans had announced it. Listening to the short-wave radio was an offense punishable by death, and the Germans launched an investigation to find out who had learned of the invasion and spread the word about it.

One day a German army staff car stopped in front of their house and two SS officers got out and came up their walk. They entered the house and one of them jammed that door open, pinning M. David against his bookcase, where he was unable to get his hands on his radio. The other one listened for a minute and then said "BBC." They hauled M. David out of his house with no chance to say anything to his wife. He was taken to an area of Champlon where he found out that all of his friends had been rounded up and they were loaded into German army trucks for transport to some unknown destination, probably a concentration camp.

M. David found that his friend who was good with trucks and engines was seated across from him in the truck on the street side.

M. David was on the curb side and both of them were at the rear of the truck directly under the armed German guard who stood on the tailgate. M. David soon noticed that his friend kept surreptitiously looking at his watch and seemed to be looking intently at M. David every time he did so when the guard was not watching.

M. David said the Germans would drive three hours straight with a short break for the guard. This surprised Rickard. American Army convoys drive 50 minutes and then stop for ten-minute breaks for the whole convoy. When the truck finally came to a stop and the driver killed the engine, his friend glanced at his watch. He appeared to start measuring time when the truck engine was turned off. He signaled M. David to follow him. Suddenly he leaped backward over the side of the truck, landed on his feet, and ran for the woods beside the road. M. David did the same. As they reached these woods, the truck blew up. They were able to hide in the shrubbery while the guards searched for them. When the rest of the convoy finally left, they remained in the shrubbery until dark. Walking at night and hiding in the day, they walked back to Champlon. As M. David went through these towns, he noticed there were wanted posters with his picture and a large reward. This got Rickard thinking, "It was such a high figure, this told me this guy was not just some plain underground guy. He was somebody big." Around September 1944 M. David went into hiding with his wife at their home. The German ration for a single person was barely enough to avoid starvation, so there was not enough food for the two of them after M. David rejoined his wife. The Davids lived off one ration, more than impossible, but they didn't dare indicate another person lived in the house. M. David never let himself be seen, but after a while the Germans caught on and one day the German staff car pulled up and two SS officers got out and started up the walk to their house.

I'll have to admit that the next words out of M. Davide's mouth threw me off a little because he stopped talking and then said, "Do you go to the movies?" And I'm wondering what in the heck could warrant such a question at this point but answered, "Sure. Yeah, I go to the movies." M. David smiled,

"Do you believe them?" I said, "No, course not. They're stories made up in Hollywood." M. David exclaimed, "Yes, that's right, Hollywood movies." He slowed down. "You are going to think that what I'm about to tell you is a Hollywood movie, but this is actually what happened."

Suddenly there was the sound of a powerful engine down the street, followed by a burst of machine gun fire. There were two dead German officers in his front yard and an American tank coming up the street— the U.S. Army was retaking Champlon. When the Battle of the Bulge broke out, the Davids loaded everything they needed into a little cart and walked to Lièges. They were afraid they'd have to walk as far as Amsterdam, but when they heard the American 1st and 3rd Armies were pushing the Germans back, they turned around. Rickard was present for the rest of their story.

That conversation lasted until one o'clock in the morning and I had to get up at 3:00. So I said good night and went to bed in my sleeping bag upstairs. At 3:00, we got up as quietly as we possibly could, but you can't put that kind of gear together in an attic like that without making some noise. I was the last one down the stairs, and the door opened and those two were standing in their nightclothes. I got down the flight of stairs and she just launched herself at me, threw her hands around my neck, kissing me all over my face while he's pumping my hand saying, "Kill the Bosch! Kill the Bosch!"

The Sauer River forms the border between Luxembourg and Germany. Ordinarily it is a peaceful little stream but at this time it was a raging flood because of snowmelt runoff from the Alps. It was about three times as wide as usual, flowing at about 12 miles per hour, and freezing cold. Directly across the Sauer from Echternach was a bluff in which the fortifications of the West Wall, or Siegfried Line, were built with artillery aimed down into Echternach. This West Wall consisted of heavily fortified interconnecting concrete bunkers and was considered by the Germans to be impregnable.

The Sauer River

On the night of February 7, 1945, the 80th Infantry Division, the 5th Infantry Division, and the 76th Infantry Division assaulted these fortifications with assault boats crossing the Sauer. The spearhead element of the 76th Infantry Division was Company B of the 417th Infantry Regiment, the unit Rickard had been in before he was transferred to the Division band.

The next day, the only unit hanging onto a bridgehead on the German side of the Sauer was Company B of the 417th. No other outfit was able to get across the river and hang on. The casualties were horrible. The 417th guys had to be supplied by airborne Piper Cub. It was several days before the crossing was secure. Because the 76th was the newest, or greenest, of the divisions that took part in that assault, and because they were the only ones that held on, they were removed from the secret list and an article appeared in the "Stars and Stripes," the Army newspaper, under the heading: "They came in green but sure ripened fast." After the war, when the Division's combat history was written in a book, that book was entitled *We Ripened Fast.*

Rickard was standing guard in front of General Schmidt's office inside division headquarters a few days later when a polished jeep appeared. Out came a rigid man in a polished helmet, fitted riding pants, with two nickel-plated revolvers. Rickard recognized General Patton right away, but when he called out "Halt!" as was mandatory to guard duty, Patton didn't even acknowledge Rickard's presence. Rickard sang out once more, "Halt!"

I was faced with a dilemma because the third

time you shout "Halt" and the person does not stop, you are ordered to shoot to kill, but I didn't think it would be wise for me to kill General Patton so I saluted him and he went into the building and came right out again. A buddy of mine was standing guard in General Schmidt's office, and when we got off guard duty, I turned to him and said, "Hey, did General Patton go into General Schmidt's office?" "Did he *ever.*" "So what happened? He came right out again." My pal said that the door flew open and General Patton walked right up to the situation map, put his finger on it, turned to General Schmidt, and said, "By 6:30 tomorrow night you and the 10th Armored Division will have taken the city of Trier." Then he was out the door and on his way. Schmidt turned to his captain, "I have two questions for you that I want answered right away. Number one, where the hell is Trier, and number two, where the hell is the 10th Armored Division?"

By 6:30 the next night, the 10th Armored Division and the 76th Infantry Division had taken Trier. After spearheading to a town on the northwest banks of the Moselle River called Wittlich, the 76th Division was given R & R—rest and recuperation, or repair and replacement. "They brought up the shower trucks and we had the first shower on March 20 that we'd had since January 8. And the clothes—when we took off our clothes, they stood up by themselves!" Patton suddenly cut their ten days to three and they were on the move again.

Forward echelon Division C.P. was being moved forward from Wittlich to Pfalzfeld, a considerable distance. Rickard was the first of the ten men to make the move and was in the town of Pfalzfeld when officers in Wittlich decided they'd had enough. One man was glassy-eyed and another couldn't remember where he put his rifle. The 10-man detail was finally relieved. So Rickard settled himself for a long drive back to Wittlich on a back road, which both he and the driver found ridiculous since there was a perfectly good highway that would cut their time in half. Figuring this was the better way to go, they ran down that highway, perfectly pleased with themselves that they had outwitted the system. "So we took this highway and were buzzing down it and we take this curve to the right. We look up and coming right at us is this huge column of American tanks with their guns aimed at us and their infantry on both sides of the road! We jumped out of the jeep faster than we could blink and threw our hands up. I am one of the few American soldiers who has surrendered to the U.S. Army!" Rickard and the driver had a heck of a time trying to convince the commander they were legitimate soldiers and not infiltrators, but the commanding officer could not understand how Rickard and his companion could travel on a road which reportedly was heavy with German forces. "We had come all this distance where we were behind enemy lines and didn't know it!"

The 76th Infantry Division crossed the Rhine River in the vicinity of St. Goar-Boppard in late March 1945 and proceeded to the Frankfurt-Dresden autobahn and fought along the route of this superhighway all the way into Saxony. "From there on the fighting got to be altogether different. We went from one town to another. We'd come to a town and there'd be a white sheet hanging out in surrender; we'd come to another town and they would offer resistance but our infantry backed out and the artillery flattened the place and then we would go on." The Americans were running over the Germans so fast that oftentimes they'd lose track of parts of their regiment or they'd have to have the Air Force drop in maps to the forward elements of the division because they had run off the pages of their previous maps.

The Germans would not admit defeat; they "played dirty." Small children fired on U.S. soldiers. "No American guy wants to shoot a kid, but the bullet doesn't know who pulled the trigger and it's going to have the same effect." The sight of the concentration camps and POW camps and the sheer destruction is clearly remembered. "The Germans took the prisoners that they captured and they treated them in the most God awful, torturous ways you could imagine. We would come upon these camps and see these guys that looked like skeletons with skin stretched over them. You'd assume that they were dead and move on when the guy would say, 'Hey buddy, you got a cigarette?'" Rickard and the men had to leave the victims where they were because they didn't have the proper supplies to treat them. The food the men carried would kill these starved skeletons. They would have to wait until following U.S. Army units arrived to help them, which was very soon.

"The German soldiers were surrendering so fast that at one point I remember that I was with two other guys opposite me across a big field guarding what must have been at least a thousand German prisoners. On occasion we had a little trouble with civilians resisting us and I had to fire a few shots over some heads but generally it was pell-mell across Germany until May 7 in Glauchau when we were ordered to cease all hostile activity." The next day the Germans surrendered to the Allied forces. That night the lights were turned on again and they were moved to Limbach for a U.S. flag-raising ceremony featuring music by the 76th Infantry Division Band! The Russians and the U.S met on the banks of the Mulde and Elbe Rivers.

76th Infantry Band at Russian ceremony

The 76th Infantry Division had made the deepest penetration into Germany of any unit on the Western front.

The 76th Division was stationed in a small town called Crimmitschau in Saxony, Germany, on an extremely pleasant occupational duty. The band was reassembled as a unit. The Army came out with the point system. The 76th Division was considered a high-point division and was detached into two segments. The high-point guys were sent home while the lower-point guys were transferred to the 30th Infantry Division. The 76th "Onaway" Infantry Division was deactivated in Hof, Bavaria. The 30th Infantry Division was based in Heppenheim, far to the west of Saxony.

During the time Rickard was in Company B of the 417th Infantry Regiment at Camp McCoy, there were 200 men in that Company. Including Rickard, 30 of them survived the war. Rickard considers that his life was saved by a French Horn.

When we arrived at 30th Division HQ in Heppenheim after a long day's trip, the 1st Sergeant came out and said, "Don't unpack your gear. We are moving out at three a.m." We said, "Wait a minute. This is too much." And he said, "Too bad. We're still at war!" "Where were we going?" There were all these rumors flying around among the Army in Europe at that time. "Are we going to France?" "No." "There are problems in Denmark. Are we moving there?" "No." "Are we going somewhere in Germany?" "No." "Where the hell are we going?" "Well, you guys are too stupid to figure it out so I'm going to have to read you the orders."

The orders declared that the 30th Infantry Division was to initiate movement to the United States! "Wow! You cannot imagine what that did to us." They were told they would be given 30 days' R & R at their homes and then reassembled at Fort Jackson, South Carolina, for transport to the Pacific for the invasion of Japan.

Rickard and the 30th Division made its way through Germany and France, stopping in places like Camp Lucky Strike and Camp Oklahoma City, and finally crossed the English Channel. While stationed at Tidworth Barracks, the atomic bombs laid waste to Hiroshima and Nagasaki and the Japanese surrendered. "That night, I happened to be on pass in London in the Piccadilly Circus, a wild place in London where you couldn't believe what was going on. Strange

women came up and grabbed you and kissed you and they upset double-decker buses! It was complete pandemonium because to those people, the British since 1939, the wars were finally over and the lights were back on. It was wonderful." It was now obvious they would not have to invade Japan but were told they were going there for occupation duty. This was later rescinded.

During peacetime, the two superliners *Queen Elizabeth* and *Queen Mary* were in transatlantic service sailing between Southampton, Cherbourg, and New York. When war broke out, they were put in troopship service and no longer sailed from Southampton because that port was on the English Channel and exposed to the German submarine menace. August 16, 1945, was a big day for these ships because it was on that day that the first of them, the *Queen Mary*, was to return to her home port of Southampton and sail for New York with the troops of the 30th Infantry Division, the first troops to return to the United States from Europe after the war ended with the Japanese surrender.

As the *Queen* approached New York on the afternoon of August 20, the Captain announced they would be going through the Narrows and entering New York Harbor the next morning. Then a dense fog set in and nobody could see anything. The ship slowed down as required by the rules of the sea and sounded its foghorn every three minutes. It was now impossible to get to the entrance of New York Harbor by the next morning, and because the ship needed to go into the harbor on a high tide, it meant the entrance into the harbor would have to be put off until evening.

The ship was still feeling its way slowly through the fog the next afternoon and the troops were not able to see anything to indicate how close they might be to the shores of the USA. Suddenly without warning a huge sign formed by incandescent light bulbs appeared on the water to the right of the vessel saying "WELCOME HOME! WELL DONE!" This was on the shore at Fort Hamilton, Brooklyn, which still could not be seen because of the fog. Then as the ship rounded the Brooklyn shore and entered the Narrows, the fog suddenly lifted and the harbor was beautifully clear in the dark of the evening. Lights were flashing everywhere, many of them saying, "Welcome Home," and "Well Done." All the New York City fireboats were shooting streams of water into the air. "Small boats were crowding the harbor so we wondered how the huge *Queen Mary* could navigate. All the buildings in Manhattan and Brooklyn had their lights on, many of them flashing and sending rockets off their roofs. Bands were playing everywhere. It was the most joyous madhouse I had ever lived through."

The only thing missing was the Statue of Liberty, which all the troops had dreamed of seeing again ever since they left for overseas. The Statue was kept in darkness so it could not be seen until the prow of the *Queen Mary* was abreast of it. Then the lights went on and it seemed to the men that this beautiful Lady held her brightly lighted lamp of liberty extended over the returning troops.

The ship proceeded slowly up the Hudson River to Pier 90, its home pier in New York Harbor, where it disembarked 15,000 deliriously happy soldiers. They were home again.

PFC David M. Rickard spent time on temporary duty at his home and was then discharged on November 11 and returned to Rensselaer where he got his Chemical Engineering Degree in January 1949.

He did not have to go to Japan.

Sign in the harbor welcoming returning GIs

Jack Ricketts

April 1941 - August 1972
Guadalcanal, Japan

Jack's Story
An Interview with Jack Ricketts
By Alex Doss and Jack Ricketts

Humor rides hard on the classic features of this weathered Navy aviator, whom I had the good fortune to meet one Wednesday afternoon in September 2006. We sat in his living room at Classic Residence in Scottsdale, Arizona, along with Hazel, his wife of 63 years, and the Arizona Heritage Project advisor, Barbara Hatch. As a 14-year-old student of history, some of Jack's stories escaped me: World War II Pacific battles and airplanes with numerous letters and numbers in places hard to find on a map. But fortune smiled on me that day, because Jack has written his own story. Humbled, I stand aside to let you hear his memories directly. This is Jack's story:

In 1938 I was in my second year in college at New Mexico State, then called New Mexico A & M, studying to be an engineer. Every once in a while the class would get the professor off the subject and discuss other topics, such as the possibilities of our country getting involved in war. It was beyond my imagination, ever having to go to war. However, by the time I entered my senior year in September of 1940, my name was drawn in the very first draft call. But I was deferred until June of 1941 so I could finish college. With rather a dismal prospect hanging over me, I continued my studies. In the spring, I interviewed with a number of job recruiters that visited our college. I wanted to be an engineer.

In March, a Navy aircraft, an SNJ, buzzed the college and got a lot of attention. That was Ensign Hilton's method of "recruiting" possible future naval aviators. I had always wanted to learn to fly, and with the draft staring me in the face, I thought, "Why not?"

I signed up with the promise that I would not be called to start flight training until the 15th of May so I could finish college. As many often found out, military promises can be suspect. When I went home to Farmington, New Mexico, on spring break, a letter from the Navy was waiting for me, telling me to report to the Long Beach Naval Air Reserve base for flight training by April 15th. I immediately returned to college so I could gather my belongings and talk to my professors to see if I could still get my degree. They all cooperated, considering the semester was close to being over and I had a good record.

That started my journey on a career in the Navy that lasted 31 years, through three wars, a Masters Degree in Engineering from Rensselaer Polytechnic Institute in Troy, New York, and the rank of Captain when I retired from the Navy in 1972.

I received my Navy Wings of Gold and was commissioned an Ensign in the U.S. Navy in March of 1942. I received orders to report to Patrol Squadron VP-51. This squadron operated the Navy's Catalina seaplanes, designated the PBY. VP-51 had moved from Bermuda to Ford Island at Pearl Harbor, soon after it had been bombed. When I reported for duty in San Diego, I was told to proceed immediately to San Francisco to await surface transportation to Hawaii. So much for the six-week transition training we were promised, and any idea of having Hazel come out to San Diego so we could be married before I deployed. VP-51 was housed in one of the bomb-damaged hangars on Ford Island. Daily patrols were conducted, which covered sectors of 700 miles out, 100 miles cross leg, and 700 miles back to base.

Unknown to me, while I was waiting transportation in San Francisco, Hazel's brother Robert Lowell Hite, whom I had never met, was loading his B-25 aircraft and crew aboard the US Navy carrier *Hornet* docked nearby at NAS Alameda. Lowell was one of General Doolittle's raiders that bombed Tokyo. His plane ran out of fuel over China after the bombing run; the crew bailed out and was captured by the Japanese. He spent the rest of the war, 40 months, in prison. When I did meet Lowell for the first time, I was attending the Navy's Post Graduate School at MIT in Boston. The family was never sure whether or not Lowell was one of the four raiders that had been executed by the Japanese. I will never forget the day that I picked up and brought home to Hazel the San Diego paper with big black headlines stating that four Raiders had been executed. But Lowell's mother never gave up the feeling that Lowell would one day come home. Lowell's story can be found in the book *Four Came Home*, written by Colonel Carroll V. Glines.

Back to my story.

Our squadron participated in both the Battle of Midway and the Japanese troop landing and occupation of the Aleutian Islands in Alaska. Why the two campaigns at practically the same time many miles apart? What had happened was about six crews had returned to the States to pick up new aircraft.

The more senior crews, including our skipper, were chosen for this trip. The executive officer and the junior crews were left behind. But just as the crews with the new aircraft were preparing to take off for the return flight to Ford Island, they were recalled and sent to Alaska. It was a toss up as to who ended up with the toughest assignment. I was probably one of the most junior of the juniors. I drew the Midway contingent and later the South Pacific detachment. The Battle of Midway was short-lived. However, one of our crew had the distinction of dropping a torpedo at night off the wing of a PBY in an attack against one of the Japanese troopships carrying troops that were to land at Midway. Midway was the first success we had, a turning point and certainly a morale builder.

The detachment that went to Alaska eventually transitioned to the first Navy squadron to operate the Army's B-24, known as the *Liberator*. Five of our crews that stayed at Ford Island were sent to the South Pacific area in August of 1942 to support

Cover of Jack's Flight Log

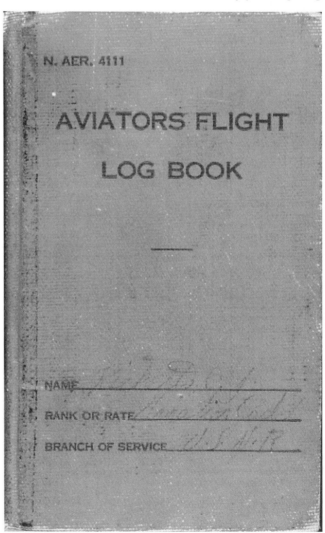

the Guadalcanal operation. We operated from the *USS Curtiss*, a seaplane tender which was anchored in the harbor at Espiritu Santo in the New Hebrides Islands.

Again our patrols were sectors 700 miles out, 100 miles cross leg, and return to base. Our schedule called for one day patrol, one day off, one day standby to be available to investigate any sighting of enemy ships that needed further evaluation. One such day, October 14, 1942, our crew was called to investigate a contact. We went to the latitude/longitude of a reported sighting, but found nothing at that position. On our way back to the base, our flight path took us close to what we called "The Slot," a waterway between the islands of the Solomon chain, such as Tulagi, New Georgia, Guadalcanal, and the rest. It was getting late in the day when we sighted an armada of Japanese troops not far from Tulagi. We attempted to radio the Marine base at Tulagi but had no response. We then tried relaying a message by blinker. Still no response. Since it was getting late, our Patrol Plane Commander Gene Long elected to land in the harbor and advise the Marines of the ships that were in the slot heading their way.

Upon landing in the harbor, a Higgins boat came out from shore and motioned us to follow him. He led us deep into the harbor, where the plane would be difficult to see from the entry into the harbor. After securing our aircraft, we were taken ashore and advised that the Marines were well aware of the Japanese troopships and a possible invasion. The main body of Marines was back up the mountainside. We were led to a series of foxholes, given some infantry-type C-rations, and wished the best of luck. Here we were, a flight crew of nine with only our automatic .45 sidearms, scattered around in different foxholes between a possible Japanese invasion and the Marines back in the hills. During the night, sure enough a Japanese destroyer made a sweep of the harbor entry and fired off a couple of flares, ready to destroy anything they found in the harbor. Finding nothing, they left.

At first light, the crew was more than ready to leave. We were slightly delayed because the Marine Colonel wanted our patrol plane commander to come up on the hill and have a look around before we took off. He wanted him to see the air battle that was going on near Henderson Field over on Guadalcanal so we could steer well away from the action as we

departed. We took off and stayed as low as possible and kept away from the action as much as we could. The Marine squadrons at Henderson Field were desperately low on aviation fuel. C-47 transports had been flying in as much fuel as possible just to keep the fighter planes in action. We also saw a ship towing a fuel barge that was getting close to Guadalcanal. We just hoped they made it. The end result of this operation was the last big effort the Japanese made to recapture Guadalcanal. They landed 20,000 troops on shore that night. There was certainly one patrol plane flight crew that was mighty happy they decided not to land on Tulagi that night.

Since the flight from Tulagi to Espiritu Santo was only 6.1 hours, our crew was scheduled the next day, on the 16th of October, for our regular return to patrol. This flight turned out to be 12.7 hours, two of which were regular night hours. The normal average time for patrols usually ran 11 hours. On the return leg we first ran into a single Japanese scout-type aircraft. He took a shot at us, and one single bullet landed inside the cabin and fell on the catwalk between the radioman's station and the navigator's table, which I was manning at the time. No damage was done. We picked up the spent shell as a souvenir. Shortly thereafter, we sighted a Japanese task force consisting of destroyers and cruisers. We sent our encrypted message to our base. We tracked them for about three hours in an effort to more accurately determine the composition of the force and their course and speed.

The cloud cover was so sparse, we stayed as close to the water as we could and out of visual contact. Periodically the plane commander would pop just high enough to check the bearing on which they were steering and their estimated speed. When we made visual contact, it appeared the force was constantly on a heading of 160 degrees at an estimated speed of 15 knots. This would position us at the time we departed to be about 45 miles closer to our base than when we started tracking them. As we later determined, the Japanese force was simply circling around the position about where they were when we sighted them. As the navigator for the crew this day, I was quite concerned when landfall did not show up at the time my dead reckoning predicted. The sun was fast disappearing and of course in those days, our navigational aids were minimal. No radar either on the plane or ashore was available. The *Curtiss* would only send a radio signal when an emergency was declared. It wasn't quite dark enough to obtain star sights with our trusty sextant, nor was the sun high enough to get a sun line. Fortunately, in that part of the world, when the breakers hit the shoreline, they cause a brilliant fluorescent light. We maintained the course we were on, and I sweated a lot, but eventually the shoreline was marked for us by this light from the waves. Within the last few miles, the *Curtiss* momentarily turned its searchlight on, and we knew we were home. Unfortunately the next day's patrol crew from another squadron drew that same sector for their patrol flight and never returned.

Our detachment of VP-51 was relieved in mid-November of 1942 and returned to Kaneohe Bay on the leeward side of Oahu. The detachment of VP-51 that returned from the Aleutians had been reformed and designated VB-101. They transitioned to the Army's B-24 *Liberator*, having trained at Barber's Point, and were in the process of readying to deploy to the Guadalcanal area. VB-101 was the first Navy squadron to replace the PBY for patrol duty with the Army's bomber, and was redesignated the PB4Y-1. The squadron, however, was short four crews and aircraft. I was assigned as one of these crews and sent back to NAS North Island to train and transition to the PB4Y-1.

First, I was given 30 days leave prior to reporting for training at North Island. This was a dream come true. Hazel and I were married on February 3, 1943, at my folks' home in Farmington, New Mexico. After my leave, we went to San Diego and had three wonderful months, during which I trained in the new type aircraft. We were given extra time in San Diego because VB-101 had been employed to not only operate patrols as we had in the PBY, but also to conduct daylight bombing raids on a Japanese airfield in Bougainville. Due to losses in these raids to Japanese Zeros approaching the Raiders head-on but just under the nose, in such a position that the free 50-caliber machine guns in the nose of the PB4Y-1 could not fire on the Zeros, an order was issued that any new planes coming to the combat area must have a nose turret. The later ERCO nose turret was not yet available. The Overhaul and Repair facility at North Island installed the tail configuration turret in the nose of the four aircraft we were to ferry out to the squadron when we returned. It was a very cumbersome configuration and reduced the cruising speed of the aircraft significantly. Our four-plane detachment left North Island on May 30, 1943, arriving at the bomber strip on Espiritu Santo on June 3, 1943.

VB-101 soon moved to Carney Field Air Base, located on Guadalcanal a short distance from Henderson Field. By the time I arrived, the commanding officer of VB-101 had convinced the upper command that the squadron could either fly patrols or the daylight bombing runs but not both because with the recent attrition rate, he would soon be out of crews. The compromise was patrols and occasional night raids. That was the order of the day when I arrived.

Life at Carney Field was far different from life aboard the *USS Curtiss*. Quonset huts for shelter, no laundry service, SPAM three times a day, mud everywhere when it rained, and sleeping under a mosquito net was a must. As the saying goes, The Navy lives like kings and dies like rats, the Army just the reverse. Nor does the comfort of the PB4Y-1 compare to the comfort for the flight crew of the PBY. The PBY had four bunks, a galley, and a large navigator's table where you could spread navigational charts and plot the entire sector route from start to finish. We could carry four pilots and did on occasion quite comfortably. The PB4Y-1 was strictly a bomber: no bunks, no galley, no hot meals, just SPAM sandwiches, two pilots, and a bombardier who also served as navigator. So as a pilot, you spent most of your time in the cockpit. However, you could carry a large bomb load and you did have the firepower of three to four gun turrets with high maneuverability. And the patrol sectors were covered in less time. We used to sarcastically say that the PBY took off at an airspeed of 90 knots, climbed at 90 knots, cruised at 90 knots, and the landing approach speed was 90 knots. But it could land safely and often did. This compares with the PB4Y-1's cruising speed of 165 knots, except for the four planes with the modified tail turret installed in the nose. Its cruising speed was about 145 knots. Most pilots cringed when they were scheduled to fly a patrol in one of these aircraft. And, of course, when you had to ditch at sea, the PB4Y-1 sank like a rock.

The patrols we flew as VB-101 were very similar to those we flew as VP-51, except that we extended much deeper into enemy territory. The night bombings on occasion could become exciting.

On one night that we were scheduled for a raid, we were first visited by what we called "Washing Machine Charlie." A single Japanese bomber would fly over the base, chase everyone into foxholes, and maybe or maybe not drop a bomb. This particular night, as we sat in our foxholes, old "Charlie" was quite visible to us because he passed up-moon from us, making a sitting duck for anti-aircraft gunners.

When the all-clear signal was sounded, it was our turn to proceed with our mission over Bougainville airstrip. We had a number of aircraft, including units from a sister squadron, and had a pattern we were to fly one after another, directly over the landing strip, and drop our bombs. Once we reached the area, it was realized we should come in from a different direction so we would be down-moon and wouldn't be silhouetted as "Charlie" was when he made his run over Carney Field earlier. We dropped our bombs and headed out away from the field. As we did, we saw the plane that we followed in the bombing run was attacked by Japanese night fighters. This was something they had not done on previous raids. The plane was hit and became a ball of fire from wingtip to wingtip and nose to tail. We saw it plunge straight down. Our gunners saw some of the fighters, but we were not attacked. According to our plan of attack, this plane that preceded us would be one of the VB-101 aircraft. All the way back we all felt pretty sad about the loss, particularly since it was one of our squadron's crew. But after we landed and headed for the mess hall for breakfast, the first person we saw was the pilot of the crew we thought we saw go down in flames. When we changed the pattern of our approach on our bombing run, the plane ahead of us was one of our sister squadron's crew. But it was still a loss to all of us.

Our squadron was relieved and departed for Pearl Harbor on August 25, 1943. There was some talk of leaving those flight crews who had ferried the new aircraft from San Diego and joined the squadron late in the tour cycle as replacements for the incoming squadrons. But fortunately it was decided that we should return and be the nucleus of reforming a new squadron that had been designated VB-101. As it turned out, I was detached from this squadron early in the organizing and training phase of the new squadron and sent out to Kaneohe Bay on a special radar mission. I stayed there until January 1945. This was the end of my combat experience.

I was accepted to attend the Navy's Aeronautical Engineering Post Graduate course at MIT and Rensselaer Polytechnic Institute. The RPI course specialized in the newly developing jet engine. I graduated from RPI in June of 1947 with a Master's Degree and was ordered to the newly established Naval Air Missile Test Center at Point Mugu, California. My status in the Navy was changed from reserve status to regular Navy and redesignated as an Aeronautical Engineering Duty Officer.

I have had many very interesting assignments in the field of guided missile development, testing, and evaluation. I also spent a number of years in the aircraft carrier catapult and arresting gear development and fleet support. The highlight of my career was returning to Point Mugu twenty years after my first assignment there in 1947 to serve two years as Commander of the Naval Missile Center at Point Mugu.

After 31 years of service, I retired from the Navy on August 1, 1972. Hazel and I have three wonderful children and two grown grandchildren, all whom we love dearly. We started out our marriage with only seven months together our first two years of marriage, but we will soon celebrate our 63rd anniversary. Our first son was five months old before I saw him. But I made sure I was around for son number two and our daughter.

Herman Rosen

November 1942 - January 1947
Italy, Switzerland

A Round Peg in a Round Hole

An Interview with Herman Rosen
By Greg Gorraiz

The self-proclaimed "luckiest guy in the Army," Herman Rosen was drafted in November of 1942 by the U.S. Army. It would have been earlier, but he already had two brothers enlisted and a third brother who died a few months earlier. Because of this, the military gave Herman six months' extra time.

When the time was up, Herman reported to Fort Devens, Massachusetts, to be interviewed for placement. As fate would have it, the sergeant interviewing him happened to be good friends with Herman's parents. The man knew Herman went to accounting school so the sergeant put him in the Finance Department. "I would venture to say it was one of the few times they put a round peg in a round hole."

Herman did basic training for the Finance Department at Fort Benjamin Harrison in Indianapolis. He then passed the requirements for Officer Candidate School. In nine months at Duke University Herman became what was commonly referred to at the time as a "90-day wonder." He became a 2nd Lieutenant.

After training at a few air bases in the South, Herman was sent overseas in October 1943 on the *USS Mauritania* with 10,000 troops. In five days Herman arrived at Tunbridge, Northern Ireland. Surrounding the area were 8th Air Force bases. He met another officer and eight or nine enlisted men with whom he would work.

To put it shortly, Herman and the other men were in charge of payrolls. Company commanders in the area had Air Force troops training for the invasion of Normandy. The commanders did their payrolls and brought them into Herman and the other men, who converted the dollars into pounds, shillings, and pence. After that, the men had to make "change lists." This meant they broke down the money into certain denominations. Specific amounts of five-pound notes, one-pound notes, and shillings were required for payroll; one of their jobs was to do this. Herman made arrangements with the Bank of Belfast to pick up their money so it could be counted. He was escorted by rifle-carrying guards provided by the bank, because of the huge amounts of money they were hauling. Herman and his men simply couldn't count millions of dollars at the bank, so they took an estimated sum back to their base to count. "We had an arrangement: if they were short, they'd make good, and if we were over, we'd reimburse them. We never had a problem with it." Once they had the money, the men spent the night around a table, sorting the money into denominations. Each man had a sack of a certain denomination. Herman called off the change list for each company and the men dumped the amount of shillings, pounds, or pence into sacks. "At the end of the day or early morning, we'd come up short. This guy says, 'I'm short a pound.' This guy says, 'I'm short three shillings.' This one says, 'I'm over three shillings.' And they'd dump it in and come out even."

Russ Johnson, a good friend and fellow officer of Herman's, called him up one day. "Didn't you tell me you had a brother stationed up in Iceland with the Air Force?" Herman said he did. "Was his name Mel?" Becoming apprehensive, Herman said yes. "We got a group in here, just came in from Iceland after two years up there." Herman said, "Well, get him a Jeep and get him over here!" The sergeant laughed and told him Mel was on his way. He stayed overnight with Herman. This was a joyous occasion for the brothers, who hadn't seen each other since they left for war and would see each other only once more before they both returned to the States at the end of their service.

Three months after the Normandy invasion, 1st Lieutenant Herman Rosen was sent to France to open an office for General Spotts, Commander of the 8th Air Force. Herman and his company were paying the troops out of field safes, since they had to be paid no matter where they were, and no banking was available. "It made them comfortable knowing their allotments were going back home." After a couple months, a colonel told Herman to "close up shop" because he was being transferred back to England. It was just around the time of the Battle of the Bulge. "In fact, I got out of Orly Air Field about four or five hours before the Germans bombed it."

In England, Herman met another officer and a "handful of GIs" from a different cavalry. They waited patiently in an apartment. Suddenly, a much-improved and completely silent V-2 rocket blew up the building right beside the one where they were staying. "You didn't even know they were there until 'boom!'—they came down." Shortly afterward, they received word to go to Switzerland.

They were flown to the border of Switzerland, where they would "more or less sneak in." Herman

and the others went into London and bought civilian clothing so they wouldn't be recognized. They were bringing their uniforms with them to Switzerland, but that was it. They took off from London but the

Boats in Le Havre harbor.

weather was dreadful, so they were forced to land in Marseilles with very little fuel left in the plane. After a few days waiting, the Army decided they couldn't wait any longer, so they packed Herman and the others into a big truck and drove for hours upon hours to the border. "It was horrible, I'll tell you." At any rate, the men arrived at the border, worn out and tired from the trip. They got into Geneva, Switzerland, the next day. After years of blackouts, the sights in Geneva were surreal and beautiful. The lights were blazing, there were jewelry stores and camera shops, and everything was alive.

Herman and the others took hold of themselves and went to their hotel, where they stayed the night. The next day they traveled to a military attaché's office in Bern and reported for duty. They were needed in Switzerland because many displaced soldiers were stranded there. In the beginning of the war, the U.S. Air Force bombed oil fields in Romania but didn't have any escorts for the bombers, so many of them were shot down or damaged. They were told to try to make it to Switzerland. Over time the amount of soldiers swelled. Herman's job was paying the soldiers stuck in Switzerland and helping them get back to the United States.

While Herman was stationed in Switzerland, there were numerous bombings along the Swiss border. Sometimes, if bombers were up in the clouds and couldn't see their targets, they accidentally did some damage in Switzerland. Once, the bombers hit the

Zurich railroad station. The U.S. Army paid the bill. "I even had to pay off some guy that claimed somebody stole his bike while he was doing rescue work." The 1700 U.S. internees who ended up in Switzerland were put into camps. "They weren't exactly concentration camps… a little bit better than that." Eventually the internees ended up in Swiss hotels, and "somebody had to pay for all this."

At the U.S. military attaché's office a select staff was made, with Brigadier General Legge at the top as attaché. The superior ratings Herman gathered as he transferred from station to station were likely what got him the job. Herman and the other officer wrote initial reports as to who should be reimbursed for damage and who should not. The other officer only lasted a short while, however, and all the man's crew ended up joining Herman and his men.

American internees caused several sticky situations for Herman's office. Some internees bought items from local merchants just before they were sent back home, so the merchants were never paid. Herman had to write letters to the internees so he could reimburse the shop owners, but many of the American GIs were less than eager to do so. "One guy sent a real nasty letter. I sent him back a *real* nasty letter telling him, 'You're damn lucky you had these people [selling things to] you.'"

Eventually, most of the American internees returned to the States. Herman's job didn't slow down, however, because his camp started getting claims from the Swiss authorities. They wanted to be reimbursed for taking airplanes off mountains and out of lakes. "It became pretty overwhelming."

Herman was "locked in" while he was in Switzerland, meaning he couldn't be promoted. Three times General Legge put Herman in for promotion. Each time it came back denied, saying, "He's on temporary duty." Herman's work didn't go unappreciated, however. He was promoted to Captain when he returned to the United States.

World War II ended; Herman was still in Switzerland. The U.S. government wanted to know how much Nazi money was in Swiss banks. Although the president of the Swiss National Bank was very friendly with Herman while the U.S. was making payments to the bank, when it came down to telling Herman how much Nazi money was in the Swiss banks, "they clammed up." Jim Mann, a U.S. Treasury representative, was sent to help resolve the dispute.

He provided the pressure while Herman provided the financial information. "We were getting nowhere." Consequently the United States froze all Swiss assets in the U.S. The Swiss reciprocated by freezing U.S. assets in Switzerland. Now, instead of gaining any ground, neither side provided banks to the other. Not until after Herman left Switzerland was this problem solved and the banks reopened, likely by an under-the-table payment. The U.S. never found out how much Nazi money was held in Swiss banks.

Eventually, Herman decided he had had enough. He wanted to go home. He'd been overseas for years without seeing his fiancée, Vivian. He had enough points to go home, so he requested a dismissal. Of course, the Army didn't want to see Herman go. He spoke Sweetsudeutsch fluently, had contacts with the Swiss, and had dutifully performed his job. The men tried their best to get Herman to stay, even sending a colonel over from the States. "I don't know where I got the guts, but I said to him, 'I'll tell you what. You get my fiancée over here, I'll stay as long as you want.'" The colonel said he would see what he could do. Permission was granted from Eisenhower's office in the European Theatre and from the State Department. The only catch was Vivian had to pay her way over, which did not cause any problems. The necessary papers were filled out, the wedding gown was packed, and Vivian got ready to depart for Le Havre, France, where Herman would meet her.

When the time came, Herman was given a staff car and departed for France. He waited at a bar when he got to Le Havre, knowing the ship hadn't come in yet. He was chatting with the local men when all of a sudden he realized the ship must have already arrived. He sped to the port and was forced to wait behind closed guard gates. Everyone had already disembarked from the ship—everybody, that is, except Vivian. Finally, the gates opened and Herman zoomed to the ship in his Army car. After years away, the two embraced each other on the ship in the port of Le Havre.

Vivian and Herman stayed the night in Paris before driving back to Switzerland. Vivian told Herman about the voyage over, how a young man heading to Geneva to become an eye-doctor asked for her hand in marriage. Apparently the man saw Vivian several times throughout the trip and had gotten to know her. When they arrived in France and all the passengers were getting off, the man noticed Herman hadn't yet arrived. He asked Vivian if she needed a ride to Bern. Vivian told him her fiancé was coming to pick her up, but that didn't stop his persistence. The young man boldly proclaimed that if her fiancé didn't show, he would marry Vivian. Of course, Herman picked up Vivian and the man was denied. He mustn't have been very heartbroken, since Herman and Vivian saw the man at a Geneva dance club shortly after they were married, dancing with his newfound girlfriend.

The Swiss men working for Herman gave the couple a welcome-back gift by decorating their apartment with floral arrangements. The men also hauled in a full-size bed, an item not even sold in the area of Switzerland where they lived. The next day was Passover. When Vivian and Herman tried to get married in the synagogue, they were forced to wait a week. Half the town turned out for the wedding, with many members of the legation wearing their uniforms.

Vivian was able to get by in Switzerland. She couldn't speak any of the main languages there but got by on Yiddish, a "bastard type [of] German." She went shopping and spoke regularly to a group of bakers in Yiddish, thinking the women didn't know English. Only long after, when Vivian and Herman were leaving Switzerland, did Vivian find out the women actually spoke English, but didn't tell Vivian because she was doing so well speaking Yiddish.

Despite the romantics, work continued at a feverish pace for Herman. He was getting nowhere with the Swiss bankers and the bills were pouring in. The International Red Cross wanted reparations for various duties performed. The Swiss wanted to be paid for their airplanes and their fields that were damaged. "And poor me, I didn't have the authority to do that."

Equally devastating was a policy instated by the U.S. Army shortly after the war. They didn't have enough transportation to get the troops home, so the soldiers were given vacations or leave time throughout Europe, some of it occurring in Switzerland.

Somebody also made arrangements that would allow soldiers to take courses in Swiss colleges. Herman "sat" men around the border to exchange money as it came in. A full colonel came to Herman in need of money. The colonel had made arrangements in Geneva for colleges. Herman, however, never received any sort of authority or money for that program, so he denied him. The colonel repeatedly demanded the money, but Herman held his ground. He simply could not give the man any money. The colonel stormed off. Herman ran up to General Legge, telling him the story. General Legge promised to protect him. The program ended up falling apart in the end.

Herman was also involved in selling off used Army equipment after the war ended. Many countries bought from them, in particular Turkey. They wanted to buy 500 Jeeps in the Egyptian desert. Payment had to be made in Switzerland in cash, nothing larger than a twenty-dollar bill. Once the payment was made, Herman signed off and let the people in Egypt release the Jeeps to the Turks. The matters were complicated since the Swiss banks were still shut off to the Americans. Herman had $300,000 in twenty-dollar bills and nowhere to put it. General Legge's office had a safe, but it only held about $30,000. Herman consequently approached General Legge and told him he needed to go to the Bank of France to deposit the money. The problem wasn't getting there; the arrangements were made and the trip approved. The problem was a requirement that any officer carrying money must also carry a gun, and they were in a neutral country. General Legge scrounged up a revolver, but told Herman it didn't have any bullets. "Good enough," said Herman. Arrangements were made to meet a representative of the Bank of France in Paris, so Herman and the other men went on a Swiss train. After a long ride, they got to Switzerland. "Where the hell's the guy? He's supposed to meet us." They sat helplessly with two briefcases, each containing incredibly large amounts of money. "Finally some kid shows up in a Jeep." Herman and the other man threw the suitcases and themselves into the Jeep and rode to the American Finance Office in Paris. They deposited the money, got a receipt, and stayed a few days before returning to Switzerland.

Arguments between the Swiss and the U.S. for reparations continued. Herman still couldn't get promoted, so he continued to get the less-than-glamorous jobs during these talks. Finally, he decided it was time to return to the States and retire from the military. He and Vivian packed the household items they acquired during their married life and traveled by car to Lovorno, Italy, where they sat in a "crummy hotel" waiting for transportation. They ended up on the *Zebulon B Vance*, a converted Liberty ship. For seventeen days they traveled and, despite the fact that officers like Herman received better quarters than the regular troops, Herman recalls the trip as "miserable." On the seventeenth day, they arrived in New York Harbor. "I'll tell you, when I saw that Statue of Liberty, it really does tug at your heart after all that time."

Herman was given a week at home with his parents and new parents-in-law before being sent to Washington to make a report on the situation in

work and war service with a sense of pride and satisfaction from serving his country while doing a task he was well-trained and pleased to do.

Herman and Vivian leaving synagogue after marriage ceremony

Switzerland. By this time he was a Captain. In Washington, the CIA asked Herman to work with them, but he refused. He was done with military life, simply wanting to get his CPA and become a non-Army accountant.

Herman worked privately until retiring a content man. He is now able to look back on his

Pete Rovero

August 1944 - May 1946
Kwajalein, Eniwetok, Okinawa

139th NCB: We Get It Through

An Interview with Pete Rovero
By Patrick Ward

The bombing of Pearl Harbor on December 7, 1941, was the beginning of America's involvement in the war against the Japanese in the Pacific. The bombing also led to the forming of a new branch in the Navy, formerly the Civil Engineering Corps, now called the Naval Construction Battalion.

A young man growing up in Connecticut, Armand "Pete" Rovero enlisted in the Navy at 17 years old in New Haven, Connecticut, with his mother's permission. Pete was assigned to the Naval Construction Battalion, better known as the CBs, or Seabees. He completed his basic training at Camp Endicott in Rhode Island. While he was there training, he met a man they all used to call Pappy Lenore. "He was from Texas, but he just couldn't march. He couldn't keep the time no matter how hard he tried, and we left him behind."

Pete completed wharves and dock school and truck driving school while at Camp Endicott and received a driver's license. They were all divided into different companies and platoons; Pete was in the 139th Seabee Battalion, Company D, 2nd Platoon.

After Endicott, the battalion was shipped cross country to Port Hueneme, California, for continued training. They spent three months awaiting their new assignment. While they were there, Pete and a few of his friends hitchhiked their way up to Camp San Luis Obispo, where they were trying to meet Pete's brother's friend, Al Dwyer. Al was a member of the National Guard in Waterbury, Connecticut, and was stationed in San Luis Obispo. He ended up not being in, so they only stayed a few days. They were fed meals by Italian POWs from the Eastern Front of the war and were served on china plates.

An incident Pete had at Port Hueneme was when he got into a boxing match with one of the camp jokers, a man they called Tiny Steiner. In Pete's words, "Man, I danced a hole around him. I guess I was pelting him all over the place." Pete got along with all of the guys great after that.

After leaving Port Hueneme, they were sent to Hawaii. They were there for one week for necessary repairs to the ship. During their break in Hawaii, Pete and two of his buddies put together the few dollars they had to buy a case of fresh pineapple juice from a local merchant. When Pete boarded the ship out of Hawaii, he had no idea where their course was taking them, but as he stated, "When you're a young kid, seventeen, eighteen years old, you don't ask questions. You just do what you're told." On the long voyage to their unknown destination, Pete and his friends sipped their pineapple juice while the other men ate sandwiches that were prepared in a garbage can up on deck.

> We would punch a hole in that thing on the way over, and every now and then we'd just take a sip out of it and pass it around between the three of us; we weren't sharing it with anyone. We said, "Well, we don't know where we're going." At that point, we didn't know where we were going until we left Eniwetok. And we were saying we don't know where we're going, we don't know what we're going to do, so let's just take it easy. And when we got there, we still had a half a dozen cans left…

It was then announced their final destination was Okinawa, an island about 350 miles from the homeland of Japan. The Marines had seen heavy fighting in the southern part of Okinawa. When Pete arrived, he was one of those chosen to stay on board for the first few days and unload the ship, or in his words, he was "one of the lucky ones." While on board they received regular runs by *kamikazes* straight from Japan, and when the LCTs in the harbor shot down the Japanese suicide attackers, the men were up on deck cheering.

> When we were out on the boat unloading, at that point when we first got there, there was quite a few of them that'd come in [kamikazes], and most of the guys would be up on deck just yelling just like it was a ballgame, you know, when they downed 'em.

When Pete finally went ashore, he rejoined the rest of his battalion and got to work right away. Most of the CBs in Okinawa were in their forties, since the military needed men who had trades. One of Pete's best friends was a guy named Bill Harter and he was in his forties, too.

Pete was a truck driver delivering much-needed supplies to the Marines in the southern part

of Okinawa and the Army guys in the north. He would haul anything and everything in his truck, from food, to bombs, to power generators. The roads on Okinawa were not paved, which made travel difficult. They were generally coral dust and, as Pete described it, "more slippery than ice." The landscape was not just a flat ride, either; it was a series of many hills and mounds that Pete had to maneuver. In his truck, he had to "shift like crazy." All the gears got a workout.

CBs had to work 12-hour shifts day in and day out. Driving on the powder-fine coral dust was not just hazardous, but also very dirty.

> You'd go out in the morning and you'd be all fresh, and you'd come back in the afternoon, and it was all coral dust 'cause that sucker got all up in the air. And heck, as a young kid 17 to 18 years old, you looked as if you were about 35 to 40.

When Pete's truck dropped off its cargo, it went back down to the dock and refueled, and then was immediately sent out. The CBs loaded the trucks with what they called "Cherry Pickers," miniature cranes that had a continuous cable. They then cinched up the cargo and dropped it in the truck. Pete's most

Pete on his truck in Okinawa

remembered day on Okinawa was once when he was waiting for his truck to be loaded at the dock.

[The] time we were hauling ammunition and one of the LCTs that they unloaded—and I'll never forget the number of this thing; it was 560—and that was loaded with all the bombs and stuff. That thing just blew apart. When they hauled that thing out of the water, it was just a tangled mess. It actually just blew the vessel in half.

Pete and buddies in Okinawa.

Sometimes when the trucks were resupplying, Pete even saw Japanese POWs coming back looking like "sumo wrestlers," stripped of everything but their underpants.

When the trucks were finally resupplied, they found others going to the same place and formed a convoy. Sometimes convoys stopped to go off the designated secure path so the men could get out and look for souvenirs. One of Pete's buddies, Stan Schaunessy, stepped on a land mine and nearly lost his leg while "souvenir hunting."

After a long day, the CBs looked forward to a hot meal. They had a chow hall and pretty good cooks, by military standards. The eggs at the camp were from the 1930s; they had been kept in cold storage. Pete said what they used to do was break an egg in a ladle, and if it was rotten or bloody, they simply tossed it aside until they got a good one.

To combat malaria, the men had to take an Atabrine tablet on a daily basis. It seemed to help with malaria, but turned the men's skin yellow.

When it finally came time for Pete to go home, he sailed on what was considered a "luxury liner" compared to the Dutch merchant vessel they came over on, called *Kota Agoeng*. The returning ship was the *SS President Adams*, a converted freighter. It even had a 24-hour-a-day soda and ice cream bar for the men on board. It was a two-week journey to come back to San Francisco.

The ship reached its destination in San Francisco, California. When Pete and his buddies got onshore, the first thing they did was go out to eat fresh milk and tomatoes. This was because they hadn't had either in a year and a half while on Okinawa.

The CBs were finally on their way home, going cross-country on the military sleeper trains. When Pete arrived back home in Waterbury, he decided he would take advantage of the 52/20 club, as the men called it. This was only for servicemen. The veterans received $20 a month for 52 months if they didn't work. After several months, Pete got bored of sitting around the house doing nothing. He went back to work and began an apprenticeship in the tool and die business.

After 8,000 long hours of apprenticeship work, Pete moved out to California and went back to work the very day he got there. He worked two jobs for three years and eventually got married. He then started up his own local tool and die shop. The shop was very successful and all of Pete's hard work paid off when he retired at the age of 53 years old. Pete took up many hobbies after the war, including flying the airplane he built, and fishing. He now resides in Torrance, California with his wife of 55 years, Irene.

Pete Rovero is not only my hero. He is my grandpa.

Oscar Schwartz

January 1941 - October 1945
South Pacific

Keeping Them Flying

An Interview with Oscar Schwartz
By Carolina Nick

On January 21, 1941, Oscar Schwartz left his home in Rochester, New York, to join the Air Corps. Little did he know that Pearl Harbor was to occur almost a year later. For his basic training Oscar was sent to Maxwell Field in Montgomery, Alabama. At the time, his records hadn't caught up with him, but once they did, Oscar received a World War I uniform "with the high collar like you see in the old movies. They wouldn't let me off base wearing it." Finally, Oscar received a "beautiful blouse" and was able to get off the base to embark on his new career.

Oscar and the other newcomers were given aptitude tests. He was sent to Aircraft Mechanic School along with his best friend, with whom he had joined. Oscar and his friend lived in the same building across the hall from each other, although his friend was two weeks ahead of him and in a different squadron. Once they arrived at Chanute Field, a technical school in Rantoul, Illinois, Oscar's friend was a class ahead, so his friend purposely missed several days and was set back one class. Now Oscar and his friend were together. After graduation, the two of them hitchhiked back home to Rochester. "It was really tough hitchhiking because there was a man about every six feet for hundreds of miles." After they got home, they went to visit Oscar's older brother, who lived in New York City and was later part of the 8th Air Force in England. They then hitchhiked down to Georgia.

Once it was time to get back to work, Oscar returned to his squadron in Albany, Georgia, at Turner Field. Before Pearl Harbor, Oscar usually had one shift during the day, but was off at night. After December 7th everything changed. "When Pearl Harbor occurred, we had machine guns out there on the outside next to the barracks. Who's gonna drop in on Albany, Georgia, I don't know." Oscar and his friend applied for Aviation Cadet Flying. Oscar failed the eye exam, but his friend passed it and became a fighter pilot in the South Pacific.

Later on, Oscar's squadron was sent to Morris Field in Charlotte, North Carolina, and shortly after went to Camp Stoneman in Pittsburgh, California. At Camp Stoneman, Oscar trained by "running up and down hills and things with a

125

pack on, carrying a rifle." The time finally came when they were going to be sent out of the States. They boarded a train and "pulled all of the shades down on the train so the Japanese and German spies wouldn't see." They rode around the Bay Area all night and finally pulled up to a dock and got off the train onto a ship, which weighed 27,000 tons. Oscar's bunk was five holds below the water line. "The bunks were seven high. I had a top bunk and the ceiling was right here—the pipes, everything, about a foot from my face." Oscar spent 38 days on the ship and had two meals a day, "and they weren't too good."

They eventually got to a point where the convoy split. Part went to New Caledonia; part went to the New Hebrides. Oscar went to the New Hebrides and was stationed on the island of Espiritu Santo, where his squadron members began making fuel dumps. The military shipped aviation gas over in 55-gallon drums. On board the ship, some of the men worked "the winches and stuff" while others loaded and unloaded trucks out in the jungle so the Japanese couldn't see.

Oscar spent several months in the New Hebrides, and then got shipped to Guadalcanal. After setting out on their voyage, they were stationary in the harbor for 20 days due to a sea battle off Guadalcanal. The ship had neither bathrooms nor troop accommodations. Luckily Oscar was able to find a place to sleep on the deck under the overhang. After 20 days at sea, there was an air raid and all the lights on the ship were on and the portholes open. "There were big beams of light going up in the sky, and the men kept screaming, 'Turn off the lights!' and nobody turned them off." The lights remained on and the ship was a perfect target, so a few men grabbed some metal buckets and smashed the lights. "Each light had a vapor-proof glass globe over it and a metal cage around that, and if you hit it with a big heavy bucket, you smashed it. So we turned off all the lights ourselves."

Once the ship was able to move again, it took four days to reach Guadalcanal. The first thing Oscar did when he arrived was look for souvenirs. He found a Japanese rifle, currency, and dead Japanese. "When you're in war, they do some pretty mean things. There was no sorrow." After their arrival, they unloaded their equipment and set up camp right next to Henderson Field. Almost every night, Japanese planes dropped bombs on the area. "We started setting up

engines for B-17s. It was the old Japanese hangers that they built at Henderson Field, and we used them to set up new engines to put in B-17 bombers." Later, Oscar moved to a new bomber strip about fifteen miles along the northern coast of Guadalcanal at Carney Field. Oscar stayed on the island for a year and a half, the days full of air raids. One of the biggest air raids Oscar experienced was when 120 Japanese planes flew over. Oscar had difficulty finding shelter because his foxhole was "full to the door with Seabees," men who built a neighboring camp. He decided to put his helmet on and sit down on the roof of his foxhole. "I felt a *little* safer." During the raid there were planes shot down right overhead.

I saw one fighter shoot a Japanese bomber down and then he dove down under him and got one about ten seconds later. There were Japanese planes falling all over the place. We lost a few planes, but they lost 80 shot down, and they figured of the 120, a big proportion probably never got back, probably ran out of fuel.

In moving from Guadalcanal to Vogel Kopf, the Dutch part of New Guinea located on the western end of the island, Oscar's squadron joined a new outfit from the 6th Service Group and became an Aircraft Tech Inspector. Days on New Guinea weren't easy, and most definitely weren't trouble-free. "It's the worst place in the world. It's one minute of latitude off the equator, and it rains four hundred inches a year… It would rain for weeks at a time, and sometimes we had to pull the planes out of the mud. They'd be right up to the axles; they'd sink right in." While on Guadalcanal, there was one particular air raid that occurred when Oscar and the crew were changing an engine on a B-24 at Henderson Field. It was dinnertime so the crew decided to wait until morning to finish the job. They went inside to eat, leaving the old engine off, with the new one standing in front of the plane.

When morning came around, that night Japanese planes came over and knocked out thirteen of our planes, and that one wasn't there anymore. It burned right to the ground; it was a big puddle of aluminum… The new engine was sitting in front of the airplane. We walked around the back of it. We found that part of the bomb went through the back of the engine, and the gears and everything were hanging out. All our tools were wrecked 'cause we piled them under the wing. The wing wasn't there anymore; it burned right down. All the tools were ruined, so I never got another set. They made me the inspector, so all I needed was a pencil and a little crescent wrench.

Several months later, Oscar journeyed on to Palawan, a small, narrow island right above Borneo, supposedly the most primitive of the Philippines. "The Japanese had built an airfield there and they used American prisoners. When our convoy was going there, they heard [the Japanese] took the American prisoners and put them in a cave and burned them." While in the Philippines, Oscar and a friend decided to do some exploring of the island so they set out north of the camp. After some time exploring, they saw movement in the bushes and went off to see what all the commotion was about. They found two headless Japanese and two other men who were playing with the heads like a ball. "I didn't feel too sorry for them after they had burnt up the Americans."

Despite what happened on Palawan, Oscar was able to set up camp on a "beautiful" beach, where the climate "was like Sonoma Park." They had a "nice camp set up on coconut logs about eighteen inches" high and built wood frames.

Both pictures: a crashed B-24.

They finally got screens some time later, which made it "pretty pleasant."

While at Carney Field, Oscar and a Tech Inspector from another squadron were instructed to go to Stirling Island in the Treasury Group. They were supposed to check on a B-24 that had been shot up and made an emergency landing on an unfinished airstrip there. Oscar and the other tech inspector were told to look for *Coos Bay*; little did they know it was a ship. "We thought it was a bay so we spent the whole day running around looking for Coos Bay!" They were able to hitch a ride aboard a Navy boat on a mail delivery route and "after several

hours, a sailor pointed to a seaplane tender out in the middle of the bay, so we got aboard it." Oscar and the tech inspector were then taken to the chief's quarters.

Talk about nice living. They had bunks with mattresses about a foot thick, a big double door refrigerator filled with pie, cake, and all sorts of fruit… We were served our meals there by seamen along with the Chiefs. I decided right then and there that in the next war I was going to be a Chief Petty Officer. I did become one in the Naval Reserve after the war ended, but they didn't call me during the Korean War. Just as well. By that time I was married and had a son to think about.

The next morning, Oscar and the tech inspector boarded motor launches that took them out to one of the seaplanes that flew them to Stirling Island. They were finally able to get a ride over to the half-finished airstrip to check on a plane that had been struck by many bullets, yet had no engine troubles. With some free time, Oscar had a chance to look over the surroundings. "The island was so beautiful. Most of the trees were mahogany. They had a few palm trees, but most mahogany. Everything was mahogany: the tent floors were mahogany, the bridges were mahogany."

Several days later, a PBY-5 Catalina flying boat landed in the lagoon and it was time to leave the island. On board the plane was a Marine pilot they had just picked out of the water near Bougainville. They took him to Vella Lavella to rejoin his

crew. It turns out he was one of Pappy Boyington's group. The plane landed and waited for the boat to come and pick him up. When the boat didn't arrive, they finally decided to blow up the pilot's raft by mouth.

B-24 tail

slightly in one way or another." It took twenty-six days to reach San Francisco before they were off to Camp Stoneman, then flown to Fort Dix to get discharged in October of 1945.

After returning home from the Air Corps, Oscar worked for Hughes Aircraft Company for 35 years. "I was always associated with airplanes, so it was my expertise. The airplanes—that's why I went to Hughes Aircraft Company." Oscar was in charge of the maintenance of company airplanes. Many were ex-military planes with which he had a lot of experience. "I went on a lot of test flights as flight engineer, and it was kinda fun."

Even after coming home from World War II, Oscar joined the Navy Reserve during the Korean War and pursued his dream of becoming a Chief Petty Officer. He got his wish after all—to sleep on a thick mattress and eat the "good" food he always dreamed of.

"He threw his chute in and put the raft in the water and swam ashore pushing his raft in front of him. We took off." Shortly after, they got word by radio that there were Japanese planes in the air. Luckily Oscar and his crew had a four-plane fighter escort both ways. They finally arrived right across from Guadalcanal at Halavo Seaplane Base on Florida Island and left the next morning to go to Guadalcanal. "It was like going home. When we got back, we found out we had gotten the Northern Solomons Battle Star. What a battle!"

Shortly after, the war ended. "All of a sudden there were rockets flying. They were shooting up big rockets all over the place. There was like 500 ships in Leyte harbor… The war finally ended!"

It was time for Oscar to return home. Twenty-five days into the journey, his ship broke down in the mid-Pacific. The ship had previously been a German cruise ship. Once the war began, the Germans sabotaged the engine by throwing emery dust in the bearings. "They never seemed to get it right after that." Oscar was put in charge of the bay of walking wounded. "We were in their cabin. They were all infantry, but they were all wounded men—wounded

James Vivian

July 1938 - November 1970
Europe, Korea, Vietnam

"Just Call Me Jim"
An Interview with James Vivian
By Chelsea Ferguson

James A. Vivian, also known as Jim, is a man of honesty and integrity who possesses many beliefs. He was born, raised, and currently lives in Arizona. Jim served his country during World War II, the Korean War, and the Vietnam War. He has had many positive experiences and learned many things. Jim admired his father and wanted to follow in his footsteps to become a doctor.

However, Jim was inspired to join the Navy after one of his neighbors came back from Annapolis looking very handsome and accomplished. After seeing this, Jim wanted to go to the Naval Academy. He took the competitive examinations for an appointment. Jim finished number two in the state. "In his great wisdom," his congressman decided that Jim would go to West Point instead of Annapolis. Jim eventually ended up agreeing with the congressman and decided to stay. He enrolled at West Point in July of 1938, where he endured a difficult plebe year followed by four interesting years. Jim was due to graduate in June of 1942, but World War II came around on December 7, 1941, so his graduation time, which was supposed to be two months' vacation, was decreased to one week. In that time, Jim had to go to a friend's wedding in Indiana and ended up in Arizona for flight training at Thunderbird Field, which is now an international management school. He went through primary training very well and faced a complicated aircraft in basic training compared to the simple biplane used in primary training—a Stearman. At this time in the war, Jim was told *that* need precluded spending any more time teaching him to fly so, being anti-aircraft artillery, Jim went to Camp Davis, North Carolina, where he became Platoon Leader, Battery Commander, and Operations Officer, as well as an instructor at the anti-aircraft school.

Jim had a great start. From Camp Davis he was picked to go to the Pentagon to train for a job as the briefing officer for General Wedemeyer in the China-Burma-India theatre. Jim was not fond of working in the Pentagon. "We went to work in the dark, and we were surrounded by concrete walls all day and went home in the dark." This was not his favorite assignment.

The job in China fell through so Jim ended up going to the Second European Officers Study Course at Columbia University for several months. In the course, he was faced with some huge reading assignments and tough tests, but Jim overall thought it was a wonderful course. It covered political, economic, and sociological aspects of Europe and Russia.

After everything he had done in the States, Jim went to Europe and joined the staff of the U.S. Forces European Theater, where he was in counter intelligence. The job he enjoyed most was Chief of Interrogations. Jim had the job of locating war criminals and finding witnesses to testify in war crimes trials all over Europe—with the help of the British, German, and French authorities, even Italian in some cases. Jim dealt with some very famous and interesting people during this job. For example, he had to escort Field Marshall Albert Kesselring and a German major general from Frankfurt to Rome for the "Ten to One War Crimes" Trial around Thanksgiving of 1947. A German SS colonel was being tried for the Ardeatine Caves Massacre, which occurred when the Italians dropped a bomb on some marching German occupiers. The Germans massacred ten Italians for every German killed; Kesselring was called as a witness since he was the overall commander.

After Jim and the Sergeant took Kesselring to Rome for the trial, they checked out and enjoyed Rome for a week while Kesselring and his major general were being interrogated by the War Crimes Tribunal. It is a very interesting story how they got back. The four of them—Jim, his Sergeant, Kesselring, and Kesselring's major general—had taken a plane to Rome, but it failed them on the way back so they were forced to land in southern France. They had to get to Frankfurt with two prisoners on their hands! They were picked up at the airport and taken to Strasbourg by an ambulance from the place where they had landed near Marseille. The commander in Strasbourg said, "Well, I can get you a two-and-a-half-ton truck to get you to Heidelberg, but no farther."

So we took the two-and-a-half-ton truck, and it was kind of cold in November. We managed to get onto a train in southern France to get to Strasbourg, but we had to sit up all night on wooden seats on this train to make that trip. The French had joined us with two members of the Sûrete Nationale to be sure no incidents occurred, and we had an incident-free trip except that in the morning we had nothing to eat. There were no dining facilities or anything on the train, and we had sat up all night on these wooden seats. Field Marshall Kesselring fished out of his coat a couple of sandwiches. I'm not positive, but one of them I might have given him a week before, and we split them eight ways! It was our breakfast!

After enduring the breakfast, they got in the two-and-a-half-ton truck and drove to Heidelberg, where Jim turned the Field Marshall and his general over to the British Authorities. Jim and the Sergeant went back to Frankfurt in style in a sedan. "The Sergeant and I were armed with pistols, and of course, they were unarmed. We saw no need of handcuffs or any means of detention. They were very friendly. Field Marshall Kesselring was, as we called him, 'Smiling Al.' He smiled a lot. He was very, very pleasant. Whether or not he was a Nazi, or a bad guy, I couldn't say. All I can say is he was an easy person to be with, when I was with him."

Another situation proved that people and situations can always surprise us.

Jim had a lot of interesting people under his "net." Some of the war criminals he had to find and move were traitors during World War II. One of them was the infamous "Axis Sally." Axis Sally was an American and, like Tokyo Rose in the Pacific theater, broadcast anti-American propaganda on Radio Berlin during the war. She was in the American jail north of Frankfurt, Germany. Another traitor Jim's people had to find and transport to trial in the U.S. was Robert Best, an American who broadcast Nazi propaganda from Germany during the war. Jim had them escorted back to the United States for trial—one to Boston and the other to Washington D.C. "I heard that Axis Sally was very attractive, but I didn't get to see or meet her. Should have taken the time to do that."

After three years in Germany, Jim went back to the States and received a Master's degree in Civil Engineering at Cal Tech in June of 1950 and became the Assistant District Engineer in the Philadelphia Engineer District. Jim was in Philadelphia when the Korean War broke out, and he had to direct a lot of emergency construction for the mobilization. Jim particularly remembers Fort Dix and the urgent contract to repair and reopen it. He also had to build a shell-case production facility to manufacture 105-millimeter shells in nearby Burlington, New Jersey. Unfortunately, there was a shortage of copper; therefore, these were to be produced out of steel bullets about eight inches in diameter and one-half inch thick. "It was an interesting project and one of the most urgent projects in the United States at the time."

Jim was encouraged by "Uncle Sam" to go to Korea and "enjoy the climate for a while" as commander of the 62nd Engineer Construction Battalion near East Gate, just outside Seoul. In Korea, Jim built light aircraft runways and maintained others. He finished construction of a M.A.S.H. hospital and, in all, maintained 210 miles of roads in case the Chinese decided to cross and attack. Actually, the battalion could only handle about 90 miles effectively. The U.S. Army would have to

Jim working at his desk in Okinawa

use those roads to stop the Chinese. Jim stayed there for a year and then became the Chief of Air Force Construction on Okinawa, which had been torn up by a typhoon. Jim's job consisted of building the flying facilities on Okinawa and neighboring islands, including several jobs for the Air Force and the Navy. There was a lot of Army construction as well, done by others.

Later, Jim became the Chief of Operations for the Okinawa Engineering District, so he started out with Air Force construction, ended up as Chief of Operations, and then was transferred back to the U.S. as Chief of Engineers of the U.S. Army, one of the most interesting jobs he ever had. That job originally consisted of writing a plan for the Corps of Engineers participation in the civil defense of the country in case of a big disaster. "Since we've just been through the terrible disaster in New Orleans [Hurricane Katrina, 2005], we know that you have to be ready for something like that." For some reason the plan he authored was not accepted and FEMA was called to assist with disaster relief. The remainder of his tour in the Chief's Office was spent as Liaison Officer to the congressmen in the northwest and central United States. As such, he testified before congressional committees and answered questions for congressmen about navigation and flood control projects.

After that, Jim went to the Intelligence Schools at Monterey and Washington, D.C. and studied French. From there he went to Paris as the Assistant U.S. Army Attaché in the embassy, was promoted to Colonel, and became the Deputy Army Attaché. Afterwards, Jim arrived in Germany and became Commander of the 37th Engineer Combat Group. The group was part of V Corps during the Cold War and part of our defense team in case the Russians attacked. They had many plans for that possibility.

Not only did Jim enjoy jobs around the world, he also enjoyed one right back here in the United States. As the U.S. Army District Engineer in Memphis, Tennessee, he was in charge of the levees, flood control, and navigation of the Mississippi River from Cairo, Illinois, to Helena, Arkansas, for a three-year period until he volunteered for Vietnam.

In Vietnam, on January 18, 1968, Jim was assigned to the 20th Engineer Brigade as Deputy Commander, in a cantonment near Bien Hoa Airbase. Bien Hoa Airbase was separated by a narrow area of barbed wire from Bien Hoa Army Base. Jim arrived in Vietnam just in time for the biggest battle of the Vietnam War to that date—the Tet offensive of 1968. He didn't actually encounter combat, but he was sitting in the Tactical Operations Center when a few miles away, the Vietcong decided to attack in the middle of the night. Unfortunately for the Vietcong, they were in the open while they were attacking Bien Hoa Airbase, so they were "decimated." They had no chance. "Our engineers had cleared the rubber trees they had planned to use as cover before the attack."

The closest Jim came to being hit in combat in Vietnam, as far as he knew, was when the Vietcong launched unguided missiles, similar to the ones used by Hezbollah against Israel, hoping to kill someone in Bien Hoa. Jim had one land at a nearby generator. The Korean who tended to the generator was sleeping in a nearby tent; he lost a couple of toes. "It made us nervous, but that's life in the big city."

Jim's organization—he was now Engineer for the II Field Force—did a lot of road and bridge work, rebuilding bridges that the Vietcong had blown up. One specific one was about two o'clock in the morning. Jim was awakened to go to a blown-up bridge just north of Saigon. This bridge was on a main supply route from Saigon up toward Cambodia so it was very important that it be put back in order. His organization had a floating bridge up by noon, with traffic moving across it.

Overall, Jim thought that being in the Armed Forces was a worthwhile experience. It was an interesting and even a trying experience, but a good career. It had lots of opportunity for him, and he had the desire to stick with it. He also stressed to me the importance of education in every person's life.

I think people should take every opportunity to get the best education that they can. That's another thing about the Armed Forces. They'll see to it that you get a GED if you don't have it. Because of my service, I not only received a BS from the Military Academy [West Point], but later on they sent me to Cal Tech for an MS. They sent me to Gunnery School and several others. I went to ASU and got a Masters in Public Administration. I think you should take every advantage that you can to obtain a good education. Some people are not inclined that way. Go as far as you can.

Jim showed how he took his experience from all three wars and used it during his own life. "Well, I guess in World War II, I found that 'the world doesn't revolve around Jim Vivian.' It's a pretty complicated place, and you have to learn to give and take."

Jim has many interesting and inspirational beliefs. He believes that even modern situations, such as Iraq, can be related to the wars and experiences he has gone through.

You have to think long-term of what's going to come out of an action. We talk about nothing good coming out of Iraq and Afghanistan. Well, what do you think happened to Germany? What do you think happened to Japan? What do you think happened to Korea after our wars? What happened? They've become powerful, powerful economic giants, democracies! We have defeated Japan, defeated Germany, and almost defeated Korea. Very successful outcome. Nobody talks about that now. They talk about we've lost 2,500 men. I feel for every one of them and for the parents and their siblings. But we've lost more than that in five minutes of World War II at the landings of D-Day. The price of freedom is hard. The president had a vision, and I think he's carrying it out. Democracy has budded in parts of the Middle East—Lebanon, Israel, Afghanistan, and a landslide vote in Iraq under dangerous conditions. May it be nurtured.

Jim not only has beliefs on the military; he has morals and a vision he believes are important to living a fulfilling life. "Have a good ethical base. Belong to a church. Do what the church teaches you and use that as your basis for your actions. Then practice patience, prudence, integrity. Try to get an insight into what makes the world go round."

The price of freedom is hard. The vision of freedom is the future.

Fred Westlund

February 1943 - December 1945
North Africa, Europe

Algerian Interlude
An Interview with Fred Westlund
By J. Caitlin Campbell

Fred Westlund wanted to be in the Navy. "This is how it is," he says. "You go through a line. I went through the line, and they said, 'What service do you want?' I said, 'Navy.' They looked at the sheet and they said, 'It's filled up.' So I went back in line again. Well, they asked your age, so I went back in line again, and I changed my age. I thought maybe I'd get in the Navy, and the guy looked up and he said, 'Get back over there!'"

Fred ended up in the Army, at age 20, in 1943. He went to Fort Bliss for his basic training, and after three months he boarded a troop train from El Paso to New York City and then took the *SS Monterey* to Algiers, North Africa. It was a long journey, made even longer by zigzagging to avoid the German depth charges and submarines in the Atlantic. They spent about 13 months in Algiers and didn't have much combat action except for the French Foreign Legion, who weren't friendly.

Fred didn't have any problem with theft, because as he says, "If the Arabs wanted to steal our stuff, they got shot dead." A few tried, but they were shot and killed, and that quickly put an end to that.

There was always a lot of mail, and at mail call the corporal in charge of the mail would call your name and give you your package. Parents often sent cigarettes along with letters. Fred got Lucky Strikes from his parents. Everyone back then used to smoke, and cigarettes were used as a form of money. They even had a lot of girls mail them to keep the men's spirits up, and of course the soldiers had to write back in order to keep the chain of mail going.

"One time I had some cigarettes that my folks had mailed me, and they had also mailed me some foot powder for my feet. And the package of foot powder broke open in transportation, and the cigarettes got all the foot powder in them. So what did I do? I sold them. Somebody else smoked cigarettes with foot powder in them."

There was an officer in charge of checking all outgoing mail, and if he saw indications of troop location, he blacked it out without anyone knowing. "People back home knew more of what was going on than we did. I mean, we

133

didn't know what was going on half the time. Now it's different. If you have something going on, you know it instantly. Back then you might have had to wait two days, but now the war, you look at the war right away. It's a lot different now."

While over in Algiers, Fred met a girl named Fatima. She was from a small village near where Fred was stationed at the time. He wrote a story about his experience with "Princess Fatima" called "Algerian Interlude." It describes a departing G.I. giving Fatima to Fred to settle a debt. Uncomfortable with this arrangement, Fred hired Fatima and her village to do laundry for the soldiers. When missing buttons were traced to the women having beaten the clothes on rocks to remove the stains, Fred brought Fatima buttons and thread to reattach them. This is one of his favorite memories of his time in Algeria.

It seemed to Fred all these plans were made, but they functioned the way you expected them to. They didn't function well. The troops had planned to cross the English Channel but encountered very bad weather and had to turn around and wait for the weather to get better before crossing to France. Once he arrived in France a funny thing happened to him. The invasion had already been going on for two weeks. Fred and his regiment went in combat-ready, only to encounter Red Cross girls serving him and his fellow soldiers coffee and doughnuts! "That's really combat, isn't it?!"

Fred in Marseilles, France

His unit proceeded on to Paris, riding in trucks. Fred noted everything was blown out but the French people were very friendly. They continued on to Liege, Belgium, where the Battle of the Bulge occurred. As the aircraft battalion leader, Fred was right in the middle of the battle. Through the ice, snow, and fog, they were shooting at tanks and airplanes and any German opposition they saw. The allied infantry was ahead of Fred's regiment, although Fred's regiment was ahead by aircraft. They

shot down many enemy planes with their artillery. "See, you don't know you're shooting down an airplane until you confirm you shot it down." What happened was this: Fred's regiment had radar and they would see a pip on the screen, when all of a sudden it disappeared. They didn't know what happened to that plane. Officers had to go out and find the plane that was supposedly shot down, because if they didn't confirm who shot it down, that soldier did not get credit. The officers rode all over the area looking for these planes.

Fred was on the radar and the Germans were pretty smart people. They would take the kind of tinsel you put on a Christmas tree and drop it from their airplanes to jam American radar. Fred's radar could not detect the German planes with this interference.

The Germans also had buzz bombs, called V-2s. They aimed these at ports where the ships were unloading, though not directly at Fred. The bombs flew overhead very fast, and at first Fred tried to shoot them down. He soon figured out they were either too fast or too low to shoot and stopped trying—no need to waste ammunition on them. Not all the bombs made it there, of course. Even these German rockets weren't perfect. Some of them just fell; Fred couldn't see where. "But they were enough to scare people."

Fred said some landed near enough to follow. "I've seen them land. In fact, one thing I remember is one of them, or maybe two, hit the electrical towers and knocked out the power. You saw sparks all over and all, but it was more like in a farmer's field, you know, so it didn't hurt anybody. It most likely knocked out the electricity. Then across the port in Belgium, I've seen one of those so-called buzz bombs go right down the chimney of a house once, and the people just disappeared. Just blew up the whole house."

The Americans didn't win the war on the ground; we won the war from the air because we had so many bombers. In springtime, towards the end of the war, bombers came over from England. Raids came over fast, and Fred would look up and the sky would be blackened by bombers going over. "They just bombed the cities, and the cities disappeared. All rubble. We drove through those cities afterward—just a lot of brick, and old ladies out sweeping the street, picking up the brick and rebuilding."

As the Germans started advancing they ran out of gas, which was good, Fred says, because if they hadn't run out of gas the Americans would have run out of ammunition. "The weather had most everything to do with it, except that they ran out of gas."

Gas wasn't a problem for Fred's regiment. They had plenty, enough that they used to wash their clothes in it! They carried 5-gallon tanks of it around called Jerry cans, and when their clothes got dirty and greasy they dipped them in gasoline, wrung them out, and hung them up to dry. They didn't have water to wash them; it was all ice and snow. The soldiers had to wear all the clothes they had to keep warm. It was extremely cold and there was always a minimum of two feet of snow on the ground, making transportation difficult.

Pontoon bridge over the Rhine River, Germany

The soldiers lived outside all the time, even in the winter, but were served very good food by the Army cooks. Sometimes Fred's regiment went into town and spent some of their money on assorted food, drinks, and occasionally movies. He saw Russian soldiers there too, but the Russians didn't get very good pay, and in town they didn't know what to do with themselves because they didn't have any money. The officers, on the other hand, were different. They went around town and spent their money.

Fred next continued on to Germany, staying along the Rhine River. He crossed the pontoon bridge and proceeded into Bad Godesberg, the capital of Germany at the time. There were hundreds and hundreds of German refugees leaving Germany because the Russian troops were coming in from the east. The refugees were civilians and weren't armed. They walked in huge waves.

The war ended in April while Fred was still in Germany along the Rhine. "There was a German plane that came over after the war. He dropped some bombs, just to get rid of them, I guess. He wasn't dropping them at, or on, us. He just dropped his bombs and went home. It was really weird."

After the war Fred thought he was going home. Instead he was taken down to Marseilles, France,

where he was put to work as a support guard, helping the troops load up and head toward Japan. This would have been Fred's next adventure, but the war ended and he never got to go to Japan. "Thank goodness," Fred says.

While in Marseilles, Fred's regiment didn't have anything to do so they were put in charge of guarding the German prisoners of war—not that the Germans minded being prisoners of war because they got fed. "In fact, I used to go in there as a guard. I used to like to go there in the morning because they had better cooks than we did. And I had breakfast in the German prisoner camp because our cooks weren't as good as theirs."

In fact, when the Americans came to take over the POW camp, the Germans were greatly relieved because the Russians had been guarding them and they didn't treat the Germans very well. Many of the prisoners cried, they were so happy. Furthermore, the Russians didn't have a lot of extra food to give the Germans. Once the Americans took over, life improved for the German prisoners, and the Russians were happy because they got to go home. But the Germans were well organized and pretty much took care of themselves. When the war ended and the Americans couldn't afford to keep feeding all the German prisoners, they were released.

Fred took a ship back to the U.S. and landed in New York after a 12-day journey. He was 23 years

Fred and buddies in North Africa measuring height of shell to be projected from gun.

old and had been in the service for three years. He was rushed back to Chicago and was discharged within two days at Camp Grant. He was given $300 as a sort of bonus. One of his buddy's parents came to pick him up and gave him a ride back to Chicago. He was home in time for Christmas.

After being discharged Fred, and many other veterans, received this letter thanking them for their noble service.

To you who answered the call of your country and served in its Armed Forces to bring about the total defeat of the enemy, I extend the heartfelt thanks of a grateful Nation. As one of the Nation's finest, you undertook the most severe task one can be called upon to perform. Because you demonstrated the fortitude, resourcefulness and calm judgment necessary to carry out that task, we now look to you for leadership and example in further exalting our country in peace.

Signed,
Harry S. Truman, President of the United States.

Fred got back his old job of working on the railroad and returned to a normal civilian life. He had no financial problems because while in the service he wired money back to his parents, who put it all in a bank account for him. He also had his job, which was good.

Fred met his wife Doris at a ski club called the Windy City Ski Club. They're both avid skiers and they still cross country. They often visit Telluride and once went to ski in the Alps. Their daughter also skis.

When Fred heard the Dial Corporation was going to move to Arizona, he told his wife he was going to get a job with them. He did. He worked in Chicago for one year and then he and Doris moved out to Arizona in 1975.

Fred's viewpoint on World War II is that it was a great adventure. He got to travel. When he lived in Chicago the only place he'd ever traveled had been Wisconsin. While in the Army he went to New York City, North Africa, England, France, Belgium, and Germany. He got to see all that part of the world and learned a lot.

"When you train for combat action, it is exciting and not real. When you're actually in combat, it is hurry up and wait."

Paul Wise

February 1942 - August 1945
South Atlantic, South America

Brasileira Blues

An Interview with Paul Wise
By Lindsey Anderson

Throughout his flight training in Kansas City, Kansas, Paul Wise's flight instructor called him three names: single-cell, knot-head, and dopey. The instructor, Lieutenant Bergen, a veteran of the recent Spanish Civil War, would bellow, "Get that starboard wing up, knot head." Paul would frantically churn the stick in the back of the open cockpit bi-plane, attempting to meet the demands of his instructor. After failing his first flight check to solo the airplane, Lt. Bergen asked, "Think you can do any better with three more hours?" Paul hesitatingly replied, "Well, if you wouldn't get on my back so much." After three more hours with a young instructor who ineptly bounced a few landings, Paul's confidence and technique improved and he passed the flight check.

All of America was thinking about the military draft after the attack on Pearl Harbor on December 7, 1941. Only five-foot-six, Paul did not relish engaging in any hand-to-hand combat with the enemy so he hoped to join the Navy as a pilot. He visited the local post office in Topeka, Kansas, to test his eyes on a military eye chart. He was told he would never make it into the Navy, much less accomplish his goal of becoming a pilot. Later, his brother urged Paul to join him in getting complete Navy physicals in Kansas City where he lived. The two brothers completed their exams successfully and were enlisted in the Navy on December 31, 1941. To celebrate with his brother, Paul had his first drink of alcohol, a rum and Coke.

After elimination training in Kansas City, where Paul grew accustomed to the rigors of military life as a Seaman 2nd Class, he was shipped off as a cadet for advanced training to Jacksonville, Florida. There the new Navy cadets began training in an open field, practicing takeoffs and landings an open cockpit low-wing monoplane nicknamed the Maytag Messerschmitt. Messerschmitt was the name of a German fighter plane. One day, Paul's instructor said, "I'm gonna do something I don't want to ever catch you doing." Instead of taking the longest available way down the field into the wind, the instructor tried to pull the nose of the plane up to clear a fence; the plane stalled. It cartwheeled onto its back into the next field on top of the two pilots. Luckily the crash post sticking out above the front cockpit saved both from serious injury or death. Paul's instructor treated him very nicely after the crash, for during an official inquiry, Paul backed up his instructor by agreeing that the plane appeared to be underpowered. The instructor escaped any charges.

After concluding his training in various planes as well as formation and instrument training, Paul elected to go into P-boats, patrol planes that landed only on the water. Looking back, Paul frankly admitted it was probably the decision that may have saved his life. Though his military time did not involve direct involvement with the enemy, his service would not be without danger.

Paul visited his sister in Decatur, Illinois, after receiving his wings. There he met a "very nice girl," his future wife Kack. During their first date out on a lake, she allowed him to pin his wings on her as a sign of their engagement. Soon after, he was reassigned to Banana River, Florida, to fly the Martin Mariner, a twin-engine P-boat known as the PBM. Kack flew down a few months later and they were married the day following her arrival. Paul was required to report for a training flight early the next morning.

PBY Catalina *and natives in boats*

In 1942, Paul was assigned to Patrol Squadron VP211, a squadron of Martin Mariners in the South Atlantic operating from various ports in Brazil, from Belem on the Amazon River and Natal in the north, to Bahia and Rio de Janeiro in the south. At these various locations, his squadron had a variety of assignments. The squadron provided escort to convoys to protect them from submarines. It was also involved with rescue work searching for survivors of downed aircraft and sunken merchant ships. This included providing the survivors with provisions while they waited for rescue. Much time was also spent searching for dangerous German submarines between Brazil and Africa; these subs preyed on merchant ships that dominated the Atlantic during the early part of the war. The closest Paul came to experiencing direct contact with the enemy was about midnight in the mid-Atlantic near Ascension Island when a companion plane about five miles away made a futile searchlight attack on an enemy submarine.

There were long periods of boredom between rigorous training and intense patrol duty. It was not like the repetitive deadly combat other segments of the Navy or Army were subjected to during the war.

Due to the concentration of Germans in Brazil, high quality beer was easily accessible, but due to the prevalence of Germans in the area, the planes were not equipped with the latest secret anti-submarine technology for fear of German discovery. For night flying, the squadron did have the advantage of the "Leigh Light." Before the advent of the Leigh light, flares were used to attack submarines at night. After a flare was dropped, the plane had to be in a position on the far side of the submarine and fly down the flare's path before the submarine submerged, a challenging task. With the eighty million candlepower Leigh light, the PBM could follow a surfaced U-boat and make a radar approach undetected. The blinding light was turned on several hundred yards away and attacked the boat even before the crew knew it was sighted. Yet the light required a significant amount of training in order to use it safely. Vertigo was a common problem. Planes were lost before successful techniques were developed to combat it.

As you saw the light moving across the water, you'd think the plane may be moving in a certain way, and it wasn't. If the Leigh light operator missed the target and moved the light across the water, you might think maybe your wings were dipping or the plane was moving in an incorrect way. If you tried to correct it based on inaccurate perception two or three hundred feet above the water, it could end catastrophically.

The pilots on the whole, however, were more concerned with Mother Nature than submarines and human enemies. Since many flights were between Brazil and western Africa, the intertropical fronts presented perilous weather challenges. Towering cumulous clouds with powerful up and down drafts were formidable, particularly if you did not have adequate training. "Obviously we didn't have to worry about other combat planes," stated Paul, "but you had the weather."

Both the climate and the rigorous flight schedule affected Paul's attitude. Though each pilot was allowed a maximum number of hours to fly in a month, for some periods of time they flew from twelve to fifteen hours every third night. "When you fly every third night, it gets rough," Paul recollected. "Psychologically, you are on edge. You begin to think, 'Does that engine sound just right? Am I over single-engine weight?'" The worry was the weight of the plane, which much of the time was a weight above what a single engine would support. Though the large load was needed for the customary sixteen-hour night flights, if one of the engines malfunctioned and died, the plane, if above single-engine weight, could not stay aloft. If there was a single-engine failure, crews were doggedly trained to dump everything possible to keep the plane in the air.

The impending possibility of accidents one witnessed and heard about could prey on the mind. "Every time there was an accident, you'd ask, 'How'd it happen?' 'Cause you worry. You don't want it to happen to you."

The best man in Paul's wedding died in an accident during training. According to one report, his friend Tom Donahue flew too low over the water and crashed, but Paul remembers it differently.

> The way I remember it was that they were dropping depth charges in training. Instead of the depth charge going under the water, it went off on contact with the water, which blew the tail off the plane. The plane hit the water. Fortunately there was another plane in the air and it was able to rescue half of the passengers, but my very close friend Tom Donahue didn't make it.

The surrender of the Germans was cause for celebration. Paul's Atlantic squadron was no longer needed. When the worry of being transferred to fight in the "bloody" Pacific was eliminated with the surrender of the Japanese, champagne was opened and passed around at the Officers Club in Norfolk.

PBY Catalina *in Rio de Janeiro, Brazil*

Paul had accumulated enough points to know he would soon be discharged.

Though Paul is of small stature, he is no less spirited. This gracious, humble man now lives with his second wife Fran in Scottsdale, Arizona. Kack, Paul's first wife, and Fran's first husband both died some years ago. Paul had known Fran since high school and the two couples had lived near each other for some time in the suburbs north of Chicago. After the death of their spouses, Paul and Fran married. Their home is decorated with Paul's service pictures, models of airplanes he flew, and an unassuming piece of artwork depicting his favorite constellation, Orion. Paul had taken navigational readings from the constellation.

> Cruising in the black of night suspended between heaven and its twinkling eyes and the somber blackness of the sea below, you gain a serenity and peace that only that ethereal world can give. Orion was like a beacon providing the way home and reminding you of the blessings and the wonder of life.

Long night flights fostered a familiarity with the stars. "The moon would be out and it's just beautiful," remembers Paul. "You can fly over the white-capped ocean and see the stars at night and the clouds. It can be the most beautiful thing."

Korean War

Most Korean veterans say the same thing. "It was the coldest winter I've ever spent." Wars are difficult enough, without adding to the misery. Sub-zero temperatures were just one hurdle American troops had to jump in order to prevail in the "conflict." At the 38th Parallel there were more problems than simply trying to keep warm: fighting on foreign soil, and being undermanned against the "Sneaky Chinese." Chosin Reservoir fighters all talk about this. Escape from Chinese encirclement took a great display of American resilience and determination.

Korean veterans often speak about being a part of "the Forgotten War." How can this war be forgotten when analyzing the aftermath of the attacks fifty years later? Like any other war, men fought and died. More than 50,000 United States troops died between 1950 and 1953, and the border is still policed today. Today Communist North Korea is an impoverished nation led by an overbearing dictator, while Capitalist South Korea boasts a healthy economy and maintains ties to the western world.

American soldiers fought a hard war and improved the lives of South Koreans. That alone deserves enough recognition to not be forgotten.

Kirk DiGiacomo

James Hickok

June 1950 - June 1953
Korea, U.S.

Keeping the Lanes Open

An Interview with James Hickok
By Brittany Van Bibber

Bertrand Russell once said, "War does not determine who is right, only who is left." This interview is dedicated to Navy sailor James Hickok, whom I interviewed on August 24, 2006, and to whom I made a promise: I would not forget the Korean War, in which he served.

Jim Hickok is a very important man. Now, you may not have heard of him in the newspapers or magazine tabloids or perhaps even on TV. No, he is not that type of "important" person. Jim served in the Navy during the Korean War for three years, from June 1950 to June 1953. This makes him important to many, many people.

Jim entered the Navy before the war, thinking it would be a fun time serving for America next to his buddies, but little did he know that just weeks later North Korea would invade South Korea and make his life a lot more difficult than suspected. Jim was not only active in serving America then, but he still is now. He votes, stays informed and participates in politics, and pays taxes. The life he led, and still leads today, contributes to society. This makes him an important man in my book, and it should in your book, too. This is his story...

While serving in the Korean War, Jim played a very big role in the U.S. Navy. He was commissioned on the 14th of June in 1950 and expected to cruise around for a couple of years to get some time in the service. But all of that changed 11 days later on the 25th of June, when the North Koreans invaded South Korea. At the time, Jim's orders were to pick up the *USS Eversole* (DD789), which was on deployment in Hong Kong, but instead he got expedited. Orders were to meet the *Eversole* and the other ships of the 7th fleet in Okinawa. The Navy's role in the war was to keep the shipping lanes open, to protect the sea around Korea from submarines, and to protect the carriers as they launched and recovered carrier aircraft. Jim stated that "this got to be very, very boring duty," occasionally interrupted by shore bombardment.

His normal duty consisted of going to sea for 40 days at a time, primarily providing anti-submarine screening to aircraft carriers launching and recovering aircraft. The amount of sub contacts they had was plentiful in number, but none could truly be identified as Russian submarines. When the ship returned to port, it went to a port called Sasebo. It was a port found in the southwest part of the most remote island in the Japanese chain. The port had been used during World War II by the Japanese Navy. Jim's ship would go into Sasebo to load up on supplies, oil, and fuel. Then they'd be off to sea again for another 40 days.

On the 15th of September, 1950, General MacArthur led an invasion of North Korea by sea in a pincer movement to take over the communications center at Seoul and begin to drive the North Koreans out of the capital. It was incredibly successful and was the start of offensive activities against the North Koreans. Also, when MacArthur threatened to drop nuclear bombs on North Korean bases in China, China sent in troops. That caused a massacre at the Chosin Reservoir, where the American Marines suffered their first defeat.

The tides in Inchon, where the invasion was planned, were especially hard to maneuver because they could get to be up to 30 feet. The amphibious boats would go in meeting little resistance, but if the tide went out, the LSTs were stuck on land until the tide came in 12 hours later. This left the men on the ship vulnerable to North Korean attack. Those who claimed the invasion was not feasible must have been surprised when it succeeded and American troops began to push North Koreans out of the South.

During the summer of 1950, when Jim had to spend most of his days locked up on the *Eversole*, the weather rose to extremely hot temperatures on the ship. There was no air conditioning. Most of the time it was better for the men to sleep through the heat. During the winter, the ship was freezing cold. Waves broke over the bow and frequently turned to ice, which had to be chiseled off by the sailors so as not to disrupt the stability of the ship from the ice's weight. The *Eversole* took a side trip down to present-day Taiwan—Formosa, at that time—but it didn't last long. Back in those days deployments only lasted about six months, so Jim's fleet got sent back and forth constantly from San Diego to Japan and Korea.

Communications were not always reliable, neither was the radar, so ships had occasional collisions at sea. Jim's destroyer left port in San Diego in April of 1951 to a place called Mare Island Naval Shipyard to get checked with the latest equipment.

They returned to San Diego two months later, their homeport.

Jim was named the assistant communications officer. In this position, in addition to standing watch, he went up to the coding shack to decode all the messages coming in from various sources. The coding shack was even hotter than the rest of the ship because it was a tiny room, and he had to lock himself in so nobody else could get the codes. When he got to San Diego he was sent to Air Control School, which he finished.

Next Jim was sent to Green Cove Springs, Florida, to take a ship, the *USS Howard D. Crow* (DE252), out of mothballs. The ship was "a piece of junk." More than half the guys on the ship were Reservists who had been called back to active duty. This caused them initially to be quite bitter. The rest of the ship mostly consisted of inexperienced people. Since Jim was more experienced, he often did double watches as officer of the deck. Also, at that point in time, he had been promoted from assistant communications officer to communications officer. Once the ship finally got going, it was obsolete. The equipment was old, and the ship speed was slow. The ship went to the Jacksonville Shipyard and did some modernization, then reported immediately to the rest of the fleet.

During the Korean War, Jim had many memorable experiences. One time, when his "school

USS Howard D. Crow *in dry dock*

ship" was in Key West, Florida, for the summer, he witnessed a very funny happening. They were providing ASW training for a group of NATO officers.

In those days President Truman had his summer White House down in Key West. It wasn't located too far from the piers where the ships returned each evening after training. Occasionally, President Truman would go down to the pier to watch the ships go in and out. On one particular day President Truman had decided to watch the ships come in. It was very windy, so maneuvering into the pier was a difficult task. Jim's

North Korean swimming towards the destroyer

ship was second in line entering the pier, and the ship ahead of his was turning into the pier and turned right into it! The ship sheared off its bow. President Truman stood there and witnessed the entire accident unfold. He had a light humor about him, though, and started to laugh. It's more than likely the incident finished the career of that particular commander.

Not all of Jim's incidents in the Navy were humorous. One of the most difficult jobs he ever had happened during his Korean service. North Koreans who wished to flee South often tried to get aboard American ships by either swimming to them from the pier or trying to gain passage some other way. But since the Koreans were not considered part of the Navy, they were not allowed on the ships. Jim and his crew had to refuse their passage on board. They could not give them anything, not even food. It was a fleet-wide directive to avoid any terrorism. This makes perfect sense, but it didn't make it any easier for Jim and his crew members to turn back desperate refugees swimming toward their ship to escape a brutal government in North Korea.

Another interesting experience Jim had while serving in the Navy was refueling the ship at sea. In

order to do so, you have to come alongside a fuel ship, maintaining a distance of about 100 feet, and pass the hoses over the water. Men then had to connect the hoses. If the hose snaps, someone can get hurt. During his time serving in the Navy, Jim learned lots of life lessons through these experiences and even his mistakes.

Being in a war gives someone a lot of responsibility, and it gave Jim a lot at once. Jim also said something that moved me when we were discussing the topic of responsibility. "Here I am now, I'm up as an officer of the deck, and 300 people are down below, and their lives are in my hands, so to speak. I found that very exhilarating. I really enjoyed it." He described the important decisions he had to make as a young naval officer. "Somehow you find a way of settling down, and growing up when you have to grow up. There's too much at stake with something like that, and if you don't watch what you're doing, then you're not simply endangering your life, but you're endangering all our lives." When Jim said that, it put my responsibilities in perspective for me.

Jim thought about staying in the Navy, but his wife Ginny had other plans. She grew up a "Navy brat," moving each time her father was reassigned, having to make new friends. She did not wish that life for her children. "'You have no idea how cliquish it can become, and just about the time I'd break in and be comfortable with my friends, boom, off we are to somewhere else. I don't wish that on any of my kids.' And so that was sort of that."

I think it is wonderful Jim joined the Navy and learned a lot about being responsible and a lot about life in general. The Korean War is also looked upon as the "forgotten war." Jim says the fact that it was called that didn't bother him much because he got used to hearing it being referred to as a forgotten conflict. This moniker also helped him empathize with the vets from Vietnam. They gave the war their all, but all they received was criticism when they returned, and they had to take it hard.

Towards the end of the interview Jim had a few last words about young people today and what they should remember most. He hopes they don't forget the Korean War and other wars of our time. He was also quite disturbed by the lack of American willingness to stand up and be counted as a country. Getting involved is important, and the more involved you are, the more change you can make for yourself and the people around you. Young people in particular need to make a difference.

According to everything Jim has done in society and in the war, he is definitely an admirable person in many people's lives. His contribution in the war kept people safe, no matter how you think of it. The thing that surprised me most about Jim was his willingness to serve and his upbeat aura about the entire war. He didn't think war was necessarily a good thing, but he enjoyed his life while he was in the service and that shows a lot of integrity. It's great that he could stay positive through everything. I certainly look up to him.

Jim reminded me what many men who served in Korea frequently say. "Remember that even freedom is not free."

Waves crashing over bow

KH

Bob "B.J." Johnson

May 1948 - February 1952
Chosin, Korea

Stone Cold: BJ "Bad Jokes" Johnson
An Interview with Bob Johnson
By Kirk DiGiacomo

The Korean War produced not only astonishing and unexpected heroes, but also men of great endurance and perseverance, perhaps even more diligent than warriors from World War II, Vietnam, and other military conflicts. Not only did back-breaking and body-swelling cold stab at Korean veterans during their trip to the 38th parallel, but extreme strength disadvantages at the Chosin Reservoir crippled the 25,000 U.S. soldiers who battled 120,000 Chinese troops. As if these conditions weren't harsh enough, there were also uneducated Chinese bullets flying at self-proclaimed "Jeep drivers" like Robert "B.J." Johnson, because Asian combatants had no idea that most American men knew how to operate a car by age sixteen. Tenacity would save the Marine Corps, a group seemingly "loved by no one," not even Harry Truman, president during the Korean Conflict.

Obviously, a typical day in Korea dealt with freezing cold temperatures. It's painstakingly difficult for an Arizonan like me to grasp just how cold. Not far from Siberia, temperatures were so cold—40 degrees below zero—that B.J., sent to war with an average size-ten shoe, was forced to put his enlarged swollen foot into a size-fourteen shoe before he returned home. Swollen hands wouldn't even allow B.J. to eat, much less live as soldiers do in most wars.

B.J. was deployed to Korea without the benefit of full training. After a mere two weeks at Camp Hamilton, North Carolina, he was sent to wage war in Korea. "I knew which side of the gun was to be fired, and they needed bodies, so they sent me." The sixteen-day "Aleutian route" journey across the Pacific followed his rudimentary training, and he landed at Inchon, Korea, on September 19, 1950. While onboard, great storms ravaged the furiously rocking ship and injured many soldiers; it threw many passengers across the cabin. This occurrence gave B.J. an advantage over his fellow troops: he never became seasick during the tempests and was able to eat more than his fair share of the *Beefield's* food.

"Things got hot right away" after his arrival in the Orient. B.J., along with fellow troops, had to march north to Seoul and capture the grand city before American troops could continue the offensive. After capturing Korea's major city, the troops marched back down to Inchon and took a ship bound for the other side of the peninsula to Wanson, a city in northern Korea. Much to the delight, and not the surprise, of his fellow troops, Bob Hope landed in Wanson before they did. B.J. remembers the situation most clearly from a Marine Corps joke, "Bob Hope always knows what to do—get there first!" Following this speck of laughter for the Corps, a series of battles ensued, much more horrendous than Hollywood writers or Tom Clancy could dream up.

The troops believed there would be no opposition from the coast to the Yalu River, where they would meet the Chinese and fight. "It didn't turn out that way, though," B.J. remarked. Raging gunfire was aimed at B.J. during the march to the Chosin Reservoir; they didn't make it to the Yalu River. So many bullets were intended for Jeeps he drove that they were thrown off to the side of the cow paths they traversed throughout Korea.

B.J. celebrated his birthday like no other on November 26, 1950: struggling to stay alive. By many official accounts, this is the official starting date of the Battle at Chosin. "They surprised us; they really did. They somehow camouflaged themselves and we didn't see any of them." He and his troops faced encirclement from the massive "Chinese Trap" at the Chosin Reservoir, the climax of B.J.'s service. Over the next fourteen days this ferocious bloodbath developed, leaving the Marine Corps survivors with honorable names such as "The Chosin Few" and "The Chosin Frozen."

"Lady Luck was on his side," however, while B.J. was travelling to the reservoir—definitely not the only time he was lucky in Korea. In one of the most infamous Jeeps he drove, he encountered his only battle scars. Riding on a glorified cow path, an officer lost visibility and slammed into an immense truck during a dust storm. B.J. flew headfirst out the windshield. "It destroyed the Jeep, but I was okay. Like I've always said, I had Lady Luck on my shoulder many times." All that came of the accident was a gash on the head.

Perhaps the greatest gift on this day was being on the right side of a tent. The area was quiet surrounding the reservoir. All MacArthur had heard about Chinese troops were minor reports, so he figured they were "only a few laundrymen, and could easily be taken care of." Moments later, after walking around in the silence surrounding the reservoir, "all hell broke loose." Troops sprinted to their positions and waged

war. B.J. took part in the alternating schedule of fighting for a while, then retiring to the "heat tent" for five minutes. While in the tent for his five minutes of heat, an officer walked in and informed everybody on one side to follow him into combat. B.J. wasn't on that side of the tent, so he stayed where he was. He returned to the battle shortly after. At the time, he

Red Cross evacuation point

didn't realize how lucky he was; none of those who followed the officer would ever be seen again.

As a runner for supplies, ammunition, and a carrier of corpses during the battle, the Jeep became a good friend. "You couldn't shut it off; it was all over if you did. The engine was frozen solid if that happened." Like his counterparts, he never slept during the battle, or on his way back down. "You were afraid to go to sleep. When guys fell asleep, their bodies got too cold and they died. Or sometimes Chinese would sneak up from behind and they got killed."

While driving through no-man's land, B.J. drove into a huge ditch. Great fear spread through him because on areas with roads, foot traffic was generally safe, but as soon as one stepped off the road, he faced the imminent danger of land mines. Thankfully, B.J. made his way out of the ditch and was able to hitch a ride all the way back to camp. When he reported to his officer that the Jeep was abandoned, his commander showed great concern— for the Jeep. B.J. thought to himself, "I wonder why he cares so much about a stupid Jeep?" The officer sent B.J. and four other men back to the previous town and forced them to lift the Jeep out of the ditch and haul it back. They might as well have left it there. When they returned, the troops received a scolding from the officer. After he inspected the Jeep, B.J. finally found out the reason for the officer's concern. The whisky hidden beneath the driver's seat had been mysteriously removed. Needless to say, the officer was enraged.

Following fourteen of the hardest days of his life at the Battle at Chosin, B.J. hardly felt a reprieve from his misery. Afterward came a gruesome trip back down the mountains. Battles every twenty feet forced the Corps to move at a sluggish pace. "You could only go about fourteen miles in a day." The ailing Chinese and North Korean troops were hardly an issue when compared to the drastic cold the Marines faced. The harsh winter made the 78-mile return far harder than it would have been otherwise. "There were no tents, and many people had no sleeping bags, or anything! And it was forty below. People had frozen feet—everything. People couldn't even eat!" Luck was one of the main emotions B.J. felt when he finally reached Pusan. Both the media and his fellow troops deemed the Americans' miraculous return to the city a Christmas present, left under the tree for them in their "Miracle Christmas."

B.J. was released from service after being loaded onto the *Missouri* with thousands of other passengers. He was "replaced and released" and sent back to the United States the September after his arrival in Korea. When he arrived at the harbor, B.J. was immensely happy because "it felt hotter than Hades. Rather than forty below, it was forty degrees above Fahrenheit," blissful after battling the horrendous cold. Like the others who escaped from Chosin, B.J. too had acquired the "forty-mile stare," a sign of combat fatigue, or shell shock.

Evacuating a wounded soldier

On July 27, 2006, a news article about B.J. and his wife Arlee, whom he married after his return from Korea, appeared in the *Arizona Republic*. The article beamed of the communication B.J. kept during his year in service. As often as possible, they responded to one another through mail. They wrote letters that proved to be invaluable in later life, especially useful helping him link his service memories together and remember them today. "It's brought back a lot of memories I don't even remember doing or saying. That's the most wonderful thing I have," B.J. remembered. "She was my lucky star while I was there." The letters helped him bear the miserable combat. One letter stands out because B.J. wrote it right after his evacuation from the Chosin nightmare.

It seems so strange to hold a pen or pencil in my hand again. It's been over two weeks since I've had a chance to write a letter. I wrote one to you, and one to my folks since then but I doubt if you will receive it as a lot of mail had to be destroyed.

You probably know all about how we were trapped way up in the mountains. We had to destroy an awful lot of gear and equipment in order to get out. All of us who arrived here safely are sure thanking our lucky stars. Quite a lot of our buddies never made it. We were all on the front lines all the way down and it was really an ordeal. I wanted to write you but I just couldn't take the chance or time either.

Right now we are at the seaport of Hungnam, about twenty miles from Hamhung. We are going aboard ships, I guess headed for Pusan. I sure wish it was stateside. As I said before, "Maybe next time."

We arrived here night before last, and right away had mail call. I received three letters from you and that certainly made me feel good. I got some sleep last night, the first in a long time, so now all I want is a shower and a change of clothes and maybe I'll feel somewhat back to normal, haven't even washed my face or hands since the 24th of November. I hardly look like a white man. I hate to look at my *white longies*. By the way, I have two pair on. It is supposed to be warmer in Pusan so maybe I can take off some of this gear. From the waist up I have on three tee shirts, 2 longie tops, 2 wool shirts, one sweater, two parka fur vests, one field jacket and my heavy parka. Down below I have 2 pairs of skivvies, 2 pairs of longies and 3 pairs of pants plus 4 pairs of socks inside of my shoe packs. It takes a lot of effort to move, believe me. Though even with all this on you're still cold, especially at night. I told you, you can't have a blanket so there's no use asking for a parka.

I guess I sound like I'm in pretty high spirits, and I am. Boy it's a good feeling being in a safe place again. It was worse than hell up there.

Finally aboard ship, B. J. wrote to Arlee again the next day.

I feel pretty sharp right now. After I got aboard ship yesterday I took a shower, shaved, put on some clean clothes and put two double square meals under my belt and hit the sack at 7 last night and didn't get up this morning till after 10 A.M. It sure felt good to sleep warm for a change even if it was on the floor. This is a cargo ship from Portland, Oregon. They don't have berthing space so you have to sleep where you can. They make up for it in chow, though.

I'm one of the lucky few who still have all their gear. Most everyone lost everything but what he was wearing. We only have three jeeps out of 15 left, mine and two others. The rest were shot up and had to be left.

The ship pulled out at about midnight last night and now there's no land in sight. There's a rumor floating around that we may not stay in Pusan very long. I hope it's true, but you know how rumors go. "Don't you believe it."

If the UN gets on the ball, for a change, this ought to be all over with by then and I'll be able at least to be in the states. Every time something happens to prolong our stay over here, it hurts because then we know we'll be here longer, especially when they tell us we'll be going back to the states on a certain date and then not get to.

You probably won't get this till close to Christmas so I'll wish you and all your family a very merry Christmas, at the same time wishing with all my heart there was some way I might spend my Christmas with you.

Another purpose the letters served was relieving tension back home. Robert "B.J." Johnson was rumored to have died many times during his service. Why? There were three Robert Johnsons in B.J.'s camp alone. All of them were in the Marine Corps, and when men with the same name tragically died, confusion spread. The telegrams were sent to his family incorrectly suggesting *their* B.J. had fallen victim to the war. The letters, though, assured them he was alive.

In 1985, during his stay in Grand Teton National Park, B.J.'s wife Arlee recommended he go to a conference being held for persons who fought at the Battle of Chosin. B.J. made his way to San Diego and fell in love with the group. The coming together of this group helped him form a "brotherhood" with his fellow "Chosen" veterans and bring closure to the Korean War. Currently he serves as President of the Arizona Chapter of The Chosin Reservoir, and remembers the freezing valleys and plains of Korea where he fought over fifty years ago.

Bob Patterson

June 1945 - August 1975
Korea, Vietnam

An Engineer Forced To Hurry

An Interview with Bob Patterson
By Kirk DiGiacomo

Career veterans are a unique breed; thirty years of service leads them to have diverse experiences. Robert Patterson served in three of the twentieth century's greatest wars: World War II, Korea, and Vietnam. From these wars he brings a perspective I have never seen. As an engineer and infantryman "behind the scenes," Patterson did the dirty work few think of when imagining war—building roads, bridges, towns, and preparing the logistics of war. Modern wars make individuals like Patterson tremendously useful; without an engineer's assistance, there is no chance of troops surviving the elements nature throws their way.

In 1945, Colonel Robert Patterson graduated from high school in Coronado, California. Later that year, or during "the latter days or World War II," as Patterson calls it, he applied for Officer Candidate School, or OCS. His company commander decided he could be an officer; thus he spent 1946-1947 at Fort Benning, Georgia, in the infantry school. After graduating, he was sent to the First Infantry Division in Europe, the famous "Big-Red One." As an engineer officer he was assigned to the First Engineer Combat Battalion, at that time training and performing guard duty as part of the occupation forces.

For Patterson, "the heat was on in '47 and '48," as the Berlin airlift was in full swing. The engineer battalion commander was directed to build a tent camp in Grafenwoehr, Germany, to consist of typical mess halls, tents, and first-aid areas for medics. This tent camp was essential for the First Division to go into the field and begin training. Prior to the construction of the camp, this division was constantly on guard duty throughout the American Zone and needed a place to train as a unit. Creation of this infrastructure, which would aid in the progression of the troops, was the type of work Patterson would perform for a while. The camp at Grafenwoehr ultimately became the largest training area for the U.S. Seventh Army in Europe.

In 1952, Patterson became part of the 16th Infantry Regiment, commanding G Company, "the most satisfying event in this young officer's life." While a company commander, he decided he wanted to receive a regular commission; it took him eight long years to actually achieve this. Not until he had become airborne-qualified and had more years of service and experience under his belt could he receive the commission he desired. From there, Patterson's road took a unique course.

While in the "Forgotten War," as the Korean War is often called, Patterson, now a Captain of Engineers, was assigned to the 74th Engineer Combat Battalion. "The unit was about four hours by snow-covered mountain road from the group headquarters. The main mission was to keep over 75 miles of roads open for convoys. There was guerrilla action in the hills to further hamper the mission. Mine-clearing operations were a high priority." Patterson was the S-4, S-3, and then later company commander of Company B. S stands for Supply Operations.

The grandest achievement for Patterson in Korea was building a town. The summer after the Korean War's end, the U.S. armed forces decided to put forth the necessary resources to build a "war-replacement" town to hold 4,000 South Koreans. This is exactly the type of work expected from an Army engineer. As was typical of his service, Patterson was forced to hurry to meet military deadlines, this time building a town with a police department, headquarters for the town, and other community buildings. The reason for the rush was to enable the Americans to finish rebuilding *their* village, Young-Jung-Myon, also called Armed Forces Aid to Korea Project 8211, faster than their communist enemies in the north could rebuild *theirs*. This village was built near the "farm-line" in Korea, along the DMZ. An argument arose between the American engineers and the mayor of the town. The Americans told the mayor they believed a fire-station was appropriate. The mayor asserted they "didn't

Bob with cigar in Korea on Company Street

want a fire station," so the Americans obliged his request. Patterson found these dealings challenging, but fun. He reapplied for a regular army commission.

Returning to the United States, he found he had finally been granted this commission. At long last, while still a captain in the infantry, he was assigned to the Infantry School at Fort Benning. He concurrently began night study at the University of Georgia in Columbus. After three years of intensive study, he was sent to Athens, Georgia, to complete his studies and received a Bachelors of Science in Education in 1954. An assignment in 1960 sent Major Patterson to work at Colorado State University in Fort Collins as an assistant professor in military science. These four years on ROTC duty were spent begrudgingly; Patterson preferred hands-on military action as an infantryman to teaching college students. Even though he was "trapped," Patterson acted as all soldiers do—with humility, and willingness to work on any task.

The moment every infantryman waits for came in 1964. This was a huge year for Patterson, as well as the United States. President John F. Kennedy had recently been killed, and the Vietnam conflict was coming to a boil. On July 27, 1964, 5,000 soldiers were ordered to South Vietnam. Conflicts in North Vietnam led to the "full Americanization of the war," and one of those 5,000 called in was Patterson. He was assigned as a Brigade S-4 of the Twenty-Fifth Infantry Division, "Tropic Lightning," in Hawaii. Patterson was promoted to Lieutenant Colonel, and subsequently assigned to the United States Army Hawaii as Chief of the Plans Division, G-4. This arduous position is one in which Patterson feels great pride.

While on this job, he was sent to Vietnam on temporary duty as a logistics planner. When the Marines landed in Da Nang, Patterson found himself "thrown into" a special planning group in Saigon, where he was the G-4 planner. From this, a "secret planning mission" would ensue under the command of General Westmoreland. Westmoreland's plan to send additional troops into Vietnam left Patterson and his fellow planners with a "big question." Simply put, "Where are these units going to go, and what mission will they have?" The group's situation was made even more difficult by aggressive Chiefs of Staff in Washington desiring immediate answers to these major questions. Waging war is never easy, especially when your job resembles anything close to Patterson's; military genius is essential, as well as diligent working capability. In fact, at times the group would be "locked in" the bunker and "not allowed to leave until the plans were settled." They were under the control of Brigadier General Bob Duke.

Logistical planning for the units to be deployed to Vietnam happened very quickly as Patterson, along with other planners from Japan, Okinawa, and Korea, achieved with merely six men what 200 planners were generally asked to accomplish. The moving of 300,000 men was strenuous, but finding necessary resources was one of the problems they were forced to solve. Already extremely undermanned, another obstacle in the way of the group's success was redundant and pointless questions coming from the Joint Chiefs of Staff and other concerned affiliates with the group. Perhaps the greatest obstacle was the constant ground attacks of the Vietcong, a group the American planners feared while busily "locked away" preparing for the arrival of American troops.

There was extreme urgency for this group to plan quickly. They only had 90 days to prepare for Secretary of Defense Robert McNamara's July 4th arrival in Vietnam with the Joint Chiefs of Staff. This led to twenty-hour days, with questions arising such as where Air Mobile Division units were to be placed, and where would this mass number of troops be lodged. After many long days and nights, the group somehow found a way to finish the task in time for the arrival of Secretary McNamara. Upon arrival, General Westmoreland briefed the group's decisions and plans to McNamara. Westmoreland told McNamara, "Sir, I recognize that you can not meet our requirements, or these units, with the forces now on hand in the United States. So you're going to have to call up Reserve forces, and you're going to have to do some tailoring of forces to meet our requirements." McNamara unfortunately responded to these remarks with, "I'm not going to recommend this plan because of the current political situation [election in the United States]." Patterson saw this response as "the beginning

of the downward spiral in Vietnam." He believes a lack of dedication from American politicians regarding Vietnam was the greatest factor in America's failure.

After a thirty-day furlough, Patterson came back to Vietnam in 1966 commanding a support battalion of the 25th Infantry Division from Hawaii.

During this run in Vietnam, Patterson spent

Engineering Battalion constructing a bridge in Korea

time in Cu Chi. Famous for a complex Vietnamese-built system of underground construction, these tunnels were outfitted with extraordinary underground hospitals, R & R areas, recreation halls, and war planning facilities. Not unlike underground metro-trains in modern cities, Vietnamese living in the region for more than thirty years before the war found refuge from the harsh action above by burrowing beneath the Earth's surface. From January to May, Patterson and his troops were forced to find these well-hidden tunnels within the Hobo Woods to eradicate their adversary. Patterson speaks fondly of pioneering "tunnel rats" who volunteered to search for these tunnels. These men had high casualty rates, but they were instrumental in destroying the tunnels which had proved invaluable to the Vietnamese.

After commanding a support battalion in the 25th Infantry Division, Patterson was assigned to Headquarters U.S. Army Vietnam as assistant to

Bob shaking hands with Korean Commander

Brigadier General Frank Miller, the Deputy Chief of Staff for Plans and Operations. "Six months in this job taxed all my talents as a staff officer." Subsequently, he attended the Command and Staff College at Fort Leavenworth, Kansas, and was assigned to the staff of the Deputy Chief of Staff for Logistics in the Pentagon. As an officer on the Army Staff, working directly for Lieutenant General Jean Engler, the DCSLOG, he again faced numerous challenges.

On the humorous side, Patterson once received a letter sent to President Richard Nixon from a concerned mother. She wanted to know "why her son couldn't bring a dog back home which had saved his life during the Vietnamese War." Nixon had a policy of a reply within 24 hours. Patterson admitted dogs played a major role in tracking the enemy through jungles and other various tasks, but dogs were left in Vietnam because they were likely to bring diseases back home against which Americans had no immunity. A blanket rule was made by the Department of Defense stating, "No dogs go home." Thus, Patterson was forced to answer this kind woman's question with the appropriate response. But this was not the end of the "dog drama." Some soldiers smuggled dogs into the United States at the war's end. A story in a Hampton Roads, Virginia, newspaper told of a soldier who found a random dog in Okinawa and decided to bring him home as a pet. In his position, Patterson was forced to deal with the issue. In order to solve this problem, he asked Major General Ray Conroy, a high-ranking official in his department, for an answer. Major Conroy was also the person who would sign the reply on President Nixon's behalf. A stern Conroy replied to Patterson's conundrum with the following. "Patterson, I want you to go around to the Navy, the Air Force, the Coast Guard, the Marines, and I want you to get their name in blood if they agree with this policy; they will *not* allow these dogs to come home." Patterson followed through. "It turned out the publicity surrounding the dog in Virginia was an error. The dog was *not* a war dog, but a pet. Thus, the DOD policy remained solid."

In 1970, Patterson left Washington for the Military Assistance Advisory Group China in Taiwan. As the J-4, his job related to an advisory position in both countries. The highlight of this portion of his service relates to when Nixon took a trip to Red China, causing "all sorts of consternation" in Taiwan. After a rough time with this group, Patterson was sent on his final run through Vietnam in 1972 as Senior Advisor to the First Area Logistics Command in Da Nang and Hue. Following this, he graduated from the Army War College in 1974. One year later, Patterson retired from active duty and served for ten years as the "big-daddy" of the Phoenix Union High School District Junior ROTC program.

Hollywood focuses on the infantrymen when it depicts its war heroes. Yet, how could the combat soldier survive without the infrastructure to house and transport him? Without team players fulfilling their role, there is no way a successful war could be carried out. From World War II through Vietnam, Colonel Robert Patterson provided the men proper housing in which to live and roads to move their equipment. A quiet, humble, and self-sacrificing soldier, Colonel Patterson brings honour to the men who served behind the scenes to guarantee the success of America's missions abroad.

Throughout his 30 years in the military, Patterson was supported every day by his wife Lou, a former Army Nurse whom he married in 1951 in Furth, Germany. Both were 1st Lieutenants at the time. "Her advice and assistance in every way was invaluable and helped in all diplomatic assignments outside the USA."

Bob's father, Robert W. Patterson, WWI

Vic Phillips

January 1951 - September 1974
Korea, U.S.

Five Star Horse

An Interview with Vic Phillips
By Carolina Nick

When Vic Phillips was thirteen years old, living in Washington D.C., he was interested in two things at the time. He was interested in playing tennis and interested in horseback riding. His parents couldn't afford to buy him his own horse so he rode a rental horse at the Meadowbrook Saddle Club and even took some equitation lessons. "One day the club manager said to me, 'I've got some good news for you. One of the club members…has this beautiful palomino (Buddy) out there in a big box stall.'" A few months earlier, the horse had broken its leg. At that time in 1941, if a horse had such an injury it would be put down. The man that owned the horse said, "Oh, no." So the horse was sent to the very best veterinarian hospital and they were able to fix his leg.

The horse's leg eventually healed and he could be ridden, but not very fast. Mr. Ashton, the club manager, said to the horse's owner, "We have a young boy here whom I've trained to ride, and if you'd like, he'd be happy to exercise Buddy." The owner said, "That would be great." Vic went to the saddle club once or twice a week. One particular Saturday Vic had been riding Buddy in Rock Creek Park and as they came back to the stables, he saw two men with Mr. Ashton standing outside the door. One of them was a tall, rather stately looking man with a Homburg hat and a grey suit. Vic wondered: Saturday? Grey suit? The other was an Army officer with many stars on his shoulders. As Vic and Buddy started to turn toward the stable, the man in the grey suit saw them and called out, "Buddy, Buddy, my boy." Vic realized Buddy knew this man. The horse's ears pricked up and he took off at a gentle trot. Vic got off the horse and stood back with Mr. Ashton. Buddy's owner said, "Well, we would like to stay longer, but we have to leave." So they came over and Mr. Ashton introduced Vic to the men. When they got into a large limousine, they said they were sorry they had to go back to work. The Army officer turned to Vic and commented, "I can see that you enjoy riding. Maybe sometime you could come over and ride at Fort Meyer with me."

The men drove away. When Vic got home, he remembered the men's names and told his parents. "I got to meet Buddy's owner and an Army officer that was with him." His father asked, "Oh, who was that?" With the innocence of a young boy, Vic responded, "Well, the man's name was Henry Stimson, and the Army officer was General George Marshall." His father pointed out the importance of these two men. "Mr. Stimson is the Secretary of War; General Marshall is the Chief of Staff of the United States Army."

Vic Phillips has always been close to the military, even as a child. His father, a purchasing manager, was an officer in the Corps of Engineers during World War I, and his mother was an Army nurse. When he was a "little bitty guy," in the afternoons his mother took him to Walter Reed Medical Center for the Retreat Ceremony when they lowered the flag. Vic got out of his walker and stood there "like little John Kennedy and saluted the flag as it came down." Vic became a proud member of the U.S. Air Force for 23 years and later pursued his dream of teaching.

Vic graduated college in June of 1950, just as the Korean War was beginning. He was in a National Guard unit and was sent to Fort Custer in Battle Creek, Michigan. Vic met his wife Ann, a senior at Michigan State University, on a blind date.

Vic applied for Air Force Officer Candidate School and became the O/C colonel and Group Commander of his class. As a Distinguished Graduate, Vic returned to Michigan, and proposed to Ann and "about fell over dead when she said yes." The two married in January of 1952 and embarked on a military career.

Vic went through flying school including navigation training in Texas, bombardier training in California, combat crew training in South Carolina, and survival school in Nevada. Bombardier training taught him to drop bombs using a piece of equipment called the Norden Bombsight, which helps the bombardier find where and when to drop a bomb, compensating for wind drift as well as the speed of the airplane. Survival school taught him what to do if he were captured. Being captured can't be replicated, but they can simulate what it's like to be captive. In this training, Vic was dropped off about ten miles from the base and had three days to get back. In the course there were aggressors with trained dogs trying to capture the men. Vic was one of the lucky ones to avoid capture. The unlucky ones who were captured were taken to a simulated POW camp, where they underwent a great deal of interrogation. "They

About to fly a mission in an RB-26 in Korea

told you ahead of time that if you were captured and taken to POW camp, there was one way to escape, but obviously they didn't tell you what it was; you had to find out. What it turned out to be is that they had these primitive johns… One of the holes there said Out of Order, and it was literally out of order and there was no sediment at the bottom of it. You could have gone down and out that way. I guess a couple of people discovered it. I wasn't captured, so I was able to get back without the experience."

After his training, Vic was "in a pipeline straight to Korea."

In May of 1953, Vic began flying combat missions, but then got grounded for a month due to a severe ear infection. He was flying in RB-26 aircraft, a reconnaissance bomber, to photograph the military installations in North Korea. They took pictures of areas and would decide if there were places, such as railroad-marshaling yards, that were worth bombing. Bomb damage assessment (BDA) was yet another job that included flying over an area that had been bombed and assessing the amount of damage that had been done. "We flew several classified missions." Vic's outfit, the 12th Tactical Reconnaissance Squadron, was able to complete the photographing of every major target in North Korea in the two nights before the end of hostilities, and received the Presidential Unit Citation for their hard work. After the war ended on July 27,1953, Vic and his crew flew combat-ready missions over South Korea, where there were North Korean guerillas in the mountains who shot at them. "We got shot at almost as much after the war was over as we did during the war."

During December of 1953, Vic returned home. Later on in January of 1954, he flew a type of triphibian aircraft called an SA-16 until his annual physical rolled around in May. Vic's hearing was checked multiple times. Unfortunately, his was below minimums and he was grounded from flying. At this point, he was faced with two options. He could either leave the Air Force or stay as a career officer in an administrative position. He made up his mind to apply for Air Force ROTC, Reserve Officer Training Corps. He was accepted and taught at the University of Connecticut for three years. He found he loved teaching. This was also where Vic and his wife Ann completed their Master's Degrees: his in Business and hers in Education.

In 1958, Vic was assigned to the headquarters of Air Force ROTC, part of a major air command called Air University, located at Maxwell AFB near Montgomery, Alabama. There he wrote a training manual, and two years later, "The clouds opened up and God said to me, 'You are blessed,'" when Vic became the aide to the two-star general who was vice commander of AU. This was done with the help of his good friend Ed Ellis. Ed, a superb fighter pilot, whom he had met in combat crew training, "has this great huge Alabama smile from ear to ear" and was like an older brother to Vic. The two-star general, Troup Miller, Jr., was later promoted to three stars and became the commander of Air University. For Vic, being the aide and executive

1st Lt. Vic Phillips with Major Ed Ellis

assistant to this man was "four years of heaven on earth… My boss had an idea that I was on track to become a general, and he was disappointed when I told him I wanted to go to the Air Force Academy to teach." He reminded him, "Vic, if you do, that may close the door to stars." Vic responded, "General, I don't really want stars; I want to teach. I love to teach."

Vic made up his mind and decided to apply for the faculty at the Air Force Academy in Colorado Springs. He was accepted, but wanted to get his doctorate before he went.

One always thinks that in management you should go to Harvard or UCLA… I talked to friends of mine who had gone to Harvard…and they said, "You don't want to go to Harvard. Living there for families in the Cambridge-Boston area is absolutely awful. Try and find a really good school in a small college town." Turned out to be Indiana University. The doctoral program is modeled after Harvard's. It's a similar program, which means you work your fanny off, except that you do it in a nice college town where your family has a lot of fun and you do too. At the time we had the last of our four children so living conditions were important.

In three years, Vic completed the course work, oral/written exams, and his dissertation. He left with degree in hand and the family was off to Colorado Springs in 1967.

For Victor Phillips, the Air Force Academy was the highlight of his career. He felt it was the most fabulous assignment he ever had, other than working for General Miller, "who was just the greatest guy in the world."

It was an experience that if you love to teach, you walk in the classroom each day and here are a bunch of young men, superb athletes, in great physical condition, good brains, always prepared with their lessons, very respectful, but not fawning or obsequious in any way. One has the perspective of students as being either stupid jocks or geeks, and there's not much in between. There are at the Academy… I mean, these guys are tough and they are in good shape. At the same time they are expected to perform in class. Now this is not Basket Weaving 101… These are courses in English, history, management, thermodynamics. We have an expression in the military: when things go so well, you say you back up to the pay table; you're almost ashamed to get paid for doing something as wonderful as this.

He was also faculty adviser to the Academy's Varsity Wrestling Team, "an enjoyable additional duty."

Vic was at the Air Force Academy for five years and got promoted to full colonel. During this period, Ann also completed her Masters in Library Science at the University of Denver.

Unfortunately, Vic could not stay at the Academy. In the Air Force at that time, he needed to move on to another colonel's assignment. When asked where he wanted to go, he said he didn't know. He was offered the job of base commander in Vietnam but refused. "I don't want any part of it, because I'm getting out as soon as I can to go teach at a college some place. Give it to some bright colonel who is bucking to become a brigadier general; let him have the experience." He was offered a position instead at the Industrial College of the Armed Forces in Washington, D.C. because he is a D.C. native. He replied, "That's why I don't want to go there. I know what it's like. The city now is not the city I remember growing up in."

Vic eventually ended up as a faculty member at Air War College back at Maxwell Air Force Base in Alabama. He was there for two years and then retired. That was the end of his military career. In 1974, he was "enthralled by Miami [University] because it was the so-called elite public university in the state of Ohio and the second oldest university west of the Appalachians, founded in 1809. Vic liked what he saw at Miami University. He was offered a job as a full professor and chairman of the Management Department in the School of Business Administration. His wife Ann got a job at Miami as the head of the Department of Humanities and Fine Arts in the library; she also directed three branch libraries. Despite the fact that Miami was a "more homogenous group" in comparison to the "diversified" group of students at the Air Force Academy, Vic and his wife enjoyed their fourteen-year careers at Miami University.

By the time Vic and Ann left Miami University in 1988, they had turned sixty and were getting tired of the Ohio weather. They decided to move to Scottsdale, Arizona. Their children, three sons and one daughter, were almost all through school so Vic and Ann decided they "could afford to hang up the teaching materials and working days. We always wanted to retire when we were sixty in order to travel and to get away from rigid schedules." Vic and Ann got just what they wanted, traveled the globe, and "managed not to let too much moss grow under our feet or in our brains."

Finally, asked what he is most proud of in his life, Vic is quick to answer: his family. "My parents were devoted to each other and to me. My wife of 55 years is an attractive, personable, devoted, highly disciplined, and organized person who while raising four children also completed two Master's degrees and maintained a great sense of humor. We have never had an argument. Among our children and their families are a former NCAA All-American swimmer, a nationally ranked equestrienne, a holder of a Masters in Educational Technology, and Ironman Triathlon finisher, and a twice-decorated Navy veteran of the Gulf War. They hold degrees from Northwestern, Harvard, Miami, and Arizona State, and enjoy a modicum of success in accounting, sales, teaching, and medicine. They are my heroes. I must also include our three grandchildren, all of whom, like their parents, have an interactive love of family."

Bill Rintelmann

September 1952 - July 1955
Ft. Sill, Oklahoma;
Ft. Carson, Colorado

Target of Opportunity

An Interview with Bill Rintelmann
By Bethany Bennick and Barbara Hatch

William Fred Rintelmann—Bill to his friends—was a graduate of Arizona State College in Tempe, sporting a polished new Bachelors Degree in Psychology. Upon completion of the ROTC program he and seventeen fellow cadets were commissioned as officers and second lieutenants in the Army Field Artillery. He reported to Fort Sill, Oklahoma, for the "Battery Officer's Course," which included an intense sixteen weeks of training in field artillery. Bill learned quite a few things there and became particularly fond of howitzers. His sixteen weeks of "fun" came to a close and Bill's class, Number 56 at Fort Sill, finally got to walk down Battery Street. The war with Korea was still going on in 1952 and every officer in Bill's class held his breath with high hopes of not being shipped off to Yokohama, Japan. The time had come for class orders to be read aloud; all ears perked forward.

The first officer to be called forward to receive his orders was sent to Germany. "When that happened, everyone whooped and hollered because that meant not going directly to Korea as a total class." Although more than half his class did retain orders to go to Korea, Bill had unknowingly received his "target of opportunity" when assigned to Fort Carson, Colorado, home of the 538th Field Artillery Battalion. Bill's new life had arrived. Placed as a second lieutenant, Bill got the duty of teaching basic trainees how to handle grenades. This was his first encounter as a teacher and one that ultimately led to his passion.

Standing in front of a bunch of "basics" sounds like a challenge in itself; teaching raw recruits to operate hand and rifle grenades was another matter. Anything could go wrong at any moment, but Bill met this challenge. Next followed work with field artillery. Battery test after battery test was conducted and unit proficiency was all that mattered. Three firing batteries with howitzers, a supply company, and headquarters company constituted a battalion. When an airplane spotted a target from above, he called in a fire mission. It was the job of the battery to get their six howitzers off the road, line up the muzzles parallel to each other, and locate their exact map position by doing a survey. Triangulating the target using survey techniques, they then called to a forward observer on a hill or in an airplane, who brought in the fire mission. The target is called the registration point. The men "bracketed" the target when shells landed long or short, or to the right or left. The forward observer could call to adjust the fire. Not only did Bill have to teach trainees this difficult skill, he had to do it with an aptitude of such accuracy that it could be completed in less than 55 minutes with 155-millimeter howitzers! To be able "to get off the road, into an area where you get your howitzers lined up, do the survey, register your fire on the registration point, and then hit the target of opportunity" is something to boast about.

Bill's good fortune was escalating. His battery had set a new record for accuracy and speed in the 5th Army. Now Bill's very own "target of opportunity" was in quick pursuit. He was asked to write a program of instruction for "Artillery Chiefs," Master Sergeants who run the firing batteries as noncommissioned officers. Bill set up a school and wrote the program of instruction. He ran the school for about eighteen months while continuing to be involved in training exercises. He also acted as an "umpire" to evaluate battalions' firing ability during training exercises. This is when Bill decided he "really enjoyed teaching" even though much of his work in the Army was in the field, with only a few classroom activities.

During his third year of active Army service, college applications were sent out. He had a Bachelors Degree in Psychology and had done some work in Speech Pathology. Bill was proud to have been accepted into one of his primary choice schools, Indiana University, a starting point for an education that led to a Masters and PhD in Speech Pathology from IU, combined with a PhD in Audiology. Bill went on to teach at the University of North Dakota, Northwestern, Michigan State, the University of Pennsylvania, and Wayne State University, from where he retired in 1995 as Audiology Department Chair in the School of Medicine.

So how does this education connect to his service years? Besides discovering a love for teaching, Bill also developed hearing loss from exposure to prolonged artillery fire. At that time the Army did not have a hearing conservation program, though the Air Force had developed one in 1956. While on the faculty at Northwestern, Bill taught Army and Air Force officers about military hearing conservation so they could start programs in their respective branches. According to Bill, the first step is assessing the noise level in a work environment with sound level meters, then testing soldiers to create baseline levels of their hearing prior to exposure. Remedies included earplugs or muffs. Believe it or not, even yawning offered minimal protection. As an audiologist, Bill learned that two muscles in the middle ear contract to attenuate loud noise by four or five decibels. Unfortunately technology did not arrive early enough to help Bill. By the time he was 25, he had worse hearing than a 70-year-old! No doubt cannon and howitzer fire contributed to this diminution.

Though work in Audiology and teaching consumed much of our interview—and 40 years of Bill's life—we asked him to explain more about training Army artillerymen. The first questions related to the difference between hand and rifle grenades. Most of us have seen GIs toss hand grenades in World War II films. Rifle grenades, on the other hand, are fired from the end of a rifle for greater distance and accuracy. A 2-by-4 window was the target. Bill's group never had any accidents with grenades, but he recalls one serious accident with howitzers that took

Bill with 105-mm howitzer at Fort Sill

place when he was at Fort Carson. To fire a 155-mm howitzer, the shell and powder bags are rammed into the howitzer by opening the breech block. Should the gun misfire, requiring the officer in charge to open the breech block, the powder can ignite when exposed to air. This happened to one lieutenant during training. "When he turned the screw to open it, it ignited, and the breech block just tore him in half… It literally went right through him. Thus, he did not survive." Normally it is the Executive Officer's job to open the breech block after a misfire; on the few occasions Bill had to perform that duty, there were no problems.

Every lieutenant in training spends time as a forward observer. Bill was no exception. At times he directed fire from a hill; sometimes he plotted targets

Bill with survey equipment at Fort Carson

from the air. He admits that in combat the forward observer is really in the "hot seat," since he is the first person the enemy will take out in order to cripple their ability to direct artillery fire. He also worked in the Fire Direction Center with maps used to plot the targets to be fired upon.

The Mountain and Cold Weather Training Command used the smaller 75-mm howitzers, called "mule pack howitzers" because they were easier to haul up the mountains. It took six mules to haul the gun and all the ammunition. Moving larger howitzers was a challenge, and most are moved by tractors getting about "four miles to a gallon." Training used live ammunition, another expense. On occasion they fired 75-mm howitzers to save the cost of larger shells. Captain Rex Welty, Bill's battery commander, referred to firing these weapons as "the sport of kings." He laughed. "Where else can you have so much fun shooting at targets and spending hundreds and hundreds or thousands of dollars on this sport?" Helicopter pilots we interviewed have been known to make similar comments about flying "big expensive toys." According to Bill, if the weather were decent

and there was no real enemy to contend with, "it was fun."

We wondered how the locals felt about the constant noise this "fun" brought to the community. The 280-mm guns were so large they had to be fired from one range to another across the Post. No doubt that put out quite a bang. One 280-mm shell landed on the Post, but fortunately didn't kill anyone. The officer in charge immediately had orders cut for Korea; he was gone in two days. But most residents near Fort Sill accepted the inconvenience because the base was the "lifeblood" of the town of Lawton, Oklahoma. The military provided jobs. The Army base at Fort Carson, on the other hand, was quite a distance from Colorado Springs. Bill never heard too many complaints.

Bill enjoyed his years in the Army but did not make it a career. Teaching pulled him in another direction, though his work in Audiology helped him maintain contact with the armed forces. He extended his two-year Army commitment to three to give himself time to make a decision and honored his promise to stay with the Reserves for ten years. His teaching schedule interfered with Reserve training until he switched his MOS from Field Artillery to Civil Affairs and Military Government. Ironically, one of their simulations as a training exercise was taking over a Middle Eastern country.

Bill stays in touch with a few of the officers he trained in the hearing conservation program, but since he's been retired for eleven years, he has lost touch with most of the men. He admits that computers have opened up new applications in measuring electrical activity in the human auditory system, technology he wishes was available in the '50s. Locally, he was on the Planning and Zoning Commission of Carefree for six years and is a docent at the Cave Creek Museum. He is active in Kiwanis and his church. But he has not forgotten his time in the Army. Learning to relate to people while maintaining discipline for 127 enlisted men in an artillery firing battery who "didn't want to be there" helped him become a better teacher. His time in the Army "was a life experience that I would not have given up. Other than the fact that I have this hearing loss, I never regretted spending three years in the Army. I thought it was a good experience."

A positive target of opportunity.

Cold War

The "cold" split between two former World War II partners, the United States and the Soviet Union, was a struggle caused by jealousy over world influence. It was a "war" of shifting powers and frightening strength, showcasing the advancements in weapons and warfare and paving the way for much of what we know of war today and where it is headed tomorrow. Sadly it was an unseen war to many, "fought" beneath the ground in missile silos and under the sea in stealthy submarines. With the fall of the Soviet Union, one asks if this "war" is over. More than that, how did it happen? What pressures and dangers were the soldiers faced with in this "battle"? Here are those stories, those that you will not find in the textbook, that present the good and bad as only the men involved could relate.

Kevin Hildebrandt

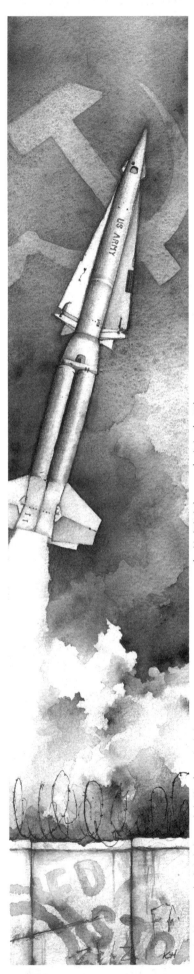

Len Lai

June 1959 - July 1989
Germany, Korea, Taiwan, U.S.

Oh, the Places You Will Go
An Interview with Len Lai
By Kevin Hildebrandt and Barbara Hatch

Childhood is the time when our morals are formed and what we believe in becomes steadfast. What is learned and experienced during these young years is what carries a person to who he is going to become. This was the case for Leonard Lai. He came to serve just after the Korean War, but this was not his first experience with war.

As a Hawaiian native, Len grew up during World War II; he was only five years old when Pearl Harbor was attacked. On December 7, 1941, his family had just left Lanikai on their way to see a doctor in Honolulu when they heard the news. Their beach house was located between two military air bases, "both of which were attacked."

On that particular morning I had gotten sick and my parents took me into Honolulu to see my uncle to get some prescriptions. When we got there, we could see the airplanes buzzing around, the smoke and everything else. My uncle and my father decided: maneuvers. By the time we got to the pharmacy, however, the pharmacist said, "We're under attack. I have a son at Pearl Harbor and we are being attacked by the Japanese."

It just so happened that in crossing the island from the beach house in Lanikai to their home in Honolulu, the Lai family missed the destruction at Bellows Army Air Base and Kaneohe Naval Air Station on the east side of the island as well as at Pearl Harbor on the west. The war with Japan had begun. The United States had finally entered a war that began in Europe with the invasion of Poland in 1939 and in Asia with Japanese incursions in China. When police stopped the Lais from returning to their beach house where they were hosting an office party luau where 100 guests had already gathered, the family convinced the police they were returning home and were allowed to pass.

Lanikai's gentle beaches made it a likely target for Japanese invasion. The military subsequently quilted the beach with concertina and barbed wire. To get to the beach from their beach house, Len's family had to attach serial numbers with American flags on their boat in order to pass through the checkpoints. They were under martial law. Security police would stop a movie to spot-check IDs. All the paper money in Hawaii had the words "Hawaii" overprinted on it in case the Japanese captured the islands and got their hands on the currency. Blackouts made night driving hazardous. Headlights were hooded, exposing only a tiny sliver of light by which to navigate; fortunately the speed limit was a mere 35 mph so accidents were few. Gasoline and food were rationed like in the U.S., but from a child's perspective, life didn't seem that bad. Kids sold war bonds and found many aspects of the war adventurous. Len and his young "entrepreneurial" friends sold coconuts for a dime to officers and enlisted men at the two rest centers near Lanikai.

On Hawaii, in their serene spot on the beach, the Lais played host to many Marines, offering their private facilities for them to use. In return, the Marines, who did not suffer from rationing, offered their steaks and delicious meals in exchange for beachfront barbeque equipment and bath houses. These groups came and left but each left a lasting impression. Some Marines even sent back souvenirs from the war.

I can recall one day an irate father came to talk to my dad and said his daughters apparently had asked for some souvenirs, and somehow in the mail, got delivered to their house a package. In it was human ears, and apparently these guys had cut the ears off dead Japanese soldiers, I guess, and shipped them.

It was amazing these "souvenirs" had arrived to the young girls' homes for at the time the entire island was under strict rules and regulations on what they could or could not do. The mail was censored, but somehow these Marines had found a loophole. When the angry father approached Len's father, he replied, "Well, what do you expect me to do? These are Marines, and your daughters asked for souvenirs and that's what they got."

Natives of Hawaii were often criticized for looking like the Japanese. So many Hawaiians were of Japanese descent, there surfaced a lot of hatred among the Americans. Americans of Japanese descent on the west coast of the United States were put in internment camps. Locking up Hawaiians of Japanese

descent was impossible. Where are you going to put them? In the center of the island? On a boat? The businessmen on the islands convinced the military governors of Hawaii these people were Hawaiians and loyal; they were not Japanese sympathizers.

All during my school years growing up, you know, we had kids of Japanese ancestry in school with us the whole time, and nobody thought anything about it. I mean, nobody ever really questioned their loyalty. I mean, these are kids. In Hawaii, you can tell. I can meet a person of Asian ancestry and pretty much say, "Japanese, Chinese, Koreans," just because I have been around them all the time. So no, I was not given any kind of special treatment because I was an Oriental. I wasn't Japanese.

With Kaneohe Air Station close by, Len went to school with military kids. His father worked as a logistician on loan to the military. Military kids "came and went" as their fathers were transferred, but local kids stayed. This was their home. Len remembers the McCool brothers, whose father was an Admiral but was never at home; luckily he survived. Len's survival might have been less sure when he and a friend found some unexploded ordnance in an empty lot on their way home from school and decided to take it home. When one of the neighbor ladies saw them and began "screaming her head off," the boys dropped the bomb and ran. Len laughs when he recalls his last assignment at the Pentagon as staff officer in charge of unexploded ordnance disposal. Ironically, exposure to that bomb in Hawaii as a child was "the closest I'd ever got to actually trying to detonate anything like that."

Growing up surrounded by military in a wartime atmosphere, Len went into the United States Army as a 2nd Lieutenant in infantry after graduating from the University of Hawaii's senior ROTC program. He had been working "part-time" 40 hours a week in college while 2nd lieutenants in the Army made $222.30 a month. When he was commissioned, he earned less than he did before he entered the Army. So began his long list of assignments and lengthy resumé in his thirty years of service. He served in Germany when the Berlin Wall went up, in Korea through three coups, and in Taiwan during the

Vietnam War. Fortunately, "I never had a shot fired at me in anger that I know of."

Len happened to be in Germany when the Berlin Wall went up. He had just transferred out of the infantry. While going to work one day he saw his old unit, 1st Battle Group of the 18th Infantry, going down the autobahn to relieve the Berlin garrison. He had been an infantry rifle platoon leader and a weapons platoon leader and then had just been "detailed back" to the Ordnance Corps to become operations officer of an ordnance maintenance company when relations with the Soviets heated up because of the wall. He heard of the incident at his base in Mannheim. There had been practice alerts regularly, but on the day the wall went up, members of his old unit were informed, "We are rolling to Berlin as soon as daylight. And we're going 'locked and loaded.' We will not stop at any checkpoint.' So the units rolled right into Berlin. The Soviets knew they were coming. It was no big secret. I mean, they rolled down the autobahn. The Soviets just waved them right through and they went right into Berlin, and they reinforced the Berlin Brigade." Len did not assist in this operation but he saw them go by. Controls were tighter for all Americans stationed in Germany as they were constantly on the lookout for Soviet "liaison plates." Though these "accredited" Soviet troops were assigned to Germany, American GIs still had to report their movement. "You couldn't stop them, but you were supposed to report where they were. And these were overt intelligence people. I mean, they wore uniforms, and they weren't spies. They were spies, but they were in uniform so you knew what they were doing." Going into Berlin was difficult so Len and the other GIs skied in Austria and Italy instead. For German natives, life changed more dramatically. When they tried to send canned milk to their relatives in East Germany, the soldiers at checkpoints punched holes in the tops of the cans. "I don't know whether it was just to see what was in it or it was just for spite, nobody knows, but they could never get a can of milk through the postal system or the delivery system to their relatives in East Germany." Len never did see the Wall.

In Korea, Len "wore three hats." He was part of a combined Republic of Korea (ROK)/US Forces Command, U.S. Forces Korea, and the 8th Army. Among his other jobs in his three tours was defending the Demilitarized Zone (DMZ) between North and South Korea. He was also the Chief of Ammunition Division, in which his job was to check every ammunition site that stored U.S.-owned ammunition, including the Korean storage sites.

> [That] was kind of exciting because we had to fly in by helicopter, and usually the helicopter pad was on some flat place on the top of the mountain. And the ammunition storage area was down below. So the steps carved on the side of the mountain were pretty small. Now, one other thing that they liked to do was I guess a challenge to the Americans. They liked to run down the mountain, and of course you were expected to run down the mountain and run back up the mountain when you were through. I never broke a leg, but I came close a couple of times.

Naturally the South Koreans were always on the alert for North Koreans crossing the DMZ, trying to get into Seoul. Sometimes they would dig tunnels. What made it difficult was that even the South Koreans could not always tell the difference between a North and South Korean. There was no significant change in dialect, they might be in Western clothes, and of course they looked alike. Any soldier who discovered a tunnel or captured an infiltrator became an instant hero and received a cash award, even though it was the duty of the South Korean military to catch the intruder.

During his tours in Korea there were three coups so eventually it became routine. The first time, President Park Chung Hee was assassinated and a military regime took over. "Actually, the head of the Korean CIA took over. And then they had another coup and they threw *him* out. And President Chun Doo Hwan took over. So there were shots fired." Len lived right up against the fence line of the Ministry of National Defense, so the military compound in Yongsan was right next to the Ministry of National Defense. They had no warning whatsoever. They went to bed the night before and heard shots fired early the next morning, commenting, "'Oh, somebody's taking over.' Nobody knew who was doing what to whom. Obviously somebody was overthrowing the president, but nobody knew who was coming in." His work continued as usual even though there had been a change in the government.

They knew it was not North Koreans because they had seen South Korean tanks rolling down the street and they would have been awakened much earlier if there had been a North Korean invasion. There were a few new faces among their South Korean counterparts, a few men were relieved and never seen again, but not much else changed. Len was never involved in how the South Koreans disposed of North Korean infiltrators. That was a South Korean responsibility, not American.

Next it was on to Taiwan where Len spent two years supervising troops stripping down and overhauling equipment damaged in Vietnam to send it back into the war. The Taiwan Materiel Agency contracted with the Taiwanese military, with American staff expertise, to do the job. Taiwan had volunteered to send troops to Vietnam, but the Americans declined, preferring to have them provide support services instead. While rebuilding personnel carriers, trucks, and communications equipment (they didn't work on airplanes) to depot standards, resetting the odometers and the like, the men found all sorts of "souvenirs." Besides ammunition that had not been removed, they found flags and personal war memorabilia the GIs in Vietnam had left. Since it was impossible to return these items to the men in Vietnam, Len let the American maintenance men in Taiwan keep them. Len said that if it wasn't in their inventory, he didn't want to hear about it. Some items had most likely been taken off dead North Vietnamese or Viet Cong. Len did this job for two years.

Len was in Taiwan when Generalissimo Chiang Kai Shek died. His funeral cortège passed right in front of Len's house. With no military housing to speak of, Len and his family lived "on the economy." As part of Defense Command, he moved in "pretty high circles." Len's wife Diane got to meet Mrs. Chiang Kai Shek through the Wives Club and Len got to meet an Air Force 4-star who was Chairman of the Joint Chiefs of Staff, coincidentally also named Lai, who was convinced he and Len were related because their name shared the same Asian letter, or character. Len and Diane had quasi-diplomatic status with special license plates indicating their important role—plates Diane referred to as No Go To Jail plates. As such, they were not subject to the martial law regular troops had to endure. Len and Diane's two sons could ride their bikes up and down the streets when no one else was about. Fortunately the Taiwanese guards recognized the boys were American despite their Asian looks; they only spoke English. Besides, they were only 10 and 12 years old and carried American identification.

Tensions were fairly high in Taiwan while Len was there because mainland China would trade artillery rounds with some of Taiwan's outer islands. Whenever things would "get nervous," the U.S. 7th Fleet would sail up and down the channel separating the two Chinas until things would calm down. Though the United States is no longer the main protector of Taiwan and has recognized mainland China, the U.S. is still their primary source of armaments. While Len was there, the U.S. was already very cautious in providing equipment, "nothing long-range, everything was for defense, nothing offensive, nothing that would encourage them to actually attack the mainland of China."

Finally Len had two assignments with the Pentagon. The first time he worked for the Office of the Chief of the Army Reserve as a logistician. He told the General he had only been active Army, never Reserve, and thus lacked experience, to which the General replied, "Well, this will be an experience. This is the way you're going to learn about Reserves. Get out there in the field and talk to these guys and find out what they do." Len enjoyed it. He got promoted so he felt he must have done a good job. His second job was Chief of Missile and Munitions Division in the Department of the Army, Office of the Deputy Chief of Staff of Logistics, now called G-4, in charge of the missiles and munitions "from birth to death, from the acquisition to the demilitarization." They would monitor the path and status of the missile or munition from its design to its disposal.

When he retired, he "floated a couple resumés," but nothing interesting emerged so he retired and traveled. Diane got bored so went back to work. Len decided to spend time volunteering. Locally he is on the board of the Desert Foothills Library in Cave Creek, Arizona, in charge of the Veterans History Project; on the board of the local chapter of the Association of the U.S. Army; and on the Veterans Service Committee of the Phoenix Elks Lodge. He returns to Hawaii less frequently as his immediate family has passed away; his children live here in the States.

Overall, Len's service totaled 30 years of active duty. He had two assignments to Europe, four in Asia, two at the Pentagon, and one in Hawaii that got curtailed. He retired as a full colonel with outstanding awards: two Legions of Merit, two Defense Meritorious Service Medals, one Army Meritorious Service Medal, and three Army Commendation Medals. It is amazing the different viewpoints and observations he was able to get from growing up as a child in Hawaii during the attacks on Pearl Harbor, observing the changes in Germany as the Berlin Wall went up, witnessing three coups d'état in Korea, and being the only one of his family in that generation to remember it all. This insight from Mr. Lai is an unbelievable account of how one man could be in so many critical places at exactly the right moment to take in the changes in the world.

We thank Len for sharing his story and continuing to serve the community as a volunteer. "These were the times that I grew up in, and I just had a memory of World War II that I probably will never forget." But still in all, "retired life is good."

Interviewer Kevin Hildebrandt and Len Lai after the interview

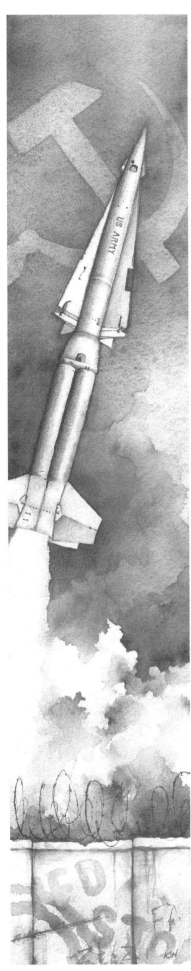

Hugh Shoults

March 1944 - June 1972
Japan, Vietnam, U.S.

Pulling the G Forces
An Interview with Hugh Shoults
By J. Caitlin Campbell

The first time I went solo in the T-6, I was going to do a three-turn spin from 8,000 feet. When I stopped my spin recovery and pulled back on the stick, I pulled back too hard and fast. I blacked out so badly that I did not know where I was. I had pulled too many G forces. When I started coming to, I heard this noise in my ear. I was wondering where I was, and then I realized I was in the airplane. I forced myself to see the altimeter in front of me and heaved a sigh of relief because I was back up to 8,000 feet by that time.

Hugh Shoults joined the Army Air Corps during World War II. On his birthday, October 29, 1943, he went to Fairchild Air Force Base and took the test to enter the aviation cadet program. Since he volunteered, he was drafted into the Air Corps. He was specifically interested in the Air Corps because his brother Lee was an aviation cadet at that time, learning to fly. In May of '44, Hugh's brother completed his pilot training and was commissioned a second lieutenant.

Hugh wanted to follow in his brother's footsteps, but by 1944 there were so many pilots in training, it was difficult to get into the aviation program. So after basic training in Amarillo, Texas, Hugh went into the electronics program at Truax Field in Madison, Wisconsin. He specialized in radio mechanics to learn code as a radio operator. From there he went to Chanute Field in Rantoul, Illinois, for more electronics. During the winter of 1944 and 1945 he was at Boca Raton, Florida, training to be a radar mechanic.

Hugh was shipped out to Williams Air Force Base near Phoenix, Arizona. As a radio and radar mechanic, the idea was to train navigators and bombardiers to use radar. Victory in Europe had just been declared so the big emphasis was on bombing Japan. Hugh did not have time to do much training, because three months later the war in Japan was over, effective August 14, 1945.

Hugh stayed at Williams Air Force Base for another year until he was discharged in June of 1944. He spent a couple years trying to find out what he really wanted to do, working at a logging camp and for Western Electric as an electrician and equipment installer. After those two companies went out on strike at different times, he decided it was time to go to college. He attended Washington State College, which later became Washington State University. He intended to take Air Force ROTC and go back into the Air Force, so later on that year he joined the Air Force Reserve. When the Korean War started in June of 1950, he was just entering his senior year, but he had already received his reserve commission as a second lieutenant. Upon graduation in June of 1951, he was supposed to be called to active duty, but he applied to navigators' school because his eyes weren't good enough for pilot training.

On October 7, 1951, Hugh married his wife Betty, whom he had met a couple years earlier in Oakesdale, Washington, where his brother Lee got married. Betty had been working in a local cafe and made him a milkshake. She started college in September of 1950 and he'd see her around campus once in a while, but they never dated until he graduated from college. About three weeks after the wedding, he got orders to go to pilot training at Marana Air Base near Tucson. By then Hugh's eyes had improved and were almost 20/20— from "reading less," he says.

The Marana airport today is not the original training base. The original facility is a base the CIA uses for special operations and also storing airplanes. For a long time, Marana was a maintenance repair depot for many airplanes that needed special repairs. Hugh was at Marana before it became a CIA base. At Marana, Hugh had basic pilot training. He arrived there the weekend of Veterans Day, thinking he had to be there before that date, but since Veterans Day came either on a Friday or Monday at that time, he arrived several days before the class started. He and Betty lived in the back part of a house belonging to a very nice couple in Tucson, Al and Vicki Carrillo.

In training, Hugh started out in the AT-6, also called the Texan. He'd flown in the back seat previously because his brother had taken him up on his flights. Now, Hugh was in the front seat, and to him it looked like an awfully big airplane. He was required to solo somewhere between 20 and 25 hours; he soloed about 21 hours. Each time he went flying, he was supposed to do spins, and that was when he had his blackout incident. Needless to say, he never pulled back on the stick that hard again. But each

time he went solo he did at least a three-turn spin, and he was supposed to have done 30 spins by the time he graduated. He completed a lot more than that. Hugh also did aerobatics during training to learn how the airplane performed. He did maneuvers such as the lazy eight and a barrel roll. Hugh only blacked out once during all his years as a pilot, thanks to a body maneuver he learned to do. He tightened his stomach muscles so the blood didn't all go down to his feet, which can cause a blackout. The Air Force later developed the G-suit, which pressurizes around the legs to keep the blood in the upper body. The planes Hugh started out in weren't pressurized, but later on, as he got into jets, they were, since they flew much higher. A pilot can ascend to 14,000 feet without oxygen, but normally he stays somewhere below 12,000 feet.

From Marana, part of Hugh's class went on to fly multi-engine airplanes, but those who went on to fly fighter jets, like Hugh, were assigned to Williams Air Force Base. There he flew T-6s for another 20 or 30 hours of flying time and then transitioned to the F-80, which was a single-engine and single-seat jet airplane. He had at least two or three flights in that, prior to going solo in the T-33 jet. Finally he went on to the T-33 two-seat jet training plane with an updated fuel control system that was a much more comfortable airplane to fly.

Hugh graduated from Williams just before Christmas of 1952. His wife Betty was pregnant and due in February. Not wanting to spend all his leave time, he went back to Williams Air Force Base after two weeks' vacation. Some of his class at Williams were going to Nellis Air Force Base for training in the F-86, but he went to Luke Air Force Base for gunnery training. When he first reported to Luke, they had so many pilots going through training, they were automatically held back two weeks to enter another class. With the baby due in February, Hugh approached the colonel to see if he could get held back another class and go home when the baby arrived. The colonel agreed, and Hugh went home. His son was born March 5, 1953.

The class Hugh entered at Luke was the first class that didn't go directly to Korea as planned. While at Luke, training consisted of formation flying, strafing targets with fifty-caliber machine guns, dropping practice bombs at different angles, and shooting rockets into targets at a place now called the Barry M.

Hugh with T33 at El Centro, California

Goldwater Air Force Range. Most of the time Hugh hit his targets. He shot rockets at a big panel.

> I remember that the instructor pilot said, "After you shoot your rocket, don't wait to see where your rocket goes because you're going to end up hitting the ground just after the rockets do." So, after you released your rockets, you broke off and climbed back up to altitude.

Firing the rockets and bombing took practice.

> Normally you fly to the range in a formation of four airplanes. Then you break formation and enter the bombing pattern. The gunnery/bombing pattern is similar to an airport traffic pattern. You enter on the downwind leg, turn base, and then turn final to line up with the runway or to sight on the target to fire your guns, rockets, or drop the bombs. When you complete the gunnery or bomb release, you pull up, turn crosswind, and then re-enter the pattern by turning downwind, and set-up for the next pass. The gun sight or bomb release sight is a reticle that reflects on the windscreen and may be adjusted for the type of weapon to be used. The target may be a circle on the ground for dropping the bombs or firing the rockets, or a large panel like a canvas sheet for shooting the guns.

Hugh never knew if he hit a bulls-eye because the targets weren't that accurate. The trainers simply told him if he hit the target or not.

Over the 4th of July, 1953, Hugh drove to Bergstrom Air Force Base in Texas to join the 27th Wing of the Strategic Air Command as a fighter bomber pilot flying the F-84G. There he took a course in celestial navigation. Supposedly during the Cold War, pilots would need this training to fly out to a target to bomb with a nuclear weapon.

During the Cold War, Hugh was never able to talk about his training. He attended nuclear indoctrination in Texas and Sandia, New Mexico, to learn how nuclear weapons operate, how they're designed, and their limits. He was there a little over a year, training in navigation and aerial refueling. He then converted to the F-84F, a special swept-wing version of the F-84G. He had gotten about 10 or 12 hours in the F-84F when he got orders to go to Japan.

In Japan, Hugh was stationed at Itazuke, which is near Fukuoka, on the southern island of Japan. He spent a year there before his wife came over to join him. After that year he came home and brought Betty, along with his three-month-old and the two-year-old sons, back to Japan. They traveled on an Army troopship, the *USS General Billy Mitchell*. Duty in Japan was nice for Hugh, but sometimes difficult for Betty since he was gone a lot of the time. He was on TDY (temporary duty) one week out of every 6 weeks. At that time he was a member of the 49th Fighter Bomber Group and the 7th Fighter Bomber Squadron, the "Secret 7th."

The 7th Fighter Bomber Squadron shared a base with another squadron of F-86Ds, which was an air defense type F-86 night fighter. Supposedly if the Russians came, the F-86Ds could shoot down the incoming Russian airplanes. The 49th Fighter Bomber Group was also composed of the 8th and 9th squadrons—the 9th at Misawa, in northern Japan, and the 8th near Nagoya. Hugh's 7th was at Itazuke. Hugh and his squadron practiced deployments, because if they ever had an alert, they would have to deploy to another base. That way, if the Russians came to bomb them, they wouldn't all be located at one base. So they practiced going to the different bases throughout Japan, and three or four in Korea. They also flew down to Kadena Air Base in Okinawa, or Clark Air Force Base in the Philippines.

Each of these places had a nearby bombing range to practice dropping 8-pound chunks of iron. When the bombs hit the ground, white smoke came up to indicate how near the pilot was to the bulls-eye.

During this time the Air Force had an exercise to evaluate the pilots' efficiency. The 80th squadron had also become part of the 49th group. In those four squadrons there were over 80 airplanes qualified to drop an atomic weapon, equivalent to a 20-kiloton atomic bomb. The bomb dropped on Hiroshima, called Fat Boy, was approximately 20 kilotons.

When Air Force Headquarters Team came to evaluate the 49th group, most of the airplanes in the four squadrons deployed to different bases throughout the Far East. The next morning the airplanes took off so they could fly a navigation route, descend and find a tanker, refuel, fly another navigation route, and arrive over the Tokyo radio beacon in five-minute intervals. As they would approach Tokyo radar, the pilot would request clearance to descend to the Tokyo bombing range. The descent was called a "tear drop" pattern. The pilot would start a let-down from 20,000 feet, flying outbound over Tokyo Bay. At 10,000 feet they would make a descending left turn and track back into the radio beacon and level off at 500 feet or below. As he passed over the beacon, he made a right turn onto the heading toward the bombing range.

At this time the pilot would set his switches for an automatic bomb release. He would locate the target, which was a white tower in the middle of the range. As the plane passed over the tower at 100 feet, the pilot would pull back on the control stick and hold a four G force to continue climbing up through the clouds. When the plane was at approximately 90° pointing straight up, the bomb would release and continue up to approximately 9,000 feet and then turn over and come back down and hit near the tower for a bull's-eye. The pilot would continue to fly with the four G force to complete one-

half a loop and roll out level at about 5,000 feet. This maneuver is called an Immelmann.

About every five minutes an airplane flew over the range. Out of 80 airplanes, only one or two didn't hit the target. With a 20-kiloton bomb, any bomb within 1,000 feet of the target would be considered close enough to be a bull's-eye. The Air Force rated the 49th Group a 10—the first time a group ever received such a high score. A 10 was considered perfect.

During the Cold War, each pilot had a target in some part of Russia or northern China, either an airfield or a factory on which they would release one of these atomic bombs. Each of them also had a secondary target, just in case they couldn't hit their primary one because of weather or some other complication. This was highly classified information at that time. Even Hugh's wife didn't know about it.

In the summer of 1956, Hugh took a peaceful trip to Bangkok. SEATO, or Southeast Asian Treaty Organization, was having a show-of-force exercise in Thailand. The 49th Group was invited to bring twelve airplanes for a fly-by. Hugh was one of the lucky four selected from his squadron to participate. He flew down to Kadena, where the four squadrons joined up, then on to Clark AFB in the Philippines. There were twelve airplanes scheduled to go to Bangkok, and four airplanes that were airborne spares, in case any of the original twelve had a problem and couldn't continue to Bangkok. On the way to Bangkok, after the airborne spares had turned around and gone back to Clark Air Force Base, three of the planes declared emergencies, including him. Hugh's flight commander, Bill Finkey, had a tip tank that wouldn't feed, and the one that wouldn't feed was getting heavy while the functional tank was getting light, making the airplane unable to fly correctly. Another pilot from the Ninth Squadron, "Blackie," had the same problem. Hugh had an oxygen leak, causing the high-pressure oxygen system to go down rapidly. Since they were flying at high altitude and needed oxygen, he had to declare an emergency.

It just so happened the air base they had to use was Nha Trang, in South Vietnam. The three of them landed, having no idea what kind of support they were going to receive or what was going to happen when they got there. Hugh was the third to land. He kept his engine going so he could talk on the radio to the airborne C-54 that was transferring communications between Hugh and other planes. Hugh told the C-54 what kind of support they needed. After Hugh shut down the airplane, a South Vietnamese officer approached his airplane and asked, "Parlez-vous Français?" When Hugh said he didn't, the officer got a big smile on his face, "because if I couldn't speak French, he figured I was probably a pretty good person." The Vietnamese were not too fond of the French.

Mr. and Mrs. Evans, representatives of the United States State Department from Seattle, Washington, were there to assist the South Vietnamese in agriculture, and they served Hugh, Bill, and Blackie a good meal and put them up in their servants' quarters. Hugh was taking a shower at 0700 the next morning when he heard an airplane. "I ran out and looked and yelled at Bill Finkey. I said, 'Bill, there's a C-119 in the traffic pattern coming to help us.' So we quickly got dressed and rushed down to the airfield." The ground crew mechanics were there, sure enough, with all the equipment they needed to get airborne. They pumped fuel into the planes and hooked up the JATO bottles, which are Jet Assist Takeoff containers that give the airplane extra thrust on a short runway. The mechanics fixed the oxygen leak in Hugh's airplane with a piece of hydraulic hose and filled the oxygen tank. At 1100 hours they were airborne. "I'm sure we surprised a lot of people because other types of airplanes had landed there and they were still parked along the side of the runway. But we were accustomed to this kind of support. I thought it was terrific that we were able to get out of there so quickly." Hugh flew to Bangkok to join up with the rest of the airplanes.

Colonel Gil Pritchard led the group, but he had lost his radio enroute and didn't know that three of his airplanes had suffered a forced landing. Consequently, when the planes joined up to make their landing, he only counted nine airplanes and had to wait until they landed to know what had happened. The next day they made their fly-by with twelve airplanes.

That night was a big banquet at the Thai presidential palace, which the 49th Group attended in their summer dress uniforms. In those days the president or prime minister of Bangkok was a five-star general. One of the generals in the Royal Thai Air Force had been at West Point with Colonel Pritchard, so General Toby escorted Hugh and his

fellow fighter pilots around; they were given first-class treatment. At the banquet, the 49th Group sat inside a large dining room, while the overflow of people was outside on the grass. The food was plentiful—a pig with an apple in its mouth, turkeys that had been cooked and sliced and put back together, and more. When the 49th Group went through the line, they got the top pieces off the turkey and first choice of the other foods. "It was an experience you just don't often get to participate in." Although Hugh couldn't tell Betty where he was going or what he was doing in Bangkok, she read it in the *Stars and Stripes* newspaper the next day. Even though it didn't mention Hugh's name, she knew where he had gone.

Meanwhile, Hugh and Betty and their children were living in an off-base house, since at the time there wasn't enough housing on base. The Japanese had built the house according to what the military wanted. The house didn't have central heating, though, so they had to keep warm by an oil tent stove in a sandbox, the kind you see in the TV program *M.A.S.H.* The baby had to be kept in the playpen so he wouldn't touch it and burn himself. Unfortunately the older boy fell against the stove and was burned badly on his arm.

The Shoultses lived in a row of five houses of five military families; all around them were two-story Japanese houses. Living off base, they didn't get much news or weather information. If a typhoon were coming, they wouldn't necessarily know it, but they could look across the street and see the Japanese men putting poles against their houses to keep them from blowing over—a sure sign a storm was coming.

Transportation while "living on the economy" was another issue. Betty had to contend with driving on Japanese roads. "We had this big American car over there; we obtained it after we were there. It was almost wider than the road, and it frequently rained. Their roads were not paved and they turned to mud—deep mud—and I got stuck. I had the two small boys in the car and me. The minute I got stuck, men came out from I don't know where, and they pushed and they pushed and they got me out of the mud. They laughed the whole time they were doing this, probably thinking, 'This dumb American woman got stuck!'"

Living in Japan wasn't as easy as living in the U.S., but it wasn't too hard because a lot of Japanese people spoke English there, says Betty. There was a well-stocked commissary where they bought most of their food because they couldn't eat the fresh food grown in the dirt fertilized with human "night soil." They didn't have a stove, but they cooked on a hot plate or on a kerosene camp stove.

When we were off base, we lost our oldest boy, who was two-and-a-half, or three. So we went down the street looking for him, and he was in one of the Japanese houses playing; they were making a lot of noise. And I knew he was in there because, lined up at the door, were all these Japanese *getas*, which were the wooden shoes with the built-up piece underneath. And then at the end of the line were these red leather corrective shoes.

Another challenge of Japanese housing for Betty and Hugh was the weather. In Japan, the walls were not connected and sealed to the floor, so when Betty looked, she could see it snowing between the walls and the floor, although none ever got inside. She plugged up the bottom space as best she could.

A third challenge was communicating with her Japanese maid, which everyone living on the base hired. "I had to have a maid—everybody has a maid there—and the maid I had off base couldn't speak English, so I'd write her a note. She'd take it home to her kids who were going to school learning English, and her little boy would read the note to her and she'd know what I wanted."

After living off base for about six to eight months, Betty and Hugh finally got an apartment on base. On base, Betty had a lot of time on her hands, so she taught swimming to children of the other dependents. Betty lived in Japan two years total before coming back to the U.S. Overall, they remember it as a good experience. "The Air Force really takes care of you." Hugh remained in the Air Force upon their return.

The Air Force was replacing its F-84G airplanes, which Hugh flew, with F-100Ds, supersonic fighter bombers. The 7th Fighter Bomber Squadron was the elite, the best squadron in the Far East, so the Air Force decided they were going to be the first ones to get the F-100D. Hugh's squadron then became the 80th Fighter Bomber Squadron, part of the 8th Fighter Bomber Group, which also had the 35th and 36th squadrons. The 80th Squadron mascot, a headhunter, looked like a wild native with bones stuck

in its ear. Hugh and his squadron sewed these patches on their uniforms to show they were part of the Headhunters—a fierce group. What also designated the 80th Squadron were the yellow stripes painted on the tail of their aircraft. During this assignment, Hugh practiced air refueling off the KB-50, an aerial tanker, following a process developed at the end of World War II. A drogue, or basket on a long hose, extended from a pod under the tanker wing. The probe on the fighter's tip tank is pushed into the drogue to receive the JP-4 jet fuel. This type of fueling was good for overseas flights, despite the fact that only two airplanes could get their fuel from the tanker at a time. Every once in a while there were accidents.

We had been flying the F-84Gs and were familiar with hooking up with the tankers. We

Headhunter's patch

didn't have any problem. But then, when the other two squadrons got their F-100s, they had never done any aerial refueling. So they were not accustomed to the peculiarities of hooking into the basket. The F-100D had an "afterburner" so that when more fuel was added and was re-lighted in the exhaust cone, the engine would have about four times as much power as normally. The afterburner was engaged by moving the throttle outboard a small amount. When this pilot was on his first hook-up for refueling, he needed to add just a little power to push the probe into the drogue, but accidentally also moved his throttle outboard and the afterburner lit. He went too fast and the refueling hose couldn't reel in, and before he could come out of afterburner, he had to push down and go under the wing of the tanker. His probe folded over the top of his wing and under the tanker's wing and immediately jerked loose from the drogue. Of course, the jerking yawed the tanker violently, and the tanker crew were shaken badly and quit for the day. The next day Bill Finkey and I called the tanker to request refueling hook-ups, and the tanker pilot wanted to make sure we weren't going to have any problems.

After three years in Japan, Hugh applied to the Air Force Institute of Technology, an advanced school. He received a diploma in aero-mechanical after one year. He anticipated working as an engineer, while also continuing to be a pilot.

His first assignment was to join a combined Air Force/Navy parachute test facility in El Centro, California. He flew along on different flights with test pilots dropping parachutes, even though he wasn't a test pilot himself, accompanied by test engineers who tested the parachutes. He flew photo missions with a Navy photographer in the rear seat. Two of the photographers he flew with were also members of the Aero Club, so they were taking lessons in a T-34 airplane. After a while, he asked them if they wanted to do some spins. They always agreed as soon as they stowed their cameras.

I would gradually increase the number of spins I did each time. I always started my spin recovery at 5,000 feet. Each time, the photographers wanted me to do more spins than I had done with the other one. At different times I would do 8,10,12,15 turns.

On one photo mission of an engineer testing a space suit with an emergency parachute, the test engineer had difficulty breathing so the mission was cancelled. I was at 12,000 feet for the photo mission, and a good way to lose altitude is to spin. The photographer stowed his camera, and I pulled up to stall and start the spin. We were at 16,000 feet and entered a very smooth spin, doing two spins each thousand feet. I recovered at 5,000 feet and had completed 23 turns. The photographer has something to brag about with his friends.

As chief of the manned parachute section at this time, Hugh got in a lot of flying time before he volunteered to return to a fighter squadron. When released to be transferred, however, the Air Force had a different idea. Since he was an engineer, they sent him to Wright-Patterson Air Force Base for development of the F-111, or TFX for Tactical Fighter Experimental. This was the first airplane in the Air Force with movable wings that could fly at supersonic speed. He stayed in this project for approximately four years, primarily responsible for crew systems and escape development—a system where, if necessary, the whole cockpit could separate from the airplane and a parachute would deploy and recover it. This was different from previous systems, where only the seat would separate.

By this time, the situation in Vietnam had heated up. Air Force Systems Command had made an agreement that their engineer pilots would go to Vietnam since the Army was in need of forward air controllers. They then would have to come back to the States to be engineers. Hugh went to Luke Air Force Base for a refresher in the F-100.

In August of 1966, Betty drove to Spokane, Washington, where she would stay while Hugh was in Vietnam. He went to Hurlburt Air Force Base in Florida for training on the O-1E "bird-dog" airplane. On Labor Day, he arrived in Fort Riley, Kansas, to join the 9th Infantry Division that was getting ready to go to Vietnam. In December 1966, Hugh flew to Vietnam. After a couple months of in-country training, he was called up to joint Army/Air Force Headquarters in Bien Hoa. There he became an assistant liaison officer to Lieutenant Colonel Arnold. Colonel Arnold flew with different units whenever the opportunity arose, and he encouraged his assistants to do the same so they were familiar with what all the units were doing and to give them any support they needed. A couple weeks of every month Hugh was out flying. In total he got over 300 hours and over 200 missions with the different army units.

When Hugh wasn't flying, he was coordinating and keeping the army informed on how the forward air controllers were supporting the Army units in the field, and the different bombers available to support the Army. From the air, he called in jet bomber strikes to targets on the ground.

One time I was up where the 25th Infantry Division was, which was outside of Cu Chi, in Vietnam. They gave me this area that the army was going to move through in the next few days, and they had some intelligence that something was up there, but they just didn't know what. So I went up there and I circled around and couldn't really find anything that looked like a worthwhile target. It was an old French rubber plantation. The trees were all broken down and there were a few foundations in the area, but nothing that you'd see was worthwhile. But I did see a trail coming up from a dry creek bed, and I thought, well, maybe there's something up there in the rubber plantation. So I had the bombers come over and I shot the smoke rocket, but it didn't go where I wanted it to. The fighter bomber dropped long from where I shot the rocket. The first bomb opened up some bunkers where there were underground rooms.

After that, the bombers began to drop bombs in different areas. By the time they got through, Hugh counted 22 bunkers that had been exposed.

Meanwhile, back in Spokane, Betty was busy taking her boys to Scouts and their daughter to ice skating lessons, and volunteered one day a week at Fairchild Hospital. She helped the boys achieve their Eagle Award. She never really knew what happened in Vietnam until years later while watching TV. "Some of these Army guys, called 'tunnel rats,' were crawling through the tunnels, and they mentioned about this place, which was just outside of Cu Chi, where an underground city had been exposed by these bombs." She realized then Hugh might have been part of that operation. When the tunnels were exposed, the Army

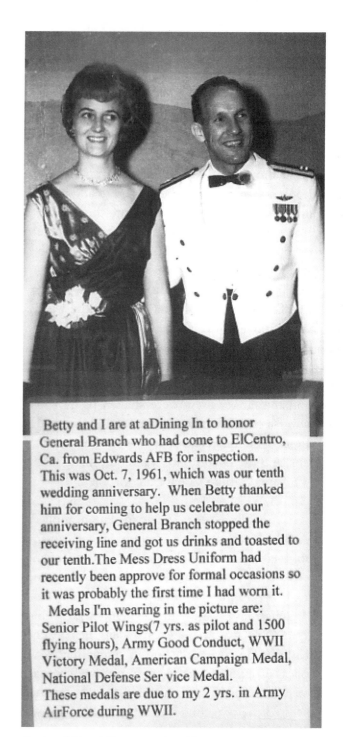

Betty and I are at a Dining In to honor General Branch who had come to ElCentro, Ca. from Edwards AFB for inspection. This was Oct. 7, 1961, which was our tenth wedding anniversary. When Betty thanked him for coming to help us celebrate our anniversary, General Branch stopped the receiving line and got us drinks and toasted to our tenth. The Mess Dress Uniform had recently been approve for formal occasions so it was probably the first time I had worn it.

Medals I'm wearing in the picture are: Senior Pilot Wings(7 yrs. as pilot and 1500 flying hours), Army Good Conduct, WWII Victory Medal, American Campaign Medal, National Defense Ser vice Medal.

These medals are due to my 2 yrs. in Army AirForce during WWII.

Hugh and his wife Betty on 10th wedding anniversary at El Centro, California

uncovered an underground hospital along with many other rooms that supported the North Vietnamese.

From Vietnam, Hugh was assigned to Vandenberg Air Force Base to work on the Minute Man III and Thor Agena missile tests. The Agena spacecraft was used for the weather satellites and the Thor was a basic rocket to launch the payloads into space, which was later replaced by the Delta rocket. After completing a Master of Science degree in

Aerospace Management through night courses at USC, Hugh retired in June 1972. He then went to work for Boeing and helped design and test commercial airliners.

In Hugh's eyes, a lot of our modern technology today is from GIs who came back from war and went to college. These engineers and technicians were available to private companies who developed all sorts of new technology, both military and commercial—the cars, tractors, airplanes, and other equipment you see today.

It was a bit hard on Hugh's family moving all the time, "15 times in the first 12 years of marriage," says Betty, but then it slowed up to maybe once every four years. The family adjusted. Today Hugh and Betty live in Carefree, Arizona. Hugh apologizes for his poor hearing, the result of flying jets for so many years, but feels fortunate to have had the experience of flying so many airplanes, having been rejected the first time for poor eyesight. It is amazing that, with thousands of hours of flying time, he never had a serious accident.

"Well, the Lord takes care of you."

Vietnam

When soldiers flew home from Vietnam, expecting the warm reception their ancestors received following World War II, their world collided with that of the American public, who had experienced a transformation in their absence. Almost immediately, the soldiers were deeply saddened to find the hostile and indifferent masses meeting soldiers at airports with the turn of a shoulder or a bucket of red paint. As the men back in Vietnam threw themselves and their newly fallen friends aboard American helicopters flying into Vietcong-ridden jungles, bullets anxiously flying in every direction, the U.S public saw the televised carnage and turned against their camouflage-clad guardians. As the soldiers overseas crawled through blood and muck, trying desperately to secure terrain from Vietcong guerrillas, Americans at home came to know their armed forces as baby-killers. The public didn't realize that political affiliation had little to do with their decision to fight the war. The politicians started it, and soldiers decided it wasn't up to them to determine whether or not it was a necessary war. Their country needed fighters, and they provided them.

The sacrifice and determination of the U.S. soldiers in Vietnam to perform their duty, regardless of their personal opinions, was truly remarkable. Even if their own opinions on the war began to sour as death and stalemate mounted, they still did what they were supposed to do, to their absolute greatest ability, knowing it was their responsibility and others' lives depended on them. Regrettably, the American public largely overlooked this. They shunned those willing to put themselves in the face of death every day. Today, many Vietnam veterans continue to sacrifice for their country. Seeing such horrific visions in such harsh and unfamiliar territory, only to come home to the unappreciative and even spiteful public, has severely damaged the resolve of some of the men who boldly performed their duty. Still, it would be wholly unfair to group every Vietnam vet in this category, as cinema has all-too-often done. Many men moved on from the war after gaining a more rounded perspective of life from their service and learned the values of companionship and responsibility through their distress.

It is our duty today to attempt to rebuild the confidence in Vietnam veterans that what they did was right. A government parade forty years after the fact won't be enough to show the men they are appreciated. The following pages are our attempt to welcome them home.

Greg Gorraiz

Virgel Cain

October 1963 - May 1968
Gulf of Tonkin

Last Resort

An Interview with Virgel Cain
By Amanda Poincelot

Having both his parents serve during World War II, Virgel Cain knew exactly what he was going to do after he graduated high school in June of 1963. His father, a Marine, was stationed at Pearl Harbor when it was bombed. The Marines were getting staged and ready to go for anything that could and would happen. Luckily, Virgel's father was one of the survivors of Pearl Harbor. Virgel's mother also served during World War II, but she was in the Navy.

My mom was in the Navy during WWII and she was just getting ready to go to Hawaii when Pearl Harbor happened, and so needless to say, back then it was a little different mindset. Back then, once Pearl Harbor happened, the women were no longer allowed to go to Hawaii—for safety sake, I guess. She was reassigned to Washington D.C, so she spent the whole war [there] until about 1945. She actually got out because she was pregnant with me in 1945. I was born in 1946, so she was discharged because she became pregnant. My folks were married in '44, so they were a married couple. There wasn't anything wrong with that except you weren't allowed to be pregnant in the military. So she was discharged, but she was stationed—back then it was the U.S Naval Intelligence, which would now be part of the Pentagon. She got to see a lot in D.C., a lot of the top brass and political people and stuff like that so it was interesting for her.

When events in Vietnam looked like they were "heating up," Virgel wanted to pick his service rather than be drafted. His father encouraged him not to go into the Marines because he was a Marine, and in his opinion the main objective of being a Marine is to kill people. Virgel volunteered to go into the Navy, and in our interview he said, "The Marines are part of the Navy anyway; just don't tell them I said that."

Virgel Cain joined the Navy at the age of seventeen on October 1, 1963, and served in active service until May of 1968. Because he was seventeen, Virgel needed his parents to sign for him. He went off to boot camp in San Diego for a three-month training session. In boot camp, Virgel was trained in every way possible to determine what would be best for him. His expertise, they decided, was in electronics and radar. After twelve weeks in boot camp, Virgel was sent to Treasure Island, San Francisco, for Radarman A School. He toughed out the cold winter weather for nine long months. After nine months of hard, grueling training, Virgel was assigned to a ship stationed at Pearl Harbor—the *USS Goldsborough*, guided missile destroyer DDG-20, where he spent two six-month tours in the Gulf of Tonkin, Vietnam.

Virgel's ship was traveling with the *USS Yorktown*, which was a carrier group. One of the duties Virgel and companions had was to follow about 1000 to 2000 yards behind the *USS Yorktown* when they did flight ops, or operations. If a plane went down, Virgel and his crew were responsible for fishing the pilot out of the ocean. Total count, Virgel's ship rescued two pilots.

> I don't remember exactly what happened with one of the guys, but he either missed the landing or he had a malfunction. I think he had a malfunction and he stuck it into the water, and of course we were right behind the *Yorktown*. When they realized he went down, we did what they call a man overboard drill. We would mark the spot and then we'd pull out to that. Keep in mind there are currents, so someone could float away pretty quickly. We actually pulled right up and caught him because he was right there. I think he ejected and came down in a parachute, and I think he realized what was happening. Then the plane hit the water; he hit it right after. And I am stretching memory again, so that is to the best of my memory.

Virgel's ship was also prepared to assist the manned *Apollo* rescue mission. They never got the chance to help rescue the space capsule, but they were always north of the Hawaiian Islands at the exact coordinates to pick them up no matter where they landed.

During the Vietnam War, Virgel's ship was in the Gulf of Tonkin, doing what they called "Port and Starboard," which was four hours on and four hours off on a 24-hour clock. For four hours he was on

duty, and then he got four hours off to try and get some sleep or drink tons of coffee and play cards. Sleep was hard to come by. When General Quarters was called, everyone had to man his battle station. GQ was called one time because a Russian MIG-19, a Russian MIG-21, or a Vietnamese

Sailor Virgel at home

PT boat was making a run at the ship. The MIGs were coming from Hainan Island, and the PT boats were making runs at the ship from Haiphong harbor. Most of the time they were only playing "cat and mouse" with Virgel's ship; they never had real intentions of attacking, but you never knew for sure and always had to be ready.

> What I mean by "cat and mouse" was they were testing your readiness; they were keeping you on edge and keeping you nervous, basically. And they didn't want you to have any sleep. They wanted you to be always on, and standing at attention, and always ready to respond. So it was part of what they were doing. When I say "cat and mouse," they really weren't really planning on attacking. Most of these runs, more than likely that wasn't the plan. The plan was to cause you to go to a higher state of readiness and just to make you nervous, basically, and they did a good job of it. Because, you got a MIG-21 coming at you at 1200 knots, you know, it kind of gets your attention. And the PT boats would literally— we would track them at 55 to 60 knots, so they were coming at you pretty good too, which was far superior to anything we could do. It was double what we could do.

As soon as the MIGs and the PT boats started to come at the ship, Virgel tracked them down on the radar, sending the coordinates over to the fire department, and as soon as it got to the fire control department, they locked on. Once they were locked on, the MIG or PT boat would scatter back to Hainan or Haiphong harbor.

Another duty Virgel had as a radar man was tracking down Russian subs with sonar. This system was another form of "cat and mouse" since many of these vessels pretended to be innocent fishing boats.

We were basically responsible for tracking all of the Russian subs that claimed they weren't there, that were—there were plenty of them—also looking out, watching after, keeping an eye on all of their Soviet Russian trawlers that were on the surface pretending they were fishing. But really there were a million radio antennas, and they were monitoring all of our communications and everything we did. So they were pretending to fish, but they were really spying on us basically. Yeah. And we got so close to some of them that we'd wave at the sailors and they'd wave back.

Virgel in front of Budokah (Judo) during Tokyo Olympics

One way the Navy tracked subs was with a sonar pod the helicopters dropped into the water. Every time they dropped it, the enemy subs scattered backward, not knowing what it was. They stayed back watching to see if it would do anything and while the Russians were watching it, Virgel's ship and its crew were watching them.

Virgel worked with a radar system that was not easy to understand. When asked about it, Virgel gave a great, but complicated, explanation.

We could detect air search well over 100 miles. On the surface you're limited because of the curvature of the earth. Line of sight for curvature is 15 miles, and we could go better than the line of sight, but it depended on what it was. If it was a land mass, like the top of a mountain on an island or a land mass, we could pick that up. We couldn't pick up the beach, but we could pick the high spot because it is over the curvature of the earth—probably 30 to 50 miles out, depending how high of an object we are talking [about]. When in the middle of the ocean, we used charts and the stars to estimate our position.

Virgel and his crew could pick up anything at these distances. Sometimes they did not know exactly what they were looking at, but they knew they were looking at something. One time the bridge did not believe the radar room because they could not visually see what Virgel and his buddies were trying to tell them was there. They knew some object was approaching; they just could not say what.

I remember one occasion—this is a true story [though] it sounds a little farfetched—but we're in radar and we are tracking something and it's coming right at us. We're in the center and this thing is going around this way and we're tracking something from, oh, a couple thousand yards out, and we kept telling them there is something dead ahead just off the bow, just a little bit off to the starboard side of the bow. Dead ahead there's something out there. And, of course, the bridge is right in front us and we are in the radar room behind. We don't have the capability of seeing with our eyes; we are seeing it with our radar on surface search. We kept telling them, "We're tracking this. There's something coming straight at us."

We were between Hawaii and Japan, out in the middle of the ocean. We had just left Midway, if my memory is correct, so we were between Midway Island and Japan. And so it kept coming, it kept coming, and the bridge kept on going, "You're crazy; you're crazy. There's nothing there; there's nothing there." So a couple of us dove out one of the hatches on the right side of the ship, on the starboard side of the ship, just to see for ourselves and eyeball it. And son of a gun, this big, humongous tree, I swear to god, this huge tree, was just bobbing in the water and it went right alongside our ship.

Virgel's ship was moving faster than the tree, but it passed perhaps 20 feet from their craft. If they had hit it, it would have created problems for the ship because it was a full-size tree, at least 100-foot by 20-foot, that had probably broken loose from a major logging center, like Seattle, and drifted for a long way. "The bridge never doubted us again after that. We were tracking the thing all the way. You know, that was about the oddest thing."

On the ship there was nowhere to spend money, only a little store the size of a broom closet. After 94 days at sea, the ship docked in Hong Kong. Because Virgel did not spend any money on the ship, he had *a lot* to spend in Hong Kong. The sailors were not allowed to go into Taiwan because they were a guided missile ship, and the U.S Government did not want China spying on those ships. Virgel and his crew were in Hong Kong for two weeks. While there, Virgel says they "probably went out and partied more than [they] should have." One of the things Virgel did was eat at a floating restaurant in Kowloon. Another event was partying at a British NCO club. Virgel claimed he partied with "the Brits, the Aussies, and the New Zealanders, or Kiwis."

Virgel's life after the war was a little bit shaky at first, but once he started getting used to civilian life, things started to settle down.

My first year in college was terrible. I ended up dropping out before I got thrown out. I mean, it was really difficult to make a change from a military environment to a community college environment. It was almost impossible. And then I went to work full time. I worked at Sears selling paint. Then I decided working full time—there is nothing wrong working at Sears selling paint, it's just not what

I wanted to do for the rest of my life. So I got a little more acclimated to civilian life versus military life and I got a little more motivated to go back to college and get serious.

Virgel went to Rio Hondo College in Whittier, California, a two-year community college. He was on the Dean's honor roll the three semesters he was there. After Virgel got his AA through Rio Hondo College, he went to Cal State University Fullerton, or Cal State "Disneyland," as the kids called it. Most of them worked at Disneyland while attending college. He earned his four-year Bachelor of Arts degree in Business Administration, Management.

Today Virgel works at Barnes and Noble bookstore as Community Relations Manager and is part of the City of Phoenix Military and Veterans Commission. Mayor Gordon asked the commission to open a military and veterans lounge at Sky Harbor because it did not have one. The lounge opened on December 8, 2006. Virgel is recruiting volunteers to work at the lounge part-time. It is located in Terminal Two and is open to all military veterans and personnel, along with their families. The commission might also build a museum at Steele Indian School Park. The City of Phoenix Military and Veterans Commission has done many great things, including building the lounge and participating in the Veterans Day Parade every year, and will keep doing them in the future. Virgel says he is on his second term, and it has been very rewarding.

When asked, "How much of the war situation did you actually grasp?" Virgel admits, "None of it." Virgel believes that war should be a last resort. He thinks we should try everything else before we declare war because war is a terrible thing. War should only be started for the right cause.

I don't know if it is your class, probably not, it was one of the history classes—remember, I do sub up in the district occasionally—but [in] one of the history classes, one of the kids was talking about the movie *Pearl Harbor* with Ben Affleck and so on and so on. And he said, "Ahh, man, it was an awesome movie." And I said, "Whoa, whoa wait a minute. Yeah, it was an awesome movie, but it was a real event. Don't forget that." The movie was one thing, but it was a *real event*, and a lot of

18 November 1963, Virgel second from the right, front.

people lost their lives. My dad was at Pearl when it was bombed. He was a Marine. He was at Pearl Harbor and they knew something was coming so they were over there getting staged and ready to go for whatever it was and he survived that. So it was a real event; it wasn't just a movie. I think reality sometimes escapes us. I never got shot at over there. I'm lucky. Like I said, the next time our ship went over, there were some people actually where I work that were wounded, and I believe some of them were killed. So we just got lucky the two six-month tours I was there. It could have

happened to us, just as much as it happened to the next crew or one of the other ships. That's not a pretty thing, and war certainly is the last resort. It's got to have a just cause.

While interviewing Virgel I realized the importance of gathering these stories and the significance of our military veterans. It is critical for Americans to support the members of our military because although our freedoms are guaranteed by the Constitution, those freedoms have been protected by veterans like Mr. Virgel Cain.

Maralin Coffinger

July 1963 - May 1989
Vietnam, Turkey, U.S.

Anything A Man Does
An Interview with Maralin Coffinger
By Emily Burke

Maralin Coffinger would never refer to herself as a feminist, but she helped pave the way for ambitious, patriotic women seeking a military career. A former military base commander, Space Command Director for NORAD, and one of the few women to rise to the rank of brigadier general, she continues to inspire young women both in and out of the military.

During her 26-year military career, Coffinger has traveled the world, serving in such far off places as Alaska, Turkey, and Vietnam. Her nearly two dozen awards and decorations include the Air Force Distinguished Service Medal, the Legion of Merit, the Bronze Star, the Meritorious Service Medal, the Small Arms Expert Marksmanship Ribbon, and the Space Badge.

Born Maralin Katharyne Morse on July 5, 1935, in Ogden, Iowa, she clearly recalls the pride and emotion of the World War II years. "If you think you saw patriotism on 9/11 a few years ago," she reminisces, "[that was a] pittance compared to what it was like during World War II. I mean, everybody was lined up trying to get into the armed services to serve—lines two, three blocks long at the recruiting stations. That was real patriotism back then."

That particular feeling stuck with Coffinger into adulthood. Her interest in the military was spurred, in part, by her two brothers' involvement in World War II and the Korean War, respectively. However, she did not immediately act on this interest. She first became an English teacher. During this time she was a flutist for the Phoenix Symphony Orchestra as well. Even after five years working as a teacher, she felt a strong draw to the military, and after much consideration decided to enlist in the Air Force. She considers it the "best decision of my life."

Coffinger began her outstanding career as a second lieutenant at Keesler Air Force Base in Mississippi. Heading a large program to mechanize personnel records, she achieved the highest success rate within the Air Training Command. At the end of her time at Keesler she was informed her next assignment would be Hawaii. A few days later, Coffinger learned she had been denied the position because the colonel in charge did not wish to have a woman working for him. Similar incidences of prejudice towards women would be experienced by Coffinger in the years to come.

Instead, Coffinger went to Ankara, Turkey, where she served as the Chief of Quality Control, handling promotions and effectiveness reports. Later she took over managing assignments as well, shouldering the responsibilities of two different departments at once. At this time, Turkey was one of the few NATO countries in that part of the world, but even so Coffinger recalls, "I found many of them to be very hostile people." At that time, some people in Turkey were not fans of Americans, with the exception of the popular U.S. president John F. Kennedy. Coffinger remembers two specific occasions when she was on the receiving end of those anti-American feelings.

I was coming out of choir practice one night, which was in a building downtown rented by the military. Some kid came along and threw a Coke all over me from behind. All I was doing was walking out of the building. I didn't even see him until it happened. Then there were a couple other times, some friends and I were walking along the street. We were downtown shopping…and we were standing on a corner waiting for the stoplight; a car went by and someone spit at us.

Coffinger describes her experiences in Turkey as "interesting." "It was not a pleasant place while I was there. When the bombings of the Pan Am building started happening, they wouldn't let us drive to work anymore. We had to ride on buses, and there were Turkish guards on all our buses. It was just not a good place."

Coffinger's job did not keep her only in Turkey; she also traveled to Greece, Pakistan, and Iran for short visits to give briefings. Once, while in Pakistan, she and a few friends took advantage of a day where they were not needed for any official business and accepted an offer to take a trip to the Khyber Pass. "It was very dangerous, because all along that whole road to the Khyber Pass, everybody, I mean everybody, all the people walking

along the road, carried rifles. But the thing about Pakistan was—it was really grim; thousands and thousands of people walking along the roadside, sleeping along the roadside, no homes, no nothing."

Her next assignment was meant to be Sandia, Albuquerque; however, a week after she was informed of this, the assignment was changed to Scott Air Force Base in Illinois. Her boss made inquiries into the change while passing through Randolph Air Force Base in Texas and relayed the following to Coffinger. "They said the people in Sandia didn't have facilities for women, which is not correct, because they had lots of civilian women working in that agency. But I was a military woman."

By this time, Coffinger had become a captain, and while serving at Scott Air Force Base, she headed a three-year project to implement an entirely new computer system throughout all of Military Airlift Command. Over the previous years, she had volunteered for an assignment to Vietnam, but due to the importance of her project at Scott Air Force Base, her request was not honored until the end of her tour there.

Coffinger went to Vietnam in a dual position: Advisor to Women in the Vietnamese Air Force, and Personnel Data System Advisor. The project mechanized the Vietnamese personnel records, "but

Maralin shakes the hand of a Vietnamese General who has just awarded her the Vietnamese Honor Medal and Service Medal. She was taken aback when he had to put his hand inside her shirt in order to attach and tap down the two prongs behind the medals!

I was also the advisor to three male Vietnamese lieutenant colonels, and I was still a captain—but I was on the major's list. I hadn't pinned major on yet. I was very tall, and the Vietnamese in general are quite short. I was told if I wanted to be effective with these three male lieutenant colonels, that every now and then I should take them each a bottle of cognac. So that's what I did."

One aspect of her job was to meet with the head of the Vietnamese Women's Air Force, Major Nguyen. They met almost daily and traveled often to check on the women in various locations and find ways to improve living conditions. "[T]he interesting part about Major Nguyen is that she was almost as tall as me, and that was very, very unusual [for a] Vietnamese woman, towering over these Vietnamese men."

Although Coffinger never saw battle, she did experience a great deal of danger during air raids on the base. "In those days the women in the Air Force—well, all military, I guess—were considered non-combatants. So I was never issued a flak vest or a helmet or any of those kinds of things, because I was considered a non-combatant. Well, the enemy didn't care. They shot their rockets wherever they felt like shooting their rockets." The dormitories on base were old French army barracks, and she remembers running down into the recreation room of the dormitory and using furniture as a shield. "It wasn't a very well-protected place, but it was someplace to go because the French barracks were just old wooden things that would go up [explode] just like a bunch of splinters."

At the end of her fourteen-month tour in Vietnam, Coffinger got together with the chief nurse and a few others with whom she had become friends, to have a Coke. As they sat in the nurse's trailer outside the dispensary that night, they were shelled. "This was right near the perimeter fence of the base," Coffinger recollects in detail, "and there were Vietnamese houses right outside of the fence. Air raids! All of a sudden the rockets were whipping over and going tcchhhttcchhhtchtch—bang! Tchhhttcchhhtchtch—bang! Like that. There was one that landed right on the other side of the trailer. And there was one that landed right on the other side of the fence, the perimeter fence. And so [the chief nurse] said, 'Come on with me!' So there were three or four of us. We went running out of the trailer and into the dispensary."

Coffinger explains that in addition to seeking safe shelter, she and her companions attempted to comfort and distract the immobile patients in the dispensary. "I remember she assigned me to an Army lieutenant colonel and he couldn't move because the day before…he had had his hand blown off. He had his arm propped up... and they had reattached his hand because he had carried it back in his lap in the helicopter. Here we were in the middle of this rocket attack, rockets flying all over the place, and he was showing me how he could wiggle his fingers. This was a stranger; I had never met the man before, but I was trying to talk to *him*. Here was a guy just come back from combat; he should have been talking to *me*."

Modesty aside, Coffinger's service in Southeast Asia earned her the Republic of Vietnam Gallantry Cross with Palm, the Republic of Vietnam Campaign Medal, the Republic of Vietnam Armed Forces Honor Medal First Class, and the Republic of Vietnam Air Service Medal Honor Class. She returned to the United States in April 1972 and attended Armed Forces Staff College in Norfolk, Virginia. From there she received her first assignment to the Pentagon where she held the position Chief of Officer Accessions on the Air Staff at Air Force Headquarters. Then she was promoted to lieutenant colonel and became Deputy Director of Women in the Air Force. Because women were becoming a larger part of the Air Force at that time, she happily wrote the Office of Women in the Air Force off the books. Upon completion of her tour of duty in the Pentagon, she was selected to attend National War College. It was after this she became Deputy Base Commander at Elmendorf Air Force Base in Alaska. During her second year, she became Base Commander, which entailed commanding over a dozen different agencies and supporting all activities within the base.

According to Coffinger, the Alaska post was her favorite job. She notes that by comparison, in such jobs as personnel, the tasks are unvarying. "You get bored out of your mind. Now and then you have a little glitch here you have to deal with or maybe you have some trouble with one of your troops or whatever. But it's pretty much a day-in and day-out sort of situation. But the base commandering world, it's something new *every* day."

One of the more memorable problems she dealt with at her new post required a great deal of tact and planning. When the Canadian government decided to take in thousands of Vietnamese refugees who had been sitting in their boats along the coastline, Coffinger's base was asked to allow their planes to stop and refuel at the base on their way to and from Canada. It was not a simple matter of the planes refueling. There were problems of staging crews and making repairs that would require the occupants of the carriers to stay overnight. All possible worst case scenarios had to be considered and anticipated. Fortunately, the operation went well and the planes stopped and refueled successfully. Coffinger and her

Maralin at her command post inside Cheyenne Mountain in Colorado Springs, part of NORAD's defense system

deputy's efforts were specifically acknowledged and thanked by the Canadian government.

In Coffinger's experience, "a base is like a small city. Everything that can happen in a city can happen on a base." An excellent example is when she received a call from an officer informing her there was a woman in one of the housing units who was reportedly brandishing a butcher's knife. She thought, "You've got to be kidding me.'" Coffinger went to the area near the house, bringing with her a psychiatrist for negotiating and some of her security police. The psychiatrist spoke to the knife-wielder and discovered the woman was upset with her husband, who had a year of his tour left, and she simply wanted to go home. The Commander sent a few of her men to check the house and look in the windows to find out more. They reported that the knife was on the kitchen counter and the children were perfectly fine. A new Wing Commander, who lacked experience, drove up and began making a fuss, asking why the SWAT team had not been called. After Coffinger calmed him down and told him the SWAT team wouldn't be necessary, she went in and personally spoke with the woman. Then she called the woman's husband, who had been locked out of the house. The Air Force found a new assignment for him and peace was restored.

The Air Force's accommodating attitude towards keeping families together sometimes created negative consequences, as Coffinger witnessed during another incident. One day the Alaskan Air Commander called Coffinger to discuss some troubles at Shemya, a small base at the tip of the Aleutians, with the women stationed there. She agreed to accompany him and look into the problem. "The woman problem wasn't a woman problem at all," laughs Coffinger. It turned out the "problem" was not with the women; it was with some of the married *couples* on the base. The remote locale meant husbands and wives were constantly together, grating on one another's nerves. After having worked hard to make sure these couples were not separated by their jobs, the Air Force now had to reassign them to other bases in Alaska, flying them in to see each other only occasionally.

Coffinger transferred to California's Norton Air Force Base where, from 1980 to 1982, she continued her career as a base commander. After she left Norton, she was selected Air Force representative on the Fifth Quadrennial Review of Military Compensation in Washington, D.C. Here she served as the chairman of the Special and Incentive Pays Committee. Over the course of a year, from January to October 1985, she served as Deputy Director, Personnel Programs, Office of the Deputy Chief of Staff, Manpower and Personnel at Air Force Headquarters. On October 1, 1985, she was promoted to Brigadier General. During that same year, she became a command director with North American Aerospace Defense Command combat operations in the Cheyenne Mountain complex in Colorado.

After she earned the rank of brigadier general, Coffinger's current boss, who had also been her wing commander while she was at Norton, told her he wanted her to "try something new." His plan was to find a position in operations for her, an area in which she had no previous experience. He began searching for opportunities, but none readily appeared because she lacked experience in this field, or possibly because they did not want a woman. Her superior changed tactics, attempting to assign her to the command post for the Joint Chiefs of Staff down in the Department of Defense in the Pentagon. Here, too, she was turned down with the excuse that she was not a flyer.

Hoping to remedy the situation, her superior called and told her, "You know, I could force you into the job because there is no requirement for you to be a flyer, but if I do, your life would be miserable." Then he told Coffinger he had decided to put her on a one-year tour at Cheyenne Mountain in Colorado Springs. The tour was unusually short because of the extreme demands of command director duties. Put simply, the Command Director sat in front of a large "scope" at the Command Post where she and her crew monitored North America primarily, as well as other parts of the globe, for incoming missiles, while also running war games. Part of the crew was in the room with the commander, but the rest could be reached at any time by telephone. After she was certified as a Certified Command Director and spent a designated amount of time on duty, Coffinger earned the prestigious Space Badge.

Just as intense as the job, the training that preceded it lasted from a month to six weeks and involved both a written and a practical test administered by the Lead Command Director and the Commander of Space Command. When Coffinger explained this process, she referred to the command director who gave the test as "him." She explained, "I say 'him' because I was the only woman who ever did it."

Later in the year, Coffinger became Lead Command Director. It was unusual for a woman to be Lead Command Director, and in one instance the idea met with some resistance. The army needed to replace their general and were late about doing it, so they had to rush the replacement through the training process. Normally the lead director would not do the training because he would be conducting testing later on. In this case, the Training Office asked Coffinger to do the honors. She agreed to meet with the

replacement that night and take him through the practical applications.

The evening wore on and the general did not show up. Coffinger called around and learned that nobody had seen him. Finally, the officer in question walked in with the training officer, and strolled right past Coffinger to the upper level command post. Coffinger remembers, "And then it dawned on me, what was going on. A macho Army general probably didn't want to train with a woman." The training officer came back down and confirmed her suspicions. The general did not want to have a woman train him, even though she would be the one administering the test.

After some discussion, the training officer went back up to talk to the replacement office and returned with a very reluctant-looking general. They went through all the introductions. Finally, she seated him in front of the scope and began taking him through a war game. At one point during the session she saw her boss waiting to talk to her, so she told her deputy to continue training the general while she stepped outside. The general rejected this idea, informing her he would wait for her to get back before he continued. Coffinger laughed. "It took me a while, but I had won him over. He didn't want to train with my deputy. He wanted to train with me."

Since Brigadier General Maralin Coffinger first began her career, the role of women in the military has changed greatly. "[They] discovered along the way that women can do many, many more things than they ever thought they could do. They can do anything a man does!" She continued with a laugh. "Today, if you were to ask some general in the Pentagon if they could run the armed forces without women, they would say no—if they were being honest."

She herself has been a part of this change, with an exemplary career that serves as an example for young women. She has opened doors that were firmly shut to women, and was instrumental in getting women into pilot and navigator training. Looking back, she sums up her career this way.

"The military is a wonderful career for a woman. The problem is that everybody's discovered it!"

Vic Conner

February 1940 - November 1985
Vietnam, Germany

Crazy Conner Never Makes the Same Mistake Twice

An Interview with Vic Conner
By Greg Gorraiz

A young Vic Conner sat in his home watching TV. He was attending Texas A & M when he "ran out of money and grades, both at about the same time." An Army advertisement played on TV. Though seeing commercials like it many times before, Vic decided to take notice. It promised education and money, the two things he sorely needed. He decided to take advantage and joined the Army, inducted in February of 1960.

Vic began training, getting ready to join a two-battery Nike Hercules battalion being established in Abilene, Texas, to defend the Air Force base there. After his basic training he did on-the-job training to be a missile man. To join the unit and enter NORAD—North American Aerospace Defense Command—he was required to pass a test, which he did. After joining, Vic married his fiancée Sharon and had his first child.

After a year and a half, Vic applied for Officer Candidate School in artillery. Once he graduated he was sent to Okinawa as an Air Defense officer. Vic stayed in Okinawa for two and a half years, serving as a platoon leader on a HAWK missile system. For the last seven or eight months Vic held the "extremely interesting job" of aide to the commanding general. During this time, he was given efficiency reports to track his projects, which the Army does to all its officers. One report read: "Lieutenant Conner sometimes makes mistakes, but he never makes the same mistake twice."

From Okinawa, Vic was accepted to flight school. He started training at Fort Wolters, Texas, and finished training in Fort Rucker, Alabama. He graduated late in 1965, the time when "everybody was going to Vietnam." His entire class went, but Vic himself was delayed because artillery personnel were intended to go a separate course. "They thought artillery people could shoot missiles and they were getting ready, playing with shooting missiles from helicopters. So I waited for that course. [It] didn't happen, so I went on to Vietnam."

In his first tour, Vic flew over a thousand hours. On one occasion Vic was lifting off an LZ when his company "took heavy fire." The company commander got shot in the kneecap and it was destroyed. Although the man was unable to fly any longer, he became an infantryman and later became the infantry battalion commander who took Hamburger Hill.

Numerous times Vic inserted six-man Special Forces reconnaissance teams who, after he dropped them off, crept through the jungle to "find the bad guys." Fortunately these accomplishments came without the death of one American. In fact, Vic's helicopter never "lost" a Special Forces soldier. Some were wounded, but fortunately all of them were evacuated.

The Special Forces men were inserted during the dead of night so they wouldn't be detected. They didn't even turn on the lights of the helicopter. Of course, this made it increasingly difficult for Vic. On one occasion, Vic was to get his helicopter in a 130-foot-tall triple canopy jungle with a very small hole for the helicopter to come through. The plan was for his major to lower the helicopter and Vic, with a map, to tell him where to go. The major got nervous and told Vic, "You got it." Vic threw the maps in the back and took the controls. "It wasn't quite as big as we thought it was. We were clipping tree branches going down." It was pitch-dark and Vic couldn't see a thing. He had no idea how far away the ground was. Suddenly he felt the Special Forces men jump off, so he carefully went back up. He made a couple of circles in the air just in case the men got in trouble. The team came up on the radio with the code word that they needed help. Vic alerted the vacant second helicopter and the fire team of attack helicopters supporting him that he was going down a second time. He told the empty helicopter to come get three of the six, because his helicopter only had enough power to lift three men. "It's a lot easier to land than to take off with the extra weight." The crew chief and gunner helped a little by holding "two little pin lights" as a guide for Vic. Vic's helicopter was "bouncing" because one of the helicopter blades got sliced. Snapping branches along the way, Vic got his three men evacuated. One of the Americans was wounded. It turns out that as Vic was lowering the helicopter when he first unloaded

the men, some of the "snap, crackle, and pop" everyone thought was Vic hitting tree limbs was actually the helicopter being shot at. One of the men was hit and fell out at ten feet, so the other men jumped out to help him. En route to the hospital, the helicopter flew perfectly, because on the second time going down, Vic went down evenly, with equal space on both sides and all of the blades evenly chopped.

Vic also did what are called "ash and trash" missions, where he flew supplies from one Special Forces group to another. The objective was to haul as much as possible, so they just "piled it on." On one occasion, Vic was doing this from the top of a mountain. With all the extra weight, the helicopter barely got two inches off the ground, "sliding along, not even flying." At the end of the mountain was a barbed wire fence. Beyond the fence was a 500-foot cliff. Vic managed to narrowly lift the helicopter over the fence, after which it plummeted 300 feet off the cliff, with the copilot screaming at Vic the entire time. At about 300 feet the helicopter built up enough air speed and he flew it up, "not a problem."

Vic (left) with General Creighton Abrams

Vic was able to transport many fiercely brave Special Forces men. On one occasion, Vic put in two Americans and four Chinese "Nungs," or mercenaries. They were supposed to report to their unit every eight hours via radio, but two days went by and they weren't heard from. Everybody assumed they were "got." On

191

the third day, the men finally called in, so Vic picked them up. The reason they hadn't responded is because they discovered a North Vietnamese division-size base camp, with "buildings and everything else, under this tree canopy jungle." The Special Forces men crawled inside. During the day, they lay under the buildings. At night they came out and "crawled around." By the time they left the site, they had a complete map of the facility. The next day "a B-52 strike went in on it and made sure it wasn't anymore." The same men later discovered a communications wire "running through the jungle out in the middle of nowhere." They found out it was going from North Vietnam to South Vietnam, so they came back with monitoring equipment and recorded everything coming from it for a week. After that, they destroyed the wire and left because it was no longer safe to stay.

At the conclusion of his first tour, a "fictitious organization" called the Warrant Officer Protective Association gave Vic a plaque of which he is particularly proud. It is addressed to "Crazy Conner." Vic got it in honor of some of the "crazy things" he did. "When you're young, you sometimes do crazy things." Among them, he proved a Huey UH1 helicopter, rated at maximum airspeed of 120 knots, could actually go 145 "if you were in a steep dive." He pulled this off when he got a call for help from a Special Forces unit he had inserted and who were being "chased under fire." He pulled the steep dive, picked the men up, and came back out. "My copilot was terrified—not only from my flying the aircraft significantly over its rated capability of speed, but because of the bullet holes in the helicopter. You could actually see the people sitting there shooting at you." The copilot wouldn't talk to Vic after the flight and demanded a transfer, saying he wasn't going to fly with that "crazy SOB" ever again.

Vic was sent to be an instructor pilot upon the conclusion of his first tour. For 18 months he taught young pilots at Fort Wolters, Texas. Vic, a captain at this time, would have been required to take the advanced course, but there was a high demand for helicopter pilots so they ordered him back to Vietnam. "But I did talk them into sending me to the fixed-wing qualification course to learn how to fly a fixed-wing aircraft."

When Vic returned to Vietnam a second time, he spent the first six months as a battalion operations officer. During the second half, he was able to get a command at a helicopter company. A company back then was about the same size as a battalion is today, about 30 aircraft and 260 people. It was an "extremely rewarding job." The only hard part of it, Vic said, was writing six letters home to the families of the men killed during his duty.

When Vic was commanding the assault helicopter, there was one instance where he was doing combat assault in support of the South Vietnamese army on the ground. The South Vietnamese came under heavy attack from Vietcong, so they called out several helicopter gunships, but they didn't seem to gain any ground. By the time darkness fell, Vic decided to call for Air Force fighter-bomber support. Two separate aircraft responded. To help direct them where to shoot, Vic threw out white phosphorus from his helicopter. For one reason or another, the men couldn't find it. Vic tried to show the men where the "friendlies" were so they didn't accidentally get shot, but Vic was coming under increasing attack from a 51-caliber machine gun. When the tracers came from the machine gun, it looked like "a 55-gallon drum coming up through the sky at night." Vic decided to turn on his lights so the Air Force aircraft could see him. From there he was able to direct the Air Force men by referencing the South Vietnamese to the position of the Vietcong's machine gun tracers. "They came in and did their thing." Vic and the gunships stayed for another couple hours until the ground forces let them know they had escaped. The next morning the "good guys" went back to the area, only to find trails of blood from the wounded Vietcong dragged away. For his work, Vic's co-pilot and the ground commander wrote up a recommendation for a Silver Star, which he later received.

At this time, Vic was a reserve officer. "There's no such thing now," but since he was "an OCS" he was considered in the reserves but on active duty. The rules at the time stated anyone in his situation must retire at twenty years. "I had seen one of the most outstanding officers I'd ever known forced to retire at twenty years because he was a reserve office and had never gone regular Army. So I applied for regular Army commission." Vic wasn't sure he was going to stay in the Army for that long, but it was a simple matter of filling out an application, stating his request to be in the regular Army, listing his qualifications, and getting a few "endorsements" from some singular officers. His application was approved.

Upon returning from his second tour, Vic was required to take the 9-month advanced course, "which is supposed to teach you how to be a company commander at the captain level and a battalion level staff officer... Of course I'd already done those things." During his training the Army sent out personnel managers to advise the soldiers on their careers. As Vic was being advised, the man said, "But wait a minute, you don't have a degree. How did you get a regular Army commission?" Vic replied, "I applied for it, and you guys approved it." He told Vic he would have to go to college and get a degree. For the next two years, Vic did nothing but attend classes at University of Texas, El Paso, where he earned a Bachelor in Business Administration and Personnel Management. "[I] thought that was appropriate."

Then Vic spent a tour out of school as the executive officer of the Allied Student Battalion at Fort Bliss, Texas. "Fort Bliss had as many as 16 to 17 different countries at once taking air defense courses because they had bought U.S.-manufactured air defense equipment—missiles, guns, and such." Needless to say, there was an ethnically diverse student body. It became a tradition to celebrate, or help celebrate, each of their national holidays. "At least once a month we had a party to help make it fun."

After a year Vic was selected to attend Command General Staff College at Fort Leavenworth, Kansas, for nine months, meaning Vic spent almost four out of five years going to school. "School got old." When he was told he really should have a Masters Degree, Vic said it was time to move on from school, so he went to Germany, where he was the executive officer of the HAWK battalion for two years. "That was fun, but a lot of hard work." Being in Germany allowed him to travel and see Europe during his free time. He spent his final year in Germany as the aviation officer for the Air Defense Brigade, "one of the easiest jobs I ever did." He was able to fly the UH1s, OH-58s, and U-21s at this site.

After his tour in Germany, Vic was sent to Fort Rucker, where he became the evaluation division chief of "Evaluation Standardization Directorate." Standardization was concerned with ensuring all the pilots in the world were standardized "in the way they do maneuvers and such." The evaluation division Vic was in charge of was responsible for making sure all the training materials were produced "as they should be."

In 1980, "the Army decided I needed to go to Kuwait," so he went, where he served as an air defense advisor. "Apparently I didn't do a very good job or [the Kuwaitis] wouldn't have gotten overrun by the Iraqis in 1990!" From Kuwait he returned to Fort Rucker for almost four years, "the longest assignment I'd ever had in one place." There, his division taught the ground school for most initial aviation courses for officers.

Near the end of this assignment, Vic's parents were getting very old and "not doing too well," so he looked for a way to get closer to their home in Abilene, Texas. He found out the Army was going to start a "force development test" on the Apache helicopter because it was going to be "fielded" to the Army. Vic checked into it and discovered the chief of staff who was the "third senior guy" at Fort Rucker was the one who would select the members of the team. Vic started "politicking." A few weeks later, he was called to report to the chief's office. The man said, "What the hell do you know about attack helicopters?" Vic told him. The chief ordered Vic to Fort Hood as chief of the development test. Vic put together a team and they developed the test.

One day Vic got a call from a man who had been his boss at Fort Rucker. He was going to be the McDonnell Douglas program manager at Fort Rucker. The man said there would be a job at Fort Hood doing the same thing. Vic "hadn't really thought about retiring from the Army at that time," but he didn't know how to apply for that job since he already had a job with the Army; he took out the retirement guide. In the back was an article on how to write a résumé. Vic filled it out and sent it off to the company. After an interview he was hired to be the program manager at Fort Hood, which he did for three years. "When I retired I was thinking I was going to find a job having nothing to do with the Army, and I supported doing something different... Of course, I didn't do that."

Eventually the Army began fielding the Apache in Germany using what were called REFORGER exercises, war games created to increase the United States' ability to quickly deploy forces to Germany in case of a conflict with the USSR. Vic moved to Germany to help support logistics and maintenance for the aircraft. When Desert Storm began, the Army built a force that included all the Apaches in Germany. Only one Apache remained when the war began, and it stayed in Germany only because maintenance didn't have enough pieces to put it back together.

Vic went to Saudi Arabia with "tech reps" to help coordinate support for the Apaches. He traveled in a Range Rover, helping find parts and solve maintenance problems. He arrived before the start of the war and remained until the conflict ended. One battalion was left in northern Kuwait to provide security for the forces still there. They were having maintenance problems, so Vic took his tech rep in his Range Rover and headed to Kuwait to offer help.

On his way over, Vic traveled along the "highway of death," littered with "burning tanks and turned-over trucks and big holes in the road." Scattered along the highway were about 20 Kuwaitis, searching through the rubble to hopefully find some of their property stolen earlier by the Iraqis. As Vic drove by, the Kuwaitis saw the "upside down V" that all American cars have on their doors and roofs as a marking symbol. "They came running up and stuck their hands in the door and said, 'Thank you,' and shook your hand because they had their country back. [It was] one of the most gratifying things."

Vic at his desk

Before he crossed the border, Vic parked his car alongside the road. A young private walked up. Noticing Vic's telephone, he asked if he could use it. He hadn't talked to his wife in three months and telephone stations in Kuwait were hard to get to. "I said, 'Come here,' and put him in the vehicle and showed him how to use it… That was the happiest kid I'd seen."

Eventually Vic made it to the base, where he dropped off the tech rep. Vic spent the night preparing to go home. In the morning, the tech rep asked when he could come home. Vic said, "Whenever that colonel over there tells you you can." He stayed for about three weeks. Before Vic could leave, however, the "black monsoons" arrived, known in Kuwait as "shamals." These powerful storms "rolled up" observation choppers fifty feet and turned over six Apaches, a "lot of damage." Of course, the Army wanted to get them repaired and flying before Vic left, so Vic was picked up to survey the damage. The senior Army colonel approached Vic and told him he wasn't allowed to go home until all the Apaches were up and flying. "I said, 'Colonel, you know that might take months,' and he said, 'I don't care,' because he knew I could help him get parts." Two weeks passed "and I was standing there when the sixth aircraft was getting its test flight." Vic was able to go home.

After Desert Storm, Vic became the field service manager. He supported the US Army and their foreign officers in the Netherlands, the United Kingdom, Greece, the United Arab Emirates, Israel, and Egypt. "We wound up traveling to all of these places and [I] was able to take the wife with me to Israel."

Today, Vic continues to love the helicopters he worked on and flew for so long. On the wall of his house hangs a large picture of an Apache helicopter. In his office is a toy model, fully equipped with the noises the helicopter makes. The model helicopter is representative of both the hard work he put into his career and the joy he got out of it. "It was fun—challenging many times, but it was fun."

At least if you don't make the same mistake twice.

Al Crawford

August 1946 - November 1976
Germany, Vietnam

"I am a Land Warrior"
An Interview with Albert Crawford, Jr.
By Chelsea Ferguson

We're no longer soldiers. We're "land warriors" and "sea warriors" and "air warriors." Did you know that?

Al Crawford began to look at a career in the military because of his father. His father was pulled out of school by Al's grandmother to protect their family from neighboring Indians near Safford, Arizona. It might have been paranoia, but all in all Al's father never had a real chance at an education. Al's father, whose background revolved around World War I, died in 1989 after being hit with a car at 89 years old. Due to his loss of education, he inspired Al to look to West Point for its educational excellence and a career in the military.

Al used to read Tom Swift books as a child, novels that told of heroic manly adventures. Many discussed rockets and space, but they got Al interested in West Point. During his senior year of high school, Al took and passed a series of tests to get into the Academy. After he enlisted, he was called into the Army Specialist Reserved Training Program. The Army promised to send him to a university when he turned 18. He was 17 at the time. He was subsequently sent to the University of Utah for basic freshman pre-engineering. His education there, however, he describes as a "rat race." He was bunked with 500 other cadets in a field house filled with triple bunks.

Al finally got his appointment to West Point after he finished with his "barely survivable" field house in Utah. He was recommended by Arizona Senator Ernest McFarland, but he didn't leave for West Point until July. As Al waited, he signed up for the winter semester at the University of Arizona, where he took some engineering courses. Unfortunately, Al ran into a "snag." The army called to tell him since he was 18, they were sending him to Camp Beale, California, and then to Japan for basic training. Even though Al protested he had been appointed to West Point, he was made to go to Camp Beale, where he became a bit of a "gopher" to a 1st Sergeant. Eventually Al's paperwork caught up to him and he was discharged from the Army Reserve, sent back to Tucson, just in time to make his July 4th arrival at West Point.

Like most plebes at the Academy, Al experienced six months of Beast Barracks, which was rough. The purpose of this initiation was to teach the plebes character, West Point principles, and discipline.

The motivation was that if you can't take it, you're not empowered to give it out later. It was really a test of your will and your willingness to stick it out, and I would say ten to fifteen percent of the class dropped out by the first eight weeks. I thought about dropping out myself, but I'm glad I stuck with it.

The next stage at West Point was still during plebe year. There was severe discipline and hazing, but it involved very heavy academics. At the end of the first year, there was a Recognition Day where a plebe actually became "worthy" of shaking the upperclassman's hand and being known as a "person," not just a plebe. Prior to graduation there was a 100 day and night celebration, and then according to your class rank, you got to pick your branch and first station. Al ranked splendidly, 20th in a class of 640. He chose the Army Signal Corps. He had always been interested in this field of specialty.

Al was on break after graduation in June 1950 when the Korean conflict broke out. The graduates who chose an assignment on the West Coast were shipped off to Korea, while Al luckily had been assigned to Germany. He spent his first three years in Germany with the Army's 97th Signal Battalion as a junior officer on troop duty in Bavaria. He had a delightful time. He had just married a "lovely woman" and they were given a house in Bavaria that had been requisitioned from the Germans. They even had a live-in maid, gardener, and "fireman" to keep the furnace going. Although Al had a "jolly time" in that house and warmed up to German and French culture by learning the language and eating escargot, those three years were also stressful. There were escape drills for the women and children in case the Russians attacked so they knew where to rendezvous in case of an invasion.

While a junior officer, Al picked up other assignments such as motor, mess, and supply. He was also assigned a platoon of enlisted men to put out signal communications for the 7th Army. The 7th Army was the major ground headquarters for all the army

troops in Europe. Two years into the three, Al was selected to take on the headquarters company of the battalion. This was a rare opportunity for a young lieutenant to be picked for a captain's position so Al had to quickly learn the art of command. He had not gone through branch training at West Point because the Class of 1950 had been sent straight to Korea. This turned out to be a mistake. Fortunately a 1st Sergeant took him under his wing. He taught him everything he needed to know about command. "And if you hear about noncoms being the salt of the earth of the army, I found it there. I treasured his friendship and his relationship for the rest of my time. Bill Stanton—1st Sergeant Bill Stanton."

Al learned a bit more about the German culture when he went back for his second assignment ten years later. He actually lived in an apartment above a German family. He and the landlord became very close; they are friends to this day. When Al went back with his wife Bettie to visit her in Zweibrucken, Germany, the landlord had prepared a tiny buffet. Al accidentally took one of her silver spoons back to America, but she told him she would have given it to him anyway as a keepsake.

From 1950 to 1953, Al's primary duty was communications. At one point he was called a Carrier Operations Platoon Leader. He dealt with a set of equipment that permitted one to send many telephone communications across a single cable. When Al and his team were put on alert, they would always be the first ones in the field. They had to set up and be ready in case the Russians troops came across the East German border.

In 1950 there were two kinds of communication. There was the spiral-four cable, and there was the VHF radio, which has the ability to establish a line of sight to send a radio signal from one hilltop to another. In this case, there were 12 channels of voice communication. The VHF radio was wireless from one mountaintop to another, but the wires or cables had to run back down the hilltop to the headquarters located in the valleys.

After Germany, Al went back to the States and was accepted for graduate school at Stanford University in Electrical Engineering. This is where he first learned about the emerging field of computers. He received two Master's degrees. He and two other Army captains were then called out by the Pentagon to take some coursework on data processing and industrial engineering. It turned out this was the first year Stanford had taught it, so the three of them helped write the syllabus for Stanford's master's degree in data processing.

Change of command

The Army then sent Al to Fort Huachuca, Arizona, in 1954 to utilize his computer training. Al began to apply command and control, electronics, networks, and computers to tactical military forces in the field. One of Al's classmates was designing a new project called Mobidic, the first attempt to take an enormous computer, probably half the size of a family room, and squeeze it into a couple of small trailers. It was also modified so it would be able to travel across rough roads to reach the army forces in the field. He spent three years at Fort Huachuca learning about this new computer and associated software. He was then selected to take the Mobidic computer system to Germany to apply it to an army application. Again, this was with the 7th Army. Al was able to personally select a team of six officers and 30 enlisted men—a rare opportunity. The Mobidic computer interpreted data through punch cards; thousands of cards were used. Al and his team moved the computer only once or twice to prove it was mobile, fearing it might be wrecked on the winding German roads. He spent two years around Germany with this computer so the skills he learned at Stanford and Fort Huachuca proved quite useful.

After his time with Mobidic, Al was transferred to Bavaria as part of the 4th Armored Division. He became the Assistant Division Signal Officer and gained more experience dealing with troops. He became a Major and had to switch from the relatively comfortable life of a rear echelon to living with troops sleeping in pup tents in cold weather. He also had to accommodate a few "rough, gruff old armored generals."

Al was on a project in 1956 called CCIS-70, Command and Control Information System 1970. The plan was to have the Army equipped with high technology by 1970. Al spent the next three years after 1964 working on this project, with 18 months of this time assigned to a project called TACFIRE. His next stop was Army War College in Carlisle Barracks, Pennsylvania.

In the summer of 1968, Al got shipped to Vietnam first as a project manager. Again he dealt with high technology, installing large telecommunications equipment up and down Vietnam and over into Thailand. This included a job called Project Compass, which entailed installing satellite ground terminals at Ton Sa Nhut Airport. Al subsequently learned that the project's purpose was to send target imagery from Vietnam to the White House so President Lyndon Johnson and Secretary of Defense Robert McNamara could decide which targets to bomb the next day. Al considered this a "stupid idea. I think perhaps if I had known it, I would have stuck a pin in the cable or otherwise tried to figure out something to do with that project. Nevertheless, I got it installed on time and within budget."

At this time, communications was 50 to 100 channels. Al could not figure out why the Vietcong hadn't attacked his remote hilltop facilities. He then realized the Vietcong had probably tapped into their communications and were trying to use it for themselves. A year later Al was sent to the northern part of South Vietnam to I-Corps's tactical zone, where he commanded a signal group for six months. He installed communications and supported the 101st Airborne Division and 1st Marine Division. There were three helicopters required to pick up the small huts that held the communications equipment and fly them to a hilltop because there were no roads that led to the top. The headquarters for this was in Phu Bai. Besides the fact that Phu Bai was "smelly and dirty," there were frequent Vietcong attacks. This was as close as Al came to actual combat, being with the army signal group. Very little equipment was damaged even though Al personally was given part of a cable that was near a rocket explosion that had disrupted communications for a day or so. Al was never hit, but one of his helicopters was not so lucky. Fortunately he was not in it at the time. The helicopter was on its way back from an assignment and was forced to shut the power off and just use the auto rotation of the blade to slowly, and hopefully, sink down to the ground. It landed in a rice paddy.

Al returned to the Pentagon after Vietnam to join the Vice Chief of Staff and the Office of Management Information. Their job was to provide policy and strategy for the use of computers across all of the Army. In the Army, it is said that you are never supposed to "volunteer," but Al volunteered to lead a study team focusing on the idea of making computers more accessible to the tactical troops. He became a full Colonel and "fortunately" was out of the Pentagon after just one year. The study resulted in a project at Fort Monmouth, New Jersey. Al was given the ability to again hand-pick a staff of engineers and officers and civil servants to organize a project office to oversee and manage Army tactical data systems. He spent six years doing this. The Pentagon tried to reassign him a number of times, but the Secretary of Defense refused, arguing Al was needed for working on computer accessibility for the Army. Al finished the project and got the first system deployed in Operation Desert Storm in 1991. For Al, volunteering turned out to be a good thing because he stayed on the same assignment and got promotions without switching assignments. His involvement went all the way back to Korea, looking at old World War II equipment running up and down hillsides, to sophisticated communications during Desert Storm.

By Desert Storm, the Army was just beginning to use laptop computers. Information was communicated from a backpack to a satellite to someone who could use the information. Although it has been argued otherwise, Al still does not believe modern warfare will be won by the military with the best technology. He is certainly in awe of how troops today are electronically integrated, but the reliance on technology worries him. He worries about the proper checks and balances as technology is incorporated. He would also like to see the technology used for the regular soldier, or "land warrior" as he or she is called, become even smaller and more reliable. Lastly, despite the reliability of current technology, Al does not believe high school students are properly educated in its use and particularly its maintenance.

After retiring from the service, Al's forte became "change management." "Managing change is that typical cycle of you're in denial and rejection and, kind of, okay, you finally accept it. You unfreeze and accept the change but you have to learn how to accelerate through all that." He signed up with a company called Digital Equipment Corporation in Boston. He was their chief information officer and strategic planner. After eight years he interviewed in New York for American Express. He switched jobs between Phoenix and New York a couple of times before settling in Phoenix, though he spent 80% of his job traveling to New York, Florida, England, Hong Kong, Sydney, Mexico City, and Buenos Aires. Clearly technology changes the basic processes of doing business and demands a change in management outlook.

When Al retired a third time, he did a study for the governor of Arizona on how to improve economic development using technology. For five years he also "coached" a team, along with a few other members, advising young entrepreneurs with bright ideas. Al is still on the oversight committee for state IT investment. He is also part of a volunteer advisory committee that addresses the issue of getting broadband to the state's rural areas. They have started the project using WiFi, which is broadband capability for a wide area of communications.

A native of Tucson, Arizona, Al currently lives in Paradise Valley with his wife Bettie. They have five children, four with careers in technology; one is a physical therapist. Al continues to appreciate the skills he learned in the Army. He not only learned about technology, but Beast Barracks taught him character. "Yes, any of the Army schools—signal school, command and staff school, the Army War College— they all have formal courses, if you will. They also offer you the ability to improve yourself and your outlook on social exchanges and relationships." It is because of pioneers like Al that we have been able to succeed in using technology and are moving forward with it all the time.

Dick Doubek

January 1963 - June 1972
Panama, Vietnam

None Left Behind

An Interview with Dick Doubek
By Greg Gorraiz

When *Platoon* first came onto the big screen, Dick Doubek's family asked if he would take them to see it. He had been a Special Forces Ranger in Vietnam as a young man. He agreed to go, but on specified conditions: once the movie ended, there would be no questions about his service. They would see the movie and go out to dinner afterwards, but the topic of Vietnam was not to continue when the film ended. This wasn't surprising to the family; the topic was almost never discussed. Even Dick's father—a World War II veteran—never exchanged his war stories when Dick returned from Vietnam. The jewels of Dick's life lay buried for decades. These are his unearthed stories.

Dick attended college on a football scholarship. Well, he attended most of college, at least. He didn't attend all the classes necessary to keep his scholarship because he was rehabbing a knee fresh off its third operation. "I played football and thought that was more important than attending the classes—until the draft notice showed up." With knees he could hardly bend, Dick expected no trouble with a draft notice. When he reported to the draft office, they saw his bad knee and sent him back to Champagne, Illinois, where he lived. He continued to rehab his knee in hopes of playing another year of football for the university. Six weeks later he received a call from his dad saying he had bad news. Dick had to take the physical again. Again, he wasn't concerned, so he took the train back to Chicago. When Dick arrived, the doctor told him to do a deep knee bend. "Unfortunately, without thinking, I did, and they crossed off the IV-F and stamped it I-A ... Two weeks after that I found myself at Fort Knox, Kentucky, in basic training."

Dick quickly realized this wasn't a permanent career path. Just before he left for Fort Knox, he was allowed to stay home for two weeks. He began looking at his options. Canada or Sweden, he thought to himself. Those were the common places draft dodgers left for in those days; perhaps he would join them. He only gave the thought a few seconds before turning it down. His family had a military history, and he wasn't about to duck war. All ten of his uncles and his dad served in World War II. Three of Dick's cousins were drafted within six months of his being called. "Not that we were strong military backers," but his family believed that when the country called, it was their duty to serve.

After basic training, Dick wondered in which field to apply, figuring he had "pretty good odds" of going to Vietnam, even though he "put in" for Europe. He really wanted to go to Stuttgart, Germany, to be a mechanic and truck driver. Since his chances of attaining that were slim, he chose to attend jump school at Fort Campbell, Kentucky, 101st Airborne, but after graduating Dick didn't like his options. Still wondering what to do, he found a notice on the bulletin board in the mess hall looking for Rangers and Green Berets. He decided to try it out and talked a few of his friends into going along with him. "I don't think I had any idea what I was getting myself into. . . . I soon woke up and realized that Ranger School wasn't a piece of cake." One hundred men in Dick's class entered; only 24 made it through the program.

Dick applied again for Europe, but was turned down and ordered to Oakland Army Terminal to prepare for Vietnam. For a period of two and a half days, he was given what seemed to be the 30 shots he had to receive before going overseas. The shots were administered through air guns. As he walked a line between the medics, they "shot" at him. Dick had a couple tattoos and the "sadistic" medics aimed for the center of them when giving shots; if Dick flinched, the tattoo would rip and become disfigured.

As the Army officers were processing the paperwork, they told Dick he was going to Panama

Dick at Jump School, Fort Campbell, Kentucky

before he was shipped to Vietnam. Good news, Dick thought to himself. He and fourteen others were sent to Panama. Seven stayed together through Vietnam; four made it out alive. One who survived was a Cajun, Wayne McNealy. "We never figured out how the Army got to him. He had never worn shoes or boots until the Army drafted him." Whenever possible during training, Wayne simply carried his boots over his shoulder. When a commander walked by, he quickly put them on.

In Panama, Dick went to Fort Sherman for jungle warfare school. Fortunately, Dick always had a fond love of nature and was able to adapt quickly to "living off the land." Dick completed the training with relative ease, and was sent back to Oakland. After four days, orders came for the men to head to the dock. He loaded the *USS Breckenridge*, a Navy troop transport. "I will remember that name 'til the day I die." To say the least, it wasn't luxurious. "The Navy had some wonderful ships, I'm sure; this one wasn't. You slept in racks where, if you wanted to turn over, you literally had to get out of the cot, flip over, and pull yourself back in." After a three-day stop in Hawaii, the ship left for Vietnam. Dick and the other men slowly lost track of time. To make the journey pass more quickly, Dick played cards, listened to music, and worked out—anything to lessen the boredom. Some of this was hampered by the huge waves crashing against the ship, causing severe "bobbing and weaving." It sometimes became so severe, the men weren't allowed on deck. They were often able to sneak up on deck nonetheless, since the ship personnel were so occupied they didn't care. Besides boredom, the waves also caused incredible seasickness, a disease contagious for the young men. "When you see some guys not real well, you become not real well." Dick began wondering whether being swept overboard was any worse than staying on the ship. Dick held on. Near the end of the voyage, as they approached Vietnam, the quartermasters told Dick and the others, "Boys, you'll smell it before you see it." Dick was on deck exercising on the final morning when the foul scent hit him. "Sure enough, you could smell the honeydew wagons before you could see them." It was Dick's "grand induction" to Vietnam.

Dick's crew came into Da Nang, although they changed bases throughout their tour, depending on their missions. On most missions they worked as a seven-man team, and occasionally a nine-man team. Dick's job, mainly put, was to go behind enemy lines for long periods of time to gain information about the Vietcong, sometimes as long as seven days. During the day, they did nothing but stay covered up. They waited until darkness fell to eat their C-Rations. At night, they performed their missions.

A testament to the adaptability of the U.S. soldier is how quickly the men gave up their preconceived notions of glory and molded together "as one." This was not out of kindness or brotherhood, but rather out of sheer necessity. They also found other ways to adapt, given their circumstances. For one, Dick learned never to stand next to a second lieutenant. First of all, second lieutenants were too eager to prove themselves heroes. Secondly, they all-too-often bared the bars on their chests, a perfect target for the Vietcong. Because the "Charlies" rarely hit their targets, anybody within a ten-foot radius was just as likely to get hit. The men also adapted by going on long, strenuous journeys. Dick and the other Rangers only brought what they could carry because air support was frequently impossible. "More often than not, given the option between carrying extra ammo or food, we'll always take the ammo." He could live off the land, but ammo was not available in the bush.

Sometimes when the Marines were shorthanded, Dick did search and rescue missions to find fallen helicopter and fighter pilots. The pilots usually came down when they were either wounded or ran out of fuel or, as in most cases, shot down. The Vietcong were terrible shots, but "you put enough lead in the sky, you're going to hit something sooner or later." With that in mind, helo pilots often sat on their helmets. "Any metal that you could get under you when you're flying is good protection." When the pilots were "feet dry," meaning they came to land and were shot down heading back to their carrier, they were ordered to hide as best they could, keep their transponders on, and not be "heroes." It was much easier for Dick and his team to find the pilots than the other way around. "Then at night, when they were through running the sorties, they'd bring in 'Jolly Green,' and a lot of time we'd bring in gunships to protect Jolly Green and they'd pick up the teams and whatever pilot you had and take them back to the carrier. Then we'd bunk down for the night." Dick and the men were "treated like kings" wherever they

bunked. Any supplies that needed replenishment were taken care of. Any time they were able to bring back one of the lost pilots or "Navy boys," the carrier wing was very appreciative.

Many times, base commanders at outlying bases weren't appreciative of how Special Ops worked and lived. The military is very strictly organized: hierarchies, battle plans, everything clearly defined. "There's a natural pecking order."

Vietnamese kid with A-Frame

The Rangers, who constantly came in unexpected and had the indisputable right to do so, were often looked down on. On one occasion, after John F. Kennedy was assassinated, the military bases went on maximum security lockdown. "We had been out in the bush and were oblivious to the assassination." Dick and his fellow Rangers showed up shortly after midnight after a week in the jungle and were "dead tired." The base sentry didn't know that, however. Dick and the other Rangers wore all-black, unmarked uniforms and "humping enough weapons to start World War III." The tower guards saw the team and ordered them to give the day's counter sign. If Dick were stationed at this base, he would know the code. Of course, Dick had no idea what it was, and at this point he didn't care. All he wanted was a shower, food, medical aid, and a bed. He had six other men who wanted the same. Thirty-five feet above them in the guard towers, two men ordered him to drop his weapons and put his hands in the air. Dick tried to let them know he had orders in his sleeve pocket, to which the guard responded, "You move and you're dead."

Finally, Dick got fed up and asked to see an officer who could make a decision. Successive higher-ranking officers came time after time, but without results. Finally the helpless guardsmen woke up the XO—a major. Dick said, "I'm going to reach in, and

I'm going to get my orders and my ID that says you've got to let me in this place." But once Dick started reaching, the major told the guards to take off their safeties. Dick told the major what a bad decision that was. If Dick were shot, the six men behind him would take out the major. The guard hesitantly agreed, and Dick showed a furious major the papers stating the team had to be let in. "[It] didn't make his night. . . . We weren't real popular, I'm sure."

Other missions involved taking Marine sniper teams to their assigned zones. Dick never knew what the Marines' missions were, but his job was to "cover their back door" and bring them out when they were finished. Dick's back-up training was demolitions, so the duty of blowing things up fell to him if necessary. "I got pretty good at taking bridges out with couple of golf-ball sizes of C4. That's fun to work with."

When they went out on a mission, they "rotated the point" every day. The "point" was the lead man walking. They rotated because the man on point was usually the "first to get it" in the event of an ambush. "We tried not to walk into too many ambushes, but every once in a while Charlie was pretty damn smart, too." On one occasion there was a Vietcong sniper hiding in the trees. "If there were some telepathic signals, I missed them." Luckily the man was a lousy shot and Dick got it in the leg. The medic wrapped it; fortunately they were just a day away from being picked up.

Dick wasn't so lucky on another occasion when taking a Marine sniper into Cambodia. All seven men were hit at once, and it was three days before the Green Beret team got to them. Adding insult to injury was the fact that the medic was out of morphine. Luckily all seven men survived that particular incident.

Despite Dick's courageous work, as well as the sacrifices of countless other soldiers, their efforts went largely unnoticed and unappreciated in the United States. Coming home from his first tour, Dick and a few other men traveled by airplane in full uniform, as was the rule at the time. The stewardess noticed and went on the intercom shortly before serving dinner. She said that if no one had a problem, the crew was going to serve the soldiers first, "one of the things that gave me a warm spot. Unbeknownst of what was going to happen later in the day, people stood up and applauded."

As the flight landed, the stewardess told the men to wait on the plane as everybody else exited, and a military guard would escort them off. "I'm going, 'Well, this is pretty nice. We're going to get a military guard. There's a band out there. We're coming home. It's going to be pretty neat.' Everybody gets off the plane and all of a sudden I see four MPs and a couple San Francisco cops in full riot gear get on this plane." Dick turned to his buddy Dick Keiser and asked him what the hell he had done, thinking they were in trouble. Dick Keiser, a six-foot-two-inch, 232-pound Ranger who filled "every square inch" of his uniform with pure muscle, said he didn't do a thing. The MPs came to them and laid down strict ground rules for leaving the airplane. Dick, baffled, asked if there was a ceremony. "No, you Jackass," the MP replied. "There are protestors out there. . . . Where have you been?" Dick replied, "I've been in goddamn rice paddies for the last two years. What do you mean, where have I been?" They exited the plane to find a group of Haight-Ashbury hippies waiting for them with buckets of so-called "blood" and protest signs. "Why don't you guys go have a beer and a smoke?" Kaiser said to the MPs. "We haven't had any real fun in about two and a half days." The cops were getting annoyed, and told him to shut up and fall in. One Navy SEAL let the cops know he was walking by himself and took off. The hippies were high from protest fever, among other things, so they daringly decided to break through the line and get hold of the SEAL. An instant later, the same hippies were several feet off the ground, flying through the air in every direction. The Navy SEAL straightened himself and said, "Who's next?" That was Dick's grand "homecoming."

Dick came back for a second tour, and did much of the same grueling work he did on his first. Overall, the mission for every Special Ops or Black Ops Force was to strike quickly, get done what had to be done, and "get the hell out" with a minimum number of casualties. "Having said that, you're taught from day one in any of the special schools, you leave no one behind. . . . That doesn't mean you bring their dog tags; that means you bring them home." One of Dick's proudest truths is his team never left a body behind.

Dick returned from Vietnam and moved on from that stage of his life, which is not to say his service had little effect on him. "It definitely made who I was in the corporate world. It molded my thought process and decision-making abilities. It molded my empathy for people and as a manager in the corporate world... I've had a number of people over the years tell me they didn't necessarily love me, but they respected the hell out of me, and that was probably the greatest compliment." He is also a member of Rolling Thunder, a group of Vietnam veteran "old guys" who own Harleys. These men pay their respects at their comrades' funerals and make an annual trek to the Vietnam Wall. They also work the information booth at the Wall.

The past comes to him in ways he doesn't expect. By pure chance, Dick lives a few houses away from Vic Conner, a helicopter pilot who flew him into the jungle on several of his missions.

Many veterans, including Dick, are the first to say there are no heroes. Heroes, to them, are people who "are in the wrong place at the wrong time that do the extraordinary thing." Although the military wasn't Dick's first career choice, he served when called and performed admirably in some of the most dangerous work offered by the military. He certainly fits this description of hero, as much as he may deny it. It is therefore gratifying to make his remarkable story forever available to those who did not live during this difficult time.

Like me.

Viet Cong bunker leading into tunnel complex

Rance Farrell

June 1961 - June 1993
Vietnam, Europe

Remembering the Long Gray Line

An Interview with Rance Farrell
By Barbara Hatch

Knowing Rance was a West Point graduate, Class of 1966, who served in Vietnam—the class that lost the most officers in Vietnam—Kirk and I anticipated stories of bloody firefights and harrowing helicopter rescues.

Instead, Rance chose to share his 32-year love affair with the military, a career that anchored his triangular core of values: love of family, love of service, and love of friends.

I loved every day in the military. I didn't love every job I had every day, but it was something you could believe in and work for, and you took care of each other, you took care of your troops, your bosses took care of you, and you took care of your bosses. You had loyalty up and down, the right kind of loyalty. You don't protect a guy that's a bad guy, that's a thief. And quite honestly, that's why I can't really watch most military movies 'cause they don't get it right. They got some megalomaniac as commander, and he's trying to do horrible things to the troops, and the troops are crazy and on drugs. I didn't see that. My 13 years in the military, I never met those guys. I met guys like Jim Morris and Park Shaw, and the other guys that are in your book, who I think share that same love of country and love of service and love of your troops.

The idealism of John F. Kennedy's Camelot presidency permeated Rance's high school years. We had stopped Communism. "The world was clean—good guys, bad guys—and we were clearly the good guys." Army's football team was Number 1.

Rance enlisted to try and get into West Point.

The lure of the Long Gray Line met the reality of plebe life. Beast Barracks, a tradition that stretched back 204 years, meant "bracing" whenever you left your room, and the usual harassment meant to instill discipline, like memorizing "plebe poop," the definition of leather, or changing uniforms. What bothered Rance the most, though, was not getting enough to eat. Cadets had to eat a "square meal" and were forbidden contraband snacks. "You cut a bite, put your fork down, put your knife down, pick up your fork, bring the bite up, put it in your mouth, put the fork down, then chew. And if you do anything wrong, they would stop you and ask you questions and yell at you and it just seemed like you never got enough to eat." The only way to escape was to tell a joke or perform a skit. If the table commandant granted a "fall out," the cadet could eat the entire meal normally without bracing or hazing. Rance's only joke fell flat. "Mr. Farrell, is that the extent of your repertoire? Eat. Just go ahead." His bruised ego sought a different tactic: join the track team. Athletes ate as much as they wanted at special training tables. This sounded like a plan.

Rance's track buddy did not think he could make the team. "You can't beat any of us." After a month of time trials, Rance won the quarter mile, the 600, and came in second in the 1,000 and the 60. When he asked, "Where's the mile?" the coach told him he made the team. He could eat at the training tables. And the friend who told him he'd never make the team? He never beat Rance in a race. "I'd *die* before I'd let him beat me in a race!" By the time Rance graduated, he was captain of the team and held the Academy record.

Football at Michie Stadium was a highlight of West Point life. "I mean, there's something about that place. The air is clear and you can look across the Hudson [River] and see all the castles and mansions on the other side." Beating Navy was even better. Having a *date* for the game was the best. Fortunately a girls' college named Ladycliff sat right outside West Point's gates. Mrs. Holland, the social director, was only too happy to match cadets with one of her girls. Deprived of automobiles, upperclassmen could secure some privacy strolling Flirtation Walk, a blanket hidden in a typewriter case. Plebes had to settle for stolen kisses behind the crumbling walls of Fort Putnam. Dating was called "dragging," because it seemed you had to "drag" the girl everywhere you went. "Drag D" meant an ugly date. D meant deficient in West Point lingo, such as, "I went D in Math today." Of course, if the girl was better looking than you, you got teased. "*She's* the one who drags D, not you!"

Advancing from Beast Barracks to plebe status meant assignment to a regular lettered company. Rance entered G-1, a "middle hard company." The

hardest was D-1, with some upper classmen who were "beyond the pale." Its most colorful cadet was Guatemalan Arturo Jetella, in whose eyes "the light of human kindness did not shine." Jetella did not tolerate plebes who pronounced his name with a J. One day, when a "dumber classmate, a little guy, knocked Jetella down while racing around a corner, Jetella quipped in his thick Spanish accent, "Smack, do you know who you just knocked down?" Picking Jetella up and dusting him off, "Smack" looked at Jetella's name tag and clipped, "Yes, sir! You're Mr. JAY-TELL-UH!" "No, my name is AY-TEY-UH." "But sir, you're wearing Mr. JAY-TELL-UH's name tag!" No one recalls what happened to that cadet.

Unfortunately, by the time Rance graduated, Camelot had died. John Kennedy was assassinated in 1963. We got into Vietnam. The Bay of Pigs and the Cuban Missile Crisis showed starry-eyed West Pointers the world was not the peaceful place they imagined. "Gloom period," which always followed the Navy game, when the wind and snow and ice of New England autumn set in, became a mood of "shocked disbelief" with Kennedy's death. "A light had gone out of the world, I guess, is about the best way to describe it." By the time graduation came around Rance felt completely burned out, fed up with the Academy and by extension the whole military. He considered serving his required four years and getting out. This distaste for West Point changed about a month later when Rance returned for a friend's wedding. He felt the "chill" of West Point, the overwhelming brotherhood the Academy infused. He stayed in the Army for the next 27 years.

As classmates left for Vietnam, the Army sent Rance to Germany. This "wet behind the ears" 2nd Lieutenant was given a lot of responsibility as a Battery Commander, normally a Captain's job. One day Rance signed for and delivered nuclear weapons to his unit. Nuclear weapons helped deter potential Soviet advances into Western Europe. Two-man control of these weapons discouraged reckless command or possible theft, which could lead to World War III. The funniest story about nukes Rance tells is when JFK's advisors explained their top secret, fail-safe, methods for securing these weapons. Apparently Kennedy, on hearing of America's most closely guarded secret, responded, "Wait a minute. This is our best secret? Call the Russians and tell them the secret. We want them to control their nuclear weapons as well as this."

Rance admits he made mistakes as a young 2nd Lieutenant. Mistakes were expected. They also convinced him to do better in his next command. Because he spoke French and later learned German, he was selected to be a general's aide in Holland at a NATO Headquarters, After a little over a year, he volunteered for Vietnam.

Many of Rance's classmates had already served in Vietnam during his two and a half years in Europe. Trained to lead at West Point, Rance felt somewhat guilty not using that training in combat. "I felt that if we have troops in combat, they deserve the best leaders, and I was conceited enough to think I was one of those guys." As an artilleryman, he volunteered as a forward observer, and then wanted to command a battery. He emphatically did not want to be in the rear. "I wanted to be out in the field. I somehow felt that if I was out on the job I was supposed to be doing, that's what I should be doing. And I'd get through it okay."

Rance's unit operated near Cambodia. One operation called for clearing "Charlie," the Vietcong, from the tunnels that permeated Nui Ba Den, Black Virgin Mountain. A U.S. communications site sat on top of the mountain; the Americans controlled the base of the mountain and the area around it. But the rest of the mountain belonged to the VC. About every six months a firefight erupted as U.S. troops tried to eradicate Vietcong control of the mountain, but tunneled enemy troops escaped most American artillery attacks. Rance got his highest award for valor for that fight, including helping to bring dead and wounded off that bloody mountain." Later he thanked President Nixon for sending the military into Cambodia to clean out the enemy there —a VC sanctuary previously off-limits but exceptionally damaging to U.S. troops. When Rance became battery commander, it was placed in direct support of this same 25th Division Battalion and the new forward observer that replaced him was "shot out of the sky. For a period he served as both FO and Battery Commander, which was pretty exciting. Rance's helicopter was hit numerous times and had to make several crash landings, but he survived unscathed.

Another time in Cambodia a new forward observer, who found himself in a heavy firefight, panicked when he thought he was out of radio contact.

Rance could hear him on the radio but he could not hear Rance.

He was *screaming* for help. They were getting overrun. He was literally screaming and panicking. So I jumped in a helicopter and had the pilot fly us out to him. When we got close to him we were able to bring in fire support for him. His name was Larry Ward and his call sign was Alpha Two Five. I called down to him. And instead of saying, "Alpha Two Five," I said, "Hey, Larry, it's okay. It's Rance. I'm here." I used his name and my name and that calmed him down. He heard my voice; he heard me call him by his first name. I said, "Calm down. It's okay. I'm here. We got it; we got it under control. Now tell me where you want the fire, and I'll relay it and bring in an air strike for you if you need that, too." We got him out of that situation.

Larry visited Rance 12 years later in Germany and thanked him. Rance still chokes up telling this story.

If you want to make Rance angry, focus on the "Coke kids" or the "boom boom girls" that fill the movies about Vietnam. Rance will bring you back to one of his sergeants, "an absolutely great leader who knew what he was doing and took care of his men. Couldn't salute right, couldn't march in a parade, but who cared." He gave Rance an appreciation for the American boys who came to Vietnam as citizen soldiers, then returned to the steel mills of Pittsburgh. Rance made sure these men were properly trained, "standing to" in the evenings manning the guns, wearing their "steel pots," to repel the "bad guys outside the wire," then two cold drinks, Cokes or 3.2 beer, his medic strumming a guitar as the sun sank behind the jungle.

I've never seen that in a movie, either. And that's what I mean by the brotherhood, of the love of your fellow soldier. We were fighting for each other. We were going to take care of each other and bring everybody home. We didn't really know what the grand scheme of the war was. We were there to take care of our fellow Americans, the guys from our unit, take care of them and bring them home. And we did.

When Rance left Vietnam, the only souvenirs he wanted were pictures of his men. His daughter Amy arranged them in a battered album Rance picked up in the streets of Saigon.

After Vietnam, Rance was sent to study English at the University of Virginia in Charlottesville. He did not have to wear his uniform so for once he could let his hair grow. Despite some "sullen contempt" for the military on campus, no one spit on Rance. He returned to teach English at West Point, in the tradition of Robert E. Lee, Matthew Ridgway, Norman Schwartzkopf, and Wes Clark, a classmate who was also there with Rance teaching the cadets. Unlike the Navy, this assignment did not hurt his career. Rather, it gave him the chance to instill West Point values in new cadets. While there, he wandered the grounds thinking, "This is what it looked like when Robert E. Lee was here. This is what it was like when Eisenhower was here, when MacArthur was here." Leafing through yearbooks in the library, the face of George Armstrong Custer "leaped" from the page—strange-looking, but the anchor man in his class. "And I'm thinking, this is part of the Long Gray Line."

Commanding an airborne battalion at Fort Bragg "at an age when I probably shouldn't have been jumping out of airplanes" allowed Rance to continue inspiring troops, which he loved, the chance to make a difference.

Every two years the battalion underwent a command and general inspection. About three weeks before the inspection, Rance learned they had not been conducting some of the training in the manner the inspectors demanded. When one NCO volunteered to change the records to show they had trained the other way, Rance refused. "We're not going to do that. We're not going to change anything. We did what we did. And we're going to do this inspection right. I want you to tell the inspector what we did, and explain why we did it, and if there's a problem, tell him to come see me." One lieutenant sat and looked at Rance. Rance returned the look. "Thank you," the lieutenant's look said. "Thank you for showing me the way to lead."

Another time one of his captains, who was getting out of the Army, failed to file the efficiency reports upon which a soldier's career depended, while Rance was recovering from back surgery.

I had to go in front of the commanding general

at this next meeting and all of a sudden there's my battalion with four late efficiency reports. The general said, "Rance, what the hell happened?" I said, "General, I failed to supervise one of my officers properly. It won't happen again." He said, "Okay." That's it. I mean, there's no way I'll say, "Well, sir, I was on my back, and—." I said, "It was my fault. It's my fault. I didn't supervise the guy. I should have made sure he did it." And he understood that. That's the way I believe.

Rance retired as defense attaché in Switzerland, recognizing that at the age of 50, he wasn't going to make general officer. The embassy held a retirement ceremony and Rance took off his uniform. It was a bittersweet moment but Rance joked it gave him the chance to see if Susan "really married me for my uniform or not!" Apparently not. They have been married for 27 *wonderful* years.

Rance enjoyed working for Lockheed Martin after retiring from the Army, but missed the sense of loyalty he found in the military. The zero-sum competition in the corporate world had no place in the Army, where there was a sense of "I'll take care of you and you take care of me. We'll work together. We're all going to work together."

On September 17, 2006, Rance and Susan will return to West Point for his 40th reunion. They will stay at Hotel Thayer. He will reminisce with his classmates—George Crocker, Jack Wheeler, Bob Albright—about Vietnam and the Class of '66. A medic strumming his guitar at sunset. Drinking 3.2 beer. Sitting on Jonesie's body on a helo returning to base. Beast Barracks. Dragging. Football. Taking care of each other. Bringing everyone home.

Rance and Hal Jenkins leading Navy

They will walk through the cemetery, remembering those who didn't come home. Buck Thompson. Dave Crocker. Fred Bertolino.

Rance might find a cadet, stop by a grave, and tell the cadet about his friend's service. He may hope this young man—or woman—will learn to love the Army as he did. To discover the pride of the Long Gray Line. To believe, as Rance and Susan do, the words of General Creighton Abrams.

"The Army is not a profession. It's an affair of the heart."

Steve Goldsmith

Sept. 1966 - Sept. 1968
Vietnam, U.S.

S&D, a Forty-Five, and Some Morphine

An Interview with Steve Goldsmith
By Libby Day

It was the '60s and Harvey Goldsmith, regularly known as Steve, was training to be a jockey at Belmont Park in Elmont, New York, on Long Island. Then he was drafted, but luckily for him, there was a trainer going to Santa Anita, California, who had asked Steve to come with him as a jockey. Since he was moving to a different state, the government issued him a six-month extension on his draft. Consequently, Steve motored ahead with his career as a jockey and won his first race. One week later he was reporting for duty in San Diego, California, and was bussed up to Fort Ord for processing.

In 1966, after assigned his unit, Steve was sent to Fort Hood in Texas for basic training. He went through advanced infantry training and was placed in the Second Armored Division at Fort Hood. After one year in Texas, Steve was shipped off to Vietnam with the First Infantry Division. He first arrived at Cam Ranh Bay, and from there took a helicopter to Phuc Vinh, Vietnam, where he settled in for a couple of days. Then it was off to the field.

The First Infantry Division was a unit that specialized in air assaults, search and destroy missions, and ambush patrols. Search and destroy missions were generally 10 to 13-day missions whose purpose was to make contact with the enemy. In the case of the First Infantry Division, they were looking for the North Vietnamese Army. This meant they spent most of their time patrolling dense jungle areas near Saigon in an area called the Iron Triangle in the Hobo Woods.

Steve was originally situated on the inner flanks of the patrol unit with his machine gun ammo, but was quickly moved to the outer flanks, where he remained for roughly eight months. The flanks are comprised of two columns 20 meters apart. Each soldier is 10 meters from the man ahead of him, and then there are "flank men" 20 meters out, on the outside of the columns. This is a dangerous area because the flank men are usually the first to run into the enemy and risk being caught in the crossfire. "I remember being out on the flank and walking right over a brand new bunker that was just built, just dug. Then I saw another one, and another one. I ran my ass back into that column so fast. I was just getting everybody down."

The ambush patrols, simply put, "were the scariest things of all." Ambush patrols usually began just before dark. Five or six men would start off towards an area known to have enemy movement. Once the soldiers reached the destination, all they had to do was sit and wait. On a particularly heart-stopping patrol, it had gotten dark but the men had not yet reached their destination. As they drifted through fields of rice paddies, the sergeant said, "Oh, come on. We're almost there. We're almost there." David Williams, or "Red," as they called him, was in front of Steve and almost stepped on a sleeping North Vietnamese soldier.

That guy locked and loaded, like six feet away, and just started shooting. I hit the ground, and Red emptied his magazine. Bullets flying everywhere in the dark. It was complete chaos. Red fell back. "I'm shot, I'm shot!" but I knew he wasn't. I watched every bullet go right over his head. It was close, but he thought he was hit, just completely hysterical.

Steve is still in contact with David "Red" Williams. Both he and Steve have been diagnosed with Post-Traumatic Stress Disorder, as were most of the soldiers in the First Infantry Division.

On a day in late November of 1967, the lieutenant colonel was leading a patrol through an area of rubber tree plantations with the Alpha, Bravo, and Delta companies. Steve's company, Charlie Company, had been ordered to stay in the perimeter. As Steve recalled, the soldiers were fired upon by North Vietnamese snipers. The lieutenant colonel made a crucial mistake when he decided to follow them. He and his entire unit were forced into a "U-shaped ambush" by the North Vietnamese. With North Vietnamese snipers in the trees, and troops on the ground, the American unit sustained 33 fatalities and 55 wounded out of roughly 200 soldiers. It ended up being one of the worst days in American military history and is consequently heavily documented. With spurts of firefights still occurring, Steve and the rest of Charlie Company were ordered to recover and medevac out the dead and wounded and help the rest return to the perimeter. "That was a day I will never forget, to carry out so many dead and wounded. It was just horrible, really horrible."

From then on, Steve continued with patrols, and search and destroys, which were later changed to the more "politically correct" name "sweep and clear." This sounded less violent when the order was given. All in all, it was basically luck and reaction time that got the job done and the men out okay. "You could take a hundred guys and give them the best training in the world, give them all the top stuff, but when those bullets start flying past your face, you don't know how you're going to react until it happens."

After such great loss, the unit went through a period of "regrouping." During this time they did a lot of road clearing on the Ho Chi Minh Trail. This was one of the most dangerous jobs given to the unit, primarily because of the large amounts of Agent Orange that was used to defoliate and clear large areas. They guarded the roads and did a lot of mine sweeping along the roads as well. The men often found the larger mines, and it was easy to get them out without setting them off by digging around them. On the other hand, they had to watch out for "bouncing betties," small personnel mines that were easily set off. "If you step on it and you hear a click, you can't take your foot off because once you take your foot off, it goes off."

Once the unit was fully manned again, it was back on patrol. It was Christmas 1967, and it was hot, dry, and desolate as the soldiers guarded an artillery base. With soldiers strung out along a big perimeter, most were in a depressed daze, hoping to get out alive and back to their families. As a Christmas present from the United Services Organization, the troops welcomed a helicopter full of beautiful women. When the helicopter landed, the back door opened up and out came the girls dressed in cocktail attire. They were there to raise the morale and remind the troops what they were fighting for. "They come over and they're like, 'Hi, Merry Christmas, let me give you a hug.' They're there for a little while and then they leave."

During Steve's time in the armed forces, he had many new experiences, especially when it came to the Vietnamese people and their culture. In all cases, Steve's new experiences were good ones, especially when it came to social interaction with the locals. He remembers them being a very interesting and unique people, and in most cases, welcoming to the American troops. "They're very distinctive people. I liked them. I really did. I liked their culture." Of course, Steve did not experience Vietnamese culture by sitting in the perimeter and watching; he went out and experienced it for himself. There were, to be sure, stories we were not going to hear, but some he was willing to share.

The unit had just come in from the jungle after a particularly grueling search and destroy mission. As they came back into town, which was a major base, the authorities told the troops it was off-limits because there had been Vietcong movement downtown. After spending over a week plowing through dense jungle pursuing the North Vietnamese Army, the troops were having none of it. They wanted back into a civilized area to eat some good food and enjoy themselves for a short time. "We're like, 'Restricted, my ass!' So I took a .45 and a hand grenade and I went out and had a good time."

Steve with truck before R & R

As in most cultures, particularly during wartime, there are customs no one is proud of. Vietnam was no exception. In Vietnam, smoking opium was considered a highly cultural experience for locals and visitors alike. "We went into a room covered in bamboo mats and little trinkets, and they gave us these freshly pressed, white silk pajamas." Staying alert, Steve kept his .45 and hand grenade close by. "Then this little old man comes in, looked like he just walked out of a magazine with his long silk robes, long beard, and little cap." The man quietly entered carrying a small box. He sat down and shared his "culture" with the American GIs.

Steve saw many things, good and bad, during his time in Vietnam. Fortunately he had been assigned to a very proud unit, the 26th Infantry, part of the First Infantry Division. The unit was very well-commanded and took great pride in adhering to military values. According to Steve, "We were not just an average unit out there." No soldier out of the First Infantry Division ever crossed the line. There were no atrocities committed against the Vietnamese people. Most of the carnage that occurred during the Vietnam War was isolated incidents.

Every now and then opportunities arose for promotion or a duty change, some for good behavior and some because a guy just got lucky. For Steve, an opportunity was presented to him by one of the sergeants because of his small size. He asked Steve if he would like to volunteer for "tunnel rat" school. Weighing his options, Steve asked for more details. The sergeant told him it was a week-long training school in Saigon and "you get out of the bush," so Steve said, "Hell, yeah. Sign me up!" He was flown to a large base camp in Saigon, where he stayed for one week and went to school everyday. There they taught him what to look for in tunnels and how to see if one had been booby-trapped. Once he finished the tunnel rat school, he returned to the bush and continued patrols.

For a long time the unit never ran into any tunnels, but one day they were in a city area and found a tunnel entrance. Steve didn't really consider it a tunnel because the entrance was "just sitting there in broad daylight." Usually tunnels made by the Vietnamese were in dense jungle areas, very hard to locate. You had to "accidentally" run across one. Steve got called forward. "I take my flashlight and my .45 and I go have my look around. Well, that thing hadn't been used in years. It was completely vacant, and so I made the decision to blow it." When Steve came out and gave his decision to the commanding officer, he was reluctant to take it. He told Steve to go back in and have another look, but Steve was having none of that. He told the commander he'd "gladly" hand him the flashlight and follow him in—in much stronger language, of course. The officer called in demolition. Steve did not reenter the tunnel.

After that it was rather smooth sailing until the war began to escalate, and the unit moved into Loc Ninh Province, very close to the Cambodian border, where a large number of North Vietnamese troops were believed to be operating. To this day, Steve believes they were in Cambodia, but technically they were still in Vietnam. In any case, the unit was on patrol and the flanks were ambushed by 3,000 NVA regulars—the North Vietnamese Army. Thankfully, after spending eight months on the flanks, just one day previously he had been switched into the column. This move in position ultimately saved Steve's life.

Steve entered combat mode. He fired his weapon, but to his dismay he was surrounded by dead

Misty helicopter landing

and wounded American troops. The Vietnamese fired round after round and then sent in rockets. Steve had been lucky for eight months, but his luck had just run out. A rocket landed behind him, shoving him into the ground and severely injuring both his legs and breaking his right foot. "I saw my blood all over the bushes in front of me. It felt like a bus just ran me over, like my legs weighed a thousand pounds apiece." Steve did not dare look back, but remembered a man telling him that he wiggled his toes to see if they were still there. "Well, I wiggled 'em, and they were still there. I felt good, so I looked back. All my shoelaces were blown right open, just sticking straight up in the air." Not to call it lucky, but the soldier lying next to Steve had it much worse. "Blew his hand and foot right off. He probably took some of the blast that was coming my way."

Steve lay there as flat as he could, because every good soldier knows that the flatter you are, the better chance you've got of getting out alive. The soldier next to Steve had forgotten this critical tactic.

He was hysterical, jumping up and down, and

I'm yelling at him, "Get down or you're gonna die!" but he just kept hopping around on one leg. Finally I told him, "Get the fuck down on the ground!" and he did. Hysterical as ever, but he was alive. I told him, "You're alive. You're gonna make it. Just stay there."

In the background, Steve heard chainsaws clearing a landing zone for the helicopter to medevac the wounded soldiers. As he lay there, a big black man walking past stopped and said, "Shit, I can carry you." He picked Steve up, carried him about thirty yards, then set him down where the helicopter was supposed to come. "I remember just holding onto him like a little kid. I left my gun and everything there. I figured, 'I ain't gonna need that anymore.'"

As the helicopter landed, a medic ran over and gave Steve a quick injection of morphine before loading him into one of the six buckets attached to the helicopter. As the early morning sun rose, the helicopter lifted the wounded soldiers high above the jungle canopy. Steve was flown away in a peaceful daze as he looked down at the chaotic scene of fire and smoke below, thinking to himself, "I'm getting out, and I'm alive."

The chopper took the wounded soldiers to hospital triage in Long Xuyen. There Steve was set to rest on a small cot among the injured soldiers. Once again a medic came and gave Steve an injection of morphine, took a look at him, and put a small wire tag around his toe. The medic was followed by a priest

Soldier Steve in the field

who preemptively weaved through the rows of soldiers, giving them their last rites. "[Of] course I minded, but I was thinking, 'I don't need that, but thank you anyway.'" Some time later a few men came over, lifted the stretcher, and carried Steve into surgery. The next thing he remembers is waking up to a high-ranking officer in a dress uniform standing at the foot of his bed. With casts on both legs, Steve looked at the officer, who dropped a small brown envelope on his chest, saluted, and walked out of the room. When Steve opened the envelope he found a Purple Heart. To this day, this medal is kept in the small brown envelope.

Steve was in the hospital in Vietnam for five days. He was then sent to Okinawa, Japan, where he was in a ward with amputees. "Here I am, the only one with two arms and two legs, and they're all thinking, 'What in the hell did I do?'" After a few weeks in the amputee ward, Steve was put on a large jet, most likely a 747 that was reconstructed as a hospital. He was flown to Walter Reed Hospital in Washington, D.C., where he stayed for four days before being transported to St. Albans VA medical center in Queens, New York, near his home. Steve was also diagnosed with Post-Traumatic Stress Disorder. "People get Post-Traumatic Stress Disorder if somebody breaks into their house. Try being traumatized for eight months or a year."

When Steve was discharged in September of 1968, he went through three months of physical therapy before he was able to walk properly. After fully recovering from his injuries, Steve returned to Long Acres Racetrack in Washington State, where he trained horses for many years. In the early 1990s, Steve moved to Arizona, where he continued to train horses at Turf Paradise Racetrack in Phoenix. He is currently a self-described "60-year-old exercise boy" at the track.

Years later Richard Martinez, a soldier who was in the First Infantry Division with Steve, contacted him. Apparently one of the men in the First Infantry Division had been searching the Internet, trying to reunite the entire division. He found Richard Martinez and asked him to start calling around. When Richard got hold of Steve, they began reminiscing and eventually mentioned the name Dennis Hartpence, a soldier in the First Infantry Division who was mortally wounded in combat. Richard and his wife visited Denny's parents in Ohio in 2003 to tell them how Denny died on April 19, 1968, and to bring pictures he had of Denny in Vietnam. Denny's parents took them to visit his grave. Steve sent them a picture of

Denny when he heard from Richard about his visit [see "Since You Asked Again" in the back of this book].

When Steve dug through his old war photographs, he came across pictures of "Gomez," a close friend from Puerto Rico who was killed in the war. Steve decided he would try to contact the Gomez family, whom he thought still resided in Puerto Rico. After finding and picking through the details, Steve made arrangements to visit the Gomez family. He looked up everything, even the church the family supposedly attended. "I left word for the family to meet me at the hotel where I was staying, but no one came. No one called. It was like no one was interested. That really hurt me because I thought it would be nice for the family, nice to have all the pictures and things." Steve finally came to the conclusion that the family must have moved out of Puerto Rico.

The 1960s was an era of peace and love. The Vietnam War was poorly received by the public for many reasons, and like most young men and women, Steve had no desire to take part in military service. As he looks back on his years in the armed services, however, he has developed a soft spot. "I'm proud of what I did, and I'm probably a better American for it. I appreciate this country and I really love the service. Now I'm one of those old guys who wears his veteran's hat on Veterans Day. I even have a Purple Heart license plate."

A veteran's years in the service never leave him. Whether the memories are good, bad, or both, they are there to stay. Vietnam veterans never received a welcome home parade, much less a thank you. They were shoved ruthlessly back into the economic and social institutions of the United States. Some took this hostility to heart, and some did not. "My main job was getting my ass out of there and getting back home, and I almost didn't make it. I protected my troops. I did my job, and a damn good one at that." Now, after 40 years, America's Vietnam veterans are ready to speak about their service to this country. All I have to say is, "Welcome home."

Homer Holland

July 1959 - July 1971
Vietnam, U.S.

Honored to Lead
An Interview with Homer Holland
By Spenser Robert

As Mrs. Hatch and I were busy getting lost on the way to Homer J. Holland's home in order to interview him about his time in the Vietnam War, like most kids between ages nine to sixteen I was thinking, "Homer, like Homer Simpson, cool." Two hours later we found ourselves in Homer Holland's beautiful home and interviewed him. I couldn't believe the irony. Homer Holland is no Homer Simpson. In fact, the man who was number one in his class at West Point Academy could not be more drastically different.

On November 30, 1941, World War II had been underway for two years. It is of course widely known that on December 7, 1941, Pearl Harbor was attacked, leading to the involvement of America in the war. The reason I mention November 30th is because seven days before the attack on Pearl Harbor is the day war veteran Homer J. Holland was born.

When Homer was born his father was in medical school in Madison, Wisconsin. Soon after, his father was drafted into the Navy as a doctor. Growing up with his mother in a small southern Wisconsin town, Homer, the oldest of four children, didn't see his father for many years until he returned from World War II. Tragedy struck when Homer was ten years old and his father passed away. With no support from a husband, Homer's mother had to go back to teaching high school in order to support the family.

Most high school seniors across the country are asking themselves at this moment, "What am I going to do next?" Homer was no different. His mother most likely could not support his going to college, so Homer turned to his helpful guidance counselor. The counselor encouraged him to take a variety of exams on a competitive basis. Taking those tests turned out to be one of the best choices he ever made, leading him to achieve not only a scholarship to M.I.T., but an appointment to the prestigious West Point Academy as well. Now the late 1950s, Homer had to make a decision. Weighing the fact that the draft was still in effect, and that he would most likely spend time in the Army anyway, a four-year West Point education seemed to be an excellent choice. Now, I can only imagine how big a deal this must have been to go to a school like that. The reason I say that is because Homer must have been remarkably bright in order to go to this competitive school, especially coming from a town which hardly anyone left, let alone to go to a big-name school. In the long run Homer made an excellent decision, as he told me how he benefited from a strong, male-oriented school with many role models. So off to West Point it was…

I was fascinated as Homer described the first two months at West Point, where the Academy transformed Joe Citizen into a polite, upstanding cadet. The process was called "Beast Barracks." Upperclassmen monitored and supervised the freshmen, and they were pivotal in Homer's life—pivotal because when Homer saw the upperclassmen, he saw a goal to strive for. Seeing these men gave him a driving force to propel him through school. After rigorously going through the two months of Beast Barracks, I could hear a chuckle escape Mrs. Hatch when he explained how the plebes, or freshmen, were treated provisionally, still having to prove themselves. One of the main sayings at the academy was "Cooperate and Graduate," explained Homer. There was a large pressure to get to know and get along with your classmates. At meals the plebes were forced to eat at attention at the edge of their seats: you would take a bite, set your fork down, then take another bite. However, if you wanted something such as peas,

Homer with General MacArthur at West Point

you had to say, "Homer, pass the peas." If someone said, "Mr. Holland, pass the peas," the upperclassmen would know the plebe didn't know his first name. Homer's dad was Homer as well, so from early childhood through high school Homer just went by

H.J. to help differentiate between his father and himself. That choice certainly came back around to get him. It turned out to be an issue because cadets wore name tags with their last names and initials: "Holland, H.J." When someone would say, "H.J., can you pass the peas," the upperclassmen would chew him out for not knowing his name. Thus ended the H.J. era as everyone agreed the name "Homer" meant less trouble for everyone.

In his "Academic Year" of very small classes, Homer had a test everyday. As a student I'm pretty sure I have had nightmares like this, but I'll continue. At West Point a student would go up to the blackboard and explain his answers. This actually was a neat trick by the faculty, because it made you speak in front of the class and gain the ability to work under pressure. The tests, however, proved to be the beginning of good things to come, as in Homer's first year he was second in his class. He was first in the class the following year.

Homer suddenly stopped explaining to me about "getting the ball rolling" and seemed to remember what he wanted to say all along. "A cadet does not lie, cheat, or steal." This is the foundation of the honor code at West Point. Homer was very proud of this code, so much so his classmates elected him to be the honor representative for his company, H-1. From there, continuing to do well, Homer was elected Chairman of the Honor Committee as a senior. Not only that, but Homer was the Cadet Brigade Executive Officer for the entire student body, one of the highest and most prestigious ranks at the Academy. As Brigade Executive Officer and Chairman of the Honor Committee, he held immense responsibility, with duties such as giving presentations to generals, senators, and other politicians.

After finishing his education first in his class, he graduated. Graduating was the achievement he had been looking forward to all this time, yet he was suddenly down to the significantly lower position of 2nd lieutenant. Graduating from West Point, though, with such significant honors was one of the greatest experiences of his life, and it led him to his next chapter.

After graduation Homer went to jump school at Fort Benning, and then to the 82nd Airborne Division at Fort Bragg. Just after graduating he was married to his high school sweetheart; they had romantically run off together. While at Fort Bragg his son was born. It was now 1965, and President Lyndon B. Johnson had sent troops of the 82nd Airborne Division into the Dominican Republic. As company commander he was responsible for the communications for the force that went down there. He called U.S. involvement in the Dominican Republic a "show of force." There were few casualties, and at the time there were some big worries that the Dominican Republic was going to go communist. He was on orders, however, to go to graduate school and so did not stay down there as long as many others did.

After two years of troop duty he planned to go to M.I.T. and get his Masters degree in Physics, with the desire to then teach physics at West Point. His advisor at M.I.T., also the head of the physics department, explained that he had to take the Ph.D. qualifying exam. While he didn't have as much physics as many of his peers, he found that he did quite well on the subjects he had taken. In some cases it seemed to him that he understood physics as well if not better than his peers. So after he did exceptionally well on the test, his advisor encouraged him to stay on and get his Ph.D. in Physics. It was less than a year later when he had already finished most of his course work for his Masters that someone from the Pentagon came to review the graduate programs at M.I.T. for Army officers. The Pentagon representative was asked about extending Homer's graduate schooling from two years to three years in order for him to complete his doctorate. The representative from the Pentagon explained that they weren't in need of Ph.D.s and physicists, but they were looking for people who understood operations research and systems analysis. So Homer decided to take some courses in operations research and really enjoyed them. It turned out the head of the operations research center happened to be a physics professor. In this stroke of luck Homer was allowed to write an operations research thesis for him, which counted both for a Masters degree in physics and a Masters degree in operations research.

Just prior to completing his tour at M.I.T., Homer received orders to the Officer Career Course and as expected, orders to Vietnam to join the 9th Infantry Division in the Mekong Delta. Shortly before graduating from the Career Course, he arranged for his wife and their two children to move back to Wisconsin with her family, while he sent his footlocker to the 9th Infantry Division. Plans quickly changed as

he got the sudden order that he was to first go to Fort Campbell in Kentucky for six to nine months. Then he would eventually go over to Vietnam with the 101st Airborne Division. Frustrated that he had already been prepared for deployment to Vietnam, had made arrangements for his family, and had already sent his stuff, he decided to make his case to the personnel people in Washington. Somewhere in all of it they worked it out that he would still go to the 101st but he would be part of an advance party; he would go almost immediately to Vietnam ahead of the 101st Airborne Division. This ultimately worked out and hey, he even got his footlocker back.

In September of 1967 things were going pretty well. Homer's job evolved into becoming the assistant division signal officer. This meant he would be responsible for making sure that all of the communications within the division were working right, as well as getting the call signs and frequencies coordinated. As part of the advance party, they were constantly on the move. The first place they went to was a place called Song Be, in order to help block enemy infiltration. In an effort by the enemy to harass them more than anything else, in the dark nights at Song Be they were often mortared. After many nights in Song Be, being mortared wouldn't seem too bad compared to their next location, Phu

Sitting at desk in Saigon J-2 MACV wearing glasses

Bai. I can only imagine how miserable it was as Homer described their lack of cold weather gear when their advance party was moved to the colder northern province of South Vietnam.

Showing how small a world it can be, Homer began to recount a day he decided to just go for a walk around camp. As he was walking about, he saw a Quonset hut, which looked like half a cylinder. Bewildered because he didn't know who was inside, he learned it was a bunch of Navy engineers. Lo and behold, he found out the commanding officer of this unit was somebody he had gone to graduate school with at M.I.T. The officer invited Homer and a couple of other guys over for dinner. Homer says they really learned the difference between the Army and the Navy. While their Army contingent normally ate cold C-rations, Homer enjoyed this meal with the Navy guys that included linen napkins, tablecloths, and china. The Navy men even had Philippine stewards serving their meal, right out in the jungle.

Sometime after their delicious meal with the Navy, a former professor of his from West Point learned Homer had an operations research background. The professor was in J-2, or the intelligence part of the entire Military Assistance Command in Vietnam. He needed some people with analytical backgrounds, so he arranged for Homer to get transferred to Ton Sa Nhut Air Base in Saigon. Homer recalled that one night staying in a relatively modest hotel, startling rockets woke him up. Used to ducking under sandbags when he heard incoming shells, he jumped out of bed and was surprised when he remembered he was up on the fifth floor of a hotel and not in a bunker.

Following his one-year tour in Vietnam, Homer and his family moved to Annandale, Virginia, for almost three years. He worked in the Office of the Army Chief of Staff in the Pentagon. The Army decided his operations research degree and background would be useful in analyzing Army force levels and composition to be prepared for threats five and ten years out. While Homer found the work stimulating and rewarding, he also had the opportunity to interact with many senior generals and to understand the limitations and frustrations experienced by the most successful military leaders. Homer decided to complete his military career after eight years of active duty, in part because of this window into a possible future. He had prepared for his subsequent business career by going to night school at George Washington University, earning a doctorate in business while working at the Pentagon.

Homer went to work for the First Bank of Chicago, and for eight years he found success there. He later became President of the Exchange National Bank of Chicago, where he led a turnaround of the Exchange and then later acquired Central National Bank. With four years of experience fixing banks, he

decided to set out on his own, founding Holland Partners, Inc. in 1983, a firm specializing in fixing failed financial institutions. His timing was good as hundreds of Savings and Loans were falling into insolvency after the spike in interest rates in the early '80s. Over the next decade, Homer and his team acquired six thrifts in Texas. By the mid '90s, the thrifts were all profitable and Homer sold them to larger banks.

Standing in front of barracks in Bien Hoa wearing steel pot; the barracks had metal sides to fend off the rain and mosquito netting... the Ritz!

In 1995 Homer's first grandson suffered a brain hemorrhage at his premature birth. This ultimately led to a condition called hydrocephalus, where excess fluid accumulates in the cranium. Hydrocephalus is often overlooked by major foundations and researchers. Like a true leader, Homer saw the lack of research and data in this field and took the leadership traits learned in both his military and business careers to create a foundation for hydrocephalus. Pioneering in the hydrocephalus field, the Brain Child Foundation, managed by Homer's son-in-law, has also found a bold researcher with many thought-changing theories on this condition.

Today, Homer and his son and son-in-law operate Holland Partners, Inc. as a private investment company on behalf of the family, investing in financial services and real estate firms.

For a man who came up in a small town, went on to achieve scholarships to M.I.T. and West Point, and served his time in the Vietnam War, I am impressed with Homer J. Holland. He wasn't given a Purple Heart or a Medal of Honor, but his life story of overcoming the odds and using his education to be the best he could has inspired me: to work hard in school, give everything my all, and with any luck become half as successful as he is. Thank you, Homer, from me and a grateful nation for your military service, your inspiring business success, and for the work you are doing in the medical field.

Gobel D. James

1952 - 1984
Germany,
Vietnam, United States

The Travels of a POW

An Interview With Gobel James
By Amanda Poincelot

Gobel James did not expect that serving his country would lead to being a prisoner of war (POW) for almost five years. He was born in Amarillo, Texas, but his family moved to Oklahoma when he was six months old. While in college, Gobel saw the recruitment posters for the Korean War. The posters showed jet fighter aircraft and claimed the need for pilots. This really appealed to him so he enlisted in the Air Force in 1952 as an aviation cadet. After completing pilot training and combat crew training, he was sent to Kimpo Air Base, Korea, for a year. While there he flew the F-86F fighter aircraft with the Fourth Fighter Interceptor Wing. Gobel then returned to the States and was stationed at Clovis Air Base in New Mexico. It was at Clovis that he met his future wife, Betty Payton. After four years in the Air Force, he joined the Colorado Air National Guard and started back to college at the University of Colorado. Not too long after signing up with the Colorado Guard, he joined the Air National Guard Acrobatic Team. He ended up dropping out of college to be a narrator and spare pilot for the team. About three months after he started, the pilot who flew the slot position was killed during one of their air shows and then Gobel became the slot man. He did that for about a year and a half—again, flying the F-86F. Unfortunately, the team ran into budgetary problems and in 1959 was disbanded.

Gobel finished college and was called back to active duty during the Berlin Crisis. When that duty ended, he elected to remain on active duty and was stationed in Wichita, Kansas, at McConnell Air Force Base. He also served three years in Germany before returning to the States for additional training prior to going to Vietnam.

Gobel trained to be a Wild Weasel. The job of the Wild Weasel was to seek out and destroy surface-to-air missile sites. He was stationed at Korat Air Base in Thailand. He had flown many missions before his aircraft was attacked and shot down. "I was on my 34th mission when I was hit by Triple-A gunfire and my aircraft was shot down. I was in a two-place [seater] F-105; the guy who flew in the back was the weapons systems operator, Captain Larry Martin. We were going about 500 knots when we were hit. All the flight controls froze. We rolled to the inverted position and the nose dropped below the horizon. There was nothing I could do with the airplane and I called to him and told him to eject and then I ejected. During the ejection process, because we were going so fast, around 500 knots, and due to the forces of the air stream, my left knee was broken and dislocated. I had been through paratrooper school so I had a good idea of what I needed to do to avoid further damage to my knee, and I did that. Although it was a rather painful landing, I don't think I did any further damage. My main concern was the possibility of breaking the other leg, which for obvious reasons I didn't want to do. I hit the ground and there was a slight breeze blowing. It inflated the canopy on the parachute. I rolled over on my back and actuated [activated] the quick releases to release the parachute canopy. During the descent the Vietnamese were shooting at me; I could hear the shockwave of bullets as they were going by. Those same people captured me right after I released the parachute canopy."

The beginning of Gobel's time as a POW was harsh and terrifying. He downplays the horrific time by stating that "it was not a very fun time." The Vietnamese soldiers beat and kicked him and then proceeded to strip him down to his underwear. Gobel explained that this was normal procedure so the Vietnamese soldiers could make sure the American flyers were not concealing any weapons. His account of this time is not only precise and detailed but he also seemed to maintain a positive outlook no matter how dire his situation. While the soldiers were practicing "normal procedure," Gobel noticed they seemed hurried and kept looking off in the same direction. The soldiers picked him up under the arms and carried him about 100 yards to a small shack. When they got there, they quickly barred the door with wooden beams. He found out why the soldiers had been in such a hurry when the local peasants started banging on the door trying to get in. Gobel's optimism comes across with his statement of how lucky he was that he had been captured by disciplined military men. They protected him from the peasants who were, in all likelihood, trying to kill him.

Gobel's story from this point contains all the scenes of a POW movie. He was beaten, mistreated, and pushed to the limits of his endurance. The Vietnamese soldiers transported him in a truck from village to village while enroute to Hanoi. He was often forced to spend the day in underground structures, in dugout holes. They only traveled at night to escape detection by American bombers. With Gobel's broken and dislocated knee, he was not able to move himself to and from the truck. Captain Michael Burns and Lieutenant Colonel Crumpler, an F-4 crew that had been shot down 10 days before, were assigned to carry Gobel wherever the Vietnamese indicated. All of the men started to sustain weight loss and lack of energy from the poor diet and bad conditions. Not only did they have to endure the locals hitting, kicking, and throwing things at them, but at the same time American airplanes were bombing the area. Gobel tells of one of the bombing incidents. "The American airplanes rolled in and started dropping bombs and strafing. With the flares it was almost as light as day, so they could see what they were bombing. They hit a lot of trucks and caused a lot of fire. The guards shouted at them [Burns and Crumpler] and they threw the stretcher down, [then] threw me up on the truck. Burns and Crumpler jumped up on the truck and the guards [did too]. We of course were concerned about those bombs and the strafing. The driver hit the ignition and it went 'ehhnn-ehhnn.' If you've ever gone outside when it was very cold and tried to start your car and it wouldn't start, you know what frustration is and we were a lot more frustrated. The Vietnamese that were in the truck, well, everybody started talking. I couldn't understand them, but I think they were trying to tell him how to start the truck. Finally some guy raised the hood and beat on the carburetor and the truck started up and we went off and escaped from all that was going on there."

Everyday was the same for Gobel and the other POWs. They traveled by night and stopped in villages during the day. The normal routine was to pull the truck up next to a house or hut; branches from trees were cut to conceal it. The men were then brought into the house, where they stayed all day with a guard. They were usually fed a meal twice a day. In the evening they were loaded back into the truck and the villagers came out to say goodbye. They did this with rocks and sticks and whatever could be thrown at the prisoners. The guards did not like it very much because they were hit, too. At one point the routine was broken.

The Vietnamese soldiers loaded up the prisoners as usual, went down the road two or three miles, stopped and stayed a few hours, and then returned to the same village. This occurred several times until an English-speaking villager explained the situation to Gobel and the others. The Navy was bombing the approaches to the ferry. The Vietnamese would repair them in the daytime and then the bombers would come back at night. The truck moved out again to attempt to make the crossing, but stopped in a small village on the way. While there, Gobel and the others were just lying in the truck when they heard a strange snuffling noise. They looked out of the truck and saw a water buffalo being herded down the road by a Vietnamese man. About fifteen minutes later, the flares started falling and everything lit up. The Vietnamese soldiers took Burns and Crumpler out of the truck, and while Gobel was waiting for someone to carry him, the guards indicated he should stay in the truck. He decided that wasn't such a good idea and managed to get out and onto the ground. He reminded himself, "God helps those who help themselves." He used that saying to gain the strength to get across the road into a ditch. Luckily for Gobel the bombs did not reach him, but after the shells stopped falling he realized he would have to get himself back to the truck quickly before his guards caught him. During his plight he got quite a scare, although now he looks back and laughs. "The bombs dropped down the road and up the road, none in the village. So when the flares went out, I knew my guards weren't going to be very happy so I thought I better get back to that truck. I started crawling back to the truck and I heard this snorting and puffing and all of

Captain Gobel James in office McConnell AFB, 1964

that noise again. I looked up and in the dim light I could see that water buffalo coming back down the road. I had to cross the road to get back to the truck.

I thought oh, good grief, am I going to survive all these bombings and get killed by a water buffalo? There was a [large] tree fairly close to where I was. I crawled over to that tree and managed to pull myself up, standing up, holding onto the tree, and as the water buffalo approached, I started dancing around the tree on my one good leg so he couldn't see me. Again I thought, man, what a way to die after you survived all those other things. The water buffalo got right up there and I couldn't move fast enough. He got right even with me, looked over at me and snorted, turned and went on down the road. Then I saw that guy that had been herding it before was a ways behind it. But, I thought at the time, I was in shorts and a short-sleeved shirt and I hadn't been out in the sun in a few weeks, and I thought somebody standing over there watching must think this is a ludicrous scene. I had lost probably 10 pounds at least: this skinny American, pale legs, and dancing around a tree. Well, it wasn't funny at the time, but in retrospect it was. I got back to the truck and tried to crawl up in it. Burns and Crumpler got back and they pushed me up. The guards were screaming at me [and] threw a handful of dirt and rocks in my face."

The party picked up another prisoner on the way to Hanoi. He had one leg and one arm in a cast. His name was Bob Fant, a Navy pilot. The group finally arrived in the middle of August. They actually arrived during the day because President Johnson had declared a bombing halt north of the 20th parallel, so there was no bombing going on in the Hanoi area. The men were taken to the "Hanoi Hilton," where they were separated and put into cells. Each underwent interrogation and was moved around. The cells were just large enough for two or three men. There was a five-gallon bucket for a toilet and they were kept in the cells night and day. Burns and Fant ended up being put back in the cell with Gobel to help him maneuver with the injured knee. August in Hanoi is extremely hot. The cells only had tiny windows near the ceiling that did not bring any relief from the heat. Gobel and the others just lay there trying not to move, because moving made the heat worse.

Although the men were confined to their cells, they were periodically taken out. The Vietnamese subjected the prisoners to what the prisoners called "quizzes." While they were asked questions, it was really just a session of political indoctrination. Gobel describes it like a scene from a movie, with a six-foot by six-foot room, a small rough wooden table with two chairs—one for the Commissar and one for the interpreter—and a single bare light bulb hanging over the table. The prisoners were usually taken in one at a time and placed on a small, low stool. The Commissar would drone on about the history of the Vietnamese and how they were going to defeat the Americans. The sessions usually lasted a half hour to three-quarters of an hour and then the prisoner was taken back to his cell. The other time they were let out was to bathe once or twice a week. Gobel still could not walk on his own so Burns carried him to the bathing area and then back to the cell. The bathing area was a mere concrete enclosure with a concrete water basin .

After three months, Gobel was asked if he wanted a Vietnamese doctor to fix his leg. He still couldn't walk or even stand so he said yes. They kept him in the hospital for about two weeks before they operated. His health had become bad because of his extremely poor diet and lack of exercise. After taking daily blood tests, the doctors decided it was time to operate. Unfortunately, their idea of sterilization was not as advanced as ours. People in the operating room were barefoot and equipment was not as sterile as in the United States. After the operation, unsurprisingly Gobel's leg became severely infected; he had to stay in the hospital for another three weeks. With a 107-degree fever, he could not sleep. Gobel finally spoke with an English-speaking doctor when he could no longer endure the pain or sleeplessness. The doctor provided him a shot of morphine. "That evening they came in and told me they were going to give me a shot of morphine. They did, and as they started injecting it, the lights started going around in a circle, and before they got it all the way in, I was sound asleep. That was probably the most wonderful feeling I ever had, after not sleeping for three days and nights."

Those same poor conditions continued throughout his stay at the Hanoi Hilton. Although the prisoners were fed twice a day, the quality of their meals was lacking. The men were fed soup based on what was in season. Either they were served pumpkin, cabbage, or "weed soup." Pumpkin soup was first on the list; once that was out of season, cabbage came into play. After cabbage season was over, they were served a type of weed soup that everyone in his cell called "gasoline greens." Gobel found out later that some of the other cells called it "motor oil greens," so you can imagine what it tasted like. Even though the soup left much to be desired, the prisoners did get some nutritional relief from it. The French had once been in Vietnam and they taught the Vietnamese how to make French bread. The prisoners also got half a loaf of bread with their meals.

Gobel was moved around frequently and had various cellmates. One of the ways prisoners communicated who did not have access to each other was through a modified version of Morse code, both hand signals and tapping on the wall. Gobel still remembers part of it to this day. Some of the prisoners were very proficient and had long conversations. Everyone knew the code to warn of guards approaching—a big thump on the wall. One incident Gobel recalls was just before the Vietnamese holiday Tet. The prisoners usually got a treat of meat, sometimes pork, on Christmas and Tet. When the men were taken to their "quizzes," they noticed a scrawny goose in the yard. The next day when Gobel's cellmate Mike Burns was communicating with the cell across the hall, a misunderstanding occurred. "Everybody had seen the goose the day before. Mike Burns was talking under our cell door to a guy in another cell across the hall, and I was the senior officer in the cell. They were whispering, of course, and the rest of us were watching for guards. After they had talked for a while, Mike turned to me and said, 'You have anything else?' I said, 'Yes. Tell him there's a CIA man in camp disguised as a goose.' I thought that was kind of humorous. So Mike said, 'Hey, did you know there's a CIA man in camp?' And the other guy said no, and just then someone went thump on the wall and cut off all communications. It was three days before we had an opportunity to get back in touch with him to tell him it was just the goose. I felt bad because I knew he was sitting over there thinking, 'Oh, a CIA man in camp…something big is going to happen.'"

Gobel was in several camps in the outlying areas of Hanoi and the prisoners had names for all of them: The Plantation, Little Vegas, The Zoo, Camp Hope, and several others. An interesting situation happened during one of Gobel's movements. In November of 1970 there was an attempted rescue at a camp near Son Tay. Unfortunately, the prisoners had been moved so the attempt was unsuccessful. This raised Vietnamese concern over their prisoners so all

"The Zoo," Christmas 1970

the prisoners in outlying camps were brought into the Hanoi Hilton. Previously Gobel had always been in small two or three-man cells. When this large movement took place, the men were put into large cells approximately 65 feet long and about 25 feet wide. It was very crowded, but Gobel found another man he had known when he served in Germany: John Blevins. Next to Blevins was a man named Larry Carrigan. One day while talking to another prisoner, it was pointed out that Larry's family lived in Scottsdale, like Gobel's. When Gobel talked to Larry about it, they discovered an amazing coincidence.

I walked across the cell and said, "Hey, Larry, I understand your family lives in Scottsdale," and he said yeah. I said, "So does mine," and he said, "What's your address?" and I said, "6187 North Granite Reef Road" and Larry said, "Hi, neighbor." My son had health problems—pneumonia—in Kansas City and the doctor finally told my wife, "You need to get to a drier climate." She and my daughter flew out to Tucson and looked for a house but didn't really like it there, so they came up to Scottsdale and got a realty agent and she took them out to this one place on Granite Reef Road. She ended up renting a two-story townhouse. She and my daughter went back to Kansas City to get our furniture and other belongings. While she was gone back to Kansas City **a** woman named Sue Carrigan, Larry's wife, wanted to move from Phoenix to Scottsdale. She rented a condo in this complex, adjoining the one my wife was living in. Pure coincidence: neither knew that the other's husband was a POW until later. They were sleeping inches apart, literally, through the wall, and Larry Carrigan and I were sleeping inches apart 10,000 miles away. I always thought that it was a remarkable coincidence.

While in the various camps, Gobel went through many trying times. In April 1972 the Air Force began bombing the Hanoi area with B-52s. Gobel stated it was an "interesting" time. The Vietnamese moved approximately 120 of the 500 men in the Hanoi Hilton to an area near the Chinese border the prisoners called "Dog Patch." This was actually a relief for those men, as the camp was higher in elevation and cooler. While there was no electricity, the men got by using stubs of candles when necessary.

Gobel's words were not as positive when speaking of the atrocities committed by the Vietnamese when torturing American prisoners. Some of the various punishments could be severe. One of the more common tortures was to tie a man's arms so tightly behind his back the upper arms would touch. They then ran the rope up over the man's head to pull up his arms. Many prisoners suffered broken bones. Another physical punishment was to beat the men with rubber hoses across their bare skin. While the physical punishments were horrible, the Vietnamese also performed psychological tortures. They kept some men in dark rooms for months, rarely letting them out. They sometimes made the men sit on stools for days at a time without moving. The list of terrible punishments goes on and on. Some men were cuffed by their wrists and ankles, pulled up to the ceiling on block and tackle, and then dropped. How many American soldiers died from these tortures? We will probably never know for sure.

In 1969 life seemed to get a little better for the American prisoners. They were not sure if it was due to the death of the president of North Vietnam, Ho Chi Minh, or the support for the POWs back in the United States. Whatever the reason, the food got a little better and living conditions improved. The men were allowed out more often to bathe and in the large cell where Gobel was placed, they were permitted to play chess on homemade chessboards and also to play cards. This helped the time pass a bit more quickly, but Gobel missed his family immensely. To keep his sanity, he only allowed himself to think about his family for two minutes a day. This might sound harsh, but it was what he had to do to make it through each day. He did not want to imagine the fishing trips he was missing with his son, or the days with his wife and other children. At the same time, while Gobel was trying to keep his mind positive, an emotional moment was occurring for his wife. With the improved conditions, prisoners were allowed to start writing letters to their families. He recounted an incident he found out about later when he returned home. "I was allowed to write a letter after I had been there about a year. Up until my wife received that letter, she didn't know whether I was dead or alive. The way it was explained to me, an anti-war group came over to visit Hanoi and the Vietnamese let a number of us write letters, and that group brought the letters back to the States and mailed them here. My wife had gone to the post office for some reason and the postmaster told her, 'I have a special letter for you here.' He handed it to her and she could see that it was from Vietnam. She opened the letter and she saw who it was from and almost fainted. She excused herself and went back out to her car. [She] sat there for about twenty minutes, reading the letter

Return home 1973, hugging wife Betty

and trying to compose herself. It was a very short letter... Then she went back into the post office. That was the first that she knew whether I was dead or alive."

On January 19, 1973, the Vietnamese at Dog Patch told the American prisoners to get ready to be moved. The whole situation was different from any other time the prisoners had moved to other camps. The treatment was much more lenient. When they got back to Hanoi, Gobel was sent to the Plantation, where the prisoners were informed the war was over and they were being sent home. The first group went out in February; Gobel was sent out in the third group on March 14. When they got to the airport in Hanoi, one of the most beautiful sights Gobel had ever seen was waiting for them—two C-141s. On the side of those planes it did not say "United States Air Force." It said "United States of America," and a huge American flag was painted on the vertical stabilizer. They lined up in a long row and as each man's name was called, he walked proudly to a table set up on the ramp. Seated behind the table were an American Air Force Colonel, a Navy Captain, and a Vietnamese officer. Each prisoner saluted smartly and gave his rank and name followed by, "Reporting for duty, sir." The salute was returned. Each man was subsequently escorted by an American airman to a C-141. After several stops, Gobel arrived at March Air Force Base outside Riverside, California, where he was reunited with his family: his wife, his daughters, and his eleven-year-old son. After being a POW for almost five years, he was finally home.

There were changes, but Gobel picked up the pieces of his life and started living again as if he had never been away. Today he is very close to his children. He continued his career in the military and retired to Arizona. He attends reunions with the other POWs on a regular basis and stays in touch with many of them. Gobel tries not to think very often about that time spent as a POW. He remembers how hard it was, but he also remembers the rare acts of kindness.

We pulled into a village when we were moving north to Hanoi, right at dawn. They took Burns and Crumpler out of the truck. Up to that time, they had always taken me inside with them to spend the day inside a hut, but that day they left me in the back of the truck. It was early August and it was really hot when the sun came up. I stayed down low because I wanted to maintain a low profile, but around 7:30 to 8:00 in the morning, some guy jumped up on the edge of the truck and saw me and he let everybody know. Lots of people came and climbed up on the sides of the truck and they would jab at me with sticks. And as I said, you always worried about your eyes and the knives that they carried. They would spit on me, throw things at me and so on and so forth, and it was hot as hell lying there in the sun in August. A young girl jumped up on the side of the truck and threw a piece of melon and hit me in the chest. I think she made it look like she was punishing me, but really what she was doing was giving me something with water in it. That melon… I picked it up and ate it. I thought that was an act of kindness.

Gobel retired from the Air Force in 1984 with the rank of Colonel after 32 years of military service. Being a prisoner has given him a greater appreciation for the United States of America and the freedoms our military men and women fight to keep for us. If he had his life to live over again, Gobel says he would be a fighter pilot and an officer in the United States Air Force.

Gobel with F-4 in Korat, Thailand

Tom Leard

December 1967 - June 1974
Vietnam, Thailand,
Cambodia, Laos

Fitting the Pieces Together

An Interview with Tom Leard
By Kirk DiGiacomo

Tom Leard's first experiences involving military service came during his time at Ohio State University. While attending he joined ROTC, which gave him the opportunity to fly, something he desired to do. Leard had no idea what it "would take to be a pilot," but learning in the military and the prospect of combat flying seemed exciting to him.

In December 1967, Leard went to U.S.A.F. Undergraduate Pilot Training to begin training. He remembers "every waking hour and sometimes sleeping hours were focused in one way or another on producing a qualified rated pilot at the end of fifty-two weeks." He embraced the pace and intense training. As the year progressed, his flight and academic performance allowed him to have an early selection of an operational aircraft. Tom's choice was the brand-new OV-10A "Bronco," a forward air controller and visual reconnaissance plane manufactured in the town where he attended college. After graduation from UPT, the path to qualification in the Bronco led to Undergraduate Survival School and to fighter gunnery qualification. Finally, transition training in the OV-10A and its varied missions began.

After a few months of training with the OV-10A, Leard was sent to Southeast Asia to fly combat in the Vietnam War. Upon arrival he volunteered for assignment to a base in northeastern Thailand as airborne forward air controller. The forward air controller, or FAC, flies over the battle area and identifies and directs other pilots to targets on the ground. The fighter bomber aircraft then maneuver to place their ordnance on the targets. The missions he flew from the Thai base were either in Laos or Cambodia. This was, at the time, euphemistically called the "out country" war.

Upon arrival in Thailand, Tom's first impression of the air base was that of a junk yard. The walk from the flight line through the small terminal to "base side" passed countless empty ammunition boxes and "busted up" A-1 "Sky Raider" airplanes, which had Leard thinking, "It's going to be a long year." And it was.

From his base in Thailand, Tom first flew into Laos along the Ho Chi Minh Trail. In his position as forward air controller involving the identification of targets on the ground, Tom took caution to be as efficient as possible to execute these tasks without causing unnecessary collateral damage. This posed several restrictions on the operation. At times the weather, especially during the rainy season, provided yet another obstacle in the delivery of ordinance,

Ho Chi Minh trail just south of Mu Gia pass from North Vietnam

making a challenging job even trickier. Furthermore, finding transhipment devices along the Trail from the sky proved to be incredibly difficult due to groundcover and extremely healthy vegetation obstructing an aerial view.

It is easy to imagine enemy soldiers on the ground "didn't like being bombed." Supporting the shipment of materials into Laos from North Vietnam was the enemy's large quantity of anti-aircraft weapons. These were used by the North Vietnamese to shoot down planes flying overhead. After an American plane was hit during an attack, odds of the pilot surviving were slender because of the few "friendlies" on the ground to help him. The remote nature of Laos made it incredibly difficult for an airman to walk back to any base without the aid of other personnel. Mr. Leard's role in this type of situation was to direct the long-range rescue of crew members. He coordinated the extraction of crew members from the ground once they bailed out or ejected, depending on what kind of airplane they flew. Many different close air support aircraft supported these rescue operations. However, A-1s, supporting the CH-53 rescue helicopter, were the planes Leard coordinated to conduct the actual rescue on these missions.

One of the methods the North Vietnamese used to camouflage their defenses was to house the AAA (anti-aircraft artillery) guns in caves in the vicinity of the Trail. Leard recalls a rescue mission where an unlucky F-4 was shot down. The pilot and back seater each landed on opposite sides of a river. At the end of the first day, the pilot was captured and shot. The F-4 back seater (GIB) tactical navigator survived and spent the night on the ground. Leard was involved in attempts to recover this airman. Over the following three days an armada of American fighter bombers, including many A-1s, worked to suppress AAA ground fire to make a rescue attempt. Finally, the A-1s and CH-53 rescue helicopter were able to affect a successful rescue. One can imagine the celebrations that reigned when the airman was salvaged from the calamity.

New technology was being developed for OV-10 "backseaters" who flew on night missions. Leard flew these missions in Laos for awhile. Some of Leard's GIB colleagues were assigned to the A.F. System Organization for research and development of this new equipment suite. This allowed the GIBs to acquire "hands-on" experience, which they would use when they returned to the Systems organization to define the application for these new technologies for the aircraft. On one night mission, Leard was flying over the Ho Chi Minh Trail above an AAA site when a 37-millimeter gun was fired at his plane. The 37-millimeter "AAA" gun is a large weapon which, when moved, is towed behind a truck. To operate it, one man controls the gun barrel's azimuth position, the other its elevation. At night, the gun's clip of seven shells usually contained one tracer round. Fortunately on this night, the gunners were not very coordinated. While the gunners proceeded to fire, the tracer shells illuminated a complete circle, rather than tracking a straight line to Leard's aircraft. They put on quite a show and easily gave away their position.

Another day while in this theater of operations, an American O-2 and OV-10 experienced a midair collision at low altitude. The whole ordeal began when an F-4 GIB ejected after AAA gunfire hit his aircraft. Due to the damage the OV-10 received in the air, the pilot decided to eject himself and his GIB. The ejection was low enough that Leard saw the two seats still streaming upward as the airplane hit the ground in a fireball. Meanwhile, the O-2 pilot lost one of his vertical stabilizers and part of the elevator in the collision. However, even though it was in terrible condition, it could still fly. In about 25 minutes, Leard led the O-2 plane to an emergency Laotian airfield. According to Leard, "I thought everything was going to be fine," but he quickly realized he was wrong. After reaching the emergency field, all seemed home free until a Laotian C-47 pulled in front of the O-2 as it was just about to land. The O-2 went around for another attempt at landing. Unfortunately, just prior to touchdown a second time, it fell out of the sky. While all this was happening, the airborne search and rescue command post coordinated an American CH-53 helicopter to fly to the scene and standby just in case they were needed to rescue the O-2 flight crew. The O-2, having crashed on the runway, spread wreckage all along it. To make matters even worse, a jeep, coming to assist the crew, slid into the fuselage, the largest part of the plane left intact. The "Jolly Green Giant" helicopter caught

1st Lt. Leard with OV-10A after returning from a mission

word of the goings-on, came to the emergency field, and picked up the crew. In the end, two aircraft were lost and one was damaged, but Leard's group managed to save five air crewmen from the three aircraft.

The forward air controller mission also involved Leard in other situations. During his missions in support of air interdiction operations, Leard's job was more than simply asking and reacting to questions like, "Where is the target?" It also included questions like, "What did you find today on your mission?" or "What targets of interest have you found—*if* we could find ordnance to put on it?" Leard needed to consider all the aspects of counterinsurgency operations in relation to how and when—or if—military action could or would be taken. Leard commented it was quite rewarding to help manage all the "air assets" and apply them while considering all the factors of a mission. The air rescue of a downed American airman, for example, involved so many different groups that coordinating the various assets was critical to success.

One factor that aided his service in Thailand was that his fellow airmen were also volunteers for the missions in their theater of operation. This created an atmosphere of teamwork and camaraderie. One night, the troops went to a club to wind down after a particularly stressful day when they hadn't been able to save a fallen airman. The attempt was close, and all of the pilot's fellow airmen felt the loss. While at the club, a touring USO band made some remarks to the troops with the sentiment, "Woe is you." This upset those watching. Physical removal of the band ensued. Leard said, "Those folks went off to wherever they were going to next. We never saw them again, but they literally were thrown out the front door."

Tom's work in Cambodia was less eventful. When he arrived, there was not much American activity. The number of troops on the ground was limited because technically, as in Laos, "we were not there." Of course, the North Vietnamese were moving supplies to the NVA and Viet Cong in South Vietnam through Cambodia, but the U.S. had not yet openly attacked those transhipment routes in this neutral country. So, during Leard's time, flying in Cambodia seemed like a less harried version of his experiences in Laos. At the same time, the many complexities involved in coordinating the air assets and successfully executing long-range rescue efforts were the same. The only noteworthy activity from his time in Cambodia was that one of his engines gave out while performing visual reconnaissance. Fortunately the power from the remaining engine was adequate to allow for flight over the mountainous border and landing at his base.

Tom returned frequently to the exceptional quality of the men with whom he worked and the dedication of all forces to saving each American life. One story he tells is of a young lieutenant who got shot down late one afternoon. With only a few hours left until dark, a rescue would be difficult. Someone saw him hit the ground with a parachute but they didn't hear from him, even though he had a survival radio. "So an hour goes by, an hour and a half goes by, and finally he comes up on the radio. Someone asked him, 'Where have you been? We've been looking for you. So-and-so saw you land and we've been expecting you to get on the radio. We're trying to get the rescue forces lined up.'" With daylight diminishing, the rescue pilots were obviously most anxious to get the rescue operation underway. Instead he remarked, "No, I saw you flying around...but I wanted to let everybody get in position first and I wanted to get to a good location before I called anyone." He didn't panic and he didn't want extraordinary help. Tom told more than one story of men with such an attitude.

> The amount of resources we dedicated to save one life...whether it be the maintenance guys who readied the aircraft, the aircraft crew chief that strapped you in, or all the people that nobody sees who are in supply, and administration, and food preparation...it was almost unbelievable. It just goes on and on and on. It was like a totally upside down pyramid—all pointed at that one individual that needed rescuing.

When asked how he wanted to finish his story, Tom came back to the troops. He wanted me to be sure to tell about all the wonderful men (and a few women) who served in the Vietnam War, observing that only in recent years are they getting the recognition they deserve. He hopes the men and women in Iraq will also be acknowledged for their service.

Tom is proud to be from a country where we "dedicate all those resources to save one life." And where he could, in his way, help in that effort.

Bob Littlefield

February 1968 - November 1970
Chu Lai, Vietnam

A Different Kind of War

An Interview with Bob Littlefield
By Kevin Hildebrandt

His name may sound familiar from papers and the news scene, or you may have seen this current Scottsdale Councilman in a picture of the Vietnam War, flying over the landscape above the action in the door of a helicopter, shooting down at the opposing force below. Stories of fighting in this war is not all Mr. Littlefield relayed to us; rather, it was more the relations around the world at this time and his feelings about any kind of war or combat since he was there. Bob Littlefield is a proud veteran of the Vietnam War, "a different kind of war." He is proud of his job and the contribution of the entire group of soldiers who fought in Vietnam, but he questions the judgment of those higher in authority that made this war so "unpopular" with Americans and the world.

Mr. Littlefield volunteered to cross the threshold that many men feared in the 1960s and '70s. He arrived in Vietnam at Cam Ranh Bay and was posted to a base in Chu Lai, in the "northernmost part of South Vietnam," as a helicopter repairman and leader of a maintenance team. However, he felt he "wanted to go and actually fly and be part of the fighting." In March of 1970, he was promoted to platoon sergeant for a flight platoon of helicopter crew chiefs and door gunners. His platoon was always short on door gunners and crew chiefs to man the helicopters so Littlefield often filled in on such missions, taking a spot with one of the two M60s at the doors of the helicopter as it patrolled the Vietnamese countryside. He spent much of the summer of 1970, "probably the busiest time," with Special Forces, laying the groundwork for "a big push into Laos in early 1971." They fought with the South Vietnamese Army, taking troops and fighting large-scale battles in Laos. During this time, the newspapers in America reported there were no troops in Laos.

Though there wasn't any taking of land, or advancing on territory, as there was in World War II, many of the missions Mr. Littlefield undertook could be classified into three distinct categories: Eagle Flights, combat assaults, and resupply missions. Eagle Fights were more of a strategic "cat and mouse" approach that were, in a sense, seek-and-destroy missions in which the soldiers hunted down the enemy. Then there were combat assaults, in which large units moved on the enemy with a force of "seven to twenty helicopters filled with infantrymen." What remained were the resupply missions used to get supplies to the scattered firebases around Vietnam.

Showing his amiability through his modest attitude, Mr. Littlefield admits it was not a fun time by any means. It was grueling and long, exasperating and exhausting at times. However, he follows in the next breath to conclude that he is proud, and he wouldn't have given up his time in the service. Through all the difficult hours and over eighteen months in another country, to have your entire country against you and frowning upon you, yet still have a smile on your face, is truly miraculous.

Interestingly, while Mr. Littlefield was there, it wasn't necessarily the enemy that concerned him the most, but rather, flying missions with those he could not always trust. The South Vietnamese worked for them on the base, doing simple jobs and helping out the forces. By working with them, the entire American force ran the risk of being betrayed. One time in particular was after a battle with the supposed "enemy." Among the enemy dead was the body of one of their barbers. "So we were all pretty cynical about whether the Vietnamese who were there were really on our side or not."

It wasn't as in World War II where people are capturing territory. If you look at the history of World War II or the history of the Korean War, you'll see where you expanded, and territorial conquest, and how you measured

Bob with helicopter: Bob holds an M-60 standing near a UH-1H, or Huey

the progress in the war. It was exactly *not* that way in Vietnam.

It was a war full of firefights and gore to the point where the body count became the system of measuring progress and who was winning the war. "It was a very strange war. After I left after a year and a half, I didn't really feel that we had accomplished anything other than, of course, being alive ourselves."

While in Vietnam, Mr. Littlefield recalls that many of the worst missions, because you couldn't trust those you were with, were the missions that were flown with the South Vietnamese. They were not often considerate of the benefits of the entire unit; rather, they were only concerned with their own wellbeing. No matter the mission, the flight in the helicopter was much more peaceful when there were only Americans, or troops on board that everyone, without question, could trust.

In the M60 there's a part in it called an operating rod... and when it wears out, you have to replace the operating rod. But then what you've got left is a piece of steel. And rather than throwing those away, we would all keep one with us on the helicopter. And the point of that was, is when you go somewhere with the South Vietnamese, the ARVNs, occasionally, if one of them didn't want to get off, the point of the operating rod was to use it to smack him up the side of his steel pot, which would give him the message that he was to leave the helicopter. So everybody had to have one of those just in case. That was kind of a disheartening situation, but we never did trust the South Vietnamese, and so you'd always have a heightened sense of unease because you never knew if they were on your side or not.

Mr. Littlefield left active duty in November of 1970. By that time he had been reading the papers from home and knew "there were a lot of people who not only didn't like the war, but who didn't like us [the soldiers]. We all knew that we would not be coming back to a big welcome." They didn't. Though it was far from the riots and being spit on as they returned from Vietnam, there were no ticker tape

Firebase photo from Quang Ngai province, Vietnam, April 1970

parades, and it seemed to Bob his arrival back in the United States passed without notice or consideration.

It was like, okay, we're done, "bye," and then you came home. You took your uniform off and you went about your civilian life. So it was a very strange experience... It was a lot different than what happened either before or since.

Bob was fortunate to have the support of his new wife, whom he married during the war, and with whom he lives happily 36 years later. He still feels very strongly about what he and his fellow soldiers contributed to the war and to their country, no matter what his feelings are toward the reasoning behind it.

I certainly feel proud about the service I did. I did well. I feel proud. I wasn't a big hero. I didn't get a Medal of Honor, or a Silver Star, but I think I acquitted myself well. I did my

duty, I was brave when I needed to be, I didn't let anybody down. [I] accomplished my mission so far as I knew what it was, and I believe that most of my colleagues were the same. So I am proud of myself and I'm proud of them.

In part, much of what makes up Mr. Littlefield's political campaigns today comes from his own experiences and trials in the war.

I felt that we were kind of "done in" by our political and top military leadership, and I think history has proven that that's the case. And because of that I am very cynical about Americans going to war anywhere now. I look back at the small sacrifice I made and the larger sacrifices made by people who were killed and wounded over there. And I really am distrustful of the government making those kinds of judgments and sending Americans over to be killed or wounded, unless it's a clear effort.

Scottsdale Councilman Bob Littlefield continues to fly. He resides in the town of Scottsdale, Arizona, with his wife Kathy and wonderful dog Bear. I thank him for helping a young high school student like myself understand a piece of that confusing period in American history known as the Vietnam War.

Pablo Lopez

September 1966 - September 1969
Vietnam

No Foxhole Too Deep
An Interview with Pablo Lopez
By Cindy Garcia Barraza

Some memories may fade, but many don't. This story is one of those memories that never get forgotten. "We had two thousand rounds come in that night." Pablo Lopez, a veteran in the Vietnam War, enlisted on September 26th of 1966 in the U.S. Army with a friend of his named John Blair in Florence, Arizona. Pablo was born in Casa Grande, Arizona, grew up in Florence, Arizona, and, like me, is of Hispanic background.

Pablo took basic training in Fort Polk, Louisiana, when he traveled on an airplane for the first time ever.

I remember that it was my first airplane ride ever. Being a small town kid, [I] never went anywhere. They put us on a jet to Louisiana and then—no, we actually landed in Texas. Then from Texas we took a prop plane from, I don't remember just exactly where in Texas, but it took us to Lake Charles, Louisiana, on a prop job. I remember when we landed in L.A., it was raining, and it was late at night, and from that moment on we got yelled at.

At boot camp, they got their haircuts, which, according to him, lasted about ten seconds each. The style was a burr haircut, and they had to do it every week. The sergeant was telling them that most would end up in Vietnam, but some wouldn't make it back. When Pablo told us that, I got this chill up my spine, thinking that people die for our freedom. Anyway, at training, they were running all the time, and everywhere. They always ran with their combat boots on, and held their rifles and field packs with a grip so strong it felt like it was part of their bodies. You might wonder what a steel pot is, and Pablo will tell you about it. "A steel pot is the old military helmet that weighed about 5 pounds. You used it with just about anything… And inside the steel pot is a helmet liner."

After Pablo graduated basic training, they took him to Monmouth, New Jersey, to take some electronic training. When he first saw a cryptograph, he had no clue what it was, but after they told him, he had learned something new—a cryptograph is the scrambling of radio and teletype signals. The building where he took training was secured; no one could go in unless they had a security clearance. The equipment was also secured. It had a classification of confidential; they spoke nothing of it. Pablo finished his electronics training in August of 1967 at Fort Monmouth, New Jersey.

After that, Pablo and a buddy of his, Severin, thought they might try airborne. They had to take a physical first, and they passed it. They were to go to Fort Benning, Georgia, to take jump school. The girl at personnel told them they had to report to jump school if they agreed to take the orders. They looked at each other, and Severin said, "Do you really want to jump out of planes?" Pablo replied, "No." They cancelled the order. He was sent to Vietnam on October 7, 1967, from Oakland, California. On the flight, one soldier was unwell, so they had to stop at Anchorage, Alaska. Of course, it was during autumn, but they didn't predict they would have a sick soldier. They were dressed in short-sleeved khakis, and once they opened the door, the temperature dropped to zero. The airline didn't have any enclosed terminals at that time. "So, we're in short-sleeved khakis, and they're in parkas, and they're [military] asking us if it's cold." When they finally got to Bien Hoa, Vietnam, Pablo had to do some mess hall duties; mess hall duties are the duties of a private. It was late, and he was really tired, so he just went to sleep on the ground when he was supposed to be working.

That was where I ended up, in Bien Hoa, then going through all these time zones, and all these flights. I don't really know how long it was since we had gone to sleep. But, all I can remember was when I got to the replacement battalion in Bien Hoa, I had to do some duty in the mess hall, because, you know, it was a private's duty. You had to do all these nice duties. Somehow I got assigned to the mess hall, and I remember being late. And I was so tired that I actually went to sleep on the ground. That's one of the times I got really tired, and I slept on the ground area. That was my first night in-country.

Pablo was sent to Cu Chi, Vietnam, where he was assigned to the 125th Signal Battalion of the 25th Infantry. There, they had a training lesson where he "died." They got told where the traps where, what was going to happen, and what was going on. But they still "died" because they tripped the wire and stepped on the land mines.

After the course, they got sent to their units. Pablo's job in the unit was to fix equipment. There were 25,000 men in each division, and only three were working on this job. There were four units. The first was the equipment that went on backpack radios with the infantry; the second one goes on jeeps to hook the radio; the third one was a teletype, which is used to scramble messages. Last, there was a little box to scramble helicopter messages. So, it was all that work for three men who had learned electronic training over the years.

They had some nice places when they went to fix gear, but they also had some bad ones. One of the worst, according to Pablo, was when they went to Katum, which was a dense jungle area. The growth there was so thick you couldn't see five feet in front of you. Pablo was told by one of the guys, "Don't go there." You might wonder "why?" The problem was they couldn't go ten feet before being outside the perimeter. Clearly, that's not the bad part. The shocking part was that the equipment they transferred didn't work. At first it did, but when they put it together it wouldn't operate. It turned out they had to put the new equipment together, not the old one.

The equipment that I had was in the bunker. They'd dig a hole and put sand bags. So we were always forever filling sand bags, it seemed like. Anyway, the equipment [was] in the bunker, and I checked it out. It was all good,

Pablo and GI riding in truck

but it doesn't work when we put it all together. So we checked it out again, same thing. In each individual equipment, checks out good. But, for whatever reason, it wouldn't work together. And of course, communication is very important, and secured communication is even more important. The order was that we bring in whole new equipment, so we took out all the old stuff, put new stuff, and it worked, so I got the flight back.

After that incident, Pablo got sent back to Cu Chi. On the flight back the helicopter was crowded with a wounded VC prisoner and a fuel bladder for the helicopter. When an officer wanted to get on board, he was told there was no room. He pointed at Pablo and said, "Well, I'll bump *him*." The pilot politely told the officer, "Sir, of all the people you could bump, you can't bump him." This shows how important Pablo's job was in keeping the radios working.

Another time Pablo was sent near some rubber plantations at Tay Ninh, on the other side of Nui Ba Den, a mountain area. It seemed he was always repairing radios at night, with his rifle ready in case of problems, so there was little sleep. He always traveled with his tools. "So, of course, we spent the night awake." When he could not get back to Cu Chi, he took a flight to Ton Sa Nhut and a convoy back to Cu Chi. "Anyways, I was so tired that I actually went to sleep with my rifle underneath my chin on the back of the truck." At base camp, Pablo and his crew sat close to the generals' quarters, given that they worked on communications. "Being that close to the headquarters, we were a target because at night time we were at base camp." It was almost a daily event

Base shed after rocket attack

that they were warned about rockets hitting. They were being shelled regularly for no apparent reason. Later they learned this was the beginning of the 1968 Tet offensive. The 25th Infantry was close to the Cambodia border, where supplies were coming into Vietnam along the Ho Chi Minh trail. That night when Pablo heard the rocket come in, he was at base camp. Instantly, he knew something was wrong. It was like chaos starting. That was the very first time he ever heard a 122-millimeter rocket come in. It landed right next to them. Luckily, absolutely no one was hurt.

There were trenches there we were just trying to—you just find the lowest spot. You just hunkered down and that's what you do. So it was a long night, and we sat there. And the next morning we surveyed the hooches that were hit. Nobody was hit. One guy was just going out the door, and the door knocked him down. He was the closest one to getting hurt out of the whole bunch. So from then on it was like—. Actually, they pretty much kicked our butt all the way until about April of that year. And that was from the end of January to, well, it was like January the 31st when they hit us. And then we went from there until about the end of April that they just pounded us. I mean, we were hurt, the 25th Infantry. They even sent a Cavalry unit, 1st Air Cav, to help us out at Cu Chi at the time. And during Tet, for about 3 to 4 weeks we didn't get mail.

Obviously, Pablo's crew still had to fix equipment. Pablo had to fly in wherever the 25th Infantry was located. Ton Sa Nhut was one place, about 20-30 miles away. If they didn't fly, they rode in truck convoys. When they could not fix all the radio equipment at Cu Chi, they had to ship it to Saigon, so they went to Saigon over the course of the year. Pablo even saw the American embassy on one of his trips to Saigon. After the Tet offensive of 1968, however, they could no longer travel to Saigon like before. Nevertheless, Pablo continued to fix equipment as he always had.

Having served eleven months, Pablo was eligible for a break. He went to Sydney for seven

View from the Jeep: Vietnamese woman walking along roadside

days to get his R&R. He didn't think about doing a second tour. "One was enough." Back in Vietnam, he still had to wait about 30 days to go back to the "world," which was America.

On October the 5th, Pablo got orders to go back to the United States and leave Vietnam. He was sent to Bien Hoa first, because that's where they left country. When they went to the airport, the army took their weapons away. "When we got to Bien Hoa, they took our weapons away. The last night that you were in-country, you don't have any weapons at all. So that's kind of scary after being there a year. We had to turn in all our weapons. And we sat around, just got drunk."

The flight back on Freedom Bird was awfully long, and very quiet. After what seemed like decades, they finally landed in Oakland at Travis Air Force Base. Soldiers who had less than six months of service

got to leave the Army; he had twelve months. He got sent to Fort Knox, Kentucky, with orders to do communications there too. With his ability, they tried talking him into staying—at least they gave it a try. They even offered Pablo $10,000, and they would give him a bonus for being in the MOS, and a stripe. "Why won't you give me the stripe, then I'll decide," he told them, but he had to reenlist first. He said no, just no. Then he met with Severin and Barkosky at Fort Knox after a few days in town. They went to bars, hung out, and got drunk every night.

Pablo came back to Arizona and became a police officer. He has been hurt several times. Yet, it is the Vietnam War that causes him the worst fears. Telling me the story of the rocket attack, he got very choked up. I wondered what he wasn't telling me. He summed up his Vietnam experience with this comment. "You couldn't dig the hole deep enough."

Ennis Miller

May 1945 - January 1969
Germany, Japan, Korea, Vietnam

Worth the Wait

An Interview with Ennis Miller
By Leverne and Ennis Miller and Greg Gorraiz

Hello,

My name is Ennis B. Miller. I am an African American retiree from the U.S. Army, having served twenty-two years. I intend to take you on a tour that will allow you a peek into my military past, which included three combat duty stations. My military career started in World War II, then into the Korean conflict, and finally ended in the Vietnam War period. I have many fond memories, as well as a few nightmarish ones, of those years. So here goes.

Let's start by going back to my high school years. News scripts played scenes from the war during feature films, showing storm troopers marching in Germany and American bombers dropping bombs on German targets—a pretty impressive influence on impressionable American high school boys. I, along with several schoolmates, thought it was our duty to protect our American right to freedom through serving in the military. So, on the 2nd day of May 1945, I went into the Army.

I was immediately sent to what was called a reception center, where German POWs were held. The German POWs were kept busy handing out the military clothing allowance. Not too long after arriving, five days to be exact, word came that Germany had surrendered and war, with them at least, was ended. After receiving my clothing allowance I was sent to Fort McClellan, Alabama, for sixteen (16) weeks of rigorous infantry training. While I was on my last field march at Fort McClellan, the atomic bomb was dropped on Nagasaki and Hiroshima, Japan. Japan surrendered; World War II was finally over. But, before the war ended, I had been scheduled to go to Louisiana for advanced jungle training, so that was my next military training post.

Two days after my arrival in Louisiana, my assignment orders were changed to Fort Meade, Maryland. After spending two weeks there, I was sent to Camp Pickett, Virginia, and finally ended up at Camp Stoneman, California. The military just didn't seem to know what to do with us soldiers, so we got bounced around. After a month, military leaders gathered us together to make a deal. They told us that since we were draftees, they didn't have a specific date for our release, and this was a problem. So they said if a soldier chose to sign up for a definite time commitment, he would then be let go once he served that time. I held up my hand and signed up for one year of duty. I was immediately given thirty (30) days leave and told that I would receive my orders via mail. When my orders arrived in Oxford, Ohio, my home, they sent me back to Fort Meade, Maryland. After a short time there, I was put on a transport ship to Germany via Le Havre, France. Le Havre was filled with sunken vessels. Their masts and bows sticking out of the water made a poignant statement of war's devastating consequences.

A funny note: all the camps were named after cigarette companies—Camp(s) Chesterfield, Lucky Strike, Philip Morris, etc. We were never told how or why that was done. After docking, the troops were taken to Camp Chesterfield for two days. Then we were put into boxcars and sent on to Neustadt, Germany. The U.S. military occupied barracks which earlier were in the hands of the Germans. New recruits were assigned from there to various outfits; it was called a replacement depot.

I, myself, was housed in the unfinished Congress Hall, named by Hitler. He had begun construction of this multi-thousand-room building to be the site from which he would rule the entire world. The army used it for storage of supplies as well as housing of troops and German POWs. In February 1946, I wound up in the military police, doing what was called Metropolitan Duty in the war-devastated city of Nuremberg, Germany. And although the war had ended in May 1945, the foul smell of human death was still prevalent in Nuremberg. We military police were assigned to round up the Nazis and other German military personnel hiding out in tunnels located under the city. This was truly one very important and historic time period for me, being allowed to attend the trials and observe war criminals at the Palace of Justice. I remember noting that Goering seemed subdued, with not very much movement. I was glad to see that those war criminals were finally getting paid back for the crimes they perpetrated during that horrible time period called WWII.

In September of 1946 I was given an honorable discharge from the military, but even with my military police background training and experience, I was unable to get a decent job. So, I decided to enroll in Flight School, which was located in Cleveland, Ohio. There I obtained my Private Pilot's license. At the time, I was married with one (1) child. My wife requested that I stop flying around and come back home to Oxford. She convinced me to return by saying she'd rather have me alive than getting insurance money because of my accidental death by flying. But since I was still unable to get a good job, I thought surely I could use my flying experience in the Army. So I reenlisted.

I requested to be put into the Air Cadets. The recruiter said unfortunately there was not a quota for Negro pilots (the word Negro was used during that time to identify those who today are called Afro-Americans). Instead, the recruiter told me that I could enlist in the ground forces of the Air Force/Army first and maybe later on be considered for flight training. But I chose to return to the Army Infantry. I was put into a brand new battalion in the Second Division at Fort Lewis in the state of Washington. The battalion consisted entirely of black men in an otherwise all-white regiment. I was given a Private First Class rank and put in charge of a 54-man platoon with four squad leaders under my command. I also held the title of Athletic and Recreational NCO in charge of marching the battalion out into the athletic field for their daily calisthenics. It was during this time an incident happened in which a man threatened the Captain and First Sergeant in our company with a knife. Because they knew that I had a background in the military police, they asked for my assistance to disarm the man. They were impressed with my skills and statement, "There was nothing to it." As a result of that, I requested and was granted a transfer into a military police unit. I was assigned to the ASU Unit for 16 months. I then put in a request to go to Japan. In Japan, I was assigned to the 563rd Military Police Company. When I reported for duty, the Company Commander, Captain Washington, noticed that I had "excellent typing skills" and immediately assigned me to Operations and removed the Operations Sergeant, but I remained in the grade of Corporal. My new position put me in charge of the Vice Squad, patrol duties, and traffic control. I was told they couldn't promote me because rank was frozen at that time. However, as an African-American soldier, I would encounter other times in which my race seemed to be the determining factor in what really happened.

One time when it was quite obvious that my race played a part was while I was performing my assignment duty as a military policeman, working in

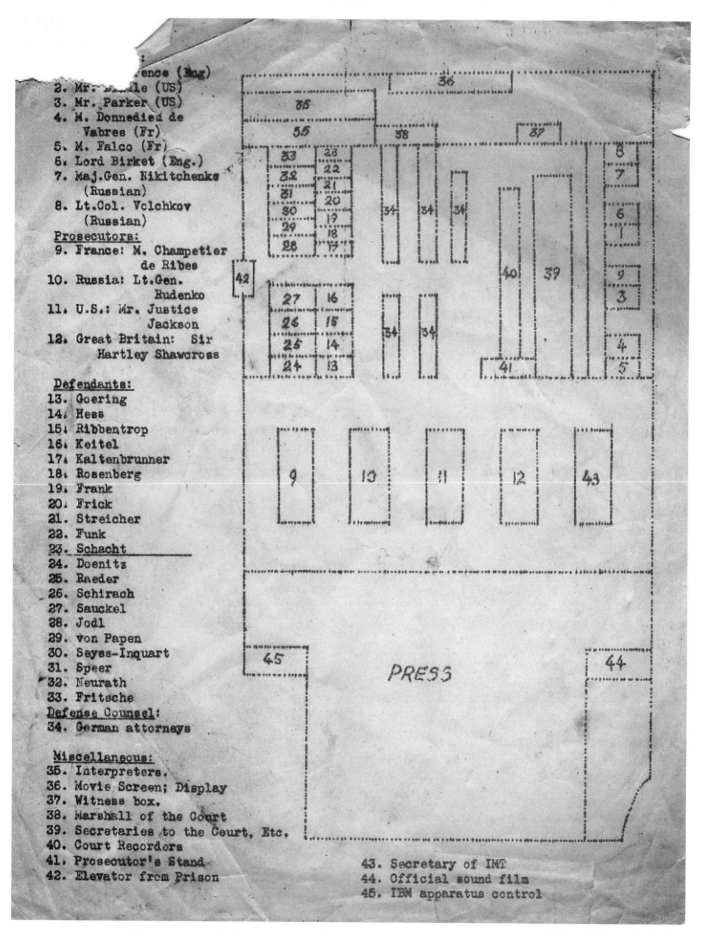

1. ...rence (Eng)
2. Mr. ...le (US)
3. Mr. Parker (US)
4. M. Donnedieu de
    Vabres (Fr)
5. M. Falco (Fr)
6. Lord Birket (Eng.)
7. Maj.Gen. Nikitchenko
    (Russian)
8. Lt.Col. Volchkov
    (Russian)

Prosecutors:
9. France: M. Champetier
              de Ribes
10. Russia: Lt.Gen.
              Rudenko
11. U.S.: Mr. Justice
              Jackson
12. Great Britain: Sir
        Hartley Shawcross

Defendants:
13. Goering
14. Hess
15. Ribbentrop
16. Keitel
17. Kaltenbrunner
18. Rosenberg
19. Frank
20. Frick
21. Streicher
22. Funk
23. Schacht
24. Doenitz
25. Raeder
26. Schirach
27. Sauckel
28. Jodl
29. von Papen
30. Seyss-Inquart
31. Speer
32. Neurath
33. Fritsche
Defense Counsel:
34. German attorneys

Miscellaneous:
35. Interpreters.
36. Movie Screen; Display
37. Witness box.
38. Marshall of the Court
39. Secretaries to the Court, Etc.
40. Court Recorders
41. Prosecutor's Stand
42. Elevator from Prison

43. Secretary of IMT
44. Official sound film
45. IBM apparatus control

Nuremberg Trial seating chart

238

traffic control. I stopped a Captain who was speeding on base. The Captain said to me in a loud voice, "What do you want, boy?" I told the Captain I was stopping him for speeding. Then I stated that he should respect my position as a military policeman, also my Corporal stripes, and not use the term "boy." The Captain then said, "Well, what are you going to do about it?" I wrote him a delinquency slip, which he took, ripped apart, and sped off. I reported this incident to my immediate Commanding Officer, who went to our higher Yokohama Ordinance base depot Commanding Officer. The Commanding Officer called me in and told me that he was issuing the Captain an official reprimand, which meant he would be punished for his actions. He would either be returned to enlistment status or given the option of leaving the service completely. Still, this type of disrespect was quite common, not only for me but also other African-Americans during this period of time.

On June 25, 1950, the "Korean conflict" broke out. I thought I was pretty secure there in Japan, but on the 21st of July my entire outfit was "uprooted" and taken to Korea. When my outfit got there, we were put into a schoolhouse. Lice was a major problem in that schoolhouse. They literally ate us up. To help ease the pain, we were given DDT dusting powder, which did a good job of killing the lice. It was during this time that unpublished history was made when I, along with six other African-American military police, were selected to set up the first POW camp in Korea. The camp was stationed in Taegu, Korea. At that time I was a mere Corporal, but put in charge of the POW camp under Major Sullivan, 8th Army Headquarters. We quickly set up the POW camp, and soon the first POWs came in; one was 16 and the other two were 14. Their names became "houseboy number one, number two, and number three." They were required only to do simple household duties. They weren't dangerous and we didn't have any problems at all, but soon new POWs started coming in "fast and furious." Because we had not been trained to interrogate, a trained unit was sent in from Japan. At that time, Major Sullivan, the officer in charge of the camp, told me and the others we would have to be relocated. The military wasn't integrated at that time, so there was no place for us in the incoming company. I asked to be sent to the 12th MP Company in Pusan, and the Major made the preparations. After the move was finished, Major Sullivan told me to give him a call if I ever had any problems at my new duty station.

My arrival at the 512th was rocky, to say the least. The First Sergeant told me he didn't need a clerk, so he sent me down to work on a nearby dock. The man in charge there, Sergeant Quarles, said he too had a clerk so he gave me a carbine and ordered me to guard a boat loaded with ammunition. I felt totally misplaced, so I called Major Sullivan to let him know what was happening. The Major told me to continue my job until my shift was over and then he would see what he could do. The next day, the First Sergeant called me up and said, "Hey, Corporal Miller, what in the heck have you done now?" I asked him what he was talking about. Then the First Sergeant told me I was ordered to report to the Provost Marshall's office immediately. I wasn't worried, since I hadn't done anything wrong. When I got there I was assigned to work inside the Provost Marshall's office. Major Sullivan had come through, as he promised. My duties included setting up files, cross-referencing files for delinquency reports, and working on anything else that came into the Provost Marshall's office. I received my promotion to Staff Sergeant at this duty station.

After a time in the Provost Marshall's office, I was sent to Japan to transport some "lifers" to the Big 8, which is the 8th Army Stockade in Tokyo. After delivering the prisoners, I was given five days temporary duty (or TDY). I went to my old stomping ground and missed my train which connects to Sasebo, where the boat that returns to Korea docks. As fate would have it, the boat was already departing, leaving me frantically trying to get on. I tried to get the personnel officer to help me and call my duty station, but the officer merely asked why I was so anxious to "get back over into that mess." Because of that, I lost my job in the Provost Marshall's office for not getting back on time. I got put on desertion, which of course was untrue. Colonel Shankle did not accept my excuses. He told me to pick an outfit, and I would be sent there. This was the way of military justice in a combat zone.

I picked the 563rd, the same outfit I was in while stationed in Japan. I was restored to rank as Operations Sergeant and then was promoted to Sergeant First Class. After 15 months in Korea, I was rotated to Fort Custer, Michigan. They had a National

Guard outfit out in Washington D.C. They didn't quite shape up like the regular Army people; they tried, but there were some shortcomings there. I was given the title of Assistant Provost Marshall with Captain Thompson as the Provost Marshall, a man known in New York as "Dick Tracy." My job at that time consisted mainly of driving to different cities and checking on MPs and their commitment to their official duties.

In 1952 the Department of Defense Center directed me to the Post Commanders to screen all personnel records to see who was qualified to go into missile training at Fort Bliss, Texas. They had a surface-to-air prototype ready but hadn't yet fielded a unit. I was one of the first three to get out of Fort Custer, Michigan, and then go west to Fort Bliss. After training there, I was supposed to go with a unit to Yakima, Washington, but I had "very unfriendly incidents" in that outfit, so I said I wouldn't go with them.

I became Battalion Operations Sergeant when I returned to Fort Bliss. After a year, I was transferred to Oakland Air Defense, and I took my family with me to California. I reenlisted in February of 1957 and was sent to a missile set-up site for defense of the cities of Chicago and Gary, Indiana. There was a Sergeant First Class there, an alcoholic maintenance chief. A stripe came down for Master Sergeant and that man was promoted over me because he had been in the outfit longer. The man didn't keep his stripe very long. The Battalion Commander then called for all the Sergeants First Class who were eligible for Master Sergeant Rank to interview for the stripe. I competed against 13 other First Sergeants for that rank and I was selected. I was promoted to Master Sergeant. It was a proud moment.

The Army ranking system had since been rearranged, while I was attempting to rise up through the ranks. Master Sergeant was the highest point a soldier in the enlisted grade could attain. After being chosen as Master Sergeant, I was sent to a suburban area, east of Gary, Indiana, as maintenance chief. The missile system I worked on, the Nike Hercules, was a much upgraded missile from my last job, the Nike Ajax, but Nike Ajax looked like a pencil compared to the Nike Hercules. I served in this unit for four years.

In 1961, I volunteered for a two-year tour of duty in Germany. This was my second tour in Germany, although I was in Stuttgart for this tour, as opposed to Nuremberg the first time. After my tour in Stuttgart, I decided to take leave in order to visit Nuremberg, my original duty station during World War II. I stopped at Parkstrasse Street, where I had once befriended a German family. During my first tour, the family and I would play games together. I wanted to see if they were still there. I went to the second floor where they lived and rang the buzzer. A man asked who was there. I wasn't sure if they would remember me or if it was even the right family, so I said, "Herr Mueller." The door flew open and I was gladly received by the family. Before returning to the States, I also visited Berchtesgaden for a few days. This was the site of Hitler's mountain retreat called Eagle's Nest. It had been changed into a GI retreat site.

Coming back home, I went through Camp Kilmer, Port of Embarkation. Lo and behold, the Provost Marshall there was Colonel Washington, my old commanding officer of the MP Company when I served in Japan. I visited with him before going home to Fort Bliss, Texas, where I was assigned. I was a Master Sergeant, and with an E-7, it didn't look like I was going to get into a position to make E-8, which was the next step. I was placed in the instructional section, teaching basic electronics in Building Two. An E-8 would have kept my stripe, so I called the Pentagon and requested an assignment that would get the E-8 status. The Sergeant at the Pentagon said there was only one assignment that took priority over my current job: learning about boats, landing, and harbor craft to serve in Vietnam. I took the job, and was willing to do it if it meant gaining an E-8 position. I was sent to Fort Eustis, Virginia, where I became a class leader. There were two Vietnamese men in the class with me, and I took them to my home in Oxford, Ohio, during the Labor Day weekend to visit with my family. After I completed my training, I was shipped to Vietnam.

When I reported to my Company, the Major told me I was late. Baffled by the statement, I told him I had arrived on time. The Major said what he meant was he already had a First Sergeant, but the First Sergeant only had five stripes on his arms. I, however, had been wearing my sixth stripe so long it was practically "tattooed" on me. The Major told me I could either stay put, endure the command of that First Sergeant, or I could take my chances and go back to the replacement depot. After a few seconds of debating, I made my choice and stayed. There, although I wasn't content with the situation, it was

Rocket hole in tug boat.

the best option at the time. I then became the First Mate on a 65-foot tugboat.

After ten days of duty, I performed the service that would earn me the Bronze Star, by saving the lives of the men on two tugboats. We were pulling ammunition up the river with the help of another boat tied onto ours. The boat was docked at Saigon, but they went to Cat Lai and hooked onto barges of ammunition to carry them to Koje-do. This river is like a snake. It's not very far to Koje-do, but by the water it's quite a ways. There were only narrow navigational passages a tugboat could navigate in the seemingly wide river. The Vietcong learned our route and planted water mines there. One went off 25 yards from our boat, close enough to rupture the boat. Almost immediately, another exploded under the barges. The Vietcong started barraging the boats with rockets and small arms. The Captain yelled, "Somebody cut the towline!" I took on the task. I went back to the towline, hacking at the stubborn nylon cord. That is so hard to cut, you would not believe. After continued striking, I got arm-weary. The second mate came up and tried to help me, but soon his arms got weary too and he gave up. I took over again. With barges sinking, burning, and exploding around me, I had to turn my back on the

incoming fire to finish cutting off the rope. I thought to myself, "God, I'm in Your hands." I finally hacked the rope completely through. We then traveled 100 yards up the river. Meanwhile, helicopter gunships arrived and were trying to clear the area. Further on the shore, Vietnamese farmers tended to their rice paddies, as if nothing were happening.

Mr. Robertson, our skipper, knew the importance of what had happened and that I had saved our two tugboats, so he put in a request for me to receive the Bronze Star. I didn't hear about it for a long time, though, so one day I asked the First Sergeant if he'd heard anything. He said he hadn't heard anything. Technically the First Sergeant was telling the truth because he and the Commanding Officer together had disposed of the request.

This was the "turn of events." For unknown reasons, the Commander and his Executive Officer got court-martialed and kicked out of the Army, and also the company clerk got court-martialed and put in the stockade. Although I can't be certain, I heard they were court-martialed for black-marketing. Regardless of what happened, the departure of the men left an absence of a leader. There was still a need for a Unit Commander. A new Commanding Officer by the name of Captain Andrews came aboard. He told me he knew I'd come to be a First Sergeant. I said, "Yes, Sir." Captain Andrews said once he got his feet on the ground and saw what was going on, he would be calling me. Within two days he had called me. He put the other First Sergeant out and gave that position to me. This was the position I was told by the Pentagon that I was sent to fill. Captain Andrews then, after hearing the missing Bronze Star story, once again put me in for the medal. Unfortunately, it came back disapproved because it hadn't been put in within the seven days of the incident, as required by official directives.

Time went by, and I made top ratings at the E-8 board. The 30th of June was turnover time, where they would "turn loose the money and everything." But this time, they didn't promote anybody. I was completely baffled. Captain Andrews had put me in the First Sergeant slot. I had a room in the supply depot with all the amenities of a First Sergeant.

That night I considered my situation. I stayed up the entire night, thinking about the next road to take. I had been through a lot since my Army enlistment so many years ago—numerous transfers, opportunities denied because of my race, hard-fought battles, and several years with military police. With twenty-two long years, I decided to hang up my hat. The next day I walked into Captain Andrew's office and said, "I know I smell like a still because I've been drinking all night, but I'm going to put in my papers for retirement." The Captain was obviously skeptical, given my state, but I stayed firm and told him it was time for me to retire. The Captain let me know he thought I did an admirable job and wanted me to stay. The next stop was personnel. "You're not going to accept this stripe?" the Warrant Officer asked. "What are you talking about?" I replied. The officer walked over to his filing cabinet, grabbing the orders

promoting me to E-8. Still, I turned it down. The order was never transacted because I didn't want to go back to the hellhole that was Vietnam, where I would have to stay for two years in order to accept the stripe. Besides, I had spent the entire night making myself sure I was correct, and I wasn't about to change my mind now. As I walked into the mess hall on my way out, the regimental commander stood at the exit. He said, "Are you sure you don't want to stay here? I understand you're doing a great job." I replied, "No, I am gone, Colonel."

I went back to Oakland Army Terminal, caught a plane to Cincinnati, and disappeared. Although I "disappeared" from Army service, I continued working for 14-and-a-half years. I was an employee of Diebold Incorporated. When the company downsized and they needed subcontractors, I became a subcontractor. With two trucks, seven employees installed vault doors, burglar alarms, ATMs, and almost anything that required my services for another five years. In 1989, I bid farewell to work and retired all together. In 1998, I married my present wife, Laverne.

"Retirement" meant little for me in the beginning, since I kept incredibly busy in retirement. I was an active VFW participant. I was a church trustee pro temp, which meant that, under the minister, I was in charge of the church's building grounds. I was President of the NAACP and President of the Oxford Advisory Welfare. So, when I moved to Arizona in 2003, I decided to take a break from work and take it easy for a while. I am currently residing in Sun City Grand and I'm an avid fishing club member there, and I volunteer services as a fishing instructor for the Arizona Game and Fish Department.

I know that I valiantly served my country, and now I'm able to enjoy the rewards of my hard work because God has taken care of me at every turn. What about that Bronze Star with "V" for Valor? Thirty-three years after being put in for this medal, I'm proud to say that I did receive it. The long wait was reflective of the hard times I endured throughout my military career. But as the mayor of Oxford handed me the award, I was truly appreciative of what is meant by being in the right place at the right time. This was the highlight of my 22-year military career, and I felt a closure in receiving the medal, even after the 33-year wait.

Newspaper article congratulating Ennis receiving the Bronze Star

A career Army man in the 1960s, Mr. Miller volunteered for hazardous duty.

The Cincinnati Enquirer/MICHAEL SNYDER

Ennis Miller displays the acknowledgement of his bravery under fire in Vietnam.

Soldier's patience rewarded: Medal came after 33 years

By Randy McNutt
The Cincinnati Enquirer

OXFORD – For 33 years, Ennis B. Miller lived with a near-secret.

Only a few people knew what happened to him on Dec. 4, 1967, on the deck of Army tugboat ST-2121. Eight men survived because of his bravery.

The crew thanked him. The federal government did not.

Last week, at age 74, Mr. Miller finally received proper recognition: a Bronze Star

with a "V" for valor. It gave closure to a faded war and a long ("22 years, three months and 28 days") military career that ended prematurely when he failed to receive the medal.

"I knew I had been cheated of what I deserved," he said. "But I didn't think so much of what I did at the time. Everybody was shook up. We didn't think we'd get away from there alive."

Mr. Miller's heroism capped a military career that sent him marching through

world history. He entered the Army in May 1945 and went to Germany, where he witnessed the trials of Nazi leaders at Nuremberg. He left the Army but re-enlisted before the Korean War. He was among the first soldiers to arrive - in a segregated unit. In 1967, he volunteered for duty in Vietnam.

"The first thing my major told me was, 'You late, sergeant.' I said, 'sir, I'm on time.' He sa

See MEDAL Page 89

Chuck Schluter

1965 - 1997
Vietnam, Taiwan, Japan, U.S.

Making Your Bones
An Interview with Chuck Schluter
By Lindsey Anderson

History books read with his father, a popular Navy poster of the *USS Constitution*, and the sailor on the box of Cracker Jacks enticed young Chuck Schluter to join the Navy. He knew almost everything about our wooden sailing Navy and our steel World War II aircraft carriers and battleships. "I always knew I was going to go into the military...and I wasn't going to hesitate," said Schluter. "John Paul Jones with his *Bonhomme Richard*—"I have not yet begun to fight"— and the *USS Constitution*, Old Ironsides, were just part of me."

Chuck entered the Navy in 1965 and took his initial training at the USN Great Lakes Recruit Training Station. He eventually reported to the *USS Colonial* (LSD 18), arriving on board December 7, 1965. The *Colonial*, a Landing Ship Dock, was a veteran of World War II, Korea, and Vietnam, and had all the comforts of a ship built for war in 1945. Chuck shipped out of San Diego enroute to Hawaii, Okinawa, and Vietnam. With a shipload of US Marines, expectations of a Second-World-War-like beach landing were quickly dashed. Vietnam was going to be nothing like World War II. As a Seaman Apprentice, and later as a Petty Officer 2nd Class (Radarman), he stood watch in the Combat Information Center (CIC) where he operated radar and sonar equipment. The CIC team tracked contacts, maintained equipment, conducted radar navigation exercises, radar-directed beach assault operations, radar-directed gunfire support operations, and pulled their share of administrative and shipboard duties. He recalls that it was interesting to receive weekly update booklets entitled "Notice to Mariners," which required that the two-hundred-plus charts that were kept within reach be updated frequently. The "Notice to Mariners" required annotation of shipwrecks, depth changes, and updates to navigation aids or hazards—including WWII-era Japanese minefields—and other modifications.

Daily routine was punctuated by several interesting ports of call, including visits to Hong Kong, Kaohsiung, Taiwan, Yokosuka, Japan, and our US Naval Base at Subic Bay in the Philippine Islands. He recalled that the entrance to Subic Bay was guarded by two huge Coastal Defense guns set low in concrete emplacements on Grande Island. Those gigantic artillery pieces are now part of a Memorial Park somewhere in Washington State. The age of the *USS Colonial*, limited ventilation, and obvious abundance of steel did leave a lasting memory of how hot things can get in that part of the world. The heat was unforgettable.

> Your bunks are suspended from chains, so it's kind of like an aluminum frame and a cot. Then, [there are] two more pieces of chain and another aluminum frame and another cot, so you [have] five guys high—five bunks. So now, the sun is beating down on the deck, which is your overhead [ceiling]… It was so hot that you could not touch the chains for almost two feet down…When you'd get into the spongy mattresses, they'd squish…because of the perspiration in the mattress. But we'd "air mattresses" every few days by lashing them to topside railings. That helped.

Some inventive men created a scoop that fit through the porthole to catch a cool breeze to bring into the compartment. This helped the men cope with their sweltering lodgings.

The men quickly learned to fend for themselves in other ways also, an invaluable part of military training. As the radar operator, Chuck had to adapt to changing circumstances. "When the radar failed, the guy responsible for the equipment had to climb the mast, and sometimes that was me; there is nobody else to call. You own your equipment." When climbing the ship's mast, he quickly disproved an old proverb. "An old adage is, 'One hand for the ship and one hand for yourself.' Baloney! Use two hands! My arms were wrapped around that mast, and I was holding onto the wrench with my teeth…and you do learn to be self-sufficient." Still, the most surprising aspect of the first cruise was not the valuable life lessons or daily Navy life, but the fact that the Vietnam War was drastically different. World War II was history,

Chuck in Hong Kong as a young sailor

and the stories he had heard in his youth were from a different age. The world was changing.

A big thing about the Vietnam experience was not necessarily Vietnam, but what was happening on the home front. The world changed very drastically in the mid-'60s. I came of age in the '50s, and grew up in the '60s. It was baseball and apple pie and Chevrolets and everything was fine. All of a sudden, we are in this war, the country seemed torn asunder… In my mind it was somewhat of a free-for-all. Values changed, ethics changed, music changed, there were Vietnam War protestors, riots occurred in big cities and on campuses. And, needless to say, during that period Martin Luther King and Bobby Kennedy were assassinated. The '60s were an unprecedented decade in that the changes wrought during those years changed culture, expectations, and the way entire generations to come would think, act, and cope. Some burned draft cards; others burned brassieres. Just think, in a few short months, in 1969, we put men on the moon, music lovers danced in the mud at Woodstock, a memory was tested by what occurred at Chappaquiddick, and The Age of Aquarius truly died at a Rolling Stones concert in Altamont, California. Dr. Tim Leary "tuned into it all" from a VW Bus in Haight Ashbury, right? Vietnam was real, but there was a lot more to it, I think.

Not only the nation changed during the war, but between Chuck's first and second cruises, his ship changed as well. Air conditioners were installed on the *USS Colonial*, so obviously he agreed that some changes were great!

During the early months of his second tour to WesPac (Western Pacific), the Viet Cong launched the Tet Offensive of '68. "Three things run together," said Chuck. "We were in Da Nang when the Tet Offensive started… We went to Hue, and Hue was one horrific battle to take back the city, street by street, primarily the Marines, but the Army too…We had plotted several enemy gun positions and were on call to direct gunfire support, but we were inboard of heavy cruisers that were firing over us." He recalls that shortly after Tet, the *USS Pueblo* was captured by the North Koreans, and the *Colonial* headed north to Korea to take part in any action that was pending. Nothing happened. That episode in Navy history is well-documented. The crew was eventually released, but that solution was political, not military.

"It's boredom, boredom, boredom, and then moments of pretty good action," Chuck recalled. His ship had earned the nickname *Vung Tau—Da Nang Express*—and was frequently engaged in duties all along the coastline of South Vietnam. An LSD is literally a sea-going dry-dock of sorts, and they were moving all kinds of small craft to selected theaters of operation, primarily into the Delta, that area of Vietnam where the Saigon Song (River) and Vung Tau Song (River) form a river delta and empty into the South China Sea. Generally speaking, they transported PBRs (Patrol Boat River) and the larger Swiftboats (PCE) to where they were needed. Other times they hauled some pretty interesting craft for our Brown Water Navy, mostly the riverine craft referred to as "Monitors"—Monitors with flame throwers were called "Zippos," a nickname taken from the Zippo cigarette lighters just about everybody had—but also the first PACVs (Patrol Air Cushion Vehicle) to ever be deployed, which could ride on a cushion of air across water and marsh areas. And one time they delivered two larger "Nasty" class patrol-raider PTFs, which were deep-water Coastal Patrol Craft. The key mission, however, was to deny the Delta to the Viet Cong, and the Brown Water Navy was an essential ingredient of the forces used. On other occasions, the mission was to evacuate damaged craft that had been shot up or crippled by mines. Finally, after "going away, coming back, going away, coming back, and going away" for two and a half tours, Chuck returned home to the States in 1969.

After the Vietnam War, Chuck took his US Navy Radar experience and put it to work at a US Army guided missile Nike Hercules base in New York. When he encountered his first RIF, Reduction in Force, he was asked where he wanted to be relocated. Chuck drew a circle on a map which encompassed his family members' homes. He found a new assignment at an Army National Guard Engineer Battalion located within the specified area, and assumed the duties of a Nuclear Biological and Chemical (NBC) Warfare Non-Commissioned Officer (NCO) in Connecticut. It was important to remain "in uniform," so he looked to Officer Candidate School, OCS, during that period.

After graduation from OCS, subsequent duty assignments included those of Training Officer, Administrative Officer, Headquarters Detachment Commander, and many more. Although he had two long tours in a Headquarters unit as a Recruiting Officer, he had also served in many line units. Primarily they were the 192nd Engineer (Construction) Battalion; 250th Engineer Company (Bridge); 238th Supply and Service Battalion, an attachment to the 1/102 Infantry Battalion; and lastly, his favorite of them all, the 242nd (Combat) Engineer Battalion.

The 242nd is where Chuck really "made his bones," or proved himself. The 242nd Battalion had enjoyed a dismal record and had failed every inspection in every category including maintenance, logistics, personnel, and training. "They had failed numerous times," stated Chuck. He thought he was "in for it," but the battalion was far from being written off. The experience level of the NCOs (Non Commissioned Officers) was at a peak, the energy was there, the desire was there, they were a "Can Do" body of men, and the 242nd motto was "Devoir," which means "Duty." "They just lacked a coordinated effort," Chuck remembered. "I set up periodic meetings, and I disallowed anything negative. I invited the recruiters and subject matter experts. I set goals and expectations, something it seemed they never had before. They needed to grasp a coordinated approach. Everybody's in it together." First, maintenance inspections were set up and *everybody* was ordered to pitch in, to scrape off paint and rust, lubricate, and service equipment—not just the people responsible for maintenance, but the entire team. "We blew that inspection away," recalled Chuck proudly. The logistics inspection came next. The five supply rooms were cleaned by everyone until each of them looked and operated the same. Again, they passed the inspection with flying colors. They did the same thing time and again with each measurable, inspection-prone area. Good units shine, and people are drawn to good units.

The taste of success is sweet, and success breeds success. National Guard units are responsible for recruiting their own members, and the 242nd strength numbers climbed too because the approach used engaged the subject-matter experts (SME) and a relevancy of interest. When the recruiting push arrived, Captain Jim Skirvin told Captain Schluter the battalion had secured management's permission to put "displays" in the entire local mall during the month of August instead of the usual single, small "Recruiters" table. Chuck required that all vehicles, weapons systems, various tent displays, mannequins with various uniforms, display identification signs, and everything possible, including a vintage World War I Renault tank, be acquired and made "showroom-floor-perfect." They wanted to ensure an impressive and durable public display. Though most military men are unwilling to volunteer for recruiting duty, with a striking exhibit, everyone was willing to participate. They stood proud by museum-quality displays, and the unit recruiting efforts capitalized upon individual training and specific interests that appealed to people.

> Where the jeep was, you would find the maintenance guy. And where the medical tent was, there would be skilled medics, and so on and so forth down the line. Weapons displays had experienced experts to explain details or answer questions, and they all wore appropriate field or camouflage uniforms. Everybody at every piece of equipment knew that item cold. And then, to talk to prospective recruits, we had our team of recruiters in full Class A uniforms, standing behind a special booth constructed by our Engineers. That booth pulled double duty at our Military Balls because it separated into two fully functional bars!

Captain Schluter had turned a capable, but under-achieving, unit into a highly motivated and decidedly successful battalion. "The 242nd was the biggest battalion and our hard luck battalion, and when I was eventually reassigned to a higher Headquarters," said Chuck proudly, "it was the biggest battalion and the *best* battalion... All I did was recognize the makings of an incredible team and energize the natural synergy that existed—I just brought them together." One thing he will always remember is that, in the process, those grizzled rough-around-the-edges NCOs taught him a few good lessons, too. "I was a better man coming out than I was going in—and I cherish the experience." Today the 242nd no longer exists, and many of its soldiers became part of the 102nd Infantry. "They are serving in Afghanistan," Chuck stated, "and I tell you what, I'd give anything to be with them."

Chuck retired from the military in 1998. He finished his career as a Colonel, US Army Corps of Engineers, while assigned as the Director of Personnel (G-1) for the Connecticut Army National Guard. "I had a good career...a great career. My friends are solid and true, and will be for life. I am pleased that I served as both an NCO and as an Officer, as a National Guardsman, and also on Active Duty as a Sailor and later as a Soldier. After leaving the military, Chuck retired to Arizona where he joined the Military Officers Association of America (MOAA).

> MOAA is wonderful. Our mission, which is dead serious, requires that we endeavor to protect the earned entitlements of our uniformed services, their survivors and families, and our retirees. It is a good, noble mission, and I embrace it with long, strong arms. We will continue to "take care of the enlisted guys" and veterans, and do our legislative research as well. It was a fluke of sorts, but I became President of the Arizona Chapter of MOAA during the first meeting I attended—and I'm glad I did. This has been a great ride and I enjoy the work.

Chuck is currently on the National Board of Directors of MOAA, Class of 2008, where he has observed several tremendous successes and a few touching and caring moments. On a recent day, a World War II veteran called the MOAA National Headquarters. He happened to speak with Vice Admiral Ryan, the President. The gentleman expressed his gratitude for the work that MOAA does for all veterans, and he was very pleased with MOAA in many regards, but he was old and ill, and regretted that he would not see the Headquarters before he died.

> So the staff got together and sent him railroad tickets, they arranged for transportation to the train station, and then picked him up upon his arrival in Washington. He toured our headquarters, and then they took him to several memorials, including the World War II Memorial, then the Smithsonian, and then to a nice hotel. The next day they took him to Walter Reed, where he could meet fellow veterans such as himself, and our current group of Iraqi and Afghanistan theater veterans.

[They] gave this guy the experience of his life. It's pretty amazing. It really is.

Chuck has a plaque hanging in his den from a surprise party that a few of the Arizona Chapter members presented to him. "That one means a lot to me," he said. The den quietly displays not only Colonel Schluter's awards and honors, but also his love of the military. Medals and plaques line the top of one wall, while bookshelves filled with American History books line another. Other plaques are in boxes in the garage. "I have a cord of firewood in mahogany in my garage… They can be pretty humbling, but you still

Chuck in a vintage car in front of a vintage P-51 Mustang

display only the ones that are really significant, or the ones with recent dates. There's no pleasure in having plaques so old that it appears you haven't done anything lately," stated Chuck.

To Colonel Schluter, the military is a group not only fighting for its country, but for each other. "That's one of the things that I think is so important about us," Chuck said. "It's a big team. Some may call it the 'brotherhood of war,' and it is true. The camaraderie is there. You'll never forget the person who stands beside you on your right and left." Chuck remains active in MOAA and serves as a member of the Arizona Committee of the Employer Support to the Guard and Reserve (ESGR). The mission of ESGR is essential, even critical today; the Global War on Terror demands much. "Stay involved, recognize others, put back more than you take, and help where

you can," he says. Chuck has also been an avid supporter of the Arizona Military Hall of Fame since its inception, and he's pleased that thus far he has written and submitted, on behalf of his MOAA Chapter, nomination packets for five highly notable individuals who have been successfully inducted into that prestigious group of men and women.

Today, Chuck feels he flunked "Military Retirement." His current job allows him to work with soldiers around the globe "24-7" as they continue their own self-development by taking online courses through the Army eLearning Program, for which Chuck is a primary consultant. Between Army eLearning, MOAA, and ESGR, "I feel pretty *good* about flunking retirement!"

A room upstairs holds more memories of a lifetime spent living and enjoying significant, but trivial and smaller, pastimes. Pieces of Chuck's life are replicated in his elaborate train room. Six trains can simultaneously snake through the three-tiered city. A majestic scene including Camelback Mountain is painted on the back wall behind the display. A model of Chuck's actual collector car, a 1948 MGTC, is parked on the miniature street along with a milk truck his father drove and his brother's first car. Rick Bishop, the first friend young Chuck made when he moved to Patchogue, New York, is honored by a small sign saying: Welcome to Patchogue, Founded 1876, Rick Bishop, Mayor. Patchogue village has a Drive-In Hot Dog stand with hot rods and vintage fire trucks near the old brick firehouse. A billboard sign is dedicated to MOAA, and another displays the emblem of the Employer Support to Guard and Reserve (ESGR). King Kong hangs from the top of the Empire State Building, while below, several yellow cabs pick up passengers from the Radio City Music Hall and Grand Central Station.

And a vintage Army post with trucks, tanks, troops, and a World War II barracks marks the home of the 242nd (Combat) Engineer Battalion, where Colonel Chuck Schluter feels he made his bones.

James Siket

June 1967 - June 1994
Korea, Vietnam, Germany

Soldier to Soldier

An Interview with James Siket
By Barbara Hatch

Brooklyn…Ohio.

Like parents in this town's New York namesake, Jim Siket's father also found college tuition for his second son hard to come by in the mid-1960s. Fortunately, Jim excelled in high school football. He was also a sprinter on the track team. His coach recommended West Point, always seeking talented football players. When a cadet on leave visited in the summer, Jim was hooked. His Brooklyn community followed the career of their native son with interest. Jim was the first to be accepted to this prestigious academy.

Life at West point was "intense." Cadets pursued academics, physical workouts, and leadership training from six in the morning till midnight, seven days a week, 365 days a year. Graduating in the Class of 1967, 2nd Lieutenant James Ronald Siket got the branch of his choosing: artillery.

Six months at Fort Sill, Oklahoma, preceded by Ranger training taught Jim basic gunnery calculations. The tools of his trade included a slide rule, booklets of data and charts, and how to account for variations of weather. A year in Okinawa as a platoon leader at a Little John missile site familiarized him with the use of conventional and nuclear weapons. When the battalion was deactivated, Jim went to work at headquarters for a 3-star general and 27 colonels, where Jim was responsible for all base equipment and a company of 250 soldiers. Unfortunately the men took orders from the colonels first and not Jim, which meant physical fitness exercises took second place to chauffeuring the officers to their destinations. Moreover, Jim, though now a 1st Lieutenant, was doing a lieutenant colonel's job. This created other challenges. "I had no idea what I was doing, but I was doing it!"

On Okinawa, Jim had the opportunity to attend airborne school. He and a buddy, Mike Spenello, one of his West Point classmates, "caught a lot of hell from the instructors" because they were already Ranger-qualified—unusual for most airborne trainees. Considered "tougher than everybody else," they did fifteen times the number of pushups. "It was a lot of fun." Jim's last two weeks in

Okinawa prepared him for Vietnam: lots of hiking and tactical exercises with live ammunition.

Jim returned to the States long enough to settle his wife and two children in New York with her mother while he traveled to Fort Sill, Oklahoma, to update his artillery skills. After that, Jim was off to Vietnam. He remembers the longer-than-long flight as a unique experience for all on board. "You could hear a pin drop." It was the quietest ride on a plane one could imagine; even the stewardesses seemed like shadows in the aisles. Fortunately for Jim and his fellow passengers, Tet of 1969 had passed with less "fireworks" than Tet of '68, but the men were cognizant of the fact that it had just been publicized that "more troops had been killed in Vietnam at that point in time than were lost for the entire Korean War."

Searing sweaty heat, not bombs, greeted 1st Lieutenant Siket when he arrived at Long Binh in May of '69. Rotor fans did little to aid sleep. "When you lay down on your three-inch thick mattress at night, it was like lying in a frying pan." You knew you were not at home. For two weeks he and his fellow officers new to the theater waited—and sweated—in anticipation of their assignments.

Eventually Jim became liaison officer from the First Infantry Division (the Big Red One) II Field Force, commanded by Lieutenant General Julian Ewell. Every day for three months, Jim would take the round-trip on a light observation helicopter (LOH) the 45 miles from Lai Khe to Long Binh. At II Field Force headquarters, he briefed the activities of all battalion-size units for the 15,000-soldier Big Red One. He briefed General Ewell and his staff on operations in this sector and answered questions, then gathered plans and comments the division would need for the coming days. On two occasions Jim's helicopter was hit by small arms fire, and once three AK-47 rounds. Fortunately, he and the pilot emerged unscathed, fascinated by the green tracers that periodically flashed by. "It always made the flight the following days a little more exciting when you took a round from the previous day."

Liaison duties prepared Jim for his next assignment—operations officer with the 8th Battalion, 6th Artillery, also located at Lai Khe. For three months Jim ran the night shift in the battalion operations center (TOC), coordinating fire support for the infantry units which were conducting night patrols and ambushes. Typically the infantry scoured a 15-mile radius from the base, then radioed their night-time ambush coordinates. Jim could then finalize the evening plan for "random artillery fires" at suspected enemy positions to help keep the "Viet Cong" (VC) off guard.

It was common practice for the U.S. force commanders to inform the local Vietnamese civilians in nearby villages not to travel outside of the immediate village after dark. If you were a Vietnamese civilian during the Vietnam War and decided to take the risk of moving outside the village at night, you were a potential moving target. Those moving at night were subject to being ambushed by the U.S. military, be it infantry, air sorties, or artillery. We had to assume that anybody traveling after dark was VC.

Periodically the artillery mistakenly fired on its own troops, either because the units reported their grid coordinates incorrectly, were lost or located where they were not supposed to be, or similar "coordinates mistakes" were made by the artillery. Jim never experienced this first-hand, but kept his fingers crossed and prayed every night that no mistakes would occur on his watch. He was among the lucky majority not subject to such mistakes.

After three months in the artillery TOC and flying live-fire missions from an aerial observation helicopter, Jim became the Delta Battery commander. At the time, all three brigade commanders wanted 8-inch gun support for their sectors, largely due to the destructive capabilities of the 200-lb. projectiles that were the most accurate artillery cannons in the Army. Jim's four howitzer sections were split between Lai Khe and the surrounding countryside. Routinely Jim left the relative safety of Lai Khe to "roam the countryside" during the day to occupy firing positions that could reach the targets designated by the infantry brigade staff. Because they occupied random positions in the middle of no-man's land and fired until dusk, they returned to base camp. The gun sections had no security capabilities other than the gun crews themselves, and night-time operations by the crews would have been a foolish risk to the men and equipment. In Lai Khe, Jim's unit received enemy incoming rocket fire nearly every night "because the Viet Cong didn't like our 8-inch artillery. We were the bad boys." Jim had several close calls. Six troops were killed by enemy rocket attacks in a division staff headquarters tent 50 feet from Jim's tent. On another occasion, Jim's entire "office" of sand-filled ammunition boxes was obliterated in a direct hit while he played volleyball. Although he did not want to play team volleyball that evening, his First Sergeant (1SG) insisted that he shut down the paperwork a little early and join his troops in a friendly game. If it were not for 1SG Morton, "I would not be here for this interview." Several other rocket attacks destroyed his small unit supply building, and another came directly through the entrance of an underground bunker and bounced across the floor. No one knew what the racket was all about until one of the soldiers awoke and turned on his flashlight. He couldn't believe his sleepy eyes. He sounded the alarm so the remaining bunker occupants could "hightail" it out of there until an ordnance crew detonated the "dud" rocket. The end result was also the loss of their bunker.

Four months later President Nixon began to "wind down" the war. Jim moved his howitzers to a depot in Long Binh, and was reassigned to a new job.

As ground operations lessened, airstrikes intensified. Jim worked for the Air Force's II Field Force helping plan B-52 strikes and U.S. and Vietnamese combat air sorties. Prior to this experience, Jim's only familiarity with B-52s was his recollection of an incident that occurred while he was on Okinawa. When Jim was in Jump School, he had seen a B-52 explode during takeoff from the local Air Force Base right on the runway, lighting up the sky and shaking the island. Needless to say, he was impressed with their power, and the Okinawans were impressed also, but not for the same reason. In Vietnam the B-52s flew at 30,000 feet, dropping 106-X 500-pound bombs in a six-kilometer-by-2-kilometer "box." After every bombing attack, U.S. Infantry would search for results of the attack. Often they found survivors walking around in a daze. "And sometimes we hit nothing. But we continued with our plans just about every night.

It took several to plan each bombing attack because we needed to have multiple and independent intelligence that we had a viable target before you could receive permission to employ B-52s. It just took a long time to make those arrangements." The enemy had no anti-aircraft guns capable of reaching these planes at 30,000 feet, nor could they even hear them coming, that is, until the bombs were exploding on target. Still, Jim has questions. "I don't know how effective B-52 strikes were, but we certainly ran a lot of them." He was not often made aware of the results of these attacks.

In March or April 1969, the existence of enemy base camps in Cambodia prompted the U.S. to deploy air and ground forces across the border. We used the U.S. Air Force's A-2 fighter bombers to destroy bunker sites and ground troops in Cambodia. Jim, as an Army officer, sat with the Air Force pilot on a few of these missions. He didn't much like the experience of dive bombing because after several runs, it began to make him sick. Although he was a paratrooper, he

Artillery firing

felt more in control with his artillery units on the ground. On every occasion flying into Cambodia, they received small arms fire. However, the Russian AK-47s that were being handled by the VC were "not too

A C-119 Gunship (Courtesy of the US Air Force library)

good at shooting down high performance aircraft fortunately." Jim also flew on an Air Force gunship called "The Shadow," a modified C-119 with Gatling guns that each fired 6,000 rounds a minute. They were used to support the soldiers on the ground and were capable of firing on pinpoint ground targets while flying in circles at 1,500 feet—in the dark. Sadly, two days after Jim flew on one of these missions, the plane on which he flew crashed, killing all on board. Despite this loss of life, casualties were less than in the early days of the war, when the life expectancy of a helicopter pilot was less than nine months. "They were the ones that had all the guts and glory, and the grunts thought they were all nuts, but we could not live without them!"

Throughout his tour in Vietnam, Jim was aware that the war was not popular at home. College campuses erupted in 1968. At Kent State, a student was killed by gunfire from a National Guard unit sent in to quell a student riot on campus. Before he left for Vietnam, he and his proud father had dinner in a hometown restaurant, where two angry family members who lost sons in the war referred to him, in the restaurant, as a "baby killer." Jim was not in uniform at the time, but everyone there knew him. In Newburgh, New York, he was spit on by a friendly passerby peace activist. "I felt like punching his lights out; however, I realized that these were the citizens I was charged to defend so they could feel free to exercise their 'freedom of speech' with a little extra spittle. I just ignored it and walked away." Most of

the hostilities encountered by U.S. military personnel at home on leave or in stateside units found most of the resentment in the large cities of the northeast or on the west coast, especially California. In what was a more patriotic south at the time, home to several military bases, the local citizens seemed to appreciate the soldiers more.

Jim's next major combat arms duty assignment took him to Butzbach, Germany. After a year at Fort Sill in the Field Artillery Advance Course, he taught artillery tactics and techniques to infantry officers and enlisted men at Fort Benning, Georgia.

In Germany, this young captain developed potential wartime plans for his howitzer battery in the German countryside. This was designed to deter the Russian threat, particularly on the DMZ near the Fulda Gap. The Berlin Wall was still alive at the time, and "Cold War" tensions were high. The senior German citizens who lived through World War II appreciated the American presence, despite the damage U.S. tanks inflicted on their communities as they rumbled along narrow cobblestone streets in small towns throughout the gorgeous German farmland. Many times American tanks lumbered up the autobahn. On one occasion, a fast-moving Mercedes, piloted by a German national, ran itself at high speed on the foggy autobahn underneath a slow-moving tank. In nearly every incident the U.S. paid for the damage. "The U.S. Government got the bill for it."

Younger Germans were mixed on the American presence. There were occasional cases of "confrontation" between Germans and American troops, but a bigger problem was racial tension between black and white American GIs—a spillover of race problems in the United States in the late 1970s. Race relations training helped somewhat as whites and blacks vented their feelings about each other. Calling each other by first names, however, whether officer or enlisted, "broke all the bounds of the structure of the Army in terms of the leadership." As a duty officer on the night shift on his German Kaserne, Jim wore a

Gunner aboard C-119 Gunship

loaded .45 at all times—for his own troops. He believed the situation was related to the low morale in the U.S. military following our lack of success and lack of victory in Vietnam. Programs like Project 100,000, a social experiment that placed disadvantaged young men in the Army, some of them school dropouts, exacerbated the problem. Still, Jim and his family enjoyed the German people and he felt good about his work there.

Jim's 27-year career gave him an appreciation for the meaning of life in the military serving his country, sometimes right and sometimes wrong. As an officer, he could see the "big picture," the role America needed to play to defend the world and itself from real and perceived threats to our democratic way of life. "Military service gave you a great appreciation for American Foreign Policy…and the relationships that America has with foreign peoples and their governments." He accepts that the United States is one of the few countries in the world today able to have an impact on world peace. But being part of the "small picture" is what Jim loved best, knowing the *soldiers* who served, leading them, helping them cope with life and duty abroad and encouraging them to pursue successful and worthwhile lives *in* the military and in their lives *after* the military. He also made friends with regular Okinawans, Vietnamese, Germans, and Koreans when he lived off-base with his family on a "citizen to citizen level." One of Jim's favorite experiences was having dinner with a South Korean businessman. While at work the businessman spoke English, dressed in western suits, and rode in a chauffeured black limousine to and from the office place. At home, his wife prepared the food and served it and then disappeared to eat elsewhere with the children, in the traditional customs of Korean family life. The man's children spoke some English; however, the businessman's major concern was his fear of losing his Korean culture and customs. "He was very fearful that his daughter would meet a U.S. serviceman, get married, and leave the country. So he was really skeptical about having us come to his house and spend time with his family. He appeared not to want his family to know Americans—not because he didn't like them, but because he believed Americans in Korea would erode the values and traditions of his country." Nonetheless, he appreciated what America and Americans had done for his country, his lifestyle, and his family during the Korean War of the early 1950s.

It was a far better alternative to life under Kim Il-Sung."

One thing Jim never had in the service was the financial resources to compete with his contemporaries in civilian life. His most colorful stories, literally, focus on the dilapidated houses and the meager service pay that dictated his lifestyle, especially in the early years. Yet, theirs was a family lifestyle that was truly an American experience. It taught him to appreciate what he thinks most Americans could never learn to appreciate. "There is often nothing like having nothing (actually we had everything important) to make one appreciate the important things in life: family, a belief in God, and the fortune to have been born American."

For $110 a month, Jim and his family lived off-base at Fort Benning. They got an extra $20 for living in a condemned house. Even on-base housing at Benning was substandard, built prior to World War II as temporary housing. "They just never became untemporary." Up until 1975, the Army only had three colors available world wide to paint an on-post home—green, brown, and pink—undoubtedly left over from painting military vehicles. You could buy your own paint for some variety as long as you painted it back to green, brown, or pink when you departed quarters. Layers of paint applied to windows over the years made them impossible to open, a routine that did not differ from one post to another, stateside or overseas. Windows painted shut was everywhere the most consistent part of military quarters.

Off-base housing in Okinawa was not much better. "The house we had was a tiny little house with two bedrooms, the plumbing didn't work half the time, there was a crack in the wall of the house that you could see through to the outside, and that was the best that I could find as a 2nd lieutenant with a paycheck of about $320 a month." Life got even more exciting during the occasional hurricane. "They just made everyone batten down their hatches and stay inside, which was a pretty scary thing in the house in which my family lived."

Jim's wife and six children "hung in there," but not all military families fared so well. Young married soldiers just out of high school, away from home in their overseas quarters, would spend up to 260 days a year "in the field." Back at home, their 17-year-old wife and baby, with no car and unable to speak the local language, had their own share of problems. Jim's wife and the other wives of officers and senior enlisted soldiers would help deliver groceries or run errands for those who needed such help. However, the stress of separation sometimes led to abuse and unhappiness and permanent separation, though perhaps no greater in military life than in society at large. At times, newly married soldiers didn't trust their wives alone, and vice versa, largely because they spent an unusually long time separated by the requirements of their military duties and lifestyle. Life in the military could be extremely stressful, especially for young married soldiers who were living overseas on their first significant exposure to life in a foreign country. It did not always end in the development of a stronger bond of marriage; it could just as easily break the bonds of any marriage.

The young soldier back in the '70s lived at a time when it was common to graduate from high school and get married. Shortly after graduation, he would join the Army and drag along his 17-year-old wife to wherever. Thinking about such a soldier with his young wife and a baby living in a little German apartment, separated for nine months of the year from her husband and family back home, unsure she has enough funds to pay the rent and feed her newborn, with no transportation, unable to speak the local German language— the situation has all the ingredients for dissolution of the family. That is why the command tries to do everything possible to help its young soldiers take care of their families under what are often nearly impossible circumstances. You have to live it to believe it.

The soldier husband and his civilian wife had to be concerned at all times about whether or not their relationship would survive. Deployed Reservists and National Guardsmen and Active Duty soldiers today in the Iraq War suffer the same hardships. "But today, it's both male and female soldiers dealing with similar circumstances in a more stressful environment than we faced in the 1970s and 1980s."

Jim believes one thing in particular has changed since he retired from the Army: the open criticism of the president and his policies among officers, mostly recently retired officers. Military officers were more discreet in Jim's day. "If you were critical of the president, it was a conversation you had over a beer, or amongst yourselves, and generally you were not conscious of making the effort to criticize the Commander in Chief. "We just did not do that type of thing." According to Jim, most Americans don't see or don't want to see the real threats to their liberties. "The world is more complicated today than it has ever been. I think in general the majority of Americans are focused on their own lives, and they don't have time to develop an appreciation for the threats to our freedom and our society. There are real threats out there. In the long run, the potential for serious injury to many Americans is not far ahead. And you can't blame 'em because they are somewhat spoiled by their freedom. They don't know what it's like to live any other way." He also detests the Hollywood producers' portrayal of American military officers as madmen ready to deploy weapons of mass destruction or nuclear weapons, men always on the edge of sanity or already out of control. In actuality, it's just the opposite. The most conservative organization in the country is the U.S. military, and the most conservative and peaceful oriented leaders are those who lead our soldiers, sailors, and airmen. Contrary to Hollywood, the military is not all that exciting most of the time. "We're not an exciting group and we do everything possible to avoid excitement for the country."

When asked to sum up his career, Jim left Jeff and me with these thoughts.

I had a great time serving my country, have few regrets, and have accumulated too many good memories to put into writing. I respect our troops and their leaders and support the military whenever it goes into action. The American military consists of dedicated soldier-citizens who are trained to engage in combat, can be forced into harm's way in unreasonably hostile environments, and are required to make life and death decisions that nonmilitary will never be able to understand or appreciate. The military of this country will always do what it can to protect and defend Americans, sometimes with and sometimes without the support it needs to be successful on the battlefield. That is when we lose. The military and its soldiers are

A line of helicopters in Vietnam

subject to the dictates of our civilian leadership, which has in the past and will in the future make wise decisions and not-so-wise decisions that require the U.S. to confront those opposed to our way of life. In my opinion, to be successful in defending our way of life, Americans must support the civilian leaders and its military so that people around the world know that when we go into combat, we will get the unsavory mission accomplished. We can be successful only if we have the full support of our political leadership and citizens. Otherwise, any lack of full support will result in serious injury to Americans at home and abroad, and will eventually irrevocably weaken what would otherwise have been a free country.

Carroll Vanik

February 1968 - February 1972
Vietnam

This Is No Shit

An Interview with Carroll Vanik
By Anthony Beckham and Barbara Hatch

Thirty-one years have passed since the United States pulled out of Vietnam. There are 58, 000 names on the Wall in Washington, D.C. The 2005 Vietnam Helicopters Pilots Association's directory estimates 2,300 pilots were killed in Vietnam and many others were "wounded or busted up." Carroll recommends *The American Tragedy* to explain why America got involved in Vietnam; it lists errors we made. *In Retrospect*, by Secretary of Defense Robert McNamara, supposedly one of John Kennedy's "best and brightest," apologizes for our misunderstanding of the Vietnamese determination to sacrifice millions to expel foreigners from their country. In sum, Carroll comments, McNamara "admits that none of them knew what they were doing," including top General William Westmoreland. Carroll served in Vietnam from June of 1970 until June of 1971.

Carroll was unable to find a job after graduating from the University of Maryland because potential employers feared he'd be drafted. Carroll chose instead to enter the College Ops Program to become an officer. He knew Vietnam would be his destination.

After basic and advanced infantry training, Carroll headed for Fort Benning, Georgia. Six months of "Spartan" living and continuous training at Benning created a "lean and mean" soldier. "You ran around everyplace; nobody walked. Everybody's running around, constantly. You got to be in good shape." Those who could not handle the pace dropped out. Carroll passed the aptitude test and headed to helicopter flight school. Waiting for classes to begin six months later, Carroll was a training officer at Fort Polk, Louisiana, until transferring to Fort Wolters, Texas, and Hunter Army Air Field in Savannah, Georgia, for helicopter training. Then off to Vietnam.

In June of 1970 Carroll got assigned to the 35th Combat Engineer Group in Dong Ba Thin, Vietnam. The Army had just added a new type of helicopter called the OH-58, which required additional training. For the next year Carroll and his team of Army aviators provided aviation support to units in the field. Unlike assault missions or troop transports, the pilots delivered ammunition and supplies, dropped mail, medevaced the wounded, even flew in chaplains for Sunday services. We'll talk about the beer later! What made their missions unique is they flew alone. While Cobra gunships generally provided cover fire for the troops, a very risky job, they also flew in teams. If one ship were shot down, the others could provide support until a rescue team could arrive. Cobra pilots thought Carroll's pilots were "crazy" to fly to remote areas in Vietnam, particularly along the Cambodian border, in a single-pilot, single-ship aircraft. On the other hand, Carroll and the engineers told their Cobra pilot friends, "You guys are nuts!"

Carroll divided the risks of his job into three categories. "The first risk was the bad guys who were trying to kill you; the second risk was the weather, terrible weather, monsoons in the afternoons, so that was another problem; and the third risk was just the mechanical failure of the helicopter." As operations officer for his unit, Carroll's job was to take the missions from headquarters in the evening, then assign pilots and aircraft for the next day. Obviously he wanted to minimize risks to keep his men alive, even if that meant flying many missions himself. If a pilot flew 120 hours in 30 days, he was grounded for three days to rest. Others would fill in.

As Carroll mentioned, the first risk was the bad guys, well-entrenched in some of the remote areas to which combat engineers flew. One incident occurred at Landing Zone Lonely near Pleiku. This engineer compound had the name because it was out in the middle of nowhere. Carroll recalls working LZ Lonely when it had come under fire from the Vietcong. The compound was surrounded. Luckily, the men had only worked there for 3 or 4 days so they got out safely. Carroll stated that this mission was primarily a medevac mission because LZ Lonely's guys were getting shot up. Carroll flew in the VIPs, then medevaced out the dead and wounded. He resupplied LZ Lonely with ammunition all day long and constantly went in and out of the "hot" LZ. "We had the fast moving F-4s coming in and doing their thing and providing fire power support and all that kind of jazz." Just as Carroll and his copilot returned to base and were about to shut down, they received a final call from LZ Lonely. It was dark, but LZ Lonely radioed in and said there was a bag of mail in Carroll and Barefoot's compound.

Just as we're shutting down, I got a call from LZ Lonely and they say, "Castle 555? Hey, we understand there's a bag of mail up there. Can you come down and deliver the mail to us for the troops?" And I looked at my co-pilot, was a guy named Barefoot, and I said, "Bruce, what do you think?" "Let's do it." So we cranked it up and we got the sack of mail. One of the crew chiefs was a guy named Chively. And now it's dark and I said, "Listen, Chively, I'm going to literally roll in over the compound, and I'm going to put it up on its side. You just throw that bag of mail as soon as I tell you." So we went down. We were redlined at 120 knots while I slid it up on the side and threw the mail down, and I went back. And on the way back the radio operator at LZ Lonely said, "Castle 555, you're too fuckin' much." You know? And we went back and had a few beers. We didn't get shot up at all on that one.

Unlike World War II, Vietnam had few FEBAs, or forward edges of battle. "The bad guys were all around you." Few men left the compound at night, and there were not many night missions. Staying inside the perimeter of the base, however, did not mean complete safety. Nightly mortar attacks were frequent in Vietnam, particularly at the beginning of the month. One night Carroll's unit earned 5 Purple Hearts when Vietcong mortared their position. Others fled to the relative safety of their sandbag "hooch," grabbing helmets and flak jackets along the way.

The second risk all helicopter pilots faced was the weather, which could cause many problems for a helicopter pilot. Carroll said the weather would come in every afternoon about 3 o'clock, the time when the ship needed to return from a remote base, perhaps along the Cambodian border. He'd be telling his passengers, "Come on, guys. Let's go. We gotta get out of here. We're not gonna get back." They would end up low leveling through the country, hoping no one would shoot at them. On one occasion, Carroll had Colonel Chidlaw and Major Cottington with him when they tried to land in Dong Ba Thin. Carroll was unable to land due to weather conditions "socking in" the LZ. Carroll and the other passengers onboard had to fly out of their way to a distant base at Phang Rang. He told Colonel Chidlaw,

"Look, I'm gonna turn all the lights out on the aircraft because we don't wanna be going through the North Phang Rang Pass with lights on 'cause the bad guys will spot us." So we went low level in the dark and we got to Phang Rang. I landed at the engineer pad.

When they got to Phang Rang, Major Cottington looked at him and said, "Fat Albert, you earned your flight pay tonight."

Clouds and darkness were not the only weather risks; sometimes dust provided a greater hazard. On the Cambodian border in a place called Bu Prang, where the combat engineers were building an airstrip, Carroll experienced this hazard. In fact, when he asked the engineers for the location of Bu Prang, they said they didn't know, to just "fly west and look for the dust coming out of the jungle." As Carroll was landing, the dust began to sweep up into his rotors, a term called "going IFR in the dust," which can cause serious damage to the aircraft. Landing was tricky. "You gotta land that thing quickly; you can't be hovering around in a cloud, okay?" For his efforts, the engineers offered him their only drink, lukewarm milk, "just disgusting." Taking mercy on these men isolated at a remote location, Carroll told them to throw an empty trash can in the back of his helicopter. He returned on a late Sunday

Carroll flying a DH-58 helicopter in Vietnam, October 1970

afternoon hauling that trash can filled with Budweiser on ice. The men were elated. "It was like we could do nothing wrong…a feel good thing."

The third risk for helicopter pilots was mechanical failure. That is why 80% of flight school focused on emergency procedures. Compared to a fixed wing aircraft, a helicopter has many moving parts that have to be well-maintained, "a nightmare." Unfortunately Carroll had one of the worst types of mechanical failures for a helicopter—a tail rotor malfunction. "We were flying in the Huey going from Dong Ba Thin to Phan Thiet," the birthplace of Ho Chi Minh. Carroll called for an emergency landing. When any American is in danger, the United States military does not mess around. Before they landed, a radio operator heard his distress call and asked if he wanted "guns." This meant support from the Cobra attack helicopters. Carroll and the men onboard set up their machine guns. About two minutes after they landed on a beach, two sets of Cobra gunships came roaring in and blew up everything in front of Carroll and his men. Two minutes after that, two medevac ships arrived. Five minutes later a whole platoon of infantry arrived on the beach and spread out. The men were safe. It gave Carroll and his men a sense of security, which he described as a "warm fuzzy feeling."

Another serious mechanical difficulty is hydraulics failure, which happened to a gunship in which Carroll was the copilot. Returning from "shooting up a mountain," they had to perform a running landing because they could not hover. Fire trucks were called to the scene. Fortunately the hydraulics came and went, enabling the pilot to land the ship without hydraulics. "And sure enough they were on until about 3 or 4 feet off the ground and they went out again. If he hadn't done that, it would have been a problem, and so he slid right on and we got out."

Despite the fearful parts of war, there were also some good times for Carroll while he was in Vietnam. The officers would hang out at the end of each day. "We'd all wind up at the end of the hooch." They had a bar and a refrigerator in their quarters, where they could sit and tell

In front of a Huey in January 1971 (left to right): Parker Goodwin, Bruce Barefoot, Carroll Vanik (Fat Albert), Dave Breedlove

jokes, or talk about what happened that day. A bunch of helicopter pilots would be playing cards. To pass the time, they told stories. Most were real; some were exaggerated. To separate the two, "Vietnam helicopter pilots, they always prefaced everything by saying, 'This is no shit.'" The reason they said "This is no shit" was because sometimes they would be accused of embellishing a story.

One funny story Carroll shared was about a pilot nicknamed "Animal." Animal was a helicopter pilot and had the rank of warrant officer. Animal was lying out sun tanning, completely nude except for a sock in a "certain place." A colonel from another regiment came up and started yelling and screaming at him. Animal stood up; the sock fell off. As Carroll said, "They gonna send you home?"

Most Vietnam veterans want to tell the funny stories. Carroll was no exception.

Besides cards, writing letters, and telling stories, the men found other distractions. One crew chief, a talented maintenance man, frequented a local brothel. While "chasing him out of there" one night, one "gal" came after Carroll and the others with a meat cleaver! All were safe but the chief's maintenance was "never the same." The only "round-eyed" women the men ever saw were the Donut Dollies, the Red Cross girls. Sadly, one of them threw up in Carroll's plane. USO shows at the officers' clubs once a month provided some distraction, but marijuana was a

problem among the enlisted. On some street corners the Vietnamese sold cocaine, or their schoolteacher sister, or whatever would bring them income. When Carroll asked if they could get him some Kool-Aid, "they'd go running off to their suppliers," thinking this was some new drug. The men even found the bright side of a typhoon that blew away their "two-holer" latrine. "The good news is the engineers built an 8-holer for us."

Carroll's favorite story, however, was an episode from the *Deer Hunter*. Right before Thanksgiving, morale was low. Men did not want to eat the mess hall turkey. A couple Southern boys proposed a deer hunt. Carroll grabbed a Huey and they were off. Two M-60 machine guns made short work of two deer out in the open. The boys cleaned them; the next night they celebrated Thanksgiving with venison and beer. The day after, Colonel Sanders—no joke; this was his name—called Carroll into his office.

He said, "Fat Albert [Carroll's call sign], shut that door." And he said, "It's my understanding that you took a military aircraft and went out there hunting. Is that true?" And I said, "Yes, sir, that's right." He said, "Captain Vanik, you understand that's a misappropriation of government aircraft, and you can be court martialed?" And I said, "Yes sir, I do." He chewed me out, then said, "Now get out of my office!" So I was leaving the office when Colonel Sanders said, "Hey, Fat Albert," and I said, "What?" He said, "You got any venison left?" And I said, "No, we ate it all." So he was not that irritated.

What they gonna do, send you to Vietnam?

Humor could not hide all the risks. By 1970 most men wanted to complete their tours and come home in one piece. This did not lessen the concern the men held for each other. "If somebody was in danger, everybody went out—everybody went out of their way. But there was nobody that had an attitude that they were gonna be a hero, you know, in that regard. There were no Audie Murphys." In the early days of the war, men did stupid things like write on their helmets or paint messages on their aircraft. By 1970 the bravado had changed, but the dangers had not. About six weeks after Carroll arrived in-country, Major General George Casey, Sr., father of the commander in Iraq today, was killed when his helicopter ran into a mountain. During the hunt for the general, a 24-year-old crew chief took a bullet in the groin from enemy ground fire. The doctor, covered in blood, wept, "I did everything I could. I did everything I could." The young man died nonetheless—along with the other 58,000 names on the Wall.

Carroll's last two weeks in Vietnam, he was grounded. As was customary, he was sent to Cam Rahn Bay three days earlier than his DEROS, or Date Expected to Return Overseas, June 5, 1971. Repeated requests to leave earlier went unanswered until he heard an announcement over the intercom requesting he report to the Red Cross Station. His father had suffered a heart attack. He was on a flight the next morning. When he visited his father in the hospital, he joked, "You know, you could have had this heart attack a month earlier. I could have come home early." His father lived for 12 more years.

Carroll returned home to his wife in Baltimore. There were no parades. "I went to the hospital, I went home, changed my uniform, got on a pair of jeans, and went to a restaurant for some steamed crabs," where he bumped into an old high school buddy who wanted to know about Vietnam. "How was it?" "How was it?" Carroll replied. "It was like a picnic!" Carroll still wonders why the military sent young men into a war without a clear timetable. He thinks about those names on the Wall.

Carroll left the service in February of 1972. He worked for Proctor and Gamble and flew for the Maryland National Guard. Today he lives in Carefree, Arizona, with his wife Susan. He showed me pictures from Vietnam and his Nomex nylon flight suit, painted orange, the international Red Cross color. His helmet has a Baltimore Colts logo monogrammed on the back. Embroidered on his flight suit is the Latin logo "Illegitimati-non-Garborundum," which stands for "Don't let the bastards wear you down." He took a match to the flight suit to show how it could protect a pilot from burns. We said our goodbyes.

Though I returned Monday to math and history class and other distractions, somehow I felt Vietnam was not a time Carroll would ever forget.

This is no shit.

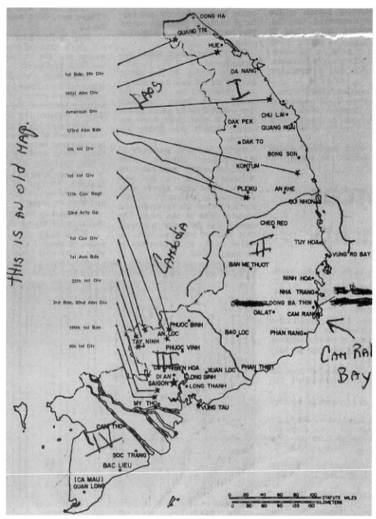

Map of various Corps sectors with Cam Rahn Bay highlighted

John Wintersteen

December 1965 - October 1994
Vietnam

With the Gear in the Rear

An Interview with John Wintersteen
By Patrick Ward

In Vietnam over 400,000 men served in the United States Marine Corps. John's embarkation into the military started when he was in college. With aspirations of attending West Point Academy, he reconsidered and instead went to a small Lutheran college. There he was the editor of the newspaper and considered a career later in life as a journalist. A few months into his sophomore year, in December, he decided right then and there he wanted to be a Marine. After quite a few hassles he arrived at the recruiting office in the middle of their annual Christmas party. He was finally sworn in by a major who didn't even move his feet off his desk to do so.

The next evening, John had an encounter with the college pastor, who was the school's anti-war group leader, at the off-campus house where he lived and where the living room was used for group meetings.

Wednesday rolls around and it's the last edition [of the newspaper] that I would have for three weeks to worry about, and the college pastor said the same thing he'd been saying for weeks. "Hey, we're having a meeting in here—come on in and join us." And I say, "Now you know the answer. I'm really tired. I'm really hungry." And he says, "No, no, come in here. I really want you to come in here, for just a minute." And he says, "Well, we know what *we're* doing for our country. What are *you* doing for your country?" And I said, "Yesterday I joined the United States Marine Corps." I walked out, and they never spoke to me again.

Part way into his officer training at The Basic School, they announced they would need ten men to volunteer as engineers. Since John's father was an engineer, and John had experience in construction and reading blueprints, he thought he'd give it a go. John volunteered and went on to engineer training.

On March 23, 1968, John arrived in Vietnam shortly after the Tet offensive. With no flak jacket, no helmet, and only a pistol, he was on his way to the Dong Ha River "ramp" when his driver brought the jeep to a screeching halt and dove into a long trench alongside the road. Not knowing what else to do, John bailed out and dove in with him. At just that moment a soldier jumped and landed right on top of him.

> ...both feet landed right on my back and my neck and just smashed me into the bottom of the trench face-first and I got some abrasions and I could hear the rounds coming in and I thought it's kind of comforting having that soldier on top of me...

On arriving at the compound, before him lay a gruesome sight: seven dead sailors who were killed in the daily North Vietnamese rocket bombardments. He was then given a call from "some colonel," who told him to do a crater analysis—used to verify munitions and the direction of incoming fire so U.S. artillery could respond—during the next attack. Showing no hesitancy, John's attitude was simply, "I can do this." At about nine o'clock the next morning, the rockets began to come in.

> I found the nearest crater between two old metal warehouse buildings that were pretty badly damaged by the rockets. I could hear the fragments and the shrapnel going Ping! Ping! in one wall and out the other. When a rocket hit in the middle, I could hear it going outward. I could hear the stuff, and it was all over the ground.

John found four nails and some string and ran out into the rocket fire until he found the crater. He got down on his knees and used a rock to pound in the nails across the widest part of the crater. He then found where the fuse had gone off because it made a little deeper indentation. He put the strings across the back, his compass in the middle, and got a back azimuth on those rounds. "And then I ran/scurried/ran/crawled as fast as I could back into that bunker. I got inside the steel door and I leaned against it and was just sucking my breath. The three Marines just stared, just stared at me. They had never seen anyone go out into a rocket attack or do a crater analysis." John told them he'd get his breath back, then called the combat operations center to report they were receiving rounds and that he had a crater analysis, a back azimuth.

During his stay at the small base on the Cua Viet River, John was under rocket attack nearly every day. His unit, C Company, 3rd Shore Battalion, was in charge of security to protect the unloading and distribution of all supplies coming up the river.

Before his arrival in Vietnam, the push for "McNamara's Wall" had become a priority in Washington. A series of many outposts, sensors, and bases stretching all the way to the neighboring country of Laos would be used to stop the infiltration of supplies to the Viet Cong and NVA soldiers. McNamara's Wall was considered almost an impossibility and mostly useless to the engineers. When construction bogged down, supplies began to build up several miles away. He and one of his lance corporals decided they could put the supplies to better use.

> One night, I just went there and cut the wire. The lance corporal had come up with a high-bed semitrailer every night from some other unit so, in the dark, I used one of the Army forklifts to load what we needed. We built a whole new line of bunkers for the compound and strengthened all the other bunkers that we had from those materials that had been sent over there for "McNamara's Wall."

The most perilous time at the port came whenever they had to unload explosives—whole boatloads of artillery ammo, small arms, or demolitions—because then they were prime targets for North Vietnamese rockets.

> Oh, we had massive amounts of artillery ammo, and when we started taking those rounds, we knew that if one of those LCUs [Landing Craft Utility] or YFUs [Yard Freight Utility] got hit by a rocket, we were going to have an explosion they were gonna' hear in Da Nang! And we would probably all be dead.

Their port got many convoys of trucks going back to the field. The men loaded those trucks as fast as they possibly could get them out of the bull's-eye of incoming fire. When the truck drivers argued they were *only* taking food, John didn't give them much of a choice. He got that artillery ammo off as fast as possible.

South Vietnamese soldiers guarding bridge

The bunker next to John's housed an older Vietnamese soldier, a former university professor with a PhD from the Sorbonne, who had fallen from grace politically. Every week that soldier went out and bought himself a luxury, a fresh crab. One week he asked John if he would like to share it with him. John kindly refused. The next week the soldier came back with two crabs and said they were going to eat together. Every Wednesday after that, John and the professor, who spoke excellent English, squatted around a stove made from an old bucket and boiled and ate the crabs.

John was also responsible for guarding the south end of the Route 1 bridge over the river, with the other end guarded by the Vietnamese National Combat Police. Considering none of his men spoke Vietnamese and only one of the combat police knew a select few English words, it made for a very interesting experience.

They welcomed me, they fed me, played volleyball, they took pieces of ice that had been made out of river water that you could see green stuff frozen into and put it into cups and poured warm beer over it to make me feel welcome. They fed me the food they were eating and they were some tough soldiers. They obviously had great respect for Marines and all forces, but the National Combat Police, they were, to my way of thinking at the time, the equivalent of SEALS and Rangers. They

went out on long patrols, had their own killed, several times a week.

After a month John was to be transferred to Khe Sahn to run the aircraft loading and unloading, but when the relief of Khe Sahn occurred, he was instead assigned to C Company, 3rd Engineer Battalion, stationed at the end of Route 9. In a sequence of events, his captain suffered a nervous breakdown. The captain shut himself in his personal Alpine tent, and when he was told some decision had to be made, he opened the flap and just stared, not saying a word. Then one day, without a word, the captain walked to the LZ and never came back, ultimately medevaced out of Vietnam. John had been serving as executive officer.

A 1st Lieutenant was sent in to replace the commander. The new CO reassigned John immediately to the field as a platoon commander and told him it was because he was not "authorized" to be executive officer and carry out the orders of the previous captain. As the platoon commander of 2nd Platoon, he built fire support bases with 2nd Battalion, 9th Marines. John traveled all over northern Vietnam and his mission was usually:

We need a fire support base there. Go out by a helicopter with a couple of your engineers, do a reconnaissance, order the stuff, build a fire support base, tell me when it's time for the artillery to start airlifting in.

After six weeks in the field as platoon commander, the new company commander sent out a newly arrived 2nd Lieutenant—unannounced—to be platoon commander. The lieutenant arrived with only instructions to John to "report to the CO ASAP." John expected some sort of "bad news." However, the company commander greeted him with a smile and told him, "I made a mistake. You're now the XO [executive officer], so just do what you were doing before I sent you out to the platoon." Soon after John was promoted to 1st Lieutenant, he was assigned as the company commander—with four other 1st lieutenants in the company.

As company commander, John had a good 1st lieutenant named Rusty Hughes. While working on the landing zone at the top of the Rockpile, Rusty stepped on a mine and had part of his foot blown off.

John flew out to the platoon and said to the senior guy, a corporal, "You're the platoon commander. Take charge. Give the orders." With the end of his tour approaching, John felt he still had responsibilities in Vietnam and extended his tour for six months. As company commander, he instructed the clerk to change his rotation tour date, or RTD, to one that would give him 20 months "in country."

When John traveled all over Northern I Corps, he spent a lot of time with his platoons and was very close to his Marines. "I paid them, I brought them beer, I brought them their mail, I did all the haircutting the whole time I was company commander. I would jump off the helicopter, check with the battalion commander or the company commander from 9th Marines that was in charge, and if he didn't have anything to pass on to me, I'd see my troops. I'd bring them maybe a six pack of beer and a couple sodas and some candy bars and I'd pay them in military payment certificates and I'd cut their hair. I just had a hand-operated clipper, and they'd just sit on their helmet or sit on the grass and I'd kneel behind them and I'd cut their hair and we'd talk. I just had such a great time with those Marines."

As John's adjusted tour date approached, he knew it was time to come home when he received a letter from his wife saying, "It's time. Come home." John said to himself that in 48 hours he would be home in his wife's arms. That prediction changed to 72 hours when he learned of a typhoon brewing off the coast; it was "raining cats and dogs." John was instead sent to the *USS Iwo Jima*, a helicopter carrier

Loading and unloading supplies at the dock

returning to the United States, where 72 hours turned into 28 days. In their first two years of marriage, he and his wife had only spent several weekends, two six-day R&Rs, and a month of leave together.

After his time in Vietnam, John served almost 30 years with the Marine Corps, including assignments like Japan, Korea, Virginia, Pennsylvania, Hawaii, Georgia, and even the military maximum security prison in Kansas. A graduate of the FBI National Academy in Quantico, he retired as the head of the Security and Law Enforcement Branch at Headquarters Marine Corps.

After Vietnam, for those of us who stayed in the Corps, it made it far less likely that we were going to have post-trauma stress disorder or drug problems or alcohol problems. So I spent the next 28 years in this marvelous support group that they call the United States Marine Corps. And I'm very proud of all that service.

John is still serving the country he helped to defend. Today he is Chief of Police of Paradise Valley, Arizona.

When asked whether his service in Vietnam was worth the sacrifice, John responded with pride in his service, representing himself and all the Marines with whom he served.

Vietnam was a battle in the larger Cold War. Ultimately, we forced the Russians to spend themselves into instability, so I felt I was, all those years, doing something that was very important, not just for the United States, but I believe for the world.

John Wintersteen firing from outer perimeter at Quang Tri

Operation Iraqi Freedom
Gulf Wars

America's involvement in Iraq is long and complex. The war has spanned seventeen years and has ignited two different wars. America's interests have changed as political and military necessities have evolved.

In the first Gulf War, the United Nations approved the use of military forces designed solely for expelling the Iraqi army from its defenseless neighbor Kuwait, which it had invaded. The second Gulf War, also led by America, was not sanctioned by the United Nations, but instead encompassed an entirely different motive: the Bush administration had reason to believe Saddam Hussein and his corrupt government were developing Weapons of Mass Destruction, which could have come into the hands of terrorists.

The technological advances used in these wars have assisted the American military in swift and decisive victories. Unlike previous wars, the implementation of "smart" weapons has reduced casualties of war and civilian deaths by the hundreds of thousands.

The men and women who currently serve in the U.S. military find themselves on the forefront of the global war on terrorism. Credited to their dedication and heroic actions, there have been no terrorist attacks on American soil since September 11. Although there are many lingering problems in Iraq today, the acts of our brave soldiers have not diminished.

Amanda Poincelot

Steve Marshall

July 1981 - August 2003
Pacific and Indian Oceans,
Arabian and Caribbean Seas

"They Would All Start Flooding Back To Me"
An Interview with Steve Marshall
By Callie Adair

At the age of 15, Steve Marshall was being groomed for sea service, hired as a navigator to sail from Tampa, Florida, to Washington, D.C. on a 30-day voyage. Steve started down the road of the Coast Guard Academy but "kind of lost interest" and "never quite made it."

After living in Iowa for a few years, Steve decided he "had enough of winters" and decided to join the military. Since the Coast Guard was full at that time, he joined the Navy. Steve knew only one thing he wanted in the Navy—to be a diver. He had grown up on Jacques Cousteau and was certified to dive at 15. He decided to become a Navy SEAL.

After his final interview with the SEAL Master Chief at boot camp, Steve changed his mind. "Where do you see yourself in five years?" the Master Chief asked Steve. "I am pretty sure I will be a commercial diver out in the oil rigs down in the Gulf of Mexico," Steve responded. That's not what a SEAL does, so the Master Chief explained there are other diving programs in the Navy. The one that appealed to Steve was EOD, or Explosive Ordnance Disposal. In order to apply to those programs, Steve had to be in the Navy for a while.

Steve went to school and learned to be a Quartermaster. Finishing first in his class, he continued on to submarine school and Submarine Quartermaster School. After almost a year in the Navy, he applied for the dive programs but found out he had to first spend a year aboard a submarine. Steve ended up on a sub in San Diego being sent to Hawaii to undergo refitting. It would be in the shipyard 18 months to two years, so Steve worked on his Personal Qualification Standards (PQS book), trying to qualify in Submarine Warfare, a prerequisite imposed by his supervisor to enter the dive program. Unfortunately, it is hard to get your submarine pin, or dolphins, in a shipyard so he stood extra watches, worked hard, and "made deals."

His break came while waiting to deploy on the *USS Tautog*, a submarine heading to the North Pole. A message came across the wire and was posted to the bulletin board. "Do you want to parachute, SCUBA dive, and blow things up with explosives? If so, contact Explosive Ordnance Disposal Mobile Unit ONE in Barber's Point, Hawaii, and we'll see if you've got what it takes." Eager to move on with his career in diving, Steve approached his supervisors, who did not want to let him go. Quartermasters on submarines were not easy to replace. When they tried to list the qualifications needed to make the transfer, and told him he'd never be approved, Steve listed all the tests he had already passed, and then commented, "Well, then you won't mind signing this saying that I am approved to go because you are positive that Washington is going to disapprove it. So your approving it won't hurt." The Bureau of Personnel (BUPERS) in Washington did approve Steve to attend EOD School in November. His supervisors were not pleased. Out of spite, Steve's PQS book, 80% complete, was torn up. "You are not going to need this 'cause you are going somewhere else."

After three years in the Navy and EOD training in Huntsville, Alabama; Panama City, Florida; and Indian Head, Maryland, Steve finally reported to his first EOD command, EOD Mobile Unit TWO in Fort Story, Virginia. His first mission was the 1984 Summer Olympics in Los Angeles. Qualifying soccer trials were held in Annapolis, Maryland. With a long waterfront vulnerable to terrorists, military assistance was needed to guarantee the athletes' safety. "We had Iranians, and Iraqis, and Lebanese, the Saudi Arabians were there—just a very scary mix of people from a terrorism point of view." Annapolis sits right next to the Severn River, and the hotel where the players were staying was over the water on a pier. Checking the seawall along the fields, and the barges surrounding the hotel, for terrorist devices were everyday jobs for three weeks.

After the Olympics, Steve went back to his normal routine. When his team was not inspecting an aircraft carrier or some other ship, they were training. There was a lot to know. "We worked on everything from firecrackers to nuclear weapons because we had to know about improvised explosive devices, or IEDs, or had to know about landmines, grenades, rockets, missiles, guided missiles, intercontinental ballistic missiles, and other nukes so it was a lot of information to know." They had to keep current on diving techniques, parachutes, and any changes in the field. It was important to be

prepared. "So training, training, training, if you weren't actually working."

In 1985, Steve was deployed to the *USS Forrestal* after a diving accident in the Chesapeake Bay, where a fellow diver got caught up in some lines while searching for training mines, and drowned. It was Steve's job to take the diver's wife to the recompression chamber to see him. Steve became the replacement diver on the team. While serving on the *USS Forrestal*, the United States attacked Libya. Planes from the *USS Saratoga* destroyed Muammar Qaddafi's palace and killed one of his sons. Steve wondered if his ship would be next to go.

After the *USS Forrestal* work-ups, Steve was reassigned and headed for Grenada after the U.S. invasion. It was Steve's first experience in a war zone. He accompanied Vice President George H.W. Bush on a Secret Service mission to speak to the Grenadians about how fortunate they were to be free of the Cuban influence. Steve was shocked by the damage he observed, "Cars flipped over and burned and rocket holes in them. The entire top floor of this hotel—there was a two-story hotel down there that had the entire top floor basically shot off of it by small arms fire and rockets from the invasion. That was pretty sobering."

After 2 years in Virginia, Steve was sent to San Diego, where he hoped to be detailed to the Marine Mammal Program. He tried it out for two weeks. After two days he found out it was "not so glamorous." His supervisor had warned him.

We have dolphins that would find mines, we had the anti-swimmer dolphins, and we had the sea lions that were really deep-ocean water recovery units. The sea lions are actually the bread and butter of the whole program because they can find things that are really deep down on the bottom of the ocean floor, deeper than a man can go with the current technology. The problem with the dolphins was that some of the dolphins had switched from anti-swimmer to mine-hunting, which I found out first-hand one time. Our job was [to] dive down and see if the dolphin had placed the explosive charge, which was inert, just a training charge, next to the mine where he was supposed to. After the dolphin would come back to the boat and essentially let us know that it was done, we would dive down and find out, yes, it's close enough or it's too far away or he totally missed it, he just dropped it, whatever. We were essentially scoring or grading the dolphin's progress. And one time I came back to the boat after doing that and was forcibly grabbed and thrown into the boat. I said, "What's going on?" They said, "We just put Oscar in the water." Well, Oscar was previously [an] anti-swimmer [dolphin] and apparently was hot for my tail at the time, so they helped me out.

Steve happily went back to the North Island shore detachment.

In San Diego, Steve's unit responded to IED threats. He reported there were "only about 300" threats in the San Diego area per year! Fortunately, most of them were hoaxes. But after six years in the Navy, Steve was ready for a change. He was not interested in cleaning ship hulls, a common job for ex-Navy divers. Instead, for eight months Steve worked with a company called UXB International, which hired EOD technicians to clean up an old Marine firing range in Tierra Santa, a San Diego subdivision, where they planned to build houses. Two children had been killed and one maimed on the property when a 30-year-old 37-millimeter projectile they were playing with detonated. The job seemed more risky than military EOD, however. Steve realized, "That was probably the first time I ever really worked on something that I was concerned was gonna blow up in my face because it was so old." Since he now had a son, he decided it would be safer back in the Navy.

Steve was detailed to the brand new EOD Mobile Unit NINE in Mare Island, California, and was deployed to the Persian Gulf on August 20, 1990. His was the first EOD team over there during the war, arriving in November. The war didn't start until January 17, 1991.

The EOD team moved into the Gulf and had to start worrying about SCUD missiles and sea mines. Steve found out Saddam was using old World War II mines to defend his coast; the Iraqis just threw a lot of them in the water as floating obstacles. No one knew quite what to do with these mines. As the senior EOD tech on the team, Steve had to figure out how best to deal with the floating mine problem. Knowing

the twenty pounds of C4 the SEALs had been using to detonate and deactivate the mines was excessive and wasteful, the EOD team used less and less to find the right amount. They settled on seven and a half pounds of explosives, even though Steve believed 2.5 pounds would have worked.

Essentially when the ship lookouts or helicopters would spot the mines, we would get in a helicopter, and then fly over to where we could see them. And then with our explosive charges we jumped into the water, swam over to the mine, strapped our charge onto it, pulled the igniter, and we had about 5 to 7 minutes to get out of the area. Then the helicopters would pick us back up and we would take off.

Sinking the mines by shooting holes in them from the surface only made ships passing overhead vulnerable in the shallow water. Three hundred pounds of

Fast rope

C-130 jump to search for mines

explosion when Steve's team detonated the mines because it was not flashy enough for the cameras. So the team substituted a tomato buoy and a forty-pound explosive charge about a foot under the water after ensuring nothing metal would fragment and injure anyone. They then pulled the boat as close as they could to the exploding charge and a huge geyser of water landed on the boat.

> We got the boat as close as possible, as close as we felt comfortable, while they were filming. We had it all ready and yelled, "Fire in the hole! Fire in the hole! Fire in the hole!" Whoof! This huge geyser goes up and we got totally soaked on the boat and they were so happy. They said, "That's exactly what we wanted!" Completely false the way that it worked out. It would never—it's not really that impressive when you take out a mine. But they wanted that.

The cameras also wanted a more dramatic entry for the EOD team, so asked the team to parachute in and use a larger boat. Adding the parachute drop completed the desired Hollywood effect. Steve realized "guys in the know" wouldn't think much of their film, and he took "a lot of ribbing" for it afterward.

Steve's EOD team deployed to Guam to assist EOD Mobile Unit FIVE in the Philippines after the eruption of Mt. Pinatubo. The Air Force had to close Clark AFB and the Navy left its base in Subic Bay, due to the disaster. Steve's team was there to assist with the missions of the Subic Bay EOD unit while they transferred equipment and personnel to Guam. In the name of international support, they taught tactics to other EOD units. Steve was deployed to Japan, Malaysia, Singapore, and Thailand. The United States, the British, and the Israelis have the best-trained EOD units, because unfortunately they deal with bombs on a day-to-day basis. While in Guam, Steve experienced the 170-mph winds of Typhoon Omar, which "tore down almost every palm tree on the island," yet few Americans noticed it because it occurred at the same time as Hurricane Andrew.

Steve became the Senior Enlisted Advisor to EOD Mobile Unit FIFTEEN, a reserve unit on Mare Island until BRAC, a series of base closures, caused his departure. His next assignment was assistant

explosives "rolling around on the bottom" of the Persian Gulf was not acceptable. Mines did inflict serious damage on two U.S. ships, the *USS Tripoli* and the *USS Princeton*. A mine creates a large gas bubble under a ship. Unsupported by water, the ship will crack. That's what happened to the *USS Princeton*. Damage crews were able to shore up the *USS Princeton* with heavy cables and weld it together and then tow it to port. The *USS Tripoli* hit a floating mine that blew a 15-foot hole in the hull.

Returning to the United States in May, Steve's Mobile Unit got a call from ABC. They wanted to do a TV special on the Navy EOD and their role in Desert Storm. For ten days in Monterrey, California, the EOD Mobile Unit NINE team worked with a Hollywood crew. "Well, let's say they embellished quite a bit on what we really did." First off, they didn't like the officer in charge of EOD Mobile Unit THREE Detachment Point Mugu, responsible for the Pacific Missile Test Range near Ventura, California. He became a Tomahawk missile trainer and worked with General Dynamics on the EOD portion of the program. What he enjoyed most was the opportunity to go to Japan's Missile School. The Japanese, by World War II treaty, cannot have any offensive weapons, but because they are so close to Russia and North Korea and need to defend themselves, they are allowed to test their defensive missiles at Point Mugu. Steve's biggest challenge in Japan was finding an interpreter who understood the language of weapons.

Steve left the west coast to work in Washington, D.C. in Research and Development, but that was too much of a slow-moving job. "I could not deal with the five years until you get a prototype, and then five more years until it's perfected, because by the time something was perfected and then ready to go into the system, it was obsolete. It was just much, much too slow for me and I couldn't handle it." Fortunately a friend at the Navy Annex next to the Pentagon was already seeking a replacement to fill his job. Steve became the Enlisted Community Manager for EOD; SEALs; Navy fleet divers; the Special Boat Units which work with the SEALs, sometimes called the Brown Water Navy; and the Navy band.

Then September 11th happened. A lieutenant told Steve that CNN had reported a plane had crashed into the World Trade Center in New York, but wasn't that concerned, thinking it was a small plane that had lost control. Then the second plane struck. After seeing the Twin Towers ablaze on TV, Steve was dumbstruck. He went outside for a moment, but for some reason decided to go back inside. The moment he sat in his chair, he heard "what sounded like a jet at full throttle right over my head. And then a thud, and the vibration, and the shake, and the explosion." He immediately ran outside, beating the sirens and the fire alarms. He was standing there looking down on the Pentagon and realizing the plane had passed only a few feet above his building because it had to dive down past the Sheraton Hotel to reach the level of the Pentagon. Steve stood in the parking lot looking down upon the fireball that erupted when the airplane's two wing tanks exploded.

Steve and others from the Navy Annex ran toward the Pentagon to see what they could do. They had to go up over the freeway ramp, where they found a cab driver sitting on his car. When the plane dove, it hit a light post on the freeway and the light post had fallen on the cab. The cab driver was shaking so badly he couldn't light his cigarette.

By the time Steve got to the South Parking lot of the Pentagon, everyone in the area was coming out to help, both civilians and military. An announcement said there was another plane inbound and everyone needed to take cover. People scattered, not knowing what to do. Steve went under the overpass, thinking the plane wouldn't hit a road. After several minutes, they decided they needed to help.

Some of the people in my office, because we were the Community Management office, we had hospital corpsmen, we had doctors, and they had sprinted down there to see what they could do. We had people—civilians and enlisted and military people in general—that had friends or family in the Pentagon, obviously upset, and they were headed down there, too.

The area of the Pentagon the plane hit was the Navy Operations Center. That meant no communications between all the Navy bases. So Steve's Admiral went to the Virginia Department of Transportation Traffic Control Center down the street and commandeered the place so the Navy could reestablish communications. Ironically, Steve was unable to reach his wife locally, but able to call his father in Phoenix to let him know he was all right. His father then contacted his wife. After that, Steve was dispatched to a local hospital to collect casualty information. He sat for four hours with little to do. When he asked why there weren't more casualties, he was told the people in the Pentagon were either "green or black"—green, no serious injuries; and black, dead. Steve went home. Because he had "slugged," or hitchhiked, to work that day and didn't have a car, he got a ride with someone who lived nearby, but walked the last mile home to have some time to himself. When he got home, he and his family were very emotional and upset.

Steve asked his wife if she had heard from one of the neighbors who worked where the plane hit. She hadn't. They had no idea what to do so they decided to walk over to the house to see if the husband was home yet, even though they didn't want to be the "first ones to break the bad news." The funny thing was, the neighbors were thinking the same thing. As they saw Steve and his wife walk across the lawn, they also came out with a six pack of beer and met in the street, relieved to find each other alive.

The next day, Steve started maintaining the database on the remains of those killed, as they were identified. He would call to Millington, Tennessee, where all the personnel records were and tell them who had been identified. Handling the database for approximately 180 casualties from the Pentagon was hard, but easier than actually going in and recovering the bodies. "It's funny. I don't remember any of the names now, but I am sure, if I saw a list of them, they would all start flooding back to me."

About two years after September 11, Steve retired from the Navy—partly because of September 11 and partly because he didn't want to move his family around any more. Today Steve works for the state of Arizona, making sure it is ready for terrorists and natural disasters. He helped with the Katrina evacuees who came to Arizona in 2006 after the hurricane in New Orleans, and he works with local emergency management. "I don't do EOD per se any more... but I still have a hand in emergencies."

Water jump from a C-130

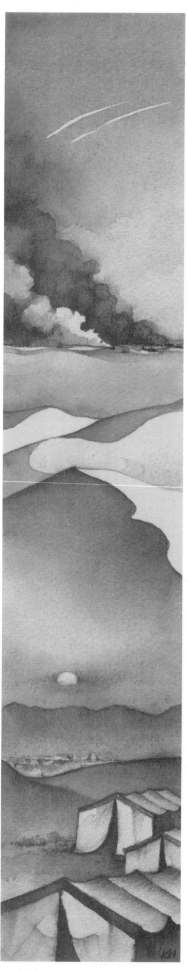

Michael Marzano

May 1999 - May 2005
Okinawa, United States, Iraq

Sergeant Sport

A Tribute to Michael Adam Marzano
By His Mother, Margy Bons

Michael Adam Marzano. I loved the name from conception—Michael. Its Hebrew meaning, "Who is like God," and Adam, "Man," made it quite clear in the beginning this was a baby born to be honored. With those vocal chords as a baby, we could not argue. His fate was to be a Man of Men and a Marine of Marines. We would have arguments later in life about the use of nicknames for Michael, but to us, he would not be shortened to Mike or Mickey or any one of a few names. He was our Michael. His only other aliases were Sergeant Sport and The Rock. Those nicknames were both fitting for this athletic young man. He was active in football, wrestling, boxing, and, we would find out much later, his expertise in hand-to-hand.

When Michael was two years old he would wear his dad's Marine Corps dress blue jacket. His dad, Al, had served in Vietnam and was proud to see his son as a future Marine. Since Al had survived Vietnam with only shrapnel wounds, he was not worried about Michael following in his steps.

Moms are different.

We think the worst could happen and want to protect our cubs, but Michael was strong-willed and would not be deterred from his dream of being a Marine. A selfish reprieve of peace occurred, for me, when Michael was in high school. He had gone to a sectional competition in wrestling and torn his ACL. This knocked him out of being able to be a Marine. So Michael concentrated on his boxing career as a heavyweight and won many titles for his talents.

Michael was training to go to the 2000 Olympics when he was finally accepted into the Marines. Michael "The Rock" Marzano put aside the gold medal for the brass buttons on that Marine Corps uniform. He was happy and proud. I was scared. But with no war going on, my fears weren't as strong. My pride on his graduation from Parris Island boot camp in 1999 was strong. My son beamed a smile so full of pride that we did not need the sun to shine that hot and humid August day in South Carolina.

Michael settled into the Corps as a natural. His unit, the 1/6 from Camp LeJeune, North Carolina, was deployed to Okinawa, Japan, a couple of times.

He liked the deployments but he wanted to see the world. He did not think the residents of Okinawa appreciated what having a Marine base was doing for their economy and security.

Then September 11th, 2001, happened. Michael was waiting for his nation's urgent call to protect and serve. He and his unit left for California for a training mission and while there, he slipped on some rocks carrying an 81-millimeter mortar barrel down a mountainside. He was knocked unconscious but came to find out he had hurt his back and was going to need treatment. His unit was later called up to deploy to Iraq, but he was not able to go with them due to his injury. As any Marine will tell you, there is a strong brotherhood with these men and to not be able to go with your brothers to combat was the worst thing that could have happened to Michael. He fought the orders and could not win. His time to be discharged was around the corner and they would not send him overseas. He was devastated.

Michael decided to move to Arizona and make his home here. I was overjoyed at having him living only a few miles away. He joined the bulk fuel reserves and tried various civilian jobs. He really wanted combat and was not content that the 1/6 and the bulk fuel units had gone to Iraq without him. He said it was a waste of training. He was a warrior and needed to help his fellow comrades. He finally decided to go to college and went for a history major in the fall of 2004. I finally breathed a sigh of relief, thinking he had given up going to war.

The holidays were approaching and Michael decided to go to Pennsylvania to spend them with his dad. They were to drive back out to Arizona and find a place to share since his dad had retired. Michael received a phone call while in Pennsylvania saying that a unit, the 3/25 out of Brook Park, Ohio, was looking for bodies to go to Iraq. Michael volunteered. He did not want me to know for fear of ruining my Christmas, so he kept it to himself and made his dad keep his secret.

On January 3rd I found out Michael had volunteered to go to Iraq. I collapsed. I screamed and cried and felt empty. I could not wait for Michael to tell me to my face so I could talk him out of it, but he went to Luke Air Force Base and signed his papers before he came out to tell me. By then I knew he was not going to be happy unless he went. I also knew, deep down, that these were going to be the last days

we would have together. Moms know these sorts of things. At least I did. On January 10, 2005, he left for Twenty-Nine Palms in California for training and to meet up with the 3/25. He ran into some of his comrades from the 1/6 and told them he wished he would have gone with *them*, but at least he was going. They wished him well.

February 22nd, Al and I drove to see Michael while he had R&R in Las Vegas. We spent three days together as a family, which made Michael so happy and me sad, knowing this was to be our last time together. I don't know how I knew, but I did. When I drove back to Phoenix after watching Michael wave his final wave to me, I screamed until I could scream no more. I begged and bargained, hoping my feelings were unwarranted. Michael called me from Iraq on March 2nd, my birthday. He forgot it was my birthday because he was so excited to be over there. Two weeks later his tone changed. He had been involved in a roadside bomb and was left carrying the leg of a fellow comrade. He realized then, I think, the seriousness of this mission.

He was promoted to Sergeant on April 1st. How ironic that his dream of being a Sergeant like his father happened on April Fools' Day. He was now known to me as "Sergeant Sport." The pictures we have of him being pinned a sergeant are amazing. He

The Marzanos together in Las Vegas

is standing at the Hadithah Dam, in Iraq, being promoted. He mugged the biggest smile I had ever seen. These pictures were on the camera that was returned to us when we found out he wasn't going to return—at least not in the same condition that we sent him.

Michael in Iraq receiving promotion to Sergeant

humor rubbed off on everyone around him. Sergeant Aaron Cepeda always welcomed new members to his platoon like they were part of the family. Finally one Sailor who we will always call Marine because he continually acted like one, Petty Officer 3rd Class Jeffrey Wiener, all gave their lives that day. They had the job of protecting the force as the Quick Reaction Force and many more lives were saved due to their sacrifice. All four gave the rest of the platoon precious minutes that allowed the Marines to return fire immediately resulting in the insurgents going on the defensive.

On May 7th I was volunteering with Packages from Home at the Safeway in Anthem, trying to get donated items to send to our troops overseas. I had joined this organization when Michael went to Iraq. I remember telling people to buy mouthwash because I was sure Michael was not using proper oral hygiene while in Iraq. I had no idea at the time that my son was on his way to rescue Iraqis being held hostage at the Hadithah Hospital. Here is an excerpt of what transpired:

On 07 May 2005, enemy insurgents fired from built-up positions within the local hospital attacking U.S. Marines in the city of Hadithah, Al-Anbar Province, Iraq. Patients and the medical staff were forced to remain in the hospital while enemy forces triggered this attack that included a Suicide Vehicle-Borne Improvised Explosive Device (SVBIED). The SVBIED exploded approximately 30 feet from the hospital patient ward killing four Marines from 3d Battalion, 25th Marines and igniting a fire within the hospital. Already we knew those Marines throughout the Battalion as heroic figures even though we dare not admit it in front of them. The laughing would not stop for hours. Lance Corporal Lance Graham watched his platoon from above as he always did behind his machine gun. Sergeant Michael Marzano's leadership and

Several insurgents then fled deeper into the burning hospital, using the patients as human shields. Trying to protect themselves and the injured Iraqi civilians, the Marines from 3d Battalion, 25th Marines proceeded to clear the hospital of insurgents, killing one and capturing another. The Marines then conducted a sweep of the immediate area discovering several more insurgents surrounding the hospital. The Marines engaged and killed these insurgents while the Iraqi medical staff moved the patients to safety from the burning hospital.

I was told of my son, Sergeant Sport's, death on Mother's Day, May 8, 2005, at 1:45 a.m. He was my hero, not just for giving the ultimate sacrifice in Iraq, but because he never gave up trying to be one of the Few, the Proud, Our Marine...

He was a great example, throughout his life, of never giving up. His determination to protect his country, his fellow comrades, and his family prove that Freedom Isn't Free.

He paid a price and we will never forget.

Margy Bons

A Proud Marine Mom of Sgt. Michael (Sport) Marzano, who gave the ultimate sacrifice on 5/7/05 in Hadithah, Iraq

Michael (center) in Iraq with fellow soldiers

Afterword

Each year the Arizona Heritage Project (AHP) evolves and becomes subtly different. The new faces, both veterans and members alike, bring about a transformation in the dynamics of the project. I have had the pleasure to witness these changes first-hand. As a senior, and a three year member of AHP, I can recall memories of success, happiness, and on occasion, setbacks. Yet somehow the students in the Project, *Semper Vigilans,* seem to always achieve our goals and deadlines. Our main motivation is not the "grade" or the "community service" we might gain, it is the insight into history: the history of America, the history of our veterans, the students making history by publishing these stories.

We may never be able to fully thank our veterans; their service might have placed tremendous pressures upon their lives. Fortunately, *Since You Asked* attempts to thank our veterans by preserving their stories for future generations. Unlike textbooks, the information and stories we have documented provide another dimension to the already multifaceted reality of war. The stories do not necessarily unveil the repulsive face of battle, but the stories of hope, passion, and patriotism.

Since its existence, *Since You Asked* has merely covered the spectrum for all the modern American wars. Yet, merely "covering the spectrum" has only touched upon the multitudes of stories from our cherished veterans. We have heard stories of success and failure, triumph and defeat, rejoice and mourning. Nevertheless, we cannot begin to fathom the bravery and chivalry these men and women, these American veterans, have exhibited. For these reasons we thank you.

Mark A. McCullough

Long road ahead (Courtesy of John Wintersteen)

Veteran Contributors

Joseph R. Anderson was born September 16, 1921, in Minneapolis, Minnesota. After enlisting, Joe boarded a train to Marine boot camp in San Diego, California. Joe spent eight weeks at boot camp and was then transferred to Camp Pendleton, California, where he spent four to five months in training. Joe started his service on June 2, 1942. As a Marine in World War II, Joe served in Guadalcanal, Bougainville, Guam, and Iwo Jima. His service ended in July of 1945. After his military service, he was one of the first stewards for Pan American World Airways. Joe then moved to Hilton Head Island, South Carolina, and became a charter member and director of the Parris Island Museum. He and his wife Evelyn currently reside among the quiet hills of Scottsdale, Arizona.

Harold A. Bergbower was born in Newton, Illinois, on April 11, 1920. He enlisted in the Army Air Corps on May 12, 1939, and was sent to Clark Field in the Philippines to work on B-10s as a member of the 28th Bomb Squadron. He was captured by the Japanese and spent time in six different camps: Malabay and Davao Penal on Mindanao, Bilibid and Cabanatuan on Luzon, and Moji and Toyama in Japan. He returned home to his parents on Halloween night 1945. His wife Eunice passed away in May 1997. Harold lives in Peoria, Arizona, next door to his daughter Deborah and still rides horses.

William Burger Barnett was born in Beloit, Wisconsin, on August 18, 1922. After enlisting, "Barney" became a signalman during World War II, using semaphore flags to signal ships to avoid Japanese detection. He hauled cargo to and from the Gilbert and Marshall Islands in the South Pacific, as well as Eniwetok and Tasmania. He directed the communications tower in the Aleutians from 1942 to 1944. He currently lives in Fountain Hills, Arizona, with his wife Ruth.

Norman F. Butler was born in Hillside, New Jersey, on January 9, 1922. In college, knowing he would be drafted, he joined the Coast Guard because he "couldn't kill anyone." Norman patrolled the shores of Florida, passed through the Panama Canal to Hawaii, eventually protecting ships and men returning from the South Pacific at the end of the war. He currently resides in Fountain Hills, Arizona, with his wife Alberta and their 50 clocks!

Virgel R. Cain, Jr. was born February 9, 1946, in Los Angeles, California. Virgel, like many in his generation, enlisted in the United States Navy. He served two tours in Vietnam aboard the *USS Goldsborough*, DDG-20, in the Gulf of Tonkin, providing air support to the troops on the ground and patrolling the coast. He recalls the nightly guns making sleep aboard ship near to impossible! Virgel was a Radarman 2nd Class (RD2) and attained the rank of E-5. Virgel currently lives in Cave Creek, Arizona.

Maralin K. Coffinger was born July 5, 1935, in Ogden, Iowa. Maralin began as an English teacher but joined the Air Force in 1963, attaining the rank of Brigadier General. She was base commander at Norton AFB in California and Elmendorf AFB in Alaska. She earned her Space Badge for being one of five commanders at NORAD in Colorado Springs, Colorado. She also served in Vietnam, advising Vietnamese military women. Retired from the service, she still plays flute with a chamber orchestra. Maralin lives in Scottsdale, Arizona.

Victor S. Conner was born on July 29, 1940, in Bay Springs, Mississippi. Between 1960 and 1985, Vic served in the US Army in Air Defense. He also flew supplies and Special Forces men in Vietnam, earning him the title "Crazy Conner." He retired from the Army and worked privately during the Gulf War coordinating support for the Apache helicopters. He currently resides in Scottsdale, Arizona, with his wife Sharon.

Albert Benjamin Crawford, Jr. was born on February 3, 1928, in Tucson, Arizona. His father served in World War I after being pulled out of school by his grandmother to protect the family from Indian attacks near Safford. He graduated from West Point in 1950 and was assigned to Germany. Al developed command and control computer systems for tactical forces in the field. He achieved the rank of Major General. Al served in the United States Military until November 30, 1976. He now resides in Paradise Valley, Arizona, with his wife Bettie.

Richard J. Doubek was born in Chicago, Illinois, on December 15, 1944. After jungle warfare school in Panama, Dick served two tours in Vietnam as a Special Forces Ranger in the Vietnam War. He retired from the military in 1972 and joined the corporate world. He currently resides in Scottsdale, Arizona, with his wife Jackie and is a member of Rolling Thunder, a Harley group that attends funerals of fallen Vietnam vets and makes an annual trek to the Wall in D.C.

Rance Farrell was born June 15, 1943, in Philadelphia, Pennsylvania. Rance graduated with the West Point class of 1966, the class that suffered the most casualties in Vietnam. Steeped in the idealism of President John F. Kennedy's "Camelot years," Rance served the United States as an Artillery Officer in Vietnam, taught English at West Point, and retired

Supply boat moving down a river (Courtesy of John Wintersteen)

as a Colonel while serving in Switzerland (Rance speaks French and German). He currently lives in

Phoenix, Arizona, with his devoted wife Susan and is mentioned in Richard Atkinson's book about the West Point Class of 1966, *The Long Gray Line*.

Lyle A. French was born March 26, 1915, on a farm in South Dakota. After high school in Mankato, Minnesota, he attended Macalister College in St. Paul for two years before starting medical school at the University of Minnesota, where he graduated in 1939 after interning in medicine and becoming Resident in Training in General Surgery and Neurosurgery. Lyle served with the 26th General Hospital in North Africa and Italy during World War II and was also detached to the British 170th Evacuation Hospital. He operated on Bob Dole in Italy. His three younger brothers also served overseas at the same time: Elden in Germany, Leslie in France, and John Robert in the Pacific with the Navy. After 30 years at the University of Minnesota, Lyle retired to California and then Classic Residence in Scottsdale, Arizona. He died October 14, 2004, at Mayo Hospital in Phoenix.

John Philip Goan was born July 21, 1925, in Billings, Montana. Phil was drafted into the Army Infantry in 1943. After training at Fort Leonard Wood, Missouri, at age 18 Phil boarded the *USS West Point* for the trip to Europe, where he joined the 70th Infantry Division, 276th Regiment, 2nd Company. This group reached the upper Rhine River near the Colmar Pocket and saw action at the Battle of the Bulge. Phil was an assistant gunner. The 70th saw 58% casualties in the war. Phil currently lives at Classic Residence in Scottsdale, Arizona, with his wife Jo Ann.

Steve Goldsmith was born on May 26, 1946, in Brooklyn, New York. Steve was drafted in September of 1966 and served for two years in the Vietnam War as part of the 1st Infantry Division. In April of 1968, Steve was wounded in combat and sent home to recuperate near Brooklyn, New York. He was awarded a Purple Heart and now resides in Phoenix, Arizona, where he works as an exercise boy at Turf Paradise Racetrack.

Anthony William Gray was born on March 11, 1921, in Winamac, Indiana. He enlisted in the Navy after Pearl Harbor. Tony served aboard the *USS Celeno*

and the *USS Hamul*, hauling cargo to various islands in the South Pacific. On the *Celeno*, Tony survived the June 16, 1943, Japanese air raid at Guadalcanal. Tony went to Purdue University on the GI Bill and earned a Bachelor of Science in General Agriculture. He currently lives in Galesburg, Illinois, with his wife Sonia. One of his daughters, Mary Davidson, lives in Phoenix, Arizona; she inspired me to write her father's story.

James Kenneth Hickok was born on June 5, 1928, in Cranford, New Jersey. He enlisted in the United States Navy in 1950 and served in the Korean War. Jim was located primarily in Korea, where his ship,

Tank and Jeep in Vietnam (Courtesy of Pablo Lopez)

the *USS Eversole,* kept the shipping lanes open, protected Korea from submarines, and looked out for carriers as they launched and recovered aircraft. Jim achieved the rank of Lieutenant and was awarded the Korean Service with Battle Stars and China Service medals. He now resides in Scottsdale, Arizona.

Emery Vernon Hildebrandt was born on April 21, 1921, in Ramona, South Dakota. In 1942 Emery enlisted in the United States Navy and served in World War II. He was located in the North Atlantic and South Pacific and achieved the rank of Second Class Signalman. After he was injured in 1946, Emery was awarded a Purple Heart, as well as a Gold Star, Good Conduct Medal, and an Atlantic-Pacific ribbon with thirteen Bronze Stars. He now resides in Corvallis, Oregon. His grandson Kevin, a sophomore at Cactus Shadows and project member, wrote his story.

Bruce Leon Hilsee was born in Glenside, Pennsylvania, on February 10, 1927. He enlisted in the Army's Airborne Division in February of 1944 but arrived in France as the armistice was declared. At Fort Bragg he tested parachutes for the Air Force and at one point made a jump from 41,000 feet from a hot air balloon. During his career he made a total of 324 jumps. After leaving the Army he worked for Honeywell and traveled the world. He has been to 134 countries and met many people. He now lives in Carefree, Arizona, with his wife Lea.

Homer J. Holland was born November 31, 1941, just seven days before the attack on Pearl Harbor. Homer achieved a scholarship to West Point Academy and was first in his class three of his four years. During his eight years of active duty during the Vietnam War, Homer served with the 82nd Airborne Division and the 101st Airborne. He adapted the skills learned in the Army to become a successful business man. He has set up a foundation to sponsor medical research on hydrocephalus to help cure his grandson. Homer resides at The Boulders in Scottsdale, Arizona.

Richard Lee Hoover was born January 5, 1921, in Salt Creek Township, Ohio. Dick enlisted in the service December 7, 1942, entering the Army Air Corps. After training and learning how to fly the P-16, he was shipped to Italy as part of the 416 Night Fighter Squadron. "One of Few," he became one of 31 Americans who flew the English Night Mosquito. After the war he established a successful cement business. Today Dick lives in Scottsdale, Arizona, with his wife Norma.

Kenneth C. Huff was born October 2, 1920, in Porter, Indiana. He realized a "deeply felt ambition" when commissioned an ensign in the Navy Reserve in early 1941. Ken served four years on active duty, 15 as a Reservist, leaving the Navy as a Commander. During World War II Ken loaded mines and torpedoes with explosives in Yorktown, Virginia, and was rumored "dead" by the *Chicago Tribune* when the plant exploded one night. As commander of the *USS LCS (L) 35,* he assisted in amphibious landings at Iwo Jima and Okinawa. He spent several months in Formosa (Taiwan) after the war detonating mines cleared by minesweepers. His wife Peg, featured in *Since You Asked, Volume II*, passed away in January 2006.

Gobel Dale James was born August 1, 1930, in Amarillo, Texas. He enlisted in the Air Force to fulfill his dream of flying fighter aircraft. After a tour in Germany, Gobel flew F-105s and F-4s as part of the Wild Weasels, seeking SAMs, when he was shot down during his 34th mission on July 15, 1968. Gobel was a prisoner in the Hanoi Hilton and other nearby prisons for 56 months until his release in March 1973. His broken knee kept him out of the air while he served at Luke, Kirtland, Reese, and Mather Air Force Bases until his retirement from the Air Force in 1984. He lives in Scottsdale, Arizona. Unfortunately his beloved wife Betty passed away in March of 2006.

Robert B. "B.J." Johnson was born November 6, 1928, in Portland, Oregon. "B.J." enlisted in the Marine Corps in May 1948 and served with the H & S 7th of the 1st Marine Division, eventually attaining the rank of Sergeant. B.J. found himself trapped at Chosin Reservoir during the Korean War, one of those lucky to survive the brutally cold retreat while pursued by the Chinese. B.J. is President of the local chapter of the Chosin Few. Letters written to Arlee, now his wife, help him remember those difficult times. *The Arizona Republic* featured B.J.'s letters to Arlee in a Memorial Day story. The couple lives in Mesa, Arizona, surrounded by a large collection of Chosin pictures B.J. uses to tell his story to community groups.

Robert Myron Johnson was born January 31, 1920, in Wakefield, Nebraska. During World War II he was responsible for the transportation of prisoners captured by the Allies, including Ilse Koch, the infamous "Bitch of Buchenwald," whose husband Karl was the first commandant at Buchenwald concentration camp and later Majdanek. Bob was also a member of the Army Band, playing the French horn. He currently lives in Mesa, Arizona, but will soon be retiring to the Villages, Florida, with his wife Ann. He served in the band with David Rickard, also featured in this book.

George Washington Kelloff, born on George Washington's birthday February 22 (but in 1921), in Segundo, Colorado, was a member of the Navy during World War II. He sailed on the *USS Mindanao* as a

yeoman, eventually ascending to the position of chief yeoman, in charge of the paperwork and filling replacement positions aboard the ship at the end of the war. He established Movie Manor Motel, a motel that surrounds a drive-in movie, in Monte Vista, Colorado. He divides his time between Colorado and Fountain Hills, Arizona, where he lives with his wife Edna Mae. He is active in VFW Post 7507's Veterans in the Classroom program, telling his World War II stories to high school students.

Louis Kraft was born April 17, 1913, in Boston, Massachusetts. He remembers his uncle "Al" returning from World War I wearing puttees and having to sleep in his bed. Al told Louis if he was ever in the military to "keep his head down" and "never volunteer." Louis was 25 years old when World War II broke out. He used the skills learned at his father's millinery business to manage the arrival of supplies for the American military at the 5th Port of Embarkation in England, and after D+6, in Rouen, France. He lived at the Classic Residence in Scottsdale, Arizona, with his wife

A Japanese ship that ran aground (Courtesy of Oscar Schwartz)

Edythe until he passed away on December 15, 2006. A Celebration of Life remembered Louis for his love of children, sparkling wit, and perennial tan!

Allan Kramer was born January 19, 1920, in New York City, New York. He enlisted in the United States Navy in July 1940 before the draft was instated. He served in World War II, primarily the Mediterranean, the North Atlantic, and the Caribbean. Allan achieved the rank of Lieutenant Commander and was awarded the European Theater Ribbon and was discharged in February of 1946. He now resides at Classic Residence in Scottsdale, Arizona, with his wife Claire.

Leonard S. Lai was born in Honolulu, Hawaii, on September 9, 1936. On December 7, 1941, five-year-old Len and his parents were leaving Honolulu as the first wave of Japanese bombers struck Pearl Harbor. Returning to their beach house at Lanikai, the family encountered the second wave of Japanese attacking Kaneohe Naval Air Station and Bellows Army Air Base. Len went on to serve the United States as an

Divers defuse a submerged mine (Courtesy of Steve Marshall)

Army officer in Korea, Taiwan, Germany, and the United States. He retired a colonel in 1989 and currently lives with his wife "Di" in Cave Creek, Arizona, where he is the Veterans History Project coordinator at Desert Foothills Library.

Thomas Matthew Leard was born December 6, 1944, in Dyersburg, Tennessee. Tom volunteered in

the United States Air Force in December of 1967 and served in the Vietnam War as part of the 56th Air Special Operations Wing, coordinating air rescues and bomber missions. He was located in Vietnam, Thailand, Cambodia, and Laos. He achieved the rank of Captain and was discharged in June of 1974. He now resides in Carefree, Arizona, with his wife Barbara.

Robert William Littlefield was born May 11, 1943, in Southampton, New York. Bob enlisted in the U.S. Army and served with the 176th Assault Helicopter Company in Chu Lai, Vietnam, ending his service as a Sergeant E-5. Bob volunteered to accompany helicopters delivering troops to the field, serving as crew chief and door gunner. On a couple occasions, while transporting reluctant ARVN troops, he had to get them off the chopper by hitting them on their "steel pots" with a machine gun rod. Bob is currently a Scottsdale, Arizona, councilman and is married to his lovely wife Kathy.

Pablo Lopez was born June 29, 1947, in Casa Blanca, Arizona. He enlisted in the Army in September of 1966 because he had no motivation to attend school. He was in the 125th Signal Battalion and the 25th Infantry in the Vietnam War. He fixed equipment and radios throughout the war and became a police officer when he left the Army. He now lives in Mesa, Arizona, with his wife Esther.

Glen Lytle was born in Narka, Kansas, on November 1, 1917. While serving in the 12th Artillery Corps during World War II, Glen survived the Battle of the Bulge and helped relocate displaced persons in Europe in the aftermath of the conflict. Glen rose to the rank of Staff Sergeant, in part due to his contribution to a radio amplification technology that proved to be twice as effective as the previous iteration. Glen was awarded a Bronze Star for this innovation. Glen passed away on September 2, 2006, of natural causes. He will be missed by a family who loved him very much.

Steve Marshall was born in Lawton, Oklahoma, on January 11, 1961. Enlisting in 1981, Steve became a Navy SEAL specializing in EOD, Explosive Ordnance Disposal. He patrolled the Severn River in Annapolis, Maryland, during the 1984 Summer

Olympics; accompanied President George H.W. Bush to Grenada; and detonated Iraqi sea mines during Desert Storm. After 9-11 Steve maintained a database of Pentagon casualties. He currently works with terrorism readiness programs for the state of Arizona. His son Ryan is a senior at Cactus Shadows High School.

Michael Marzano was born in Greenville, Pennsylvania, on May 18, 1976. Michael wished to follow in his Marine Corps father Al's footsteps by becoming a Sergeant in the Marine Corps; Al served in Vietnam. "Sergeant Sport" was tragically killed in Hadithah, Iraq, on May 7, 2005, while attempting to rescue Iraqi hostages at Hadithah's hospital. He is survived by his proud mother, Margy Bons; his father, Al Marzano; his brother Nic Haun; his niece Mariah and nephew Nicky; and of course his fellow Marines from 3rd Battalion, 25th Regiment, 4th Marine Division.

Ennis B. Miller was born June 30, 1926, in Oxford (Butler), Ohio. Ennis served in three wars: World War II, Korea, and Vietnam. Ennis received the Bronze Star for Heroism when he saved the lives of men on two tugboats by cutting the towline attaching them to ammunition barges being shelled by the Vietcong. Discrimination against African American troops kept Ennis from being promoted more quickly, but he achieved the rank of Master Sergeant E-7 by the time he left the Army in 1969. Ennis currently lives in Surprise, Arizona, with his wife Leverne.

Robert E. Parsons was born April 18, 1916, in Lynn, Massachusetts. As a transportation expert, Bob served in World War II, Korea, and Vietnam. His proudest moment was receiving a Bronze Star for Heroism with a V device in Dong Ha, Vietnam. Under heavy attack from the Viet Cong, Bob moved vehicles out of harm's way despite flying shrapnel from the ammo dump, which had also been hit. Bob has survived his Japanese wife, with whom he has four sons, and a second wife whom he met in Kassel, Germany. Bob was interviewed in Surprise, Arizona, but has since moved to Monterrey, California, to be near his son.

Robert Wilson Patterson was born January 27, 1928, in San Francisco, California. A career veteran, "Pat" fought in two of our nation's greatest wars serving as a combat engineer in Korea and Vietnam. Bob's

service spans from June 1945 to August 1975. Throughout his thirty years as an engineer, Bob built bridges, roads, and towns. Not only did he earn a great number of medals, but also the rank of colonel. He currently lives in Phoenix, Arizona, with his devoted wife Lou, a former Army nurse. Bob is retired but still plays tennis.

Albert Pempek was born in Chicago, Illinois, on September 21, 1916. In 1940, at the age of 22, he enlisted in the United States Army Air Corps and served in World War II, flying B-24 missions from England to Germany. Albert J. Pempek was killed in combat on November 6, 1944, when his B-24 *OUR HONEY* was shot down by German anti-aircraft fire. Albert was posthumously awarded the Distinguished Flying Cross and a Purple Heart. His proud nephew Jayme Deuger, a math teacher at Cactus Shadows High School, shared his story.

Victor Frederic Phillips, Jr. was born in Washington, D.C. on December 5, 1927. Vic flew RB-26 reconnaissance bombers for the Air Force during the Korean War to photograph military installations in North Korea and later pursued his dream of teaching at the Air Force Academy. As a young boy, Vic met General George Marshall and Secretary of War Henry Stimson while exercising General Marshall's horse Buddy. Vic now lives with his wife Ann in Scottsdale, Arizona.

David M. Rickard was born March 23, 1992, in Brooklyn, New York. In basic training the Army asked for musicians. Playing in the band probably "saved David's life" as he did not join the regular infantry during the invasion of Europe. With the 76th Infantry Division, David kept advance headquarters on the move during the brutally cold winter of the Bulge. In February 1945 David's division secured crossing of the Sauer River, crossed the Rhine in March, and ceased combat in May in Glauchen, Germany. The 76th Infantry Division band played for the Russians when the two forces met in Limbach. David lives with his wife "Till" at Classic Residence in Scottsdale, Arizona.

Jack Ricketts was born on September 30, 1919, in Farmington, New Mexico. Jack was finishing his college career in 1940 when thoughts of war were in the air. He was drafted into the Army, but was given a reprieve to finish his studies in engineering. Jack flew PBYs with VP-51 and VPB-101 during the Battles of Midway, Tulagi, and Guadalcanal. His military career spanned thirty-one years. Jack currently lives quietly at Classic Residence in Scottsdale, Arizona, with his dear wife Hazel.

Bill Rintelmann was born June 22, 1930, in Chicago, Illinois. Though enlisting in 1952 during the Korean War, the Army decided Bill's teaching skills made him more valuable training soldiers to handle grenades and fire howitzers at Fort Sill, Oklahoma, and Fort Carsons, Colorado. On leaving the service in 1955, Bill began a career teaching audiology at the University of North Dakota, Northwestern, Michigan State, and the University of Pennsylvania, retiring from Wayne State University as department chair in 1995. Bill lives in Cave Creek, Arizona, with his wife Sandy and two rambunctious poodles and lives down the street from former project member Jeff Tully.

Herman R. Rosen was born August 22, 1921, in Hartford, Connecticut. With a Harvard degree in accounting, the Army sent Herman to its Finance Department, where three months after the invasion, he paid troops out of field safes using Allied military currency, not dollars. Herman spent most of the occupation in Switzerland settling accounts for the Swiss rescue of downed American pilots and other expenses. He had enough points to go home but agreed to stay on if his fiancée Vivian could join him. He met her in Le Havre, France, they were married, and 40 years later they continue to be happily together at Classic Residence in Scottsdale, Arizona.

Armand "Pete" Rovero was born October 5, 1926, in Oakville, Connecticut. He enlisted in the Navy's Construction Battalion, better known as the CBs or Sea Bees. During the war in the Pacific he was stationed in Okinawa. In his truck he delivered supplies to the Marines in the south and the Army in the north. He delivered fuel, food, bombs, ammunition, and anything else the men at the front needed. Every day he worked an 18-hour shift delivering supplies. He now lives Torrance, California, with his wife Irene. Patrick Ward, Pete's proud grandson and CSHS freshman and project member, wrote his grandpa's story.

Charles H. Schluter was born October 9, 1946, in New York. He always knew he would enter the military since he grew up hearing stories about World War II's wooden Navy sailboats and steel aircraft carriers and battleships. Chuck enlisted in the Navy and served on three cruises to Vietnam from 1965–1969. Colonel Schluter also worked for the military recruiting office and helped organize the 242. He currently lives in Cave Creek, Arizona, with his wife Marie and is an active member of MOAA.

Oscar Schwartz was born February 8, 1921, in Rochester, New York. He served in the Air Force repairing aircraft during World War II in the South Pacific and later on was a member of the Air Force Reserve around the time of the Korean War. Oscar traveled to the Philippines and Fiji and just about everywhere in between. In the Air Force, Oscar had always dreamed of becoming a Master Sergeant; his dream came true. He even worked for Hughes Aircraft Company for 35 years after he came back from the Air Force. Oscar now lives with his wife Naomi in Sun City, Arizona.

Hugh William Shoults was born in Eugene, Oregon, on October 29, 1925. In March of 1944 Hugh joined the Army Air Force and served in World War II, the Cold War, and Vietnam in the 80th Fighter Squadron and 8th Fighter Group, attaining the rank of Major. His 28-year career spans WWII T-6 training planes to Minute Man missiles. He served in the U.S., Japan, and Vietnam and finally retired to Carefree, Arizona, in June of 1972 with his wife Betty.

James Ronald Siket was born on April 21, 1945, in Cleveland, Ohio. He attended West Point. After graduating he specialized in field artillery and served in Okinawa, Korea, Vietnam, and Germany, and several locations across the United States. Jim retired with the rank of Colonel. He is proud of his 27 years of service to his country and his family of eight. He currently resides in Paradise Valley, Arizona, and works for Wells Fargo Bank.

Carroll Vanik was born December 22, 1945, in Baltimore, Maryland. He attended the University of Maryland before enlisting in the Army to train at Fort Dix, Fort Polk, Fort Wolters, and Hunter Army Air

Field in Savannah, Georgia. Carroll flew aviation support missions and resupply missions on helicopters in Vietnam as part of the 35th Combat Engineer Group, bringing the troops "anything they needed." He lives in Carefree, Arizona, with his wife Susan, an active member of the Kiwanis Club of Carefree.

James Vivian was born September 20, 1918, in Humboldt, Arizona. "Impressed by an outstanding neighbor on leave as a midshipman, wearing a white Annapolis uniform with gold buttons," Jim sought an appointment to the U.S. Naval Academy but ended up at West Point! Highlights of his 30-year career include Chief of Interrogations, USFET, Germany, in World War II; 62nd Engineer Construction Battalion Commander in Korea; and Deputy Commander, 20th Engineer Brigade in Vietnam. After serving with NATO's U.S. Military Delegation as an engineer, Jim began a civilian career in government. He lives now in Scottsdale, Arizona, with Phyllis, whom he married after his beloved wife Mary passed away.

Fred H. Westlund was born on October 23, 1922, in Chicago, Illinois. Fred enrolled in the Navy, but was told it was full so he joined the Army. Fred did his training at Fort Bliss, Texas, before being sent to Algiers, North Africa. He later landed in France and fought his way to Paris though the Battle of the Bulge and was in Marseilles ready to deploy to Japan when the war ended. Fred currently lives in Scottsdale, Arizona, with his wife Doris and enjoys skiing.

John Dale Wintersteen was born June 18, 1945, in Pittsburgh, Pennsylvania. Hopeful of going to West Point, he reconsidered and enlisted in the United States Marine Corps. During his tour in Vietnam, he found himself all over Northern I-Corps building support fire platforms and performing all the tasks of an engineer. His unusual platoon consisted of half Army and half Marines. The supply depot where he was stationed was under daily barrages of Vietnamese rockets. Many years later he is still serving the country he fought for as Chief of Police in Paradise Valley, Arizona.

Paul Wise was born in Pratt, Kansas, on July 16, 1920. From February 1942 to August 1945, he flew with a VP-211 patrol squadron in the Navy, seeking out German submarines from North Carolina off the coast of the United States to Brazil and Panama in the South Atlantic. He presently lives in Scottsdale, Arizona, with his wife Frances.

Maralin replaced the Norton Air Force Base Commander Reggie Shaleski (center). To her left is Norton's Wing Commander Duane H. Cassidy.(Courtesy of Maralin Coffinger)

Civilian Contributors

Margy Bons is the proud mother of Marine Sergeant Michael Marzano, who was killed in Hadithah, Iraq, on May 7, 2005, while serving in Operation Iraqi Freedom. Margy decided to tell Michael's story when she saw *Since You Asked: Arizona Veterans Share Their Memories* on Veterans Day 2006 in Cave Creek. Margy owns a shop in Carefree called My Unique Boutique. She is very active in Packages from Home and Military Moms, which sends items to troops overseas.

Gene French is the proud wife of neurosurgeon Lyle French, who served with the 26th General Hospital in North Africa and Italy during World War II. Lyle operated on Senator Bob Dole, saving his life. Gene continued to work as a nurse during the war while raising their son Fred. They had two more children after the war. Gene and Lyle celebrated their 63rd wedding anniversary before Lyle passed away in October 2004. Gene lives at Classic Residence in Scottsdale, Arizona.

Virginia Rewick graduated from Cornell University in 1931 with a Bachelor's Degree in Hotel Administration. She worked for Cincinnati Bell Telephone Company until 1942, when she accepted a position with the War Department's Ordnance Office in Chicago. Jinny conducted training classes at various Army

Jinny and "Pipe Guy" (Courtesy of Virginia Rewick)

ordnance plants in the United States so workers "wouldn't blow themselves up with black powder." Her most memorable job during World War II was Field Director with the Red Cross Service Clubs in Scotland. Jinny currently lives at Classic Residence in Scottsdale, Arizona, with her husband David and has never lost her sense of humor.

In Memoriam

Part of recording the stories of veterans is realizing we will lose them, particularly those who served in World War II. None are younger than 80. And so we say goodbye to the dear friends we have loved and lost, realizing, to paraphrase the expression, that we have been blessed with the opportunity to let others know the sacrifices they made for us.

Michael Owen 10/15/04	Paul Trotman 1/21/06
Ted Smith 5/15/05	Carey Wilcox 2/20/06
Ken Knight 9/26/05	Glen Lytle 9/2/06
John Falconer 1/2/06	Ed Splain 10/15/06
Peg Huff 1/7/06	Louis Kraft 12/15/06

And to those who died before we had the chance to
know them, thank you. We are proud to preserve
your stories in all three of our books,
Since You Asked.

Bob Anderson 12/7/41	Pedro Gonzalez 4/6/01
Don Wollard 3/8/44	Bob Wilcox 10/13/03
Albert Pempek 11/6/44	Lyle French 10/19/04
Bill Metcalfe 9/12/82	Charles Bradford Smith 5/23/04
George Nakis 5/25/98	Michael Adam Marzano 5/7/05

Since You Asked, Again

The following stories are from "friends of AHP" who have continued their service or have continued their stories... *Since You Asked, Again.*

Like Father, Like Daughter

By Jessica Beazley
Daughter of Cold War veteran Skot Beazley and Jackie Beazley at CCUSD
Currently at the U.S. Coast Guard Academy
Past Cactus Shadows graduate

I grew up around the military. My father was in the Navy, which moved us around until I was six years old. While growing up, my father would tell me stories about his time spent in the service. Meanwhile, my mother was a teacher and a strong supporter of education. When it came time to make some decisions about my future, I chose to attend a military academy because it would satisfy the educational drive I had and yet be a terrific venue to launch my military career. After researching all four service academies, I came to the conclusion that I really like the missions of the Coast Guard and decided to apply for the academy.

I reported to New London, Connecticut, on June 27, 2005, to begin my academy adventure. That was the beginning of Swab Summer, the academy's boot camp. It was eight weeks long, one week spent aboard the tall ship *Eagle*. The beginning of the fall academic semester marked the end of Swab Summer. The school year was a mixture of rigorous academics coupled with military trainings. Freshmen are required to carry out many different tasks throughout the year that build discipline and character.

The military trainings culminated in the sophomore summer experience. I was stationed aboard the Coast Guard Cutter *Rush*, home ported in Honolulu, Hawaii. We then went on a twelve-week patrol of Japan, China, Korea, and Alaska. I was trained in watch standing aboard the ship as well as becoming qualified to run the engine room.

This was only two of the four summer trainings that I will go through before I graduate. This coming summer I will be in charge of Swab Summer for the incoming freshmen. The summer after that will be spent attending internships all over the country. Finally, once I graduate, I will be an ensign in the Coast Guard, ready to serve my country to the best of my ability.

This whole experience has been a dream come true, and no matter how hard it has become at times, I have never for a single second regretted my decision to attend the academy.

Postscript to My Story

By George Burk
Vietnam veteran, Plane crash survivor
January 13, 2007

I was medically retired from the USAF, 1 October 1971, and left the burn unit, Brooke Army Medical Center, San Antonio, Texas, in mid-September that same year. That was the last time I saw my primary care physician, Dr. Wellford Inge.

Over the succeeding 30-plus years, I stayed in touch with Dr. Inge through Christmas packages—baklava—I'd send to him at his medical practice. Every Christmas holiday season, I called him at his office, but I wasn't able to visit with him. The receptionist would tell me Dr. Inge was with a patient or at the hospital making rounds or in surgery.

Although I hadn't seen him or talked to him in person, I never stopped thinking about him and all the many actions he took, both medical and non-medical, which helped save my life. There was no doubt then and no doubt today that had I had any other doctor of the twelve on staff, I wouldn't have survived. Even with Dr. Inge's passion, caring, professionalism, and "bedside manner," I wasn't expected to live beyond Day 14 of my plane crash. He told my family that I had at best a 10% chance of surviving, and that he'd make me as comfortable as possible.

Over the ensuing years, I had always dreamed that one day I'd get to see him again, only this time it would be outside of the hospital. I wanted him to see me as I am now, not as I was then.

On 1 November 2006, that dream and hope became a reality. Beginning in June 2006, Dr. Inge and I emailed and talked on the phone. Even now, when I talk to him, I find my throat begins to tighten and I fill with great emotion. It's difficult for me to talk because my eyes water and my voice begins to flutter. I really admire, respect, and love this man!

It was during one of our emails that we decided I'd fly to Philadelphia, Pennsylvania, and he would meet me at the airport. I would spend a few days with him and his wife Betty at their home in Dover, Delaware.

On 1 November 2006, I flew to Philadelphia and was met curbside by the doctor who saved my life. It had been 35 years since I last saw him. He looked a bit older—he's 70 years young now and retired—but I would have been able to pick him out in a crowd.

We shook hands and then hugged in a long embrace. I was telling myself, "Don't start crying, you big jerk." I was nervous but ecstatic at my good fortune. I was still alive and able to see him and thank him again.

We drove to their home in Dover, about an hour and a half south of Philadelphia. I met his wife Betty, we had dinner that evening, and I spent three wonderful and fulfilling days with them.

Shortly after our arrival, I told Dr. Inge that I had a message from my daughter Kimberly. Kimberly was four years old when I was burned and severely injured. She still recalls the few times her mother brought her and our two sons Walter and Scott, ages six and two respectively, to the hospital to visit me. This was not the usual practice. Dr. Inge believed that seeing my children would emotionally help me find a "why" to live. I don't recall them coming to the hospital or most anything else during the 89 days I was in the Intensive Care Unit.

Kimberly and Savannah, my six-year-old granddaughter, visited us here in Scottsdale for a week and left a few days before my scheduled departure to Philadelphia on 12 November to see Dr. Inge. Kimberly and Savannah live near Dallas, Texas, with Kim's husband. After they landed, Kim called me on her cell phone on her way home. Near the end of the conversation, I heard her voice begin to waver and crack; I could tell she was near tears. I thought something had happened to Savannah on the flight, or some other personal issue had arisen.

With her voice cracking and trembling, Kim said to me, "Dad, when you see Dr. Inge, would you please tell him for me, 'Thank you for you?'"

Her request caught me off guard. I was touched!

There we were—Dr. Inge, his wife Betty, and me standing in their kitchen about an hour after my arrival.

"Doc," I said. "I have a message from my daughter Kimberly. She asked me to give it to you." I prefaced sharing her message with him by telling him and his wife when, how, and under what circumstances Kim asked me to deliver her message.

"As you may remember, Kim was only four when I was injured. She asked me to tell you, 'Daddy, when you see Doctor Inge, please tell him, "Thank you for you."'"

With that, Dr. Inge placed both his hands in his pockets, looked at the floor, his face turned red, and he said, "Thank you for that. I'm very humbled."

I gave Dr. Inge copies of my second and third books. In my third book, *My Mother My Friend: The Story of a Boy and the Love of His Mother*, I wrote the following:

"To Dr. Wellford W. Inge, the doctor who saved my life. The best damn doctor in the universe! I love you. Thanks! George Burk, Dover, DE, 3 November, 2006."

On the day of my return home, we were sitting in their TV room. I told him that I've tried to live my life in a way that honored John Davieau, the man who found me on fire, my family who didn't let me quit, and him and the nurses and support staff.

In his usual understated way, he asked me, "Do you remember the time when we were making our rounds in the ICU, trying to determine who we thought was going to live and who wasn't?"

"No. I don't recall that," I said.

"We came to your bed and someone mentioned that you weren't going to make it. You would probably die. You opened your eyes and said, 'Like hell! I'm not going to die. I want to live.'"

"No, I don't remember saying that," I said.

"You caught all of us by surprise," he said.

During my 89 days in the ICU and for several weeks thereafter, when prevailing medical wisdom at the time suggested to him that he make me as comfortable as possible, on ten separate occasions my demise was only a matter of hours or days away. He never gave up. He never quit trying to save my life.

I left three days later. Dr. Inge and his wife drove me back to the Philadelphia airport. I got out of the car, leaned in the back seat and kissed his wife on the cheek good-bye, and carried my bag to the curb. Dr. Inge followed me to the curb; we shook hands and embraced.

"I love ya, Doc," I said. "Thanks for saving my life."

"George," he said nervously, "I don't remember you being this big."

"You should've seen me before I was burned," I replied.

"I love you, too. Thanks for coming to see us," he said.

He leaned back, placed his hands on my shoulders, grabbed me tightly, smiled, then turned around and hurriedly returned to his car. I noticed tears in his eyes. There were tears in my eyes, too.

I'm unable to find the right words to describe my feelings for this man. In my mind, he *is* the best damn doctor in the universe! Each time I think of him, my throat still tightens and tears well up in my eyes.

I hope we can meet again this year, 2007.

George and Dr. Wellford Inge

The Best Reunion Ever

By Rocco "Doc" DeRosa

This is my story of my time in Vietnam, many years of thinking about my time in Vietnam, and reuniting with my buddies from Vietnam.

I served in Vietnam from April 1966 to April 1967 with the 25th Infantry Division, the 2nd of the 35th B Company, 1st Platoon. My job or MOS as it was called was a combat medic. My platoon, like many other platoons, went out on search and destroy missions to find the enemy. The enemy to us was mostly North Vietnamese soldiers with a few Vietcong thrown in. Our base camp was in Pleiku, Vietnam, in the Central Highlands about 200 miles north of Saigon. That year was spent with many of the same guys and many who left for several reasons: wounded, killed, malaria, and some who just rotated back to "the world," as we called the USA. The friendships formed during that time were the best. Race or color didn't make any difference. When you needed a drink of water, it didn't matter whose canteen it came from. All you knew was it tasted good and it was from a friend. You always knew that friend would watch your back, and he knew you would watch his. When my time came to rotate back to the world, I said my goodbyes and left. Never in my wildest dreams did I ever think I would see any of these guys again. I thought about them, but that was pretty much it.

Then one day in 2002, while surfing the Internet, I typed in 25th Infantry Division and started to look at the results. To my surprise I saw a website for the 2nd of the 35th Infantry. I immediately started to check it out and found a section with a guestbook where people could write anything they wanted about the unit.

I ran across the name of Philippe Saunier. I almost fell out of my chair. Saunier was the first guy I met when I came to the 1st Platoon, B Company. He knew I was as green as could be, and he said to stay behind him while humping hills and if you get separated, don't panic. Luckily his phone number was on the webpage so that night I called him and the rest is history. He was as excited as I was. We talked for a long time. Saunier then contacted John Lorts, who was also in our platoon, and he called me and again we talked for a long time. I was told by Lorts that we have a reunion every year in July in a different state so we can get together. Let me tell you I was in after those two conversations.

Rocco (standing) at his reunion

That year, July 2002, the reunion was in Seattle, Washington. I flew into Seattle and while checking into the hotel, I noticed a lot of guys my age laughing and joking and telling stories about Vietnam. I looked around and there was Saunier, Lorts, and Stelzer looking at me with as big a smile on their faces as I had on mine. We hugged (it's a guy thing), shook hands, and started talking like we had never been apart when it was actually 35 years since we had seen each other. Later that day Holly Blankenship came in with his wife Wilda. He was also in our platoon. We spent the weekend laughing, joking, and telling war stories. It was the best weekend! We promised that next year in Buffalo, New York, we would all come and bring our wives.

In July 2003 we all showed up in Buffalo, New York, along with our wives. Sergeant Whitmier and Sergeant Norkett also came to their first reunion along with their wives. To this day I still call them both "Sergeant" instead of by their first name, out of respect. My feeling is they watched over us young guys in Vietnam and made sure we didn't do anything too stupid. They earned my respect so the "Sergeant" tag will stick with them.

We have had a reunion every year in July: Orlando, Florida, 2004; Louisville, Kentucky, 2005; Scottsdale, Arizona, 2006; and in 2007 we will be in Philadelphia, Pennsylvania. Our wives have gotten to be as good of friends as we have and also look forward to the reunions. We have formed another family.

Last year's reunion in Scottsdale, Arizona, we had 400 people at our Saturday night dinner. Every year it gets bigger and bigger. The Saturday night dinner is the big thing every year. Various awards are given out, speeches are given, and a good time is had by all. John Lorts has put together a slide presentation of all the guys who were killed in our unit—twelve pictures to a screen. When you look at these pictures, it's hard to believe we were all that young. Needless to say, you can hear a pin drop while this is going on. It's still very hard on some of the guys.

On Friday night we always have a group "doing," where any and all can participate. Last year, since the reunion was in Scottsdale, only 22 miles from my house, my wife Sandy and I had a dinner party for all the guys in my platoon and their wives. We had about 30 people. It's hard to believe after 40 years we are together again and having the time of our lives.

We all look forward to next year's reunion. During the year we call each other as well as email to see how everybody is doing.

Significant Activities
Based on correspondence with CSHS graduate Chris Stull
Son of Randy Stull, Gulf War veteran volume 1
By Barbara Hatch

Chris is a member of the 1-7 Cavalry unit stationed in Iraq, proud to let me know this is the same unit that boasted General George Armstrong Custer, a name he remembered from my American History class, and the unit celebrated in the Vietnam film *We Were Soldiers*. He is stationed at Camp Taji, Iraq, part of the military mission in Iraq called Operation Iraqi Freedom. He is "proud to be in this unit."

As part of Military Intelligence, Chris tracks insurgent activity. His duties are to prepare a Power Point presentation each day for his Captain of "Significant Activities" in his AO, or area of operations—IED attacks, Sniper Fire, Cordon and Searches—"so he can brief the LTC in the morning." His unit also has trackers of Indirect Fire (Mortars) going into a town called Saba Al Bor—an IED tracker of all the routes in his AO. These updates allow him to give the troop commanders a good idea what to expect when they do their patrols.

He also doubles as an RTO, radio operator, when everyone else is busy.

On January 26, I received news from Chris that his unit had lost five soldiers, "one from an IED [Improvised Explosive Device] and four others from just one LBIED (Large Buried IED)." The four casualties were in the same vehicle. A day later, on January 27, he reported his unit was in "commo blackout," which means that "somebody in the BDE is KIA; in this case it's 3." I have no further news to report after this date.

In some small way I suppose I guessed Chris would enter the military. When we interviewed his dad in book 1, he got choked up recalling that all three sons were serving, or would serve, in the military. His older son just returned from Iraq. Back in American History, Chris brought in a camo net to present his group's presentation on the '90s. He was proud of his father and his mother, who also wore the uniform, and I sensed he would follow in their footsteps.

God speed.

Mud-splattered Chris in Tank 168

40th Reunion West Point Class of 1966

By Rance Farrell

It had been over 40 years since we had thrown our hats into the air at graduation, over 44 years since we had first met in that terrifying experience of Beast Barracks. That was only one of the many shared hardships we had endured together over the years: we had "mucked it out" together for the cadet years, suffered through Ranger and Airborne Schools, and all gone off, sooner or later, to Vietnam. Some had left the Army upon serving the obligatory four years after graduation; others had stayed on for a career. All were bound together by these shared experiences, by the words of "Duty, Honor, Country" on our class rings and in our hearts. Some of us had come together many times again during our careers, meeting on Fire Bases in Vietnam, or on operations in Panama, or assignments in Germany or Korea. Others we had only seen at occasional reunions, enjoying each other's accomplishments in the civilian or military worlds. We had all gained a lot over the years: acquiring families, position, experience, and some girth around the middle. We had lost some

Parade salute

things, too, over these years: a bit of hair, lots of illusions, and, most importantly, some friends. Our class lost more in Vietnam than any other West Point class, and they along with others lost in hostile action are not forgotten. Something none of us had lost was our love and respect for each other, and for the bonds which still tie us so strongly together. So as we met again at the Hotel Thayer in September 2006, it was very emotional for all.

Usually a reunion is tied together with a football game or some other large event. The game was away this weekend, which turned out to be a blessing in disguise. We were able to take over the Hotel Thayer, a grand old edifice on the Academy grounds. It was a place we all knew well, at least the ground floor, from our cadet days. You could walk down Thayer Road from the Barracks to the Hotel and meet your date or parents there. If you were lucky, the parents would take you to dinner in the Hotel dining room. But as a cadet, that was as far as your luck could go. You were not allowed to go to the rooms above the first floor, and when you marked your absentee card "Authorized Absence" before leaving your cadet room, you were stating on your honor you were not going upstairs to one of the rooms in the Thayer. So it was a bit of a guilty thrill to be able finally to spend the night. The biggest pleasures of this weekend took place in locations that would have been authorized even during our cadet days—in the many meeting rooms of the hotel. We came together in a constant swirl, gripping one friend delightedly, and in mid-embrace grabbing the next old friend passing by.

The planned events gave some outer focus to these random meetings. Normally we would not even have had the pleasure of a parade, since none was scheduled. By the way, parades may be a pleasure for the spectators, but no cadet can honestly say he enjoyed marching in one. "P-rades" were a lot of trouble in preparing *for* them, involved uncomfortable rigidity *during* them, and if your "Tar Bucket"—the full dress hat still worn as a tribute to the War of 1812—blew off, it meant 14 hours marching punishment tours on the Area *after* them. But this time, the Superintendent (the "Supe") called a parade in honor of our classmate Mike Wynne, the Secretary of the Air Force. So there the class stood and watched with pride, nostalgia, and a bit of *schadenfreude* as the cadets paraded during an unexpected gap in an otherwise rainy afternoon. Besides the Secretary, our class boasts of one four-star general—Wes Clark—and numerous other three, two and one-stars. Mike had to stand on the reviewing stand, but the rest enjoyed just standing together below and connecting with the Long Gray Line. In fact, the Supe sent his Aide to ask Wes Clark if he'd like to join the reviewing party, and Wes simply replied, "No thanks. I'd rather stay here with my classmates." Right answer.

One of the things that allowed us to survive our cadet days, and in fact stood us in good stead throughout our careers, was a sense of humor and the playing of pranks. We relived some of these pranks, especially the military-type operation to steal the Navy's goat before the Army-Navy Game our "Firsty" (senior) year. The goat was stolen, and all hell was raised until it was returned just before the game. The main offenders were brought before the Commandant for a royal butt-chewing and some more hours on the Area. Then, just as they walked out of his office, the Com observed, "And unofficially, great job. I'd be proud to have you serve in my unit." Perhaps still flush from this memory, or perhaps never having grown up, several of my classmates proved that pranks were still in order during the Reunion. They were walking past the Barracks when they noticed a pair of bare feet sticking out of a second-floor window. Undeterred by the distance they had to traverse or their own dignity, they formed an impromptu human pyramid until the top man could just barely tickle the feet. When the astonished Cadet leaned out the window, he was given greetings from our Class. He was still shaking his head when they left.

The reunion lasted from Thursday through a boat ride up the Hudson on Sunday. It was filled with tours, briefings from the Academy staff, luncheons, cocktail receptions, and dinners, all of which provided wonderful opportunities to gather again with old friends. At one lunch Rick Atkinson, author of the book *The Long Grey Line* about our class, gave a marvelous talk comparing the Class of '66 to the "Greatest Generation," the subject of his new trilogy on WWII. His words were very thought provoking, forcing us to consider how we were but one small example of Americans who had been called upon during times of crisis and done our duty as best we could. At another dinner we sat together in our old cadet companies, for me E-1. At other meetings we were with branch friends. I was with my Artillery buddies. The wives, many of whom had known each other since they had dated their future husbands as

cadets, also had many wonderful opportunities to bond. One of the "rewards" of dating a cadet is getting a miniature West Point ring. Dating was not easy in those days since there were few opportunities for intimacy and lots of walking involved; in fact, a date was called a "Drag" since it seemed by the end of the weekend all you had been doing was dragging her around from one place to another. In any case, my wife Susan was with some of her old friends who were comparing those days and their miniature rings. They asked Susan why she didn't have one, and she replied that since she had not known me as a cadet, she didn't feel it was right to have one. They told her, "Girl, you've earned it after being married to him for 27 years. You're as much a part of this as we are." Susan now has her miniature.

From all these wonderful events, three stand out. The first took place on Friday in Eisenhower Hall. We were there to receive an excellent briefing from the Dean, to present our Class gift, and to conduct some class business like electing new officers and setting the course for Class activities in the next few years. All these events were great, but most of us dreaded the item on the agenda called "Class Sharing"—assuming it was some sort of fund drive. Instead Jack Le Cuyer, the reunion chairman, asked four classmates and their wives to share some life-changing experiences. The first three were Jim and Pat McCallum, Jim and Karen Jenkins, and Sam and Rusty Champi, who had been afflicted by a coma-producing head injury, bone cancer, and a cardiac aneurism requiring a quintuple bypass. They told of how they pulled together to survive these near-death events, and how important it was to be prepared in all ways—financially, physically, mentally, and spiritually—for such a crisis. They were full of praise for their classmates and other friends who rallied around to help them, and who played such an important part in their enduring these challenges. The fourth speaker, Mel Liss, did not talk about his own suffering, but that of others. He and his wife Judith shared with us how they became foster parents to over twenty abandoned kids over the years, opening their homes and hearts to these young people. Mel and Judith brought their two newest foster children to the Reunion, and we stood to applaud both children and parents. All four speakers were so modest about what they had done, and grateful for what they had received, that I find my writing now cannot do justice to the emotions we all felt then.

The other two memorable events both took place on Saturday morning, beginning at the Cadet Chapel for a service to honor our fallen classmates. This old gothic edifice sits high on the hill overlooking the Academy and is the perfect place for reflection and rededication. There were prayers and homilies, and then the Cadet Choir sang "The Corps." This wonderful mixed Choir was followed by "our" Choir, those classmates who had been in the Choir or Glee Club so long ago, joining together to sing "The Mansions of the Lord" and the "Alma Mater." Our Choir's soaring, strong male voices filled the Chapel and our hearts, and the echoes seemed to reverberate in both for a long time afterwards. After a quiet pause two classmates slowly, somberly, read the name of each of our fallen friends. Outside, the great bell of the chapel tolled once after each name. No one was ashamed of the tears that fell during this tribute.

Preserving this mood, next we went to the Cemetery to visit old friends. Mike Fry had passed away recently and his family had chosen to have him interred while we were all there. That simple service included a twenty-one gun salute and the ever-moving playing of Taps. Finally we all wandered the grave sites, stopping by special ones to recount stories of dear friends' lives and their passing. The funny stories were always the best, so that we could smile through our tears. A favorite grave was that of Art Bonifas, who had been killed so brutally in Korea in 1976. His widow Marcia was at the reunion, as well as others. The Reunion had made a special effort to reach out to all the class widows, and it was gratifying how many had come. They, too, felt the sense of brotherhood and belonging that unites us. This

West Point Cemetery

day was a wonderful, cleansing experience for us all.

There is something special about the time we spent together. Not just its length, a minimum of eight years. Not just the hardships we had endured together. There is something beyond all that that ties us together and brings us back to our "rock-bound highland home," to the "Long Grey Line." These are the best friends I have and ones I know I will always cherish. It was great to be together at this Reunion, but in some ways we are never truly apart.

After 35 Years

Saturday morning – August 9, 2003 – a very sunny and warm morning. Our lives changed this morning.
—Denny Hartpence's parents

David and Carol were down in our front year putting an electric fence underground for the yellow lab they purchased in May when a white car drove by and turned into their lane, turned around, and came up beside where they were working.

The man, a stranger, asked if this was the Hartpence home. David went over toward their car and told them it was. Then the stranger asked, "Could if be Dennis Hartpence's family?" David is not sure what he said, but with the help of Carol they finally said it was. The stranger told them he was with Denny in Vietnam and was with him when he was killed. David and Carol were instantaneously shocked as we had never heard from anyone that was actually with him at that time—and after 35 years!

They told David and Carol they needed to go to a motel and clean up and rest as they had been driving most of the night. David said, "No, as Dad and Mom are here and would want to see you now." Raymond was working at the shed and I was in the house. David told them to drive in up where Dad was. David came up to the house to get me but I didn't hear him at first. I did hear a door slam and went to see who it was. David was going out the walk and I asked him "if he wanted something." He said to come out as there was someone driving in that knew Denny.

Raymond was there at the shed working when they drove up near him. David got out there by then. Carol came across the yard as I got out there. They had introduced themselves to Raymond, etc. I think the first thing I said to him, "You knew Denny." We talked awhile all standing in the morning sun—the sweat was running off of him—Richard Martinez. It was just as hard for him as it was for all of us. I remember going over to him and giving him a big hug and he said he was so sweaty, but I told him I didn't care after all these years and finding someone that was with our beloved Denny—son and brother. I had often wondered whether we would be gone and never hear from anyone that was actually with him that day.

His wife "Lily" was standing over to the side away from us. I remember going over to her and asking something [I] don't remember now.

We asked them to come in and told them they could stay here but they insisted on going to a motel and would come back Sunday morning. They did come in and I got them something to drink, etc. and we talked some more. They told us they had been to Oregon to see his brother and also some other fellows that were with he and Dennis in Vietnam and were on their way home.

Richard was injured the same day Denny was killed and spent time in a hospital in Japan and 8 months in Walter Reed in Washington, D.C.

We asked how they found us after all these years. He never had Denny's home address and never knew how to find it until they visited a Traveling Wall in 2002 that came close to them. It just gave Edison, Ohio, when they got to Edison. They stopped at one place and they didn't know us. Went on a little ways further and he saw two more men out talking. So they stopped there and the one knew us. He told them how to get here and said, "You will know as it is a pretty place."

They left then and it was for the best as we got ourselves somewhat straightened out. They did come back Sun. morning and it was a lovely day so we had a picnic in the yard. David and Carol and children helped with all of this.

Richard had a lot of papers with him. David and Carol read the one how Denny was killed. Ray and I just glanced at some of them.

Later in p.m. we took them over to the cemetery as they had brought flowers to place on Denny's grave. Also took some pictures.

Toward eve[ning] Rick spent a lot of time going thru all the books, etc. that I had made up of all the letters and things that we received after Denny's death. They didn't get thru all of them. David came back over later and he had a lot of questions to ask Rick. I came out in the kitchen and let them talk.

They stayed with us that night and took off for home the next morn around 11:00 as they had been away from home more than 2 weeks.

We were rather exhausted and saddened, but still so glad they had found us and we were still living. It was very upsetting for David, too. That's all we could think about for a couple weeks and still it all lingers with us. We keep in contact with them.

To me, it is very upsetting to hear people say, "We shouldn't have been there." Maybe so, but our

David and Carol Hartpence

Government sent them. Over 3 million of our boys served there from 1961 thru 1975.

"We leave you our deaths. Give them their meaning. We were young. We have died. Remember us." (From "The Young Dead Soldiers" by Archibald MacLeish)

Note to Steve:

We just had the 2 boys Dennis and David. David was in the Air Force Reserve at Sheppard Air Force Base when Denny was killed.

We live in the country on a 160 acre farm that my Grandfather built in 1893. Denny loved the farm and oh how we have missed him all these years.

But our hearts go out to you and so many others that spent a whole year there.

We are indebted to Richard Martinez and wife for finding us and also for contacting others that have told what happened the 19th of April 1968 and to you for sending a picture or our beloved Denny. Not sure of the side view but it could be him.

David and family built a home here on the farm so they are close by. David works off the farm but with the help of my husband Raymond and a grandson they plant wheat, corn, and soybeans.

I understand you were a jockey for many years. That's a rough job, wasn't it?

Back to Vietnam

By Mike Metzger
September 18, 2006

In January 2006 my wife Connie and I took our eldest daughter and her husband on a trip to Asia. We began our journey in Hong Kong, then visited Thailand, Cambodia, and Vietnam. I had not been to Vietnam since my tour of duty there from March 1966 until November of the same year while serving in the Marines.

We flew into Da Nang, Vietnam, and connected with our guide. I had maps and photos of the hill where I was stationed and asked if he could find the hill. An interesting sidebar is that the hotel was filled with people like me—looking for a piece of their past. We saw numerous Americans huddled over maps with guides attempting to locate significant locations where they battled or were stationed.

Our guide took a great deal of pride in the fact that he almost always located the area his clients wanted to revisit.

My location was about sixty miles south of Da Nang. So much has changed that it was difficult to find my old points of reference. After numerous stops where our guide consulted with locals, showing them the photographs of the base and such, we located Hill 54, so called because it is 54 meters high.

As I walked up the now thickly vegetated hill with my family, I got somewhat emotional upon reaching the top. I'm not sure why. Perhaps because a part of my youth was there or because of the history of what the hill was in my life.

After that we traveled back to Da Nang and departed for Hanoi. Our guide in Hanoi had the Americanized name of "Vic." When questioned why, he said he was born shortly after the war ended and his father named him Victory (in Vietnamese). He shortened it to Vic.

I asked him about his father. It turns out he served for eight years as a Captain with the North Vietnamese army in South Vietnam. I asked him if his dad would have lunch with me. He said he would ask but doubted he would; his dad had not met any American Marines or other forces since the war.

He came back the next day and said his dad consented to meet me that afternoon at a local café. I was at the café when his father pulled up on his motorbike—almost everyone there drives a motorbike. He had his uniform on with no insignias. As we sat down, his dad was very stiff. I sensed he was ill at ease so I asked his son to kindly tell his dad I was honored to be with a patriot and fellow veteran. That melted the ice!

We quickly became involved reviewing maps and going over where each of us served, using his son as our translator. We never got within 50 miles of one another during my tour of duty. He had served for eight years without being able to go home to his village. He was wounded by a mortar fired from an American base and was allowed to return to his village to rehab. He told me he fought in Laos as well as South Vietnam. He was most reflective when he told of his starving for six months in the Highlands of South Vietnam after the Tet offensive. The

bombings of the trails and trains prevented supplies from reaching the South during that time. Thousands of North Vietnamese died of starvation in the South.

We spent almost two hours together. Upon leaving, he grabbed my arm and said he enjoyed the meeting and looked at me as a friend. This was a very special event in my life.

We left Hanoi the next day to return to the United States.

Some interesting facts about today's Vietnam:

a) When the war ended there were 32 million Vietnamese. There are now almost 85 million. Vietnam has more population than Germany.

b) Over half the population doesn't know war, having been born after the war's end.

c) Eight years ago there were no cell phones. Today there are over 13 million in use.

d) Corruption is rampant. For instance, most of the children educated in America are those of government employees.

e) Vietnam is still Communist but resembles China in that the economy is changing to a market economy.

f) Pollution is awful. They have an abundance of coal, the primary fuel for electricity. In some areas it was hard to see two blocks because of the smoke from power plants.

All throughout our trip we were treated great, especially in Vietnam. I will go back again some day as I found the people and the country fascinating.

Mike Metzger
Marine, Vietnam

Veterans in the Classroom

By Barbara Hatch

Cactus Shadows staff member and veteran Rocco DeRosa speaks to students.

Cactus Shadows staff member and veteran Rocco DeRosa speaks to students.

I never served in World War II (too young), Korea (still too young), Vietnam (I'm a woman), or either Gulf War (too old). I do teach American history, however, which necessitates a look at these pivotal events in our national story. While I can provide world context to our 20th century wars, I need the veterans to tell the stories from a ship, a foxhole, a B-24. I need them to remind students how grim war can be, humorous at times, of the camaraderie that develops between them and their fellow soldiers who have all shared a common "story." They need to tell of war's waste in lives and resources. They were there; I was not.

Besides my Fountain Hills veterans, whose formal Veterans in the Classroom program has brought students face-to-face with war for over ten years, new men and women veterans in the community graciously agree to share their memories with my classes. The students are richer for this opportunity. The veteran may have nightmares from the retelling. I have heard this comment more than once. But all stand tall as they leave Room 1112, knowing these young Americans have learned the true meaning of war and patriotism.

Jerry Anderson captivating his audience while talking about his uncle, Bob Anderson, who died on the USS Arizona.

George Burk speaking to Mrs. Hatch's US History class

Student Contributors

Asterisks indicate the number of years the student has participated in the project. The names in italics after each student's comments refer to the essays written for this book, singly or in collaboration.

Callie Adair**
Junior

I joined the Arizona Heritage Project in order to be able to learn about history from someone who lived it. Being able to personally interview veterans from WWII, Desert Storm, and Iraqi Freedom has been such an honor because I have not only learned what happened in those wars but also how those fighting the war lived and felt. With AHP I have been able to tell these guys' life stories to present and future generations.

Dick Hoover, Steve Marshall

Pablo Lopez and Cindy Garcia Barraza

Lindsey Anderson*
Junior

After interviewing Dewey Wambsganss on Veterans Appreciation Day in Mrs. Hatch's World History class, I knew I had to be part of the project. I became fascinated with the stories I heard and have recently interviewed Paul Wise and Chuck Schluter. I have learned so much about the military from plane names to Brazilian cities, but most importantly, that the military is about brotherhood.

Chuck Schluter, Paul Wise

Cindy Garcia Barraza*
Freshman

I joined AHP because my English teacher, Ms. Burke, told us about it in our class. It sounded interesting, and I liked the idea of going to Washington, D.C. So I joined, and I liked it. It's fascinating listening to the veterans' stories about their lives in war. It's like another world out there, worrying about what will happen next. I will continue doing this project for the rest of my high school years. It's a great experience.

Pablo Lopez

Anthony Beckham**
Junior

I initially joined the project during my sophomore year while in Mrs. Hatch's AP World History class. She offered extra credit for writing transcriptions of veteran interviews she conducted for Arizona Heritage Project. I took up the offer and was quickly drawn in by the story of Ed Ruhe, the veteran I was assigned to transcribe. I chose to write his essay and was thus informally initiated into the Project. I stayed past my first year because I feel much can be gained from hearing these stories, especially a person like me who is looking to join the service upon graduation.

Carroll Vanik

Bethany Bennick
Sophomore

The Arizona Heritage Project appealed to me from the very beginning, but sadly I knew I wouldn't be able to juggle that amongst everything else. I had heard the horror stories of the late nights and long interviews, and I was quick to shy away. I did not want to start any work I knew I couldn't finish. But finally I was pulled in, willingly, by Mrs. Hatch who invited me on the Bill Rintelmann interview. Had I any inclination of what I was about to experience, I would have come better prepared. Mr. Rintelmann (Bill) taught me a few life lessons I hope I will never have to endure personally. It was incredible, not only listening to honor in action, but to have the chance to memorialize it. It gave the opportunity for those with a voice and a belt laden with knowledge to finally share and immortalize their words for generations to come.

Bill Rintelmann

Maralin Coffinger and Emily Burke

Emily Burke*
Junior

I have been a member of Arizona Heritage Project since the summer after my sophomore year at Cactus Shadows. I joined AHP after having gained an interest in history and the project through Mrs. Hatch's AP World History class. I enjoy learning about history through the stories of people's lives, and especially enjoyed meeting and interviewing Brigadier General Maralin Coffinger.

Maralin Coffinger

Kasey Burton*
Junior

On February 14, 2005, Mrs. Hatch brought in several of the military veterans she knew to my AP World History class. I was nervous yet excited to talk to my group's veteran. It was a very new experience for me, but I loved it. We were assigned to write an essay about our veteran. It was probably the toughest essay I've ever written. However, in response to my essay George Kelloff wrote Mrs. Hatch a note pointing mine out and commending my work. I loved the feeling, and I knew I had to join AHP.

Bob M. Johnson, Bob Parsons, George Kelloff

J. Caitlin Campbell*
Sophomore

At first I joined the Arizona Heritage Project because I'd heard it was an interesting club and the meetings were convenient to go to. And now that I've been in it I realize what a great opportunity it is to learn from veterans. I get to hear all about their lives; it shows a very different side of war. It's much more personal, and more light-hearted. It gets me talking to some people I wouldn't normally talk to.

Hugh Shoults, Fred Westlund

Libby Day**
Junior

One of the most important skills I have gained from working on the project the past two years is the ability to communicate with people and get my point across. It comes in handy in just about every area of life. My most prominent reason for continuing on the project is the people I meet, the stories they tell me, and the relationships I've developed with some of the most amazing people I could ever hope to just sit and listen to. At 3:00 you walk into their house having never met them, and possibly never even spoken to them.

David and Jinny Rewick with Kelly Wilcox

At 5:00 you walk out knowing the name of their dog, their spouse, what their favorite drink is, where they grew up, where they like to eat lunch on Sunday afternoon. You've seen pictures of them at their worst and pictures of them at their best. You know them well enough to sit down and write a short synopsis of their life. For most this process would takes years, but being part of the Arizona Heritage Project makes it possible in a matter of hours.

Barney Barnett, Steve Goldsmith

Kirk DiGiacomo**
Junior

Working with AHP over the past two years has been fulfilling and enriching. This year I was fortunate enough to interview veterans from three of our nation's biggest wars: World War II, Korea, and Vietnam. These distinguished men told stories of battle wins and defeats which have a greater parallel to everyday life than most people know. Resilience and strength were essential to these veterans 65 years ago, just as they are today. AHP gives participants

interaction with the community they otherwise do not receive, making it a valuable use of resources.

B.J. Johnson, Allan Kramer, Tom Leard, Bob Patterson

Alex Doss*
Freshman

I, as a freshman, was naturally curious about the Arizona Heritage Project when I was "drafted" by the advisor and my AP World History teacher Barbara Hatch. My interest was immediately piqued, and I ended up establishing sort of a familial relationship with everyone. Mr. Ed Splain and his wife Nancy also, if not directly, secured a small place within the Project for me when Nancy complimented me for the poem I wrote when Ed passed away. I now have a profound background, for it was his unique story and Nancy's mentorship that got me more involved.

David Rickard, Jack Ricketts

Chelsea Ferguson*
Sophomore

Not only does this project open up many different opportunities for me such as meeting different people and hearing their stories, but I learned life wisdom from some very inspiring veterans. I learned that the price of freedom is hard and how every day people, like veterans, strive to achieve freedom. The Arizona Heritage Project taught me how to be grateful for all of the rights I have. Special thanks to James A. Vivian for showing me the value of education and integrity.

Al Crawford, Jim Vivian

Greg Gorraiz**
Junior

I am on Arizona Heritage Project because I've always been interested in the many different ways history can be interpreted, and this project brings that idea into full perspective. There are so many different sides to a single war, or single battle for that matter, that textbook summaries fail to give a satisfactory understanding. The interviews we conduct have given me better insight, and my knowledge of history increases with each veteran we listen to.

305

Vic Conner, Dick Doubek, Ennis Miller, Herman Rosen

Barbara Hatch**
Advisor

No matter how long the day, how frustrating the class, heading out to a veteran interview at the end of the day lifts me up. I put my daily inconveniences into perspective when I listen to the dangers these men and women faced. I meet with the families of those who did not return. I carry the story in my head for hours afterward, comparing it to others who served in the same conflict. These memories make me a better teacher and a humbler citizen. I wouldn't miss a single story. I only wish we could tell more.

Rance Farrell, Tony Gray, Bruce Hilsee, Louis Kraft, Jim Siket

Kevin Hildebrandt**
Sophomore

This is my first full year on the project after working the last half of the second book and I am enjoying greatly the stories and real-life experiences I hear about. I feel it is one thing to hear the concept in an overview in a classroom, whereas it is far more exciting to learn it this way from first-hand details and personal stories. Also, more than just the stories, this opportunity to work with these amazing veterans has revealed to me ways that I need to interact with the people in my own life, such as talking to my grandfathers about their experiences and getting to know a whole new side of people through better communication.

Emery Hildebrandt, Len Lai, Bob Littlefield

Kyle Hobratschk**
Senior

My rewarding high school experience is due in large part to the Arizona Heritage Project. This service to our community has taught me skills in areas of writing, interviewing, communicating, publishing, illustrating, performing, and even woodworking. But most importantly, I have learned about a significant part of my community—the veterans and their stories. Not

Bob M. Johnson and Kasey Burton

only have I had the opportunity to share their memories, but I have made intergenerational friendships with these veterans from a time and experience I will never truly understand.

Art Illustrations, Exhibit

Nicole Liebgold*
Sophomore

Out of everything I have ever learned in a history class, wars have always been the hardest for me to fully understand as well as I would like. No one in my family has ever been in a war and I know that I never will be in one either, and so the idea of war is something that has always been very foreign to me. By helping out with the project I was able to hear about World War II from the perspective of someone who was directly impacted by it. As a result, I think I have emerged with a better understanding of war as an experience rather than a chapter in a textbook.

Lyle French (as told by his widow Gene)

Mark McCullough*
Senior

It has been an absolute pleasure to serve on the Arizona Heritage Project. The memories I have gained and the great veterans I have met are worth the mammoth undertakings of AHP. In addition, it is especially interesting to view how "the project" has evolved through the years. From an immature, yet determined *Since You Asked: Volume I* to a well-balanced and experienced second year, AHP members have demonstrated their capabilities with poise. No matter how much work is entailed and no matter how many hours of sleep lost from writing essays or creating the book, the preservation of the veterans' stories is a great "fortune" for us all.

Book Layout

Carolina Nick*
Freshman

When Mrs. Hatch told our class about the Arizona Heritage Project I immediately knew that it was something I wanted to be a part of. I love hearing stories and I find war stories among the most amazing opportunity for me to be able to talk to veterans and hear their stories, and I'd even get to put their stories and pictures in a book. Several of my relatives were in World War II and my brother just joined the Air Force, so what better way for me to show my appreciation for all that veterans have done for our country than to join the Arizona Heritage Project?

Natalie Omundson and Joe Anderson

Vic Phillips, Oscar Schwartz

Natalie Omundson*
Sophomore

I am a sophomore and this is my first year with the Arizona Heritage Project. I had heard about the Arizona Heritage Project through a chain of friends last year. I love to listen to life stories and history, so the idea of the project really intrigued me. My favorite part of the project is watching the connection that one shares with each veteran. Since this is my first year on the project, I have not yet compiled memories of interviews or veterans, but I have quickly learned the value of time management, and I have already witnessed the lifelong connection shared by the project and the veterans.

Joe Anderson

Amanda Poincelot*
Sophomore

My name is Amanda Poincelot and I joined the Arizona Heritage Project to learn more about the past wars. I also have a military background and I thought it would be interesting to learn other veterans' views about what went on. Mrs. Hatch is my AP World History teacher and after learning that I had a military background, she came to me and asked if I was interested. My favorite interview was with Gobel James, a prisoner of war in Vietnam for 56 months. While working on the project, I had the privilege of moving the exhibit into the library. I had never seen it before, but once they were all set up I began to read. They were all very interesting and whoever hasn't read yet needs to go out and find it! While being in this project, I have learned that it does take a lot of time and effort, but in the end it is all worth it.

Virgel Cain, Gobel James

Spenser Robert*
Freshman

While at first I joined the AHP for the extra credit in English and the desire to make a film of it, I have noticed my interest grow in veterans as well as many of the wars. It is challenging but satisfying all in all.

Homer Holland

Jeff Tully**
Freshman ASU

Though I'm now in college, I had the opportunity last summer to interview the father of my mother's teaching colleague at Horseshoe Trails Elementary School. Carmen Sterner's father Glen was visiting so I decided to interview him. I did not know at the time he would pass away shortly thereafter. Fortunately we have his story on tape and in this book. As much as I would like to "leave" the project, it never leaves me. I have decided to start a group at ASU to interview terminally ill veterans at the VA Hospital to document their service. Members would stay involved with that

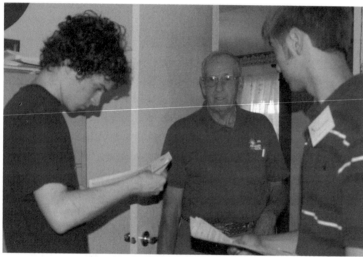

Jeff Tully, Bob Johnson, and Kirk DiGiacomo

veteran till the end. The veterans I know have made me a better person. I am grateful to know them.

Glen Lytle

Brittany Van Bibber*
Freshman

I joined the Arizona Heritage Project originally because I enjoyed writing and history. But once I started my interviews and other book work, it really sparked an interest in both subjects for me. The ambiance of the interview I did this year was very cozy and comfortable. The Korean War veteran Jim Hickok was extremely welcoming and the interview

was enjoyable. My overall experience with the Arizona Heritage Project so far was exciting and I really had fun being involved with it and its club members.

Jim Hickok

Patrick Ward*
Freshman

I joined the Arizona Heritage Project because I had heard about it from my English teacher and thought it sounded like fun. This project has opened up many opportunities for me and I feel like I am giving back to the community. My favorite memory of an interview was when I was interviewing my grandpa, Pete Rovero, and when I got to see his old war photos and hear some of his stories that he hasn't told many people before. This project has taught me that when you want to know about the stories and the lives of a war veteran who didn't think anyone cared about their service, it means a whole lot to them.

Pete Rovero, Noel Scott (ill→ 2008 book), John Wintersteen

Kelly Wilcox***
Junior

I have been a project member for three years now, and each year just gets better. You develop even stronger relationships with these amazing veterans, and you get to hear even more of their stories. It is truly a great honor for me to get to meet, let alone write, the stories of these phenomenal men and women, with hearts bigger than the world itself.

Norman Butler, Virginia Rewick

Allison Wooten*
Junior

After meeting a few veterans outside of Arizona Heritage Project, and hearing their stories, I was hungry for more. I joined the Arizona Heritage Project because I enjoy hearing the different stories and experiences of each veteran, and I feel that all these veterans and their stories deserve to be remembered.

Phil Goan

Group Picture

Photo taken at the Pearl Harbor Memorial in Phoenix, Arizona, (left to right, bottom to top): Callie Adair, Cindy Garcia Barraza, Carolina Nick, Chelsea Ferguson, Libby Day, Lindsey Anderson, Amanda Poincelot, Barbara Hatch; Kasey Burton, Allison Wooten; Kirk DiGiacomo, Anthony Beckham, Greg Gorraiz, Kyle Hobratschk

Events

Each year of the project takes on its own life and offers its own opportunities. Our third year has been no different.

Besides a few interviews that presented themselves last spring, the summer was quiet. Students took off for family vacations or immersed themselves in required summer reading. Some played sports. I graded the AP World History exam in Lincoln, Nebraska, before spending 10 days playing golf in Ireland with my husband and 22-year-old sons. R & R at last! In July I spent several days at the Sharlot Hall Museum in Prescott to help new AHP teachers learn the ropes. This "old dog" learned a few new "tricks" of her own. The weather was great and the company even better. I saw Guha again and the folks from SRP. The rest of the summer sped along as I finally paid attention to my house, but no significant painting or repairing occurred.

Some events we participate in each year, like VFW 7507's annual golf tournament in Fountain Hills; others were new. The town of Cave Creek celebrated its 20th anniversary on Veterans Day and asked us to find town veterans to sit on stage while a Stealth bomber flew over and spectators honored the veterans' service. I got to meet the governor at Harold's in a pre-event gathering. I again presented the project to the Arizona Council of Social Studies at ASU West with Dr. Ed Berger, state director of the Arizona Heritage Project. Unfortunately I could not bring students this year. But taking 15 students and Dr. Berger to Washington, D.C. to turn over 98 interviews to the Veterans History Project at the Library of Congress was the highlight of the 2006-7 year. We were also honored by the Association of the U.S. Army and shared our work with teachers at the National Council of Social Studies. The trip was, as the kids would say, "awesome"!

This spring we will travel to Albuquerque to present the project to the Rocky Mountain regional social studies conference of teachers. We hope to interview several veterans along the way. PBS called several days ago to ask us to assist with the debut of Ken Burns' documentary on World War II, planned for the fall of 2007. They wanted to know if we "had any interviews with World War II veterans"—like about a hundred! The surprises keep coming.

None compares, however, with the "out of the blue" phone calls we receive. A woman heard of our project in another state and contacted us to see if we would be interested in recording a reunion between her, her son, and the man who saved her father's life during World War II; he lives in Scottsdale. At Wild West Days in Cave Creek, Billy Schaefer asked me if we had interviewed Gobel James, POW in Vietnam for 56 months. We hadn't. Now we have. His story is in this book. At the end of each year, exhausted from finalizing essays, people ask, "Will there be another book?" With such faith in these kids and our work, how can we say no?

Barbara Hatch

Mark McCullough and Allison Wooten before "tee-off" at the Fountain Hills VFW Golf Tournament

Veterans at Wild West Days in Cave Creek on Veterans' Day 2006: Ron Green, Dick Minor, Park Shaw, Joe Anderson

Veterans viewing the exhibit in Fountain Hills, AZ on Memorial Day

311

AHP members (left to right) Carolina Nick, Kasey Burton, Natalie Omundson, Kevin Hildebrandt overwhelm Bob Patrick (left) and Tim Schurtter (right) from the Veterans' History Project in Washington D.C. with veteran information to be archived at the Library of Congress

Reception

As proud as we were of our year's accomplishments, our 2006 reception on May 7 was to celebrate the veterans whom we were fortunate to interview. We celebrated the occasion at the Terravita clubhouse, where we were able to support all of our 2005 and 2006 veterans. Other attendees included friends and family of our members and veterans, supporters from the community, and other people who have supported the Arizona Heritage Project from the start.

Students greeted arriving veterans at the door and encouraged them to sign in. After signing in, students showed them around and guided them to their designated seats. In their areas the veterans found individual place cards with their names and gift bags. We [the students] signed all of the veterans' books before they arrived and placed them in their goody bags in front of their seats. Also included in the bag was a name tag, a notepad and pen, a copy of their interview on DVD, and of course the book. Noticing the success of the veteran book signing during the 2005 reception, we dedicated the majority of this year's reception to mingling and book signing at these tables. To be more accommodating to our veterans and their guests, we arranged the tables along the outer edge of the room for signing and left the center chairs and room to mingle. The signing was once again very successful, and we have only to thank our veterans and those who came to support the project.

In addition to the book signing we had further entertainment for our guests. Before and after the book signing, we saw to it there was not a moment of idleness. A video compilation of short clips containing veteran interviews was on display, as was a slide show of pictures donated to the project by our veterans. And of course, no celebration would be complete without refreshments. Catered by Terravita, the staff provided exceptional service and delightfully delicious food and drink. A performance by the Arizona Heritage Project's own Jessica Dillon and her fellow CSHS Honors Choir members Heidi Aybar and Allison Taylor, to the tune of "Boogie Woogie Bugle Boy," kept us all in a jovial state. Congressman J.D. Hayworth, who has long been a supporter of the project, was once again present and poignant. He moved the attendees with a remarkably moving speech, stressing the importance of remembering the heroic actions of those who have served, and those who are still doing so. A veteran from each war spoke with words of wisdom and passion, as did Jeff Tully, a recent graduate of Cactus Shadows High School, and a young man to whom the project owes much of its presence throughout the community. We thank Fred Ferguson, Medal of Honor recipient Vietnam, who represented Governor Janet Napolitano; General Frank Sackton, aide to General Douglas MacArthur, who embodies World War II; Donald Schaller, who honored his fellow Korea veterans; and Mike Metzger, who shared his thoughts on Vietnam.

One of the project's finest accomplishments, the exhibit, was proudly displayed at the center of the buzzing reception hall. Members of the Project placed pictures on the exhibit of the "new" veterans from 2005-6, along with quotes. Memorabilia lent to the project was displayed on and around the exhibit, such as the Bible Tom Schaeffer poked holes in to keep a journal while he was a hostage in Iran, and the dress Bettie Smith wore when she became a radar plotter on Pearl Harbor after the attack. We also displayed General Sackton's Silver Star.

As the event progressed, AHP members were excited to know all the arduous work they put in was worthwhile. Kelly Wilcox remembered the hours she spent making and sending early postcards to the veterans, notifying them to "save the date" of the reception. She was happy to hear those were important to make, as many veterans misplaced the formal invitations students sent out later but still had the postcard. The week preceding the reception each student called "their veterans" to remind them of the occasion. To make sure the veterans found the location, students woke up early on the day of the reception and put out direction signs. Still, a few veterans didn't make it for one reason or another. Sven Keinanen misremembered the date and came the following day. George Pillmore was so hard at work in his yard he forgot altogether. For the most part, however, the veterans came and students were glad for it.

We students had the utmost appreciation for the hours Celeste Hobratschk, our organizer, put in to make sure the reception ran smoothly. She found the perfect location, organized a spreadsheet of tasks for each student, and coordinated virtually every other aspect of the event that most people would overlook or simply assume would work itself out.

Barbara Hatch, Marilyn and Mark McCullough, and Greg Gorraiz thought of the day preceding the reception, where they frantically worked to print the programs. Our own color printer decided not to work so they had to run back and forth between our computer and the printer in room 1006. Unfortunately, *that* printer didn't want to accept the card stock. At 6:00 at night they finished, weary yet satisfied.

As the event drew to a close, there was a close kinship ingrained in each guest and veteran. The formal talk from early in the evening turned to friendly conversation. We students were glad to have acknowledged the sacrifices of our veterans and the work of each other on such a fine occasion. We cleaned up, took our belongings with us, and knowing we had finished another triumphant year, had a short break to look forward to in the summer before embarking on book 3...

Libby Day
Greg Gorraiz

The Color Guard presents the Colors

Carl Schneider shares words with Bettie Smith

Veterans Mel Engen and Dave Dennison share memories and stories

AHP member Jeff Tully frantically tries to get several books signed

Dewey Wambsganss signing his page in the book

Exhibit

The desire to share these veteran stories goes past the publication of a book. Elements like photographs, memorabilia, short-stories, and quotations help complete their story. These pieces are displayed in a traveling exhibit, allowing others a glimpse into our project's mission.

A committee within the project spent almost one year designing and building the display. Producing an exhibit of this size, almost fourteen-feet long and eight-feet tall, with dramatic woodworking and attention to veteran contributions, was a daunting task. Few of us had woodworking skills, much less the experience of a museum curator. With a wood shop and extra space in my garage, we created a standing exhibit despite our learning curves.

The exhibit consists of five two-foot by eight-foot panels that serve as the "ground" for ten separate scenes. Each two-sided panel displays representational scenes relevant to a particular war. Placed on each backdrop are veteran photographs, quotations, and several informational paragraphs regarding the photos and the stories beside them. At the base of the panels lie authentic ammunition crates showcasing memorabilia on loan from the veterans. Both crates and memorabilia now serve very different purposes than they did during the wars. Dog-tags suspended from two camouflage nets recognize each veteran and his years of service. Small crates, helmets, and a 1940s radio complete the display.

To create the war scenes that serve as "ground" for the photographs and documents, we developed master cartoons from simple sketches, then projected them onto blank sheets of one-eight-inch birch. After tracing the pictures, we cut out the designs with a variety of both manual and power saws. Our favorite, the eighteen-inch scroll-saw, cut the most complex shapes—like the South Pacific Islands! Once cut, all pieces were stained in a variety of natural colors and then sealed and sanded. These "puzzle pieces" were then glued to the "ground" scenes to create a backdrop for each war. This was not as simple as it sounds. If pieces came loose, additional pressure was applied to secure the bond. The shear size of the boards prevented us from using regular clamps, so we used the largest clamping device we could find—a truck! Another board was placed on top of the glued pieces and a truck was driven on top for the duration of the drying process. Elbow grease, steel-wool, and more coats of sealer finished each board.

These boards stand vertically in a staggered arrangement with scenes on both sides. We welded five independent steel bases with three rods each to hold the panels, drilling small holes in the panel bases to fit over the rods, forming sturdy bases—unless displaying them in a strong wind, which happened on Memorial Day in Fountain Hills.

Photographs and documents from the vast collection donated by our veterans or the Library of Congress's website were selected to fill in the "ground" scenes. After printing and mounting the photographs to black foam-core, we used Velcro to secure them to the wood panels. The Velcro enables us to remove the pictures when the exhibit travels. We also used quotations from the veteran interviews to accompany text and pictures. They allow the viewer to hear the veteran's own voice. These quotations were mounted directly to the panels with transfer letters.

The exhibit has proudly rotated to various valley locations: Cactus Shadows High School, Cave Creek Museum, Carefree Chamber of Commerce, Carefree Kiwanis pancake breakfasts, Fountain Hills River of Time Museum, Scottsdale Civic Center Library, Sun City's Memorial Day, and Salt River Project Headquarters. A small, more portable "mini-exhibit" wood tri-fold traveled to Desert Foothills Library, MacDonald's Ranch, Arizona Council of Social Studies Conference at ASU West, and Salt River Project. We recently carried it to Washington, D.C. in December 2006 for the 86th Annual Social Studies Teacher Conference.

While different veterans are chronicled each year in our books, we reuse the exhibit panels to feature the new veterans. Previous photographs, quotations, and memorabilia are removed from the exhibit as we select new material to display for another year.

Our exhibit is a tribute to the veterans' service. It is a supplement to our book and a public celebration of their stories.

Kyle Hobratschk

Artist's Notes

Reading a veteran's story through a student's perspective is little different from looking at a veteran's story through a student's illustration. Both interpretations should give true feelings about the particular situation. While essays create these feelings through word choice, pictures create similar feelings through use of basic art principles. Texture, line, value, shape, and repetition spur distinct emotions.

Although war does not portray a pretty picture in most minds, it must be painted accurately according to those who have experienced it. And although these illustrations are painted accurately, they are also painted generically, so that they may be applied to more than one story. Similar to writing an essay, it is impossible to depict their entire war.

Various steps were taken when I chose certain aspects over others to be illustrated for the five wars. Basic research was the first step. What type of airplane did they fly in World War II? How did the landscape differ in Vietnam from Korea? Text and photographs answered many questions to which a list was compiled of "highlights" for each war. I interpreted hundreds of images for reference, from war encyclopedias to scenery in coffee table books. I also found myself telephoning veterans to ask them what stands out when recalling their service. For example, when composing "Korea," Don Schaller met with me to share his slide collection and recall memories from each shot.

The technical aspects of these illustrations are simple. I used only one color: Winsor & Newton's *Mars Black* - the blackest color I could find to give me the largest range of values. The media is comprised of India ink, pencil, and watercolor with a range of paintbrushes and dipping pens. These illustrations were painted on *Lanaquarelle* cold pressed watercolor paper of a larger size to be reduced for the printed version.

Each column-shaped illustration featured to the left of every veteran's essay is intended to serve as a mount for separate scenes to flow into each other, while design elements such as a peace symbol or Korean map help tie the pieces together. The following statements summarize each illustration.

"World War II" depicts a soldier in trench warfare viewing the elemental stars and stripes. The three-dimensional stars were painted from the sculptured stars displayed at the National World War II monument in Washington, D.C. The diverse terrain and machinery represent a global conflict. The Jeep was an irreplaceable addition.

"Korea" focuses on the cold and rugged landscape to which the armed forces had to adapt. Pieces included are the common and versatile truck, a group of mobile tents, an aerial view of rice paddies, snow-covered mountains, and a Korean map.

"Cold War" fits some of its icons—the graffiti-covered Berlin Wall, barbed wire, and Titan missile—into a composition yielding a hammer and sickle in the background.

"Vietnam" establishes a sandbagged tunnel with lush vegetation at the bottom. In the distance, soldiers trudge through swamps as helicopters fly overhead. A peace sign rests in the sky.

"Gulf Wars" uses sand dunes to connect the illustration. At the bottom, canvas tents are set before a Middle Eastern skyline at sunset. Above, smoke from the fires of Kuwait billows against a sky filled with tracers.

These simple distinctions have greater meanings than just an illustration. They are to accompany the veterans' stories and inspire the mind to either relive or imagine.

Kyle Hobratschk

Signature Page

Military Ranks

Army	Air Force	Marines	Navy & Coast Guard
Commissioned Officers			
General of the Army**	General of the Air Force**		Fleet Admiral**
Army Chief of Staff General	Air Force Chief of Staff General	Commandant of the Marine Corps General	Chief of Naval Operations Commandant of the Coast Guard Admiral
Lieutenant General	Lieutenant General	Lieutenant General	Vice Admiral
Major General	Major General	Major General	Rear Admiral (Upper Half)
Brigadier General	Brigadier General	Brigadier General	Rear Admiral (Upper Half)
Colonel	Colonel	Colonel	Captain
Lieutenant Colonel	Lieutenant Colonel	Lieutenant Colonel	Commander
Major	Major	Major	Lieutenant Commander
Captain	Captain	Captain	Lieutenant
1st Lieutenant	1st Lieutenant	1st Lieutenant	Lieutenant, Junior Grade
2nd Lieutenant	2nd Lieutenant	2nd Lieutenant	Ensign
Warrant Officers			
Master Warrant Officer 5			Master Warrant Officer
Warrant Officer 4		Chief Warrant Officer	Warrant Officer 4
Warrant Officer 3		Chief Warrant Officer	Warrant Officer 3
Warrant Officer 2		Chief Warrant Officer	Warrant Officer 2
Warrant Officer 1			Warrant Officer 1
Non-Commissioned Officers			
Sergeant Major of the Army	Chief Master Sergeant of the Air Force	Sergeant Major of the Marine Corps	Master Chief Petty Officer of the Navy
Command Sergeant Major Sergeant Major	First Sergeant (Chief Master Sergeant) Chief Master Sergeant	Sergeant Major Master Gunnery Sergeant	Master Chief Petty Officer

Army	Air Force	Marines	Navy & Coast Guard
First Sergeant Master Sergeant	First Sergeant (Senior Master Sergeant) Master Sergeant	Gunnery Sergeant	Chief Petty Officer
Sergeant First Class	First Sergeant (Master Sergeant) Master Sergeant	Gunnery Sergeant	Chief Petty Officer
Staff Sergeant	Technical Sergeant	Staff Sergeant	Petty Officer First Class
Sergeant	Staff Sergeant	Sergeant	Petty Officer Second Class
Corporal			
Enlisted Personnel			
Specialist	Senior Airman	Corporal	Petty Officer Third Class
Private First Class	Airman First Class	Lance Corporal	Seaman
Private	Airman	Private First Class	Seaman Apprentice
Private (Recruit)	Airman Basic	Private	Seaman Recruit
**Ranks used infrequently during wartime			

Military Units

Unit	Approximate Personnel	Composition	Typical Commander
Army	100,000	2+ corps, HQ	General
Corps	30,000+	2+ divisions	Lieutenant General
Division	15,000+	3 brigades, HQ, support units	Major General
Brigade	4,500+	3+ regiments, HQ	Brigadier General
Regiment	1,500+	2+ battalions, HQ	Colonel
Battalion	700	4+ companies, HQ	Lieutenant Colonel
Company	175	4 platoons, HQ	Captain
Platoon	40	4 squads	Lieutenant
Squad	10		Staff Sergeant
Size, composition, and leadership of military units varies with circumstances, time and place. The composition of fully authorized units may not actually re realized in actual circumstances, especially in combat. This chart is not applicable to foreign militaries.			

Resources

Each of the service branches maintains a history center containing a reference collection of books, documents, published unit histories, photographs, medals, and artifacts. The addresses and Web sites for these centers are listed below.

United States Air Force
Bolling AFB, DC 20332-111
Telephone: 202.404.2261
Web site: http://www.airforcehistory.hq.af.mil/

U.S. Air Force Historical Research Agency
600 Chennault Circle
Building 1405
Maxwell AFB, AL 36112-6424
Telephone: 334.953.2395
Web Site: http://www.au.af.mil/au/afhra

U.S. Air Force Museum
1100 Spaatz Street
Wright-Peterson AFB, OH 45433-7102
Telephone: 937.255.3286
Web site: http://www.wpafb.af.mil/museum/

United States Army
U.S. Army Center of Military History Building 35
102 Fourth Avenue
Ft. McNair, DC 20319-5058
Telephone: 202.685.2733
Web site: http://www.army.mil./cmh-pg/default.htm

U.S. Army Military History Institute
Carlisle Barracks, PA 17013-5008
Telephone: 717.245.3611
Web site: http://carlisle-www.army.mil/usamhi/

United States Coast Guard
U.S. Coast Guard Historian's Office
United States Coast Guard Headquarters
Room B-717
2100 Second St., SW
Washington, DC 20953
Telephone: 202.267.2596
Web Site: http://www.uscg.mil/hq/g-cp/history/collect.html

Coast Guard Museum
U.S. Coast Guard Academy
15 Mohegan Avenue
New London, CT 06320-8511
Telephone: 860.444.8511
Website: http://www.uscg.mil/hq/g-cp/museum/MuseumInfo.html

United States Marine Corps
Marine Corps Historical Center Washington Navy Yard
Building 58
1254 Charles Morris Street, SE
Washington Navy Yard, DC 20374-5040
Telephone: 202.433.3483
Web Site: http://hqinet001.hqmc.usmc.mil/HD/Home_Page.htm

Marine Corps Air-Ground Museum
Marine Corps Combat Development Command
2014 Anderson Avenue
Quantico, VA 22134-5002
Telephone: 703.784.2607
Web Site: http://hqinet001.hqmc.usmc.mil/HD/Home_Page.htm

United States Navy
Naval Historical Center
Washington Navy Yard
Building 57
805 Kidder Breese Street, SE
Washington Navy Yard, DC 20374-5060
Telephone: 202.433.3634
Web Site: http://www.history.navy.mil/

LOCATING MILITARY SERVICE RECORDS

Individual Personnel Files

The National Archives and Records Administration (NARA) is the official repository for records of military personnel who have been discharged from the U.S. Air Force, Army, Marine Corps, Navy, and Coast Guard.

A veteran (or next of kin) may request his or her individual military personnel file (201 file) by sending a request to the National Personnel Records Center, Militray Records Facility, 9700 Page Boulevard, St. Louis, MO 63132-5100.

Additional information about the contents of these personnel files, instructions for submitting a request, and a downloadable PDF copy of the request form may be found on the National Personnel Records Center home page of the National Archives and Records Administration Web site (http://www.archives.gov/facilities/mo/st_louis/military_personnel_records.html).

Personnel records of civilians who worked for the various branches of the military are also held by the National Personnel Records Center. The address to write for these records is National Personnel Records Center, Civilian Records Facility, 111 Winnebago Street, St. Louis, MO 63118-4199.

Acknowledgements

While we are an energetic group of hard-working individuals, many of the Arizona Heritage Project's accomplishments happen due to help from many different sources. Students have classwork to manage, but the making of a full-length book is actually an extracurricular activity. Help comes to us from several sources: the veterans who tell us their stories and donate money to publish the book; parents and community members who help with finances, proofread the book, or drive students to meetings; teachers and staff members who offer to cut checks on tight deadlines or assist with computer breakdowns, to name just a few.

Without veterans willing to share the memories of their service, and often their money to the project, the project could not exist. These men and women take time from their busy schedules to educate students with experiences they gained while in the armed forces. Their tenacity and willingness to work toward improving student essays is essential. There is no better feeling than having Mrs. Hatch or the veteran whose essay you wrote tell you that your story is "just right," or "well-written." Mrs. Hatch tells students that to the veterans we "walk on water," something we are all proud of.

Critical to our success were Cave Creek Museum, Desert Foothills Library of Cave Creek, and Sharlot Hall Museum in Prescott. They gave us support and helped us with content ideas or referred us to veterans in the community that we could interview.

The Library of Congress supported our cause once more. During our travel to Washington, D.C. we had the great pleasure to meet with Dr. Guha Shankar, Folklife Specialist of the American Folklife Center; Bob Patrick and Tim Schurtter at the Veterans History Project; and Darlene Iskra, U.S. Navy Commander (retired), who allowed us to interview her when we presented to the National Council of Social Studies. These individuals warmly welcomed us when we presented our work from the past three years. The insight from the men and women at the Library involving community research and gathering of history is greatly appreciated and constantly incorporated into what we do. The Association of the United States Army's General Roger Thompson was also very kind to us during our visit to their headquarters in Arlington. His group treated us as professionals, and we appreciate their concern regarding our armed forces. We look forward to future contact with them as well.

As a non-profit organization, the Arizona Heritage Project relies heavily on the many financial contributors to the project. These contributions arrive in several different forms: tax-credits, donations, and book sales. We see these from generous people, some who live in states other than Arizona. Local families and even the veterans interviewed often directed tax-credits toward the project, giving it the ability to progress yearly. Donations and tax-credits from these people helped form the project's financial backbone, but were hardly alone in this feat. The incredible reinforcement from the Salt River Project came in a fourth straight $3,000 grant, which our high school matched. Financial support from Cactus Shadows High School, Cactus Shadows High School's Booster Club, and Kiwanis Club of Carefree is also appreciated.

Many thanks go to the directors of the Arizona Heritage Project with their unceasing efforts for project growth. We would especially like to thank Dr. Edward Berger for his enthusiasm concerning young people's involvement in their communities. His accompaniment of the group to Washington, D.C. was kind, and we look forward to working with him next year. Individuals with his passion regarding today's world and desire to see young people succeed are essential not only in our project, but schools everywhere.

Parents of project members also make the project work. This year, two in particular stand out. Mrs. Stacy DiGiacomo became valuable to the project, especially with her contribution regarding planning and carrying out of the reception on May 6, 2007, at the Carefree Conference Resort. She has been very accommodating to the project's needs and we look forward to working with her again next year. For a fourth straight year, Mrs. Celeste Hobratschk was a "behind the scenes" supporter of the project. Over the years, there have been few people as valuable to the project as her. We thank them both for their time. We also realize that without the parents driving their sons or daughters to morning meetings or picking them up after an interview, we could not do our jobs.

Mrs. Barbara Hatch was again the most important piece in the puzzle to completion of this year's book. Our goal is to honor veterans. No one does this better than Mrs. Hatch, and her "recruits" genuinely appreciate the efforts. She lives a very busy life, yet rarely complains about the amount of work she puts in. Even when experiencing stress and exhaustion, she refuses to pull back in our commitment to honoring veterans. Mrs. Hatch is always ready to include more veterans, put in another long day of work, and simply tackle any superfluous hurdle standing in our way. The project is impossible without her. She's why there will be a Volume IV. She can't say no!

The "younger members" of the project wish to convey a special thanks to the seniors who are leaving us this year: Kyle Hobratschk, Lauren Byrd, and Mark McCullough. We are still wondering who will paint the illustrations for the book or update the exhibit. Kyle will miss Lauren's patient hand staining the exhibit boards and acting as a sounding board when he has a project problem to solve. We panic when we think who will lay out next year's book after Mark leaves. Libby and Greg have been taking notes, but they may need to start the book in the summer or put Mark on speed dial! We hope these graduates will stay in touch as Jeff Tully has done. Though he is a freshman at ASU, he contributed an essay for this book when the grandfather of his mom's coworker at Horseshoe Trails Elementary School visited in the summer. Jeff calls or stops by frequently to ask about the project. He attends veterans' funerals because they have become important in his life.

In conclusion, I would like to thank my fellow project members, both "behind the scenes" workers and the out-front people. All too often, members who do the tedious everyday tasks such as sending veteran birthday cards, making telephone calls, or archiving financial information are forgotten when it comes to acknowledging valuable project members. These people don't get "too big for their britches" and do thankless jobs asking for nothing in return. Also forgotten are the "compilers" of the book who have their names by few bylines, but make it possible to have the book published on time. Personally, I'm thrilled to work with all of the aforementioned persons as they have accorded me an experience I'll never forget.

Kirk DiGiacomo

Index

Gray, Tony 43
Green Cove Springs, Florida 143
Guadalcanal 18, 19, 43, 48, 114, 126
Guam 19
Guantanamo Bay 31

H

H.P. Law Company 76
H.V. Keltenbun 64
Hadithah, Al-Anbar Province, Iraq 276
Hadithah Dam 275
Hamburger Hill 191
Hammer Field 54
Hampton Roads, Virginia 154
Hamul 45
Hanoi 220
Hanoi Hilton 220, 221
Harley motorcycle 25
Hartpence, Dennis 213
Harvard University 73, 158
Harvey Cushing Medal 38
Hatch, Barbara 309
he Great Raid 28
Henderson Field 44, 114, 126
Henry Stimson 156
Hermann Goering 237
Hezbollah 132
Hickok, James 142
Higgins boat 22
Hildebrandt, Emery 47
Hildebrandt, Kevin 312
Hill 913 35
Hilsee, Bruce 50
Hilton Head Island, South Carolina 20
Hiroshima 110, 236
Ho Chi Minh City 83
Ho Chi Minh Trail 210, 23
Hobratschk, Kyle 4, 317
    Poincelot, Amanda 309
Holland, Homer 214
Hollywood 254, 271
Honeywell 52

Hong Kong 243
Hoover, Dick 54
Hudson River 111
Huey UH1 192
Huff, Kenneth 57
Huntsville, Alabama 269
Hurricane Andrew 271
Hurricane Katrina 131

I

Ie Shima 44
Illinois Institute of Technology 9
Indian Head, Maryland 269
Infantry Replacement Training Camp 39
Ingrandes, France 83
Invasion of Normandy 76, 117
Israel 132
Iwo Jima 20, 31

J

James, Gobel 218
Japanese Zeros 19, 48, 115
Johnson, Bob 146
Johnson, Lyndon B. 97, 197, 216
Joint Chiefs of Staff 152
Jolly Green 201
Junction, Texas 24
Junior ROTC 154

K

Kamikaze 31, 123
Kaneohe Air Station 165
Kaneohe Naval Air Station 164
Kansas State University 75
Kassel, Germany 42
Kassel, Germany. 83
KB-50 174
Keesler Air Force Base 185
Kelloff, George 64
Kennedy, John F. 156, 186, 201, 204
Kent State 251
Kesselring, Albert 130
Key West, Florida 22
Khyber Pass 186
Kings College 30
Kirkuk 52
Koch, Isle 61
Koch, Karl 61
Kraft, Louis 68
Kramer, Allan 71
Kyle Hobratschk 309

L

Lai, Len 164
Lake Charles, Louisiana 232
Landing Craft Utility 262
Landing Zone Lonely 257
Laura (movie) 73

Le Havre, France 237
Leard, Tom 225
Legion of Merit 168, 185
LeJeune, North Carolina 274
Library of Congress 79
Linderman General Hospital 27
Littlefield, Bob 229
Long Beach Naval Air Reserve 112
Lopez, Pablo 232, 303
Lufthansa 52
Luftwaffe 86
Luke Air Force Base 275
Luke Field 54
Luzon 2
Lytle, Glen 75

M

M.A.S.H. 131
M60 229
Major Conroy 154
Major General George Casey, Sr. 260
Man of La Mancha 52
Manila harbor 81
Manila Hotel 28
Marine Mammal Program 269
Marseille 130
Marshall Islands 19
Marshall, Steve 268
Maryland National Guard 260
Marzano, Michael 274
Massachusetts Institute of Technology 113, 214
Master's Degree 38
Maxwell Air Force Base 158
McCullough, Mark 4, 278, 311
McNamara's Wall 262
Medal of Honor 20, 231
Melbourne, Australia 21
Mercedes 251
Meritorious Service Medal 185
Messerschmitt 137
Metropolitan Duty 237
Metzger, Mike 300
Miami, Florida 22
Miami University 158
Michie Stadium 205
Michigan State University 156
Military Assistance Advisory Group 154
Military Government 78
Military Officers Association of America 246
Miller, Ennis 236
Mitteland Canal 86
Monmouth, New Jersey 232
Morehead State Teachers' College 60
Morris Field 125
Moselle River 108
Mountain and Cold Weather Training Command 161

Printed by Prisma Graphic Corporation, Phoenix, Arizona
Color King 2 Unit 36" Web Press/Combination Folder

Bound by Roswell Bookbinding, Phoenix, Arizona

The design and production of this book was accomplished with PageMaker 7.0 software.
The family of type used throughout this book is Adobe Garamond and Georgia.